Applied Measurement Methods
in Industrial Psychology

Applied Measurement Methods in Industrial Psychology

Deborah L. Whetzel
George R. Wheaton
EDITORS

DAVIES-BLACK PUBLISHING
Palo Alto, California

Published by Davies-Black Publishing, an imprint of Consulting Psychologists Press, Inc., 3803 East Bayshore Road, Palo Alto, CA 94303; 1-800-624-1765.

Special discounts on bulk quantities of Davies-Black books are available to corporations, professional associations, and other organizations. For details, contact the Director of Book Sales at Davies-Black Publishing, an imprint of Consulting Psychologists Press, Inc., 3803 East Bayshore Road, Palo Alto, CA 94303; 650-691-9123; Fax 650-988-0673.

01 00 99 98 97   10 9 8 7 6 5 4 3 2 1
Printed in the United States of America

Library of Congress Cataloging-in-Publication Data
Applied measurement methods in industrial psychology / edited by
    Deborah L. Whetzel and George R. Wheaton
        p.   cm.
    Includes bibliographical references and index.
    ISBN 0-89106-106-1
    1. Performance standards. 2. Performance technology. 3. Employees—
    Rating of. 4. Job analysis. 5. Psychology, Industrial Methodology.
    I. Whetzel, Deborah L.   II. Wheaton, George R.
    HF5549.5.P37A67   1997
    658.3'125—dc21   97–20366
                                                                          CIP
FIRST EDITION
First printing 1997

Contents

Acknowledgments

The beginnings of this volume go back to the close of World War II. It was then that Dr. John C. Flanagan concluded his successful leadership of the U.S. Army Air Force's Aviation Psychology Program and founded the American Institutes for Research (AIR). Dr. Flanagan's vision was to engage his colleagues at AIR in an ambitious research program concentrated in the following areas: critical requirements for successful performance of key jobs and activities; a comprehensive battery of aptitude tests; new procedures for evaluating proficiency; improved criteria for validating the effectiveness of selection instruments; modification of tasks so as to improve the effectiveness and well-being of those persons performing them; and the effectiveness of organizations and their leaders.

This year, as we celebrate AIR's fiftieth anniversary and contemplate Dr. Flanagan's legacy, it seems a good idea to bring together in one volume the applied measurement methods that are now widely used by students and practitioners in industrial and organizational psychology, human resource management, and allied disciplines. It also seems an opportune time to describe the types of tools used by the many individuals and organizations who have labored in the fields first plowed by Dr. Flanagan. In this spirit, we would like to dedicate this book in memory of Dr. Flanagan.

We also would like to recognize the contributions of many others who have participated in the development and utilization of the methods and techniques described in this text. In particular, we would single out our friends and colleagues at the Personnel Decisions Research Institutes, Inc., and the Human Resources Research Organization with whom we have successfully collaborated over many years on a variety of challenging and interesting measurement problems.

In addition, we want to express our deep appreciation to Mr. A. J. Pearson, Executive Director of the National Joint Apprenticeship and Training Committee of the International Brotherhood of Electrical Workers and the National Electrical Contractors Association. The American Institutes for Research has performed several projects for Mr. Pearson involving the analysis of electrical workers' jobs throughout the United States. These projects have involved application of many of the methods described in this book and provided a common ground for the examples we used. Throughout the studies and analyses that were conducted, Mr. Pearson always wanted to "do the job right," allowing the methods to be applied correctly, without compromise. Mr. Pearson is a man with a vision of improving the productivity of the electrical trade, and he has understood the ways in which the techniques described in this book could move his program toward that end.

Contexts for Developing Applied Measurement Instruments

George R. Wheaton
Deborah L. Whetzel

OVERVIEW

The primary purpose of this edited volume is to provide students and entry-level practitioners with practical, systematic guidance on how to develop the various kinds of measurement instruments frequently used in the field of industrial psychology to assess personnel. The book, therefore, takes a decidedly applied or "how to" approach to instrument development. Our prescriptions are logically organized to follow the process one would actually undertake to determine what constructs should be measured, what measurement techniques should be used, and how to determine the reliability and validity of the resulting assessments. Accordingly, the volume contains five major sections: (1) conducting job analyses, (2) developing a test plan for determining the constructs to be measured and how to measure them, (3) developing measures to predict job performance, (4) developing measures of job performance, and (5) conducting studies to assess the quality of the measurement program.

The context in which we discuss the development of applied measurement methods is the world of work. Thus, we want to assess the characteristics of job applicants to determine who would most likely excel on the job, both in the near term and in the longer run. Similarly, we would periodically want to assess employee strengths and weaknesses in performance, both as a basis for financial compensation and as a diagnostic tool for determining appropriate developmental courses of action. Measurement might also be used to assist in the planning of career trajectories, to support promotion decisions, and to design and evaluate employee training programs. Measurement of this latter type could be used not only to characterize how much employees have learned from exposure to various training programs, but also to evaluate the programs themselves (e.g., by determining what elements of jobs are best trained using particular training methods).

CONDUCTING JOB ANALYSES

Job analysis is the necessary foundation for all of these personnel assessment applications. For example, job analysis is essential when interest lies in predicting performance on the job. When developing a test or test battery for the purpose of selecting employees from a pool of job candidates, the first step is to conduct a job analysis that identifies the most critical aspects of the job. The next step is to identify the knowledge, skills, and abilities needed to perform the critical job operations successfully. Once the knowledge, skills, and abilities have been identified, tests that measure those attributes can be selected or developed. Thus, the development of selection instruments depends on the results of job analysis. One of the methods most commonly used to parse a job into its critical tasks and to identify important worker characteristics is the job/task inventory method.

Job analysis also is used as the basis for developing performance appraisal instruments. For research purposes, measures of job performance often serve as the criteria against which selection measures are validated. For the purpose of assessing job performance operationally, job analysis can provide an empirical basis for determining the characteristics of an entire appraisal system (e.g., Bernardin & Beatty, 1984). For example, job analysis can be used to identify the best source of information for the appraisal of different components of job performance (e.g., peers may be the best source for some components, while supervisors may be best for others). Job analysis might also provide information on the extent to which performance on different components of the job is constrained by factors beyond the control of individual workers (e.g., shortages in materials or personnel). One of the best job analysis methods you can use for determining the content of performance appraisals is the critical incident technique.

The results of job analysis are often used to support human engineering and usability testing studies (Dumas & Redish, 1993). The goal of both types of studies is to design machines and systems that can be more easily and effectively used by humans. Job analysis can be used to detect problems with machines (e.g., critical incidents are often collected to document that a control mechanism or display has been poorly designed or inappropriately placed within a workstation). Job, and especially task, analysis can also be used to describe the operations involved in using a system component (e.g., whether the task, subtask, or task element requires tracking, searching, monitoring, or decision making) and in determining the impact design will have on system operation. Again, the job/task inventory and critical incident methods are often useful precursors to these kinds of applications.

The results of job analysis are also used for job evaluation. Job evaluation is the process by which wage rates are differentially applied to jobs. The analyst conducting the job evaluation takes a number of factors into account (e.g., duties and tasks performed, required knowledge and skills, the work environment and conditions), weights those factors, and places each job at some point along a continuum. The analyst then uses job analysis results to describe the continuum in terms of a series of classes, usually corresponding to wage categories. There are several well-known deductive job analysis methods that can be used for this purpose.

Finally, the results of job analysis are often used to support curriculum design and development. The fundamental step in designing a training program is to conduct a needs analysis that specifies a set of objectives for training. These objectives may include the provision of particular knowledge, the development of specific skills, or the formation of selected attitudes. Needs analysis consists of three separate components: organizational analysis, job and task analysis, and person or worker analysis. In this book we describe job and task analysis methods that can be used to determine instructional objectives related to particular job activities or operations. When conducting analyses to support training design and development, the question being asked is, "What skills, knowledge, and attitudes may be necessary for successful performance of the job duties being considered?"

Within this broad context of work and job performance, the fundamental building block of any measurement program designed to assess the strengths and weaknesses of personnel is a job analysis. Job analysis consists of a systematic set of procedures or methods for determining what workers actually do on the job and for describing which aspects of worker knowledge, skill, ability, and other characteristics (KSAOs) contribute to job performance. In this book we consider three different job analysis methods or procedures.

In Chapter 2, we describe deductive methods of job analysis in which jobs are analyzed to determine which variables (from standard sets of variables) apply to them. The methods are deductive in the sense that the analyst starts with a predefined taxonomy to describe job requirements. Several deductive job analysis schemes are available, such as functional job analysis (Fine & Wiley, 1971), the Position Analysis Questionnaire (McCormick, Mecham, & Jeanneret, 1972), and the Occupational Information Network (O*NET), the latest and most comprehensive of the deductive job analysis methods (Peterson, Mumford, Borman, Jeanneret, & Fleishman, 1995). These and other deductive job analysis schemes primarily differ in terms of the standard set of descriptive variables they incorporate. In Chapter 2, we discuss the circumstances under which deductive job analysis is most useful, describe several popular deductive job analysis methods that preceded the O*NET, and discuss how the database underlying the O*NET can be used to streamline deductive methods of job analysis.

In Chapters 3 and 4, we describe inductive methods of job analysis in which the analyst begins by gathering detailed information about the job in terms of what workers do and what they need to know to perform the work. The data are then organized into categories and the analyst induces a higher order structure. In Chapter 3, we describe the job/task inventory method of job analysis in which several procedures (e.g., review of existing documentation, observations, interviews, and surveys) are used to obtain information about jobs. In this chapter we also describe how to assemble typical job analysis surveys, including how to define duty areas, how to write task statements, and how to describe knowledge, skills, abilities, and other characteristics. In Chapter 4, we describe the critical incident technique (Flanagan, 1954), which is another inductive method having great value in uncovering important dimensions of job performance. In this chapter, we include guidance on how to conduct incident writing workshops and how to analyze the incidents to identify underlying dimensions of performance that can be used to construct behaviorally anchored rating scales, among many other applications.

DETERMINING WHAT AND HOW TO MEASURE: DEVELOPING A TEST PLAN

Developing a test plan is the second section of the book. Though quite brief, consisting of but a single chapter, it serves as a bridge between guidance on how to conduct various types of job analysis and guidance on how to apply the results of those analyses to develop various kinds of measurement instruments. The test plan is a formal way of helping practitioners identify tests and other assessment tools that best satisfy the three objectives of a personnel assessment system: to maximize validity, to minimize adverse impact, and to enhance the efficiency of the measurement approach.

In Chapter 5, we describe how to develop a test plan in the context of developing an employee selection system. The test plan serves as a blueprint that specifies what personnel characteristics are to be measured—as determined from job analysis—and how the targeted characteristics may best be measured to satisfy the three criteria just mentioned. Although we focus on activities in the context of employee selection, similar methods could be used for designing training. For example, activities such as specifying the training objectives in behavioral terms and then determining what training methods to employ to achieve each objective most effectively and efficiently are valuable for developing training programs.

DEVELOPING MEASURES TO PREDICT JOB PERFORMANCE

When selecting employees for jobs or training programs, it is important to have predictors that are based on the requirements of the job and are valid for predicting performance on the job. Predictors can include cognitive ability tests, interviews, background data items, situational inventories, and specially constructed measures of complex cognitive skills. Each of these possibilities is discussed in subsequent chapters along with practical advice on how to develop and implement each type of measure.

Human resource planning—for example, managing growth, downsizing, and reassignment—requires the development of predictors of job performance. To the extent that jobs are changing (e.g., jobs become more technically challenging, job requirements are redefined as a result of corporate acquisitions and mergers), the constructs that predict performance on those jobs will also change. In all of these circumstances new predictors will be required to help determine which individuals to hire, which to retain, or which to reassign to different departments. Similarly, different kinds of selection measures can be used for career development purposes, determining which employees are most likely to thrive in particular assignments and which are likely to benefit most from specific training programs.

In this section, we describe five different methods that can be used to measure potential predictor constructs identified during a job analysis. In Chapter 6, we discuss the nature of cognitive ability and offer definitions of this pervasive construct domain (e.g., Carroll, 1993; Sternberg, 1988). We also explore important issues surrounding the use of measures of cognitive ability as predictors of job performance, including adverse impact and the need to investigate alternative predictors, and the concept of validity generalization as it applies to cognitive ability and the prediction of job performance (Schmidt & Hunter, 1981). In the "how to" portion of this chapter, we describe how to select an appropriate test and how to develop one should the need arise. The latter guidance includes procedures for developing test specifications, creating items, conducting sensitivity reviews, conducting tryouts of items, and analyzing item data.

In Chapter 7, we discuss employment interviews. In the first part of the chapter, we describe research on the psychometric properties of the employment interview, including reliability and validity (e.g., McDaniel, Whetzel, Schmidt, & Maurer, 1994; Wiesner & Cronshaw, 1988), adverse impact (e.g., Motowidlo et al., 1992), and the incremental validity provided by interviews beyond cognitive ability (e.g., Pulakos & Schmitt, 1995). In the second part of this chapter, we offer guidance on how to use critical incidents to generate interview questions and response alternatives for two types of interviews: situational interviews and structured behavioral interviews.

We begin Chapter 8 with a description of validation research that has been conducted on background item or biodata predictors (Stokes, Mumford, & Owens, 1994). We then discuss the theory underlying use of biodata items—that past behavior is predictive of future behavior. In later sections of this chapter, we describe methods for generating items and developing scales that have been used in several settings.

In Chapter 9, we discuss the use and development of situational inventories as a form of low-fidelity job simulation. We discuss the psychometric characteristics of low-fidelity simulations (e.g., Motowidlo, Dunnette, & Carter, 1990) and provide guidance on building situational inventories. This advice includes methods for creating items and response options that describe potential actions that might be taken in response to a particular situation.

In Chapter 10, we describe recent innovations in assessment of complex, cognitive workplace skills that represent the application of theory and research in cognitive psychology (e.g., Frederiksen, Mislevy, & Bejar, 1993). We provide a historical overview of how complex skills have been measured and present the principles that should be used to guide development of the new generation of such measures. We conclude the chapter with an example illustrating the use of these principles to design an assessment of "teamwork."

DEVELOPING MEASURES OF JOB PERFORMANCE

One of the most common reasons for developing measures of job performance is to satisfy an organization's need to determine how well its employees are performing on the job. Operational performance appraisal systems are used to support a variety of personnel decisions, such as salary increases and promotions. When jobs are redesigned or the job requirements change, companies may have to determine which employees to retain or reassign. Measures of past performance can be useful when reaching such decisions. Operational performance appraisal systems also are used as feedback mechanisms, enabling employers to explain developmental needs to their employees.

Another purpose for developing measures of job performance is to support research efforts intended to establish the validity of selection instruments or to assess the effectiveness of training. Measures of job performance, whether based on rating scales, job knowledge tests, work sample tests, or combinations of these three, provide criteria against which to validate the kinds of predictor instruments discussed in earlier chapters. Measures of job performance can be used to evaluate training. Evaluators often use paper-and-pencil measures of job knowledge to evaluate the degree to which learning has occurred. Work sample measures are used to indicate the extent of skill acquisition and the retention of that skill over time. Rating scale data can inform evaluators about further needs for improvement of performance that can be achieved through training.

Although we have categorized various measurement instruments as "predictors" in one section and "performance measures" in another, several instruments can be used for either purpose. This certainly is true of rating scales, job knowledge tests, work sample tests, and situational inventories. The use of various measurement approaches and instruments depends on the purpose of the measurement as indicated by the study design and as specified in the test plan documentation.

In Chapter 11, we describe the background and development of rating scales. Rating scales, when used to measure job performance, describe typical performance, or what an employee "will do" day to day on the job. We describe various methods for developing rating scales that make use of critical incident data (Smith & Kendall, 1963). We also give guidance on developing behaviorally anchored rating scales (Campbell, Dunnette, Arvey, & Hellervick, 1973), behavioral summary scales (Borman, Hough, & Dunnette, 1976), behavior observation scales (Latham & Wexley, 1981), and mixed standard scales (Blanz & Ghiselli, 1972). We include a discussion of rater training and the role of performance appraisal in the context of organizations (Pulakos, 1984, 1986).

In Chapter 12, we describe the development of measures of maximal performance. These measures focus on what an employee "can do" under relatively ideal testing conditions. We describe the behavioral element method of developing work sample tests and the use of performance-based written test items in job knowledge test development. We also offer advice on a number of scoring issues attendant to work sample testing, including product versus process scoring, the scorability and observability of tasks, pass/fail scoring versus level ratings of performance, and the not inconsequential matter of the logistics of testing.

CONDUCTING STUDIES TO ASSESS THE QUALITY OF THE MEASUREMENT PROGRAM

In the final section of this book, we seek closure on the topics of conducting job analyses, developing a test plan, developing predictor measures, and developing measures of job performance. Consistent with the slant on personnel selection that runs throughout, in Chapter 13 we describe the validation of selection instruments. In this chapter we discuss definitions of validity, raise issues that need to be addressed when developing a validation research plan, and offer advice on how to collect and analyze data. In this latter connection we also discuss the notion of test bias and how to assess it.

ADOPTING A COMMON THEME

The advice and guidance offered in this book are based on the experiences of a large number of applied research psychologists who have developed applied measurement methods in many different contexts for many different purposes, primarily but not exclusively related to the world of work. Within the context of the workplace, these practitioners have developed measures of many different kinds of predictor constructs related to performance on many different kinds of jobs, ranging from anesthesiologists to salespersons, from insurance agents to infantry. The challenge, therefore, has been to adopt, insofar as possible, a common context within which to provide advice and offer guidance.

Toward that end we have chosen to use the job of electrician as a running example throughout this volume so that the reader may better understand how measures are developed for a single job and how the various parts of the measurement process interrelate. The example is based on a large-scale project currently ongoing at the American Institutes for Research (Williams, Peterson, & Bell, 1994) in which we are developing and validating instruments for use in selecting candidates for a nationally based electrician apprenticeship program. As components of this project, we have: (1) conducted inductive job analyses, which included using the job/task inventory method to identify the tasks performed by electricians and the KSAOs related to task performance, and the critical incident technique to gather incidents and specify important dimensions underlying electrician performance; (2) developed predictor instruments, including measures of cognitive ability such as reading comprehension and spatial ability, and noncognitive measures such as biodata items; and (3) developed criterion performance measures such as behavioral summary rating scales. Throughout the book we make liberal use of samples of tasks, critical incidents, unused items, rating scales, and other materials drawn from this project to aid the practitioner in following the guidance we offer.

REFERENCES

Bernardin, H. J., & Beatty, R. W. (1984). *Performance appraisal: Assessing human behavior at work.* Boston: Kent-Wadsworth.

Blanz, R., & Ghiselli, E. E. (1972). The mixed standard scale: A new rating system. *Personnel Psychology, 25,* 185–200.

Borman, W. C., Hough, L. M., & Dunnette, M. D. (1976). *Development of behaviorally based rating scales for evaluating U.S. Navy Recruiters* (Technical Report TR-76-31). San Diego, CA: Navy Personnel Research and Development Center.

Campbell, J. P., Dunnette, M. D., Arvey, R. D., & Hellervick, L. V. (1973). The development and evaluation of behaviorally based rating formats. *Journal of Applied Psychology, 57,* 15–22.

Carroll, J. B. (1993). *Human cognitive abilities: A survey of factor-analytic studies.* New York: Cambridge University Press.

Dumas, J. S., & Redish, J. C. (1993) *A practical guide to usability testing*. Norwood, NJ: Ablex.

Fine, S. A., & Wiley, W. W. (1971). *An introduction to functional job analysis*. Kalamazoo, MI: W.E. Upjohn Institute for Employment Research.

Flanagan, J. C. (1954). The critical incident technique. *Psychological Bulletin, 41,* 237–358.

Frederiksen, N., Mislevy, R. J., & Bejar, I. I. (Eds.). (1993). *Test theory for a new generation of tests*. Hillsdale, NJ: Erlbaum.

Latham, G. P., & Wexley, K. N. (1981). *Increasing productivity through performance appraisal*. Reading, MA: Addison-Wesley.

McCormick, E. J., Mecham, R. C., & Jeanneret, P. R. (1972). *Technical manual for the Position Analysis Questionnaire (PAQ)*. West Lafayette, IN: PAQ Services.

McDaniel, M. A., Whetzel, D. L., Schmidt, F. L., & Maurer, S. (1994). The validity of employment interviews: A comprehensive review and meta-analysis. *Journal of Applied Psychology, 79,* 599–616.

Motowidlo, S. J., Carter, G. W., Dunnette, M. D., Tippins, N., Werner, S., Burnett, J. R., & Vaughan, M. J. (1992). Studies of the structured behavioral interview. *Journal of Applied Psychology, 77,* 571–587.

Motowidlo, S. J., Dunnette, M. D., & Carter, G. W. (1990). An alternative selection procedure: The low-fidelity simulation. *Journal of Applied Psychology, 75,* 640–647.

Peterson, N. G., Mumford, M. D., Borman, W. C., Jeanneret, P. R., & Fleishman, E. A. (Eds.). (1995). *Development of prototype Occupational Information Network (O*NET) content model* (Vols. 1–2). Salt Lake City: Utah Department of Employment Security.

Pulakos, E. D. (1984). A comparison of rater training programs: Error training and accuracy training. *Journal of Applied Psychology, 69,* 581–588.

Pulakos, E. D. (1986). The development of training programs to increase accuracy with different rating tasks. *Organizational Behavior and Human Decision Processes, 38,* 76–91.

Pulakos, E. D., & Schmitt, N. (1995). Experience-based and situational interview questions: Studies of validity. *Personnel Psychology, 48,* 289–308.

Schmidt, F. L., & Hunter, J. E. (1981). Employment testing: Old theories and new research. *American Psychologist, 36,* 1128–1137.

Smith, P. C., & Kendall, L. M. (1963). Retranslation of expectations: An approach to the construction of unambiguous anchors for rating scales. *Journal of Applied Psychology, 47,* 149–155.

Sternberg, R. J. (1988). *The triarchic mind*. New York: Viking.

Stokes, G. S., Mumford, M. D., & Owens, W. A. (Eds.). (1994). *Biodata handbook: Theory, research and use of biographical information in selection and performance prediction*. Palo Alto, CA: Consulting Psychologists Press.

Wiesner, W. H., & Cronshaw, S. F. (1988). The moderating impact of interview format and degree of structure on the validity of the employment interview. *Journal of Occupational Psychology, 61,* 275–290.

Williams, K. M., Peterson, N. G., & Bell, J. A. (1994). *Job analysis of three electrical worker positions for the National Joint Apprenticeship and Training Committee*. Washington, DC: American Institutes for Research.

CONDUCTING JOB ANALYSES

Job Analysis

Overview and Description of Deductive Methods

Norman G. Peterson
P. Richard Jeanneret

OVERVIEW

For our particular purposes in this text, we distinguish between deductive and inductive methods of job analysis. By *deductive,* we mean those methods that emphasize the use of already existing knowledge or taxonomies of job information in the analysis of the job(s) that is the focus of attention. For example, the use of a published, commercially available job analysis inventory such as the *Position Analysis Questionnaire* (PAQ; McCormick, Jeanneret, & Mecham, 1989) to study one or more jobs is a deductive approach. The information collected about the job is automatically organized within the already existing system of job descriptors and can be interpreted within a database of quantitative scores on those descriptors for other jobs, providing such a database is available (as it is for the PAQ). In contrast, we define *inductive* methods as those that emphasize the collection of new, detailed information about the focal job(s) and the use by the analyst of that information to create a coherent, structured description of the job–but one that is necessarily limited by its uniqueness.

In this chapter, we first provide some basic definitions and discuss ways of conceptualizing the domain of job analysis methods, primarily to provide the context for our distinction between deductive and inductive methods of job analysis. We follow this discussion with a description of the principal methods of evaluating the quality of a job analysis. In the third major section, we describe several widely used prototypical types of deductive job analysis. In the fourth and final section, we present some issues to consider when choosing a job analysis method for a particular use.

METHODS OF JOB ANALYSIS

At the outset, we provide a few definitions that will help communication in this arena. By *job* we mean a particular collection of work tasks that are reasonably stable and coherent across a number of job holders, and sometimes across organizations—though *occupation* is often reserved to refer to jobs that occur across more than one organization. Jobs are sometimes differentiated from *positions,* which usually are thought of as a particular instance of a job. Thus, Kelly Jones holds a position as an electrician (the job) for the XYZ Corporation. *Job families* are thought of as closely related jobs, such as a collection of clerical jobs. In effect, then, *positions* make up *jobs* which make up *job families. Job descriptor,* or just *descriptor*, is a generic term for a variable or type of variable used to describe jobs. Frequently used descriptors are job duties, tasks, generalized work activities, knowledges, skills, and abilities. Sometimes, but not always, descriptors are accompanied by one or more rating scales that are used to indicate the importance, frequency, or some other characteristic of the descriptor. With these definitions in mind, we now consider various methods of job analysis.

There are several ways to classify job analysis methods. An elemental distinction is that between qualitative and quantitative analyses (McCormick, 1976, 1979). *Qualitative analyses* result in narrative descriptions of jobs, usually containing general descriptions of the primary purpose of the job, the major duties of the job, and some of the important qualifications for the job. While such qualitative job descriptions are useful for providing a general sense of what is done on the job and what is required of a job holder, they have little use beyond that. *Quantitative analyses,* on the other hand, often provide numeric ratings of various types of job descriptors on scales like the importance of, time spent on, frequency of, or difficulty of performance. These numeric ratings generally are provided by job incumbents, job supervisors, persons responsible for training job holders, or other people with expert knowledge of the job—generically called *subject matter experts* (SMEs). McCormick (1979) called these SMEs the agents of data collection, another way in which he differentiated job analysis methods.

As noted above, the nature of variables used to describe the job, or job descriptors, usually is an important dimension in categorizing job analysis methods. McCormick (1976) used job- versus worker-oriented as a primary distinction. By *job-oriented* he meant descriptions of the work activities performed, usually in terms of what is accomplished, and sometimes how, why, and when the activities are accomplished. *Worker-oriented* activities included human behaviors performed in work, such as sensing, decision making and the like. The final way in which McCormick described the job analysis process was in terms of the methods of collection of job analysis information. These methods include observation of the job, interviews with individuals or groups of individuals performing or supervising the job, the collection and interpretation of critical incidents (the subject of Chapter 4), open-ended and structured questionnaires, and the review of various kinds of information or records relevant to the job. By using McCormick's categorization scheme, each instance of job analysis can be identified as quantitative or qualitative, using job- or worker-oriented descriptors, one or more methods of data collection, and one or more agents in collecting the information.

Although McCormick's system of categorizing approaches to job analysis is reasonably complete, some alternatives have been proposed. Peterson and Bownas (1982) used a 2 × 2 matrix to classify a special set of job analyses aimed at linking job-oriented (e.g., tasks) and worker-oriented (e.g., abilities) descriptors to one another. Classifying worker- and job-oriented descriptors as either *fixed* (a set of standard items intended to apply to all jobs) or *sampled* (generated specifically for each job or job type studied), they proposed four basic types of linkages. Type I includes the linkage of a fixed set of job tasks to a fixed set of worker abilities (the deductive approach), and they offered the *Position Analysis Questionnaire* as an example of this approach. Type IV includes the linkage of a sampled set of tasks to a sampled set of abilities (the inductive approach), one version of which is described in Chapter 3. Types II and III include the use of sampled tasks and fixed abilities, and fixed tasks and sampled abilities, respectively, both of which are combinations of inductive and deductive approaches.

Fleishman and Quaintance (1984) proposed a fourfold categorization of job analysis methods, labeled *behavioral description, behavioral requirements, ability requirements,* and *task characteristics.* In addition, they summarized a number of other approaches to thinking about job analysis and related taxonomies.

Harvey (1991) proposed a taxonomy of job analysis methods that uses two dimensions: behavioral/technological specificity and kind of scale metric. He posited three levels of specificity: high, medium, and low. For scale metric, he proposed three types:

■ *Cross-job relative*—meaningful, level-based comparisons across jobs, such as an absolute frequency scale (once a year, once a month, once a week, etc.)

■ *Within-job relative*—rating values expressed relative to the other descriptors (e.g., tasks) within a job, or on scales not anchored in terms of verifiable job behavior

■ *Qualitative*—no numerical ratings or other quantitative comparisons possible between jobs

Using these two dimensions he described nine major types of job analysis methods, three of which are qualitative while the other six types are all forms of quantitative analysis.

This brief review of ways of thinking about the various methods of job analysis is meant to drive home the point that there is no single best way for performing job analysis. Choice of a method depends to a large extent on the purpose for which a job analysis is being performed as well as on a consideration of the kinds of issues covered in the taxonomic schemes described above. In this book, we primarily are concerned with job analyses intended to provide information for the development of employee selection or assessment systems. With almost no exceptions, such job analyses will be quantitative. Beyond this basic distinction, we have chosen the fairly simple dichotomy of deductive versus inductive methods. The heart of this distinction lies in the use of an already existing system of job descriptors intended to apply across jobs *(deductive)* or the development of a new, tailored system intended to be unique to a particular job or family of jobs *(inductive).* The deductive analyses are more appropriate when a large-scale employee selection or promotion system is to be developed for a variety of jobs, and the inductive system is more appropriate when a single job or a small set of highly similar jobs is the focus (e.g., the electrician jobs used as examples throughout much of this text). Even here there are exceptions, however, since the use of job component or synthetic validation (Jeanneret, 1992; Mossholder &

Arvey, 1984) or validity generalization (Schmidt & Hunter, 1996) strategies for validating employee selection procedures might call for the use of deductive methods for a single job. And, in the future, it may increasingly be the case that inductive methods of job analysis might be carried out within the guiding framework of a given deductive system. Thus, the set of more general job descriptors found in a system such as the O*NET (Peterson, Mumford, Borman, Jeanneret, & Fleishman, 1995) or the PAQ might guide the identification of unique or more specific sets of job descriptors for a particular job or set of jobs.

EVALUATING THE QUALITY OF JOB ANALYSIS INFORMATION

Realizing that we are viewing job analysis as a methodology that goes beyond the narrative description and documentation of job responsibilities, requirements, and conditions, we necessarily are relying on some form of measurement. Accordingly, once we begin to measure job information in some quantitative manner, we can evaluate the quality of the actual job analysis data. This is important from two perspectives: Knowing something about the quality of the job information provides feedback to both the developer and the user of that information. In effect, it tells the developer how good the effort was that led to the resulting job information; also, it tells the user about the confidence that can be placed in the job analysis findings themselves, as well as the influence the findings might have if they are used for some human resource management purpose (e.g., to build a selection or performance appraisal system).

The quality of job analysis information can be assessed in many ways. In this section, we discuss reliability, validity, the effects of "analyst" characteristics, and sampling. Further, it should be recognized that these are generic topics and evaluation strategies, applicable to all forms of quantitative job analysis.

THEORETICAL MODELS OF RELIABILITY

The reliability of job analysis information describes the degree to which such information is consistent. The reliability of any job analysis procedure should be determined, if possible, because without knowledge of reliability, it is difficult to speak to the validity of the job analysis data or the utility of any results based on those job analysis data.

When addressing reliability, one begins with a theoretical model. There are two theoretical models that have been followed: classical reliability theory (Nunnally, 1978) and generalizability theory (Cronbach, Gleser, Nanda, & Rajaratnam, 1972). In *classical reliability theory,* one is estimating the degree to which the job analysis information is free from error or "noise." That portion of a job analysis score or index that is error free is referred to as the *true score.* Consequently, reliability becomes the ratio of the true score variance to the observed score variance, which is comprised of both error and true score. In such calculations, the reliability coefficient is similar to a correlation coefficient ranging from 0.0 to 1.0. The less the magnitude of the error variance, the higher is the ratio or reliability index.

Generalizability theory also provides an appropriate model for determining the reliability of job analysis data. Using this model, one attempts to systematically account for the multiple sources of variance that affect observed scores rather than casting them as either error or true score. The sources of variance one might investigate include job analyst, type of organization, types of jobs, types of descriptors, types of incumbents, and so forth, although it usually is not possible to analyze all the possible sources of variance at once. The notion of generalizability evolves from the strategy that one measures and evaluates one or more specific sources of variance in one study and then uses the results of that study to estimate the reliability in other, usually fairly similar, types of studies. Generalizability coefficients are obtained from these studies and are defined in terms of the extent to which job analysis scores can be "generalized" across the variables (e.g., analysts, organizations, etc.) that have been studied.

CLASSICAL RELIABILITY ESTIMATES

Reliability based on classical theory can be calculated in several ways. However, there are two fundamental designs that can guide the measurement of reliability for a job analysis instrument. One design considers the degree to which two or more independent raters (analysts) agree on the analysis of a job at the same relative point in time. The second design evaluates consistency of job data over time. A third possibility is to examine the internal consistency of the fixed set of descriptors included in the job analysis instrument. Finally, the standard error of measurement is an appropriate index in certain job analysis situations.

Interrater Agreement

Interrater agreement is usually calculated by determining the correlation between analysts across all the job descriptor items (or questions) on an instrument. The design can be confounded by whether a single position (or job incumbent) is analyzed by several job analysts or whether several positions (or job incumbents) having ostensibly the same job content are analyzed by different analysts. In all instances, differences in analyst agreement are considered to be error. When multiple and varied jobs are studied by a job analyst team, it also is possible to examine reliability for each job analysis item (as opposed to analyses conducted across all the items within an instrument). Using such a design, reliability is measured by the extent to which an item consistently differentiates across jobs, where the variability due to job differences is true score variance and the variability due to different analysts is error variance. A similar argument can be made if job analysis items are combined in some manner to form a dimension or component. The reliability of that component can be derived across a sample of jobs using the analysis of variance paradigm that considers job variability due to analysts as error variance.

As one develops an overall job analysis data collection strategy, consideration should be given to how reliability is going to be assessed. The following examples are presented to give the reader an appreciation of the options:

- *Analyst pair analyzes one job*—The term *analyst* is used here to indicate individuals who complete a job analysis instrument. It is recognized that such individuals could be incumbents, supervisors, trainees, process engineers, or others who have sound knowledge of the jobs being analyzed. When two analysts independently analyze the same job, the degree to which their scores agree is interrater reliability. When there are a number of analyst pairs, their respective reliability results can be aggregated to calculate an overall interrater reliability coefficient for the job being studied.
- *Many analysts analyze many jobs*—Unless every analyst analyzed every job, which is unlikely and probably not very efficient, then one would calculate all possible pair-wise coefficients within each job and then aggregate the data across all the jobs.

The interested reader is referred to an article by Geyer, Hice, Hawk, Boese, and Brannon (1989) who studied the reliabilities of ratings made by four experienced job analysts who independently studied 20 diverse jobs using standard United States Employment Service job analysis procedures. These procedures categorize job information into the *Dictionary of Occupational Titles* (U.S. Department of Labor, 1991) format. Results indicated that reliabilities calculated using both interrater reliability and analysis of variance models were generally high (.79 to .98) for work functions, educational development, aptitudes, temperaments, and interests; reliabilities were often moderate (.40 to .75) for physical and perceptual job demands. More recently, several studies of military occupations presented reliability estimates similar to those described above for a number of different kinds of descriptors and associated rating scales (Bennett, Ruck, & Page, 1996). Such research provides a benchmark that can be used to evaluate the consistency of other job analysis data, especially when obtained by deductive procedures.

Rate-Rerate Reliability

The second fundamental design under classical theory for measuring the reliability of job analysis data examines the consistency of the job information over time, and is known as *rate-rerate reliability*. Assuming that there is no reason for the job content to change from time one to time two (say a four-week period), then job analysis scores should be in agreement across that time frame. Any differences in job analysis scores indicate error in the data. Sometimes the resulting calculation is referred to as a stability coefficient (see McCormick, 1979, p. 133). The calculations can be done using product-moment correlations of scores across the two time periods, or by using analysis of variance, just as is done for interrater agreement calculations.

Internal Consistency

A third method for estimating reliability that evolves from classical theory is known as *internal consistency* (Nunnally, 1978). Under this method, one considers as error the sampling of descriptors in a job analysis instrument. The design necessary to calculate an internal consistency index (such as coefficient alpha or a split-half coefficient) requires a job analysis instrument that uses many descriptors to measure a particular component of work, and there must be many job analysts responding to these descriptors. Because the issue typically is not a critical one, there seldom is an attempt to assess internal consistency. Consequently, internal consistency reliability is not an especially useful index for job analysis instruments in the way that it is for various tests of individual differences.

Standard Error of Measurement

Another useful statistic that reflects the consistency of certain types of job analysis data is the *standard error of measurement*. This index is derived when, for example, a particular job has been repeatedly analyzed, perhaps in numerous organizations with the same job analysis instrument. Calculation of a "true job analysis score" for each descriptor of the job (e.g., job dimension or factor) would be expressed in terms of the standard deviation and reliability of the observed "scores." The standard error of measurement then establishes a confidence band (range of error) about a "true score," and given a band width of one standard error, about 68 percent of the observed scores should fall within the band.

Generalizability Theory and Reliability

As previously mentioned, estimates of reliability based on generalizability theory attempt to partition variance arising from multiple sources that may influence the quality of job analysis data. The analysis of variance design requires those developing a job analysis data collection process to consider the sources of variance that are important and should be measured, as well as the universe to which the job analysis scores will be generalized. Further, not only are individual sources of variation considered, but also the design allows for the evaluation of their interactions. Perhaps the two sources of variance most often of concern would be raters and time. Using a generalizability approach allows the inclusion of both sources in the calculation of one generalizability coefficient, unlike the separate calculations of interrater agreement and stability coefficients necessary when using classical reliability approaches.

Unfortunately, there are relatively few instances in which generalizability theory has been used to design a reliability study for job analysis research. The interested reader should refer to Webb, Shavelson, Shea and Morello (1981).

VALIDITY

When we ask if some set of job analysis data is valid, we want to know if the data adequately reflect and actually measure the job characteristics of interest as they in fact occur. In essence, the concept of validity requires us to examine the correctness of the information obtained with our job analysis methodology. However, it is not a process that is often completed in a very rigorous manner. That is to say, we typically assume the job analysis method asks the right questions, and we then are only concerned with observing consistent (reliable) answers. In many respects, our assumptions about validity are warranted, and it rarely is necessary to reaffirm the validity of our data through a post hoc validity study. The reasons for this assertion are described below as we examine certain validity concepts and strategies in some detail.

Content Validity

One establishes content validity by directly sampling from the domain of interest and then incorporating the material sampled into the design of the instrument that will be used for measurement purposes. Within the field of job analysis, a content validity strategy is often followed at the time of instrument development. When inductive instruments are prepared (e.g., the job-task inventory described in Chapter 3), they usually evolve from direct observations of the work and from interviews with subject matter experts (SMEs). Furthermore, such instruments are often pilot tested and provide other means for respondents to be sure that the job content domain has been adequately addressed. For nomothetic or, in our vernacular, deductive instruments that are intended to have general applicability to the analysis of a wide spectrum of occupations, the job analysis items typically are based on work activities that are broadly defined and have their foundation in many, if not most, well-known or high occupancy jobs. Most of these types of instruments are based on the incorporation of results of a large number of inductive job analyses and the use of theoretical knowledge derived from research in psychological or other relevant sciences.

If one is interested in trying to establish the content validity of job analysis findings in some methodological way, there are some alternatives. One possibility is to have subject matter experts independently confirm the representativeness and accuracy of job analysis outputs. A more rigorous approach may establish linkages between job analysis outcomes and objective records of productivity. For example, in many production jobs, employee time is charged to specific activity accounts for job costing purposes. Such records could be used as criteria to study the reasonableness of incumbent ratings of time spent on various job tasks or activities. Incidentally, while studies of this topic are few in number, the reported results are not always comforting. While McCormick (1979) mentions an air force study that was very positive in confirming job analysis results, Harvey's (1991) citations are more disconcerting.

One final strategy worth considering is adapting Lawshe's (1975) content validity ratio (CVR) approach to job analytic data. This method, as originally designed, uses the judgments of experts about test items in a particular equation to indicate the content validity of an entire test. For use in job analysis, subject matter experts could evaluate the *essentiality* of individual job analysis items and these data could be incorporated into

Lawshe's CVR equation to indicate the content validity of the entire job analysis instrument. Specifically, a SME panel determines for each job analysis item (descriptor) whether the item is: essential; necessary, but not essential; or not necessary for performing the job. The ratings from the panel members are pooled and for each item the following equation is calculated:

$$CVR = (n_e - N/2) \, (N/2)$$

where: n_e equals the number of panel members rating the item as essential to performing the job, and N equals the total number of panel members.

The CVR values will range from -1 to $+1$, and if the statistic equals $+1$, then all members agree that the item was essential to performing the job. One would evaluate the distribution of CVR values to decide what level would be sufficient to conclude that an item would have *content validity*. The aggregation of all item CVRs would indicate the level of content validity for the entire instrument.

Construct Validity

In a classical *construct validity* model, a new measure of a construct is compared to an established and accepted measure of that same construct and, if possible, to accepted measures of dissimilar, confounding constructs. If the degree of congruence (often measured with correlation coefficients) is high between the old and new measure of the construct, then the construct validity of the new measure has been established to an appreciable degree. The case is further strengthened if there is low congruence between the new measure and the measures of the dissimilar, confounding constructs. While not especially efficient, it is possible to compare results from multiple methods of job analysis and determine their similarity. If one method is well established and a second method is being used for the first time, such a technique could document the construct validity of the newer measure if comparable results were achieved. One example of such a strategy was reported by Harvey, Friedman, Hakel, and Cornelius (1988) who demonstrated the comparability of data obtained with the *Job Element Inventory* (JEI) to that collected with the *Position Analysis Questionnaire* (PAQ).

Summary

While it is possible to design job analysis methods so that one can evaluate the validity of the method or data resulting from application of the method, such efforts are seldom carried out. In many instances, the process could be redundant and might appear to confirm the obvious. Further, scholars in the field of job analysis such as McCormick (1979) are content to rely on reliability information and assume validity is acceptable if reliability is reasonable. We add that such an assumption is more likely warranted if care has been taken in developing the job analysis method and instruments from the outset.

OTHER STRATEGIES FOR EVALUATING JOB ANALYSIS INFORMATION

We discuss here some other strategies that may be useful in evaluating certain sets of job analysis information. Again, many of these strategies may be applied to both deductive and inductive methodologies.

Descriptive Statistics

The most straightforward descriptive indices can be very informative about the quality of job analysis data. One possibility is to evaluate the frequency distribution of responses (or percentage of responses) given to the various options of a descriptor scale (e.g., across the options of a frequency scale for performance of job tasks, like "once a year," "once a month," "once a week," and "once a day"). Comparisons can be made of the observed distribution to other distributions from similar studies or databases of job analytic information. Also, simply viewing the distribution in terms of reasonableness relative to rational expectations can be informative. Departures from prior findings or expectations should be investigated and clarified. There often is a special circumstance that explains the differences, but if no explanation can be found, then there may be some inadequacies with the study.

Calculating the means and standard deviations for descriptor responses can be equally informative. Again, both statistics should be comparable to known indices or expectations. Furthermore, standard deviations should be viewed in terms of how much variability there might be in the content of positions that have been merged (averaged) for analytical purposes. In fact, some researchers question the advisability of routinely using mean scores to eliminate the within-job variability that typically is observed in job analysis ratings (Harvey, 1991). The basic argument that opposes aggregating to a mean score is that it really is not error variance that is being discarded, and therefore the resulting mean score profile does not correctly represent any of the positions included within the job analysis. While our experience is not this extreme, it certainly is more comforting if one can compare observed mean scores with an existing database of information and verify the reasonableness of one's data. Such a strategy is particularly appropriate with deductive methods that have well-established databases such as that available for the *Position Analysis Questionnaire* (PAQ) or the *Generalized Work Inventory* (GWI).

Multivariate Analyses

Various kinds of multivariate analyses are often used on job analysis data. They usually are used to provide summaries of data at a higher level for one or another applied purpose. *Factor analysis* is used to identify higher level organizations of job descriptors to use in job descriptions or in other analyses. *Cluster analysis* is used to aggregate positions or jobs into higher level job families for any of a variety of purposes—to develop selection procedures or to form training curricula for related jobs. *Discriminant analyses* are used to identify job descriptors that contribute the most to differentiating among jobs. Each of these techniques has associated with it a considerable body of knowledge about its application and interpretation. From an evaluative perspective, these multivariate analyses should yield interpretable, rational results only if the underlying data are themselves meaningful. Thus, for example, if a factor analysis has been completed in a methodologically sound manner, but the outcome lacks meaning, then there is a strong likelihood that the original data were inadequate in some way. Additionally, with a factor analytic study one should be able to explain a reasonable portion of the variability of the descriptors being analyzed, and if this is not the case, there may be a concern about the representativeness of the underlying data. Similar comments apply to the other techniques. If clusters of jobs are unexpected or nonsensical, then the underlying job analysis data are probably not adequate for the purposes of the clustering and may cast doubt on the general usefulness of the data. We raise a note of caution here, however. The use of multivariate analyses is difficult and must be conducted with extreme care. The inappropriate choice of methods of multivariate analyses can lead to unexpected or nonsensical results, even if the underlying job analysis data are adequate. Further treatment of these topics can be found in a number of excellent sources (e.g., Aldenderfer & Blashfield, 1984; Cohen & Cohen, 1983; Harman, 1976; Harris, 1985).

Evaluation of Job Analyst Influences

One final strategy is to evaluate purposefully one or more influences that might be hypothesized to alter or bias the quality of job analysis data. Research has examined the effect on job analysis data of such respondent variables as gender, race, job experience, and/or effectiveness. Since the research results are mixed one cannot unequivocally assume that characteristics of the analyst will not affect the quality of job analysis data. Accordingly, reasonable attempts should be made to control for such influences, regardless of whether or not their specific influences are to be analyzed in a particular job analysis study.

Sampling

A primary method of exerting control over analyst influences, or other influences (wanted or unwanted) in job analysis data, is the use of sampling. When any strategy is used other than implementing a job analysis method that encompasses 100% of a defined analyst set (i.e., those who either perform the jobs or have knowledge about the jobs being studied), then some form of sampling occurs. In turn, the sampling strategy and final sample representativeness will influence the quality of job analysis data obtained regardless of the specific methodology implemented. In most job analysis studies, the sampling strategy is influenced by a number of variables. Some of the most important variables are as follows: Who comprises the job analyst set (incumbents, supervisors, some other subject matter experts, combinations of the foregoing)? Is the focal job made up of a single incumbent or does it have many incumbents? If the latter, how many? What geographical and functional divisions should be considered? What shifts do job incumbents work?

In consideration of the above variables, a sampling plan should be designed that provides for a representative and comprehensive analysis of the jobs under study. Subsequently, after the job analysis data collection is complete one should be able to document that the sampling plan has, in fact, been met. Generally there are not a lot of hard and fast rules that can be followed in making sampling plan decisions. McCormick and Jeanneret (1988) prepared several guidelines for sampling when studying jobs with the *Position Analysis Questionnaire* that might work well for many deductive approaches. These guidelines included the following:

- For large multi-incumbent jobs ($n = 100+$), a 10% to 20% sample should be adequate.
- For small multi-incumbent jobs ($n = 10$ to 100), a 50% or larger sample will be required.
- The *rule of three* should be followed whenever possible, which means there should be at least three respondents completing the job analysis questionnaire if other than trained job analysts are performing the analyses.

■ Obtain information about the organization from the top down to understand the functioning and distribution of jobs within an organizational unit.

EXAMPLES OF DEDUCTIVE
JOB ANALYSIS METHODS

There are several examples of deductive job analyses that could be chosen. We present two such examples in some detail, and then identify other systems that are available.

THE OCCUPATIONAL INFORMATION NETWORK (O*NET)

Our first example is the *Occupational Information Network* (O*NET), which currently is under development by the U.S. Department of Labor (Peterson, Mumford, Borman, Jeanneret, & Fleishman, 1995). We have chosen it because it is intended to become a national database on occupations and it contains virtually all the major kinds of job descriptors. It currently is in a prototype phase of development, with final completion expected in 2000. Interim versions are planned for annual releases.

Background
The O*NET is intended to replace the *Dictionary of Occupational Titles* (DOT) (U.S. Department of Labor, 1991). It has been developed to implement the recommendations of an advisory panel that was formed to review the DOT (APDOT, 1993). The recommendations included a considerable expansion of the kinds of job descriptors included in the system, the use of an electronic database as the primary mode for the occupational information, the use of questionnaire survey methodology as the primary mode of data collection, and more timely updating and maintenance of the database.

Description and Organization
Figure 2.1 shows the content model that has been implemented for the O*NET. The first thing to notice about this model is the large number of descriptor types that it contains and the way those descriptors are organized. There are six larger domains of descriptors (e.g., worker requirements) with constituent descriptor types within each domain (e.g., basic skills within worker requirements). Each of these descriptor

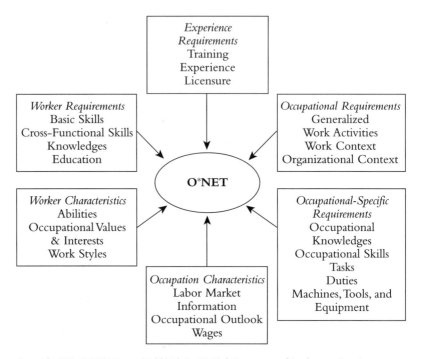

FIGURE 2.1   O*NET Content Model

types is appropriate for some uses of job analysis, but not for all. These "multiple windows" allow each user of job analysis information to select the appropriate type of descriptor for her or his purpose. The worker requirements and worker characteristics domains of the O*NET contain the kinds of descriptors referred to most often as worker oriented, while the occupational requirements, occupation-specific requirements, and occupation characteristics contain the kinds of descriptors referred to as job oriented. The experience requirements domain contains descriptors that sit between these two more general areas. All of the descriptors, with the exception of those in the occupation-specific domain, are designed to be *cross-occupational*—that is, they could be expected to apply to many different jobs, but in varying degrees of importance, frequency, or level required. Definitions of all the descriptor types and the individual descriptors themselves, with their associated rating scales, can be found in Peterson et al., 1995.

The organizational scheme of the content model, shown in Figure 2.1, is carried through in the electronic database that is the primary product of the O*NET. A specially developed software viewer can be used to examine the O*NET database; this viewer takes advantage of the hierarchically arranged multiple windows to organize the examination of the O*NET data for the user.

Rating Scales and Available Data

When all the descriptors and their associated rating scales are considered, the O*NET system contains over 1,200 separate bits of information about each occupation. These data are collected on structured questionnaires from job incumbents using a variety of rating scales, including the level or complexity of a descriptor required to perform the job, the importance of the descriptor, the frequency of performance of the descriptor, and others. The mean ratings, computed across all the available incumbents for an occupation, are the primary data entered into the O*NET database. As an interim set of data to bridge the gap between the DOT and the completion of the O*NET, trained job analysts have rated over 1,100 occupations on a subset of the O*NET descriptors by using task information derived from the DOT. The mean values of their ratings serve as an alternative, interim database.

As previously noted, the data are contained in an electronic database with a software interface that allows viewing of the data. It is intended that a large number of applications will be developed that utilize the O*NET data, including job descriptions, job classification schemes for different purposes, selection, training, vocational counseling, and others. Many of these applications, like those that have been created for the DOT, undoubtedly will be developed by independent vendors.

Figure 2.2 shows an example of the kind of information that is available from a deductive job analysis. It shows the mean level of ten generalized work activities needed to perform the electrician job, and the average of the mean ratings computed across 1,118 jobs in the preliminary O*NET database. These ratings were completed by trained job analysts. In general, the electricians show a slightly elevated profile across all the activities except number 24, which is Electronics, including electrical repair. The electricians' mean on this activity is much higher than the average across all occupations. The electrician job also is relatively high on Monitoring processes, materials, or surroundings (3), Inspecting equipment, structures, or materials (4), Updating and using job-relevant knowledge (12), and Performing general physical activities (16). Electricians are near the "All Jobs" average on Getting information to do

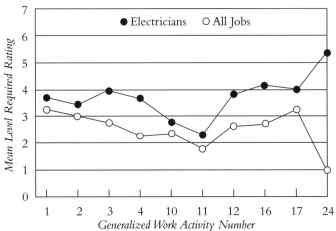

FIGURE 2.2   Sample Output from Deductive Job Analysis
Using O*NET Data

the job (1), Identifying objects, actions, and events (2), Making decisions and solving problems (10), and Thinking creatively (11). Finally, electricians are about a point higher than the average of all jobs in terms of Handling and moving objects (17). The "level required" scale used to make all these ratings has behavioral anchors at the low, mid, and high ranges of the eight-point scale. Thus, the information on electricians can be interpreted relative to the average of all other jobs, and in terms of the behavioral anchors for each of the activity scales. We note that these kinds of comparisons generally are not available from inductive job analyses.

Reliability

In the initial study of the prototype O*NET, sufficient data to conduct reliability and other analyses were collected on about 30 occupations (Peterson, Mumford, Borman, Jeanneret, & Fleishman, 1996). The primary statistic computed was the interrater agreement coefficient. There were nine questionnaires completed by incumbents, and the coefficients for the various rating scales used in the nine questionnaires ranged from a low of .45 to a high of .87, based on approximately 10 raters per occupation. Estimates for the case of 30 raters, the targeted, desired number of raters, were mostly in the .90's. Aggregate scores for the O*NET descriptors were formed by computing mean values for the descriptors that were categorized into the next highest level of each domain's hierarchy. These results were very similar to those for the base-level descriptors, except that the coefficients generally were a bit higher. The analyses also showed that the level and importance scales prominently used in the O*NET were approximately equal in terms of reliability.

The trained job analyst ratings, used in the interim database, showed comparable or higher levels of interrater agreement for those O*NET domains and occupations where both the analyst and incumbent ratings were available. The two sets of ratings showed sufficient agreement to warrant the use of the trained analyst ratings on an interim basis (the averaged correlations of the mean ratings of the analysts with the mean ratings of the incumbents ranged from .53 to .74 across the common O*NET domains).

THE POSITION ANALYSIS QUESTIONNAIRE (PAQ)

Description

The *Position Analysis Questionnaire* (PAQ)* was designed with the specific intent of developing a generic, worker-oriented, structured questionnaire that would provide quantitative information about a job undergoing analysis. The PAQ is generic in that it can be used to analyze virtually any job in any industry across the entire labor force. Since its inception in 1969, the PAQ has been used in hundreds of thousands of job analyses across the entire labor force, including all of the major jobs found in the *Dictionary of Occupational Titles* (DOT). The results of these job analyses are retained in a comprehensive database.

The PAQ is worker oriented because it focuses on the human behaviors or requirements that are involved in work activities. This perspective is in contrast to job-oriented procedures that describe the tasks, duties, technologies, or outcomes of jobs (see McCormick, 1979, for a thorough discussion of these differences). Questions on the PAQ are organized in a format whereby the respondent (job analyst) uses a rating scale to "analyze" the involvement of each of 187 questions in the job

---

*The PAQ is copyrighted and trademarked by the Purdue Research Foundation. It is published by PAQ Services, Inc. in Logan, Utah.

being analyzed. Any job is analyzed with the same set of questions, although not all questions will be applicable to a given job. The PAQ provides structured information about a job, since the rating scale responses are scored with research-based algorithms that compare the results for the job of interest to the master database of jobs. In turn, the job analysis results, which are expressed in standard score and percentile forms, can be interpreted both ipsatively and normatively.

Organization of the PAQ

The questions in the PAQ are organized into six divisions:

1. *Information Input*—Where and how does the worker get the information that is used in performing the job?
2. *Mental Processes*—What reasoning, decision-making, planning, and information-processing activities are involved in performing the job?
3. *Work Output*—What physical activities does the worker perform and what types of tools or devices are used?
4. *Relationships with Other Persons*—What relationships with other people are required in performing the job?
5. *Job Context*—In what physical and social contexts is the work performed?
6. *Other Job Characteristics*—What activities, conditions, or characteristics other than those described above are relevant to the job?

The first three divisions include questions that characterize specific types of job activities within three major categories that exist in virtually every job—receiving information from the job environment, mentally processing that information (typically leading up to a decision), and taking some form of action or creating some work output. The other three divisions characterize the involvement with others, the work context, and the demands of the job.

PAQ Descriptors

Each PAQ question describes a *general* work behavior/activity, work condition, or job characteristic. In most cases, examples (often job titles or major job features) illustrate the *central idea* of the job descriptor. However, these examples *only* help illustrate the intent of the descriptors and represent only a *few* of the possible examples that could characterize these descriptors. Extensive information on how to interpret the PAQ questions is contained in a job analysis manual (McPhail, Jeanneret, McCormick, & Mecham, 1991).

Rating Scales for PAQ Descriptors

The relevance of a PAQ descriptor to the job being analyzed is determined by a rating given by the analyst. Several different rating scales are used throughout the questionnaire, and directions are provided for each particular type of scale. The types of rating scales include extent of use, importance, time, possibility of occurrence, and applicability (i.e., a dichotomous index).

Reliability of PAQ Data

Reliability has been determined for the ratings of each PAQ question across all 189 descriptors by having two analysts study the same job and independently complete a PAQ. The ratings were then correlated, and the averages for pairs of analysts were accumulated across a wide range of job analyses to obtain an average reliability coefficient. The average reliability coefficients have typically been in the 0.80s and even as high as 0.90 across 303 different positions analyzed with the PAQ. Also, studies have been completed regarding the rate-rerate reliability of the PAQ, and the results reveal reliabilities in the high 0.70s and 0.80s. These reliability results tend to be consistent whether the analysts are incumbents, supervisors, or independent analysts, although job incumbents and their supervisors do give higher ratings on the descriptors than do independent analysts. (See McCormick & Jeanneret, 1988; McCormick, Mecham, & Jeanneret, 1977; and Smith & Hakel, 1979; for more information on the reliability of PAQ data.)

PAQ Job Dimensions

A statistical procedure known as *factor analysis* (specifically, *principal components analysis*) has been used to derive a set of dimensions of human behaviors involved in job activities, and these dimensions can characterize the structure of work (McCormick & Jeanneret, 1988). The PAQ dimensions have been replicated in several independent studies, and the set of dimensions that is used to derive various PAQ outputs (see below) is based on a sample of 2,200 jobs that characterizes the composition of the U.S. labor force. Each job analyzed with the PAQ is scored in terms of the job dimensions, and results are provided in terms of both standard scores and percentiles.

PAQ Outputs

The PAQ dimensions serve as the common denominators for comparing the similarities and differences between and among jobs, and for estimating the personal requirements and worth (job evaluation values) of jobs. Specific outputs that can be derived include the following:

- Estimates of the requirements for various mental (i.e., verbal, numerical, etc.), perceptual, psychomotor, and physical abilities
- Estimates of the requirements for certain types of temperaments and interests
- Estimates of the worth of a job (expressed as job evaluation points and a prestige score) and the probability that a job is exempt from the Fair Labor Standards Act
- Job families that can form career progressions or establish the basis for grouping jobs for some purpose

The above outputs can be used to develop or support a number of human resource management systems. Examples include developing a selection process, designing a compensation plan, preparing a performance appraisal system, or instituting a career development and vocational counseling program. More descriptive information on the derivation and application of PAQ data can be found in Jeanneret (1988) and McCormick & Jeanneret (1988).

OTHER DEDUCTIVE JOB ANALYSIS INSTRUMENTS

In order to provide the reader with a wide range of options that might be useful for a specific job analysis study, we have compiled information on instruments that fit our definition of a deductive job analysis method. By no means is it our position that we have identified all of the available instruments, nor is it our intention to endorse any method. In fact, it is important to recognize that we have obtained the information provided here directly from materials written by the developers or publishers. In some instances the information may not be completely up to date or otherwise may have changed. Accordingly, we would recommend contacting the developer or publisher for more detailed information about an instrument of interest before making either a positive or negative selection decision.

Table 2.1 provides the following information about each deductive job analysis instrument:

- *Instrument Name*—full name as well as acronym, if used
- *Types of Jobs*—the categories for which the instrument is relevant
- *Types of Descriptors*—the types and number of questions (items) included in the instrument

- *Types of Analyst*—individuals whom the developer/publisher indicates should complete the instrument
- *Applications*—uses the developer/publisher has intended for the job analysis results obtained with the instrument
- *Database Available*—whether or not a database of job analysis information is maintained
- *Year Developed*—the year the instrument was developed
- *Availability*—name of developer/publisher who can be contacted for more information about the instrument

ISSUES IN CHOOSING JOB ANALYSIS METHODS

To select from the number of available job analysis systems and methodologies, the user must make a series of decisions about the nature of the job analysis that is to be undertaken. In addition, comparisons must inevitably be made among particular job analysis options that meet the general requirements of the planned job analysis. There is no single way to go about this process, but there are some issues that should be considered along the way. We offer one particular set of ordered questions as an illustration. Other questions or differing orders of questions certainly are possible. We are assuming in the following that the decision has already been made to use one or the other of the deductive methods as opposed to the inductive method. The inductive method is generally preferred when it is desirable, for whatever reason, to generate descriptors "from scratch" for a particular job or job family, and it is described in the next chapter.

1. *What is the purpose of the job analysis?*
   This question is offered by most authors as the single most important consideration in choosing a job analysis method. Often, though, little more is said. In general terms, the end uses of job analysis information can be job classification, employee selection/placement, performance appraisal, job evaluation, job design, disability accommodation, training development, and related human resources management programs. The person responsible for conducting a job analysis should attempt to get as complete a statement as possible about the immediate, short-term, and long-term uses of the job analysis information.

TABLE 2.1 Deductive Job Analysis Systems

Deductive Instrument	Types of Jobs	Types of Descriptors	Types of Analyst	Applications	Database Available	Year Developed	Availability
Common Metric Questionnaire (CMQ)*	All	Background Contacts with people Decision making Physical and mechanical activities Work setting (285 Items)	Analysts	Job descriptions Performance appraisal	Yes	1991	The Psychological Corporation 555 Academic Court San Antonio, TX 78204 (800) 228-0752
Fleishman Job Analysis Survey (F–JAS)	All	50 Abilities Cognitive Perceptual Psychomotor Sensory Physical	Incumbents Supervisors Analysts	Job descriptions Selection Classification Performance appraisal	No	1984	Management Research Institute, (MRI) 6701 Democracy Blvd. Bethesda, MD 20817 (301) 571-9363
Functional Job Analysis (FJA) Scales	All	Benchmark tasks organized according to three primary objects of worker behavior (i.e., data, people, things)	Analysts	Job descriptions Selection Training needs	*Dictionary of Occupational Titles*	1944 Revised 1991	*The Revised Handbook for Analyzing Jobs* U.S. Government Printing Office, Superintendent of Documents Mail Stop SSOP Washington, DC 20402-9328

*Computer analysis of data available

Instrument	Population	Dimensions/Items	Completed by	Purpose	Computer scored	Year	Contact
General Work Inventory (GWI)	All	Sensory activities, Information-based activities, General mental requirements, General physical requirements, Physical activities, Interpersonal activities, Work conditions, Job benefits (268 items)	Incumbents Supervisors	Job profiling Selection Placement	Yes	1981	J.W. Cunningham Department of Psychology North Carolina State University Raleigh, NC 27695-7801 (919) 515-1703
Identifying Criteria for Success (ICS)	Managers Professionals Sales Hourly Clerical	41 job dimensions	Analysts Incumbents	Selection Career planning	Yes	1990	DDI World Headquarters—Pittsburgh 1225 Washington Pike Bridgeville, PA 15017-2838

TABLE 2.1 Deductive Job Analysis Systems (continued)

Deductive Instrument	Types of Jobs	Types of Descriptors	Types of Analyst	Applications	Database Available	Year Developed	Availability
Job Analysis Guide (JAG)	All	Major duties Work behaviors Work conditions Machines/ tools and equipment Required qualifications	Incumbents Supervisors Analysts	Americans with Disabilities Act (ADA) essential functions Job accommodation selection	No	1992	Jeanneret & Associates, Inc. 601 Jefferson, Suite 3900 Houston, TX 77002 (713) 650-6535
Job Components Inventory (JCI)	Most	Tools and equipment Physical and perceptual skills Math Communications Decision making responsibilities	Trained interviewers	Curriculum development and assessment Training design Career guidance Skill profiling	Unknown	Unknown	Manpower Services Commission Sheffield, UK

Instrument	Type/Level	Content	Respondents	Uses	Norms	Year	Source
Management Position Description Questionnaire (MPDQ) Now called FOCUS	Supervisory Managerial	Activities Contacts Scope Decisions Competencies Reporting relationships	Incumbents	Job descriptions Job comparisons Job evaluation Management development Performance appraisal Selection/promotion Job design	Yes	1974	Personnel Decisions International 2000 Plaza VII Tower 45 S. 7th Street Minneapolis, MN 55402
Managerial and Professional Job Functions Inventory (MP-JFI)	Management Professional	Organizational activities Leadership responsibilities Human resources management Community activities (140 items)	Incumbents Supervisors	Job hierarchies/levels Training needs	Unknown	1978	Melany Baehr 5555 S. Everett #E3 Chicago, IL 60637 (312) 324-8190

TABLE 2.1 Deductive Job Analysis Systems (continued)

Deductive Instrument	Types of Jobs	Types of Descriptors	Types of Analyst	Applications	Database Available	Year Developed	Availability
Minnesota Job Description Questionnaire (MJDQ)	All	21 statements about work environment given in terms of occupational reinforcers	Incumbents	Vocational counseling Occupational grouping	Yes	1968	University of Minnesota Vocational Psychological Research Minneapolis, MN 55402
Multipurpose Occupational Systems Analysis Inventory– Closed Ended (MOSAIC)	All federal occupations	Task Competencies	Incumbents Supervisors	Position description Position classification Selection	Yes	1990–1996	U.S. Office of Personnel Management Personnel Resources and Development Center Theodore Roosevelt Bldg. 1900 E Street, NW Washington, DC 20415-0001

Name	Applicability	Content (items)	Respondents	Uses	Availability	Year	Contact
Occupational Information Network (O*NET)	All	Tasks, Abilities, Interests/values, Work styles, Skills, Knowledge, Education, Experience, Generalized work activities, Context (1200 items)	Incumbents, Analysts, Supervisors	Job description, Job grouping, Job matching, Intended as a database for integrated human resources management	Limited availability until 1998	1996	Employment and Training Administration U.S. Department of Labor Office of Policy and Research 200 Constitution Ave, NW Washington, DC 20210-0001 (202) 219-7161
Position Analysis Questionnaire (PAQ)	All	Information input, Mental processes, Work output, Relationships with others, Job context, Job demands (189 items)	Incumbents, Analysts, Supervisors	Selection, Job evaluation, Job grouping, Job design, Performance appraisal, Position classification, Job matching	Yes	1969	PAQ Services, Inc. 1625 North 1000 East Logan, Utah 84321 (801) 752-5698

TABLE 2.1 Deductive Job Analysis Systems (continued)

Deductive Instrument	Types of Jobs	Types of Descriptors	Types of Analyst	Applications	Database Available	Year Developed	Availability
Position Classification Inventory (PCI)	All	84 questions tagged to Holland's Occupational Interests categories	Incumbents	Career development Vocational counseling	Yes	1990	Psychological Assessment Resources, Inc. P.O. Box 998 Odessa, FL 33556
Professional and Managerial Position Questionnaire (PMPQ)*	Professional Management Exempt	Job functions Planning Processing information Judgments Communications Interpersonal Technical Personal	Analysts Incumbents	Job evaluation Performance appraisal Job grouping	Yes	1976	PAQ Services, Inc. 1625 North 1000 East Logan, Utah 84321 (801) 752-5698
Secretary's Commission on Achieving Necessary Skills (SCANS)	Entry-level jobs in the U.S. work-force	Basic skills Foundation skills Personal qualities Illustrative tasks	Analysts	Position description Vocational counseling Selection	No	1992	Arnold H. Packer Johns Hopkins University Institute for Policy Studies Wyman Park Building 3400 N. Charles Street Baltimore, MD 21218-2696 (410) 516-7174

*Computer analysis of data available

Threshold Traits Analysis System (TTAS)	All	33 traits: Physical Mental Learned Motivational Social	Incumbents Supervisors Other SMEs (minimum of 5 recommended)	Selection/ promotion Training needs Effectiveness Performance appraisal	Unknown	1970	Lopez & Associates, Inc. One Third Vista Way Port Washington, NY 11050 (576) 883–4041
Transition to Work Inventory (TWI)	Most	Physical Psychomotor Decision making Social interaction Perceptual Equipment use Context (81 items)	Analysts	Job accomodation	No	1996	The Psychological Corporation 555 Academic Court San Antonio, TX 78204 (800) 228-0752

TABLE 2.1 Deductive Job Analysis Systems (continued)

Deductive Instrument	Types of Jobs	Types of Descriptors	Types of Analyst	Applications	Database Available	Year Developed	Availability
Work Profiling System (WPS)*	Managerial/ professional Service/ administrative Manual/ technical	Tasks Key context factors (492 items)	Incumbents Supervisors Analysts	Selection Placement Performance appraisal Job design Job description	Yes	1986	Saville & Holdsworth, Ltd. 575 Boylston St. Boston, MA 02186
Worker Rehabilitation Questionnaire (WRQ)	All	Same as PAQ (150 items)	Analysts	Disability/ rehabilitation	Yes	1986	Worker Rehabilitation Associates 4265 Corrienta Place Boulder, CO 80301 (303) 581-9778

*Computer analysis of data available

Examples of statements of purpose that are inadequate are: "Selection," "Improve skills," and "Find out why we are losing profit." Better statements are: "To develop and validate employee selection tests for every entry-level job in our company," "To find out what we need to be training our customer representatives on," or "To make it easier to transfer people across jobs with some assurance that they can perform well on the new job in a reasonable period of time." Note that each of the first set of inadequate statements is very short, very vague, or identifies an organizational outcome very distal from job analysis information. Each of the second set of statements, while not perfect, contains information about the personnel function to be implemented or changed and the range of jobs that are to be included. This usually is about as much information as persons unfamiliar with job analysis are able to provide for the general purpose of a job analysis. One very important decision to make here is whether or not a job analysis is even called for; some organizational problems definitely call for different research approaches or interventions. The purpose statement will often point toward particular kinds of job descriptors (e.g., abilities and skills if employee selection is the purpose of the analysis) or toward a system that has an already developed application for that purpose (e.g., a method for evaluating jobs for compensation if the development of a compensation system is the purpose).

2. *What is the scope of the intended job analysis?*
   Although the definition of the purpose should illuminate the intended end use of the job analysis information, the scope of people and organizations to be included has a major effect on choosing the job analysis system. Factors affecting scope include number of positions within each job, amount of diversity of jobs, number of major job families, and number and geographic scatter of organizations or organizational sites. A very focused analysis involving a few positions within one job at one organizational site argues for the use of an interview or group interview approach and, therefore, the use of a job analysis system that can be used efficiently by interviewers/trained analysts. On the other hand, when many jobs across many organizations are involved, the use of an efficient survey questionnaire that can be completed by incumbents or supervisors may be the best bet. A related question here is the availability of subject matter experts for participation. That is, will job incumbents, supervisors, trainers,

human resources experts, or others with expert knowledge about the job(s) be able to provide time for completion of question-naires or to be interviewed? Less availability calls for more targeted use of job descriptors for the more immediate purposes; greater availability allows the use of a greater range of descriptors with greater potential for long-range use. Finally, if a job analysis system has a database encompassing the appropriate kind of information for the focal jobs, then it may be useful as a substi-tute for the planned job analysis, for augmenting the information that will be collected, or as a means of checking the quality of the to-be-collected job information.

3. *Which candidate job analysis system has the technical, legal, and practi-cal characteristics that most closely match the purpose and scope of the planned job analysis?*

Given as complete a definition as possible of the purpose(s) and scope of the job analysis, there may be several deductive methods that might be appropriate. Such candidates have the appropriate descriptors, can be used by the appropriate SMEs, have appropri-ate end products or applications, and have an existing, appropri-ate database. Each should then be evaluated on its technical qual-ity, legal defensibility, and practicality of use. By technical quality we mean the demonstrated reliability and validity of the system as described in our earlier section on the quality of job analysis data. Legal defensibility is a somewhat volatile concept, changing with the passage of pertinent laws (e.g., the Civil Rights Acts of 1964 and 1991), the accumulation of court decisions (e.g., Albermarle Paper Co. v. Moody, 1975; Griggs v. Duke Power Co., 1971), and changes in accepted professional practice (*Uniform Guidelines,* 1978; APA Standards, 1985; SIOP, 1987). A demonstrated track record of accepted use by the courts and within the profession of industrial and organizational psychology provides some promise of defensibility. Practicality of use includes such considerations as training required for use by SMEs, accept-ability to SMEs and end users of the job analysis instruments and products, and the cost and time required to use the data collec-tion instruments and obtain outputs from the system.

While we have not undertaken a formal evaluative study of the available deductive systems, others have attempted to do so (e.g., Brumbach, Romashko, Hahn, & Fleishman, 1974; Gatewood & Field, 1991; Holley & Jennings, 1987; Levine, Ash, Hall, & Sistrunk, 1983). Although these studies are somewhat dated, the interested reader is referred to them for their comparative evaluations of various job analysis methods.

While the authors cited above have not compared and evaluated all of the instruments described in Table 2.1, they have covered several of them. Also, they have evaluated several methodologies (such as task analysis) which we have defined as inductive methods as discussed in the next chapter.

SUMMARY

In Chapter 5, the authors describe a generic test plan that guides the development of tests and assessments that are most likely to satisfy the multiple objectives of employee selection. Job analysis provides essential information for the creation of such a test plan.

Job analysis also contributes to the fulfillment of a variety of functions in human resources management. As a consequence, an understanding and specification of the purposes for job analysis are critical for selecting appropriate methods and carrying out productive analyses. Building on this basic premise, we reviewed the many ways that scholars and users of job analyses have categorized job analysis methods. Embedded in this rich context, we have made a primary distinction between deductive job analysis methods, the subject of this chapter, and inductive methods, the subject of the following chapter. The heart of this distinction lies in the use of an already existing system of job descriptors intended to apply across jobs (*deductive*) or the development of a new, tailored system intended to be unique to a particular job or family of jobs (*inductive*). Deductive analyses are generally more appropriate when a large-scale employee selection or promotion system is to be developed for a variety of jobs, and the inductive system is generally more appropriate when a single job or a small set of highly similar jobs is the focus.

We presented several techniques for evaluating the quality of quantitative job analysis information, including estimates of the reliability, validity, and sensibility of the information. Such evaluations are essential to ensuring that job analysis data are suitable for the purposes to which they are put.

We then presented information on two deductive job analysis systems: the O*NET, a national occupational database currently under development by the Department of Labor and intended to replace the DOT, and the PAQ, a commercially available system that has a long and well-researched history. We presented tabular information about a number of other deductive systems.

In the last section of the chapter, we presented a number of issues that should be considered in the choice of a job analysis system, chiefly, the purpose or purposes for the job analysis, the scope of the job analysis, and the technical, legal, and practical qualities of candidate systems that fulfill the purpose and scope of the planned job analysis.

REFERENCES

Advisory Panel for the Dictionary of Occupational Titles (1993). *The new DOT: A database of occupational titles for the twenty-first century* (Final Report). Washington, DC: Employment and Training Administration, U.S. Employment Service, U.S. Department of Labor.

Albermarle Paper Company v. Moody (1975). 422 U.S. 405.

Aldenderfer, M. S., & Blashfield, R. K. (1984). *Cluster analysis.* Newbury Park, CA: Sage.

American Psychological Association, American Educational Research Association, & National Council on Measurement on Education (Joint Committee) (1985). *Standards for educational and psychological testing.* Washington, DC: American Psychological Association.

Bennett J. W., Ruck, H. W., & Page, R. C. (1996). Military occupational analysis. *Military Psychology, Volume 8,* No. 3, Mahwah, NJ: Erlbaum.

Brumbach, G. B., Romashko, T., Hahn, C. P., & Fleishman, E. A. (1974) *Models for job analysis, test development, and validation procedures* (Final Report). Washington, DC: American Institutes for Research.

Civil Rights Act of 1964, 42 U.S.C. Section 2000e.

Civil Rights Act of 1991, 42 U.S.C. Section 2000e.

Cohen, J., & Cohen, P. (1983). *Applied multiple regression/correlation analysis for the behavioral sciences* (2d ed.). Hillsdale, NJ: Erlbaum.

Cronbach, L. J., Gleser, G. C., Nanda, H., & Rajaratnam, N. (1972). *The dependability of behavioral measurements: Theory of generalizability for scores and profiles.* New York: Wiley.

Fleishman, E. A., & Quaintance, M. K. (1984). *Taxonomies of human performance.* Orlando, FL: Academic Press.

Gatewood, R., & Field, H. S. (1991). Job analysis methods: A description and comparison of the alternatives. In J. W. Jones, B. D. Steffy, & D. W. Bray (Eds.), *Applying psychology in business.* New York: Lexington Books.

Geyer, P. D., Hice, J., Hawk, J., Boese, R., & Brannon, Y. (1989). Reliabilities of ratings available from the Dictionary of Occupational Titles. *Personnel Psychology, 42,* 547–560.

Griggs v. Duke Power Company (1971). 401 U.S. 424.

Harman, H. H. (1976). *Modern factor analysis* (3rd ed., rev.). Chicago: University of Chicago Press.

Harris, R. J. (1985). *A primer of multivariate statistics* (2nd ed.). Orlando, FL: Academic Press.

Harvey, R. J. (1991). Job analysis. In M. D. Dunnette & L. M. Hough (Eds.), *Handbook of industrial and organizational psychology* (2nd ed.). Palo Alto, CA: Consulting Psychologists Press.

Harvey, R. J., Friedman, L., Hakel, M. D., & Cornelius, E. T., III (1988). Dimensionality of the job element inventory (JEI): A simplified worker-oriented job analysis questionnaire. *Journal of Applied Psychology, 73*, 639–646.

Holley, H., & Jennings, K. (1987). *Personnel/human resource management contributions and activities.* Hinsdale, IL: Dryden Press.

Jeanneret, P. R. (1988). Computer logic chip production operators. In S. Gael (Ed.), *The job analysis handbook for business, industry, and government* (pp. 1329–1345). New York: Wiley.

Jeanneret, P. R. (1992). Application of job component/synthetic validity to contract validity. *Human Performance, 5,* 81–96

Lawshe, C. H. (1975). A quantitative approach to content validity. *Personnel Psychology, 28,* 563–575.

Levine, E. L., Ash, R. H., Hall, H., & Sistrunk, F. (1983). Evaluation of job analysis methods by experienced job analysts. *Academy of Management Journal, 26,* 339–347.

McCormick, E. J. (1976). Job analysis. In M. D. Dunnette (Ed.), *Handbook of industrial and organizational psychology* (pp. 651–696). Chicago: Rand McNally.

McCormick, E. J. (1979). *Job analysis: Methods and applications.* New York: Amacom.

McCormick, E. J., Jeanneret, P. R., & Mecham, R. C. (1989). *Technical manual for the position analysis questionnaire* (2nd ed.). Logan, UT: PAQ Services. (Available through Consulting Psychologists Press, Inc., Palo Alto, CA).

McCormick, E. J., & Jeanneret, P. R. (1988). Position analysis questionnaire (PAQ). In S. Gael (Ed.), *The job analysis handbook for business, industry, and government* (Vol. 2, pp. 825–842). New York: Wiley.

McCormick, E. J., Mecham, R. C., & Jeanneret, P. R. (1977). *Technical manual for the position analysis questionnaire* (2nd ed.). Logan, UT: PAQ Services.

McPhail, S. M., Jeanneret, P. R., McCormick, E. J., & Mecham, R. C. (1991). *Position analysis questionnaire job analysis manual.* Logan, UT: PAQ Services.

Mossholder, K. W., & Arvey, R. D. (1984). Synthetic validity: A conceptual and comparative review. *Journal of Applied Psychology, 69,* 322–333.

Nunnally, J. C. (1978). *Psychometric theory.* New York: McGraw-Hill.

Peterson, N. G., & Bownas, D. A., (1982). Skill, task, structure, and performance acquisition. In E. A. Fleishman (Ed.), *Human performance and productivity: Human capability assessment.* Volume 1. Hillsdale, NJ: Erlbaum.

Peterson, N. G., Mumford, M. D., Borman, W. C., Jeanneret, P. R., & Fleishman, E. A. (Eds.). (1995). *Development of prototype occupational information network (O*NET) content model* (Volumes 1 & 2). Salt Lake City: Utah Department of Employment Security.

Peterson, N. G., Mumford, M. D., Borman, W. C., Jeanneret, P. R., & Fleishman, E. A. (1996). *O*NET final technical report* (Volumes 1–3). Salt Lake City: Utah Department of Employment Security.

Schmidt, F. L., & Hunter, J. E. (1996). Measurement error in psychological research: Lessons from 26 research scenarios. *Psychological Methods, 1,* 199–223.

Smith, J. E., & Hakel, M. D. (1979). Convergence among data sources, response bias, and reliability and validity of a structured job analysis questionnaire. *Personnel Psychology, 32,* 677–692.

Society of Industrial and Organizational Psychology (1987). *Principles for the validation and use of personnel selection procedures* (3rd ed). College Park, MD: Author.

Uniform guidelines on employee selection procedures. (1978). Federal Register, 43, 38290–38315.

U.S. Department of Labor (1991). *The revised handbook for analyzing jobs.* Washington, DC: Author.

Webb, N. M., Shavelson, R. J., Shea, J., & Morello, E. (1981). General ability of general education development ratings of jobs in the United States. *Journal of Applied Psychology, 66,* 186–192.

3

Inductive Job Analysis
The Job/Task Inventory Method

Kristen M. Williams
Jennifer L. Crafts

OVERVIEW

Job analysis methods can serve several human resource purposes (e.g., work redesign, curriculum development, and selection measure development) whenever it is important to know the tasks performed by employees in a particular job and the personal characteristics or attributes required to perform those tasks. For the electrician project that we mention throughout this book, a job analysis was the first step in a multiyear project. The information collected from the job analysis served many purposes:

- Job descriptions for inside wireman, outside lineman, and residential wireman were written based on the job analysis.
- An apprentice course curriculum was analyzed to see whether the knowledge areas found to be most important, difficult to learn, and needed for the future were receiving the most training time.
- Cognitive ability tests to be used for selection were developed.

- A biodata inventory was developed that focused on abilities and other attributes considered to be important for electrical workers.
- A structured job interview form was developed to be used as the final step in the selection of new apprentices.

Job analysis frequently serves as the cornerstone of many other human resource processes.

In this chapter, we discuss an inductive method of job analysis: the job/task inventory method. It is considered inductive because one begins by gathering detailed information about the job in terms of what workers do and what they need to know to perform their jobs. The data are then organized into categories and a higher order structure is created (induced) by the analyst. Lists of job tasks and other information are developed, leading to an "inventory" of the job.

We begin this chapter by briefly reviewing the history of the inductive method and then describe how it is applied today. All of the work an employee performs on the job is considered part of the job's performance domain. We first discuss how to specify the duties and tasks that are part of this domain. Then we discuss the knowledges, skills, abilities, and other characteristics (KSAOs) that enable employees to perform those duties and tasks. Next we describe methods for collecting this information that range from interviews to questionnaires. Finally we describe how the task and KSAO aspects of the performance domain can be linked together.

A BRIEF HISTORY OF JOB/TASK ANALYSIS

The job/task inventory method of job analysis described in this chapter has its roots in the beginning of the twentieth century when work methods were studied by those interested in increasing production through development of more efficient procedures. "Scientific Management," as practiced by Taylor (1911) and others, led to studies of how workers perform their jobs, using "time and motion" methods, in which workers were observed and their performance of each job task was timed. These early studies of workers performing their jobs were often very detailed. For example, Gilbreth and Gilbreth (1917) created a system of symbols to represent each of 17 fundamental motion elements. The symbols were called "therbligs" (adapted from "gilbreth" spelled backward). Different types of industrial jobs began to be analyzed during this early period. One of the founders of industrial psychology

(Muensterberg, 1913) studied the characteristics of motormen working in the Electric Railway Service and the abilities needed by telephone operators working on switchboards.

Following World War I, interest in studying jobs accelerated. In 1927, the point method of job evaluation was first developed by National Electric Manufacturing and the National Metal Trades Association (Chruden & Sherman, 1980). The emphasis of the studies continued to be on increasing productivity. The well-known Hawthorne studies at General Electric (Roethlisberger & Dickson, 1939) began with the study of the effects of hours of work, rest, and light on productivity. Findings from the Hawthorne studies led to a change of emphasis from primary consideration of the mechanics of production to consideration of the social relations among workers. This change in emphasis gave rise to what has subsequently been labeled the Human Relations School (Mayo, 1933).

During the 1920s controversy arose between two groups, both of which performed job analysis. One group continued to conduct time and motion studies, also referred to as methods engineering, work design, and work study (Barnes, 1963). The other group conducted job analysis to specify job duties and the requirements for workers to perform those duties (Lytle, 1954). This led to a split between the intellectual descendants of time and motion proponents, who eventually became practitioners of industrial engineering and operations research, and those who analyzed jobs to determine worker requirements, who became personnel or industrial and organizational psychologists.

During the Depression, the federal government passed a law that influences the need for job analysis even today—the Fair Labor Standards Act of 1938. This act mandates overtime pay for hours worked above 40 hours per week. Some employees who are paid salaries are exempt from this law. In order to determine who is exempt and nonexempt, job analysis must frequently be performed. As a result, job analysis methods continued to be developed as more jobs were analyzed during this decade.

World War II created even more demand for job analysis—in both the military and civilian sectors. In the military, analysis of Army jobs was begun in 1940 by the job analysts at the U.S. Employment Service (Shartle, 1959). Eventually jobs in the Navy and the Marine Corps also were studied. The techniques used were published in a training manual for job analysts (U.S. Department of Labor, 1944). In the civilian sector, the Wage and Salary Stabilization Law of 1942 specified that a firm could not raise a worker's wages unless the worker, through promotion or some other change, was determined to be performing a different job.

Companies, wanting to give workers a raise to retain them, had to conduct a job analysis to justify the pay increase.

Following World War II, large numbers of military personnel entered the civilian labor force. The military developed links between military occupational specialties and private sector jobs using job titles in the *Dictionary of Occupational Titles* (U.S. Department of Labor, 1939). The military also supported further development of job analysis methods, such as Rupe's work (1956) for the Air Force Personnel and Training Research Center. Job analysis continued to be common throughout industry in the 1950s. During this time a new method of job analysis was developed by Sidney Fine and colleagues at the W. E. Upjohn Institute for Employment Research (Fine & Wiley, 1971). The Department of Labor eventually incorporated aspects of this system, which became known as Functional Job Analysis (FJA), in its approach to job analysis for the *Dictionary of Occupational Titles.*

The Equal Pay Act of 1963 and the Civil Rights Act of 1964 provided further impetus for conducting job analysis. The former mandated that jobs with particular pay status must involve equal skill, effort, and responsibility; the latter was the initial attempt to ensure that all persons had access to employment and that the personnel requirements of a job were, in fact, job related. This legislation led to a great increase in the need for conducting job analysis, and a number of new systems emerged, including deductive methods, such as the Position Analysis Questionnaire (PAQ) (McCormick, Jeanneret, & Mecham, 1972). The publication of the *Uniform Guidelines on Employee Selection Procedures* (EEOC, CSC, DOL, & DOJ, 1978) also increased the need for job analysis to support development of valid employee selection procedures. The Guidelines Oriented Job Analysis (GOJA), developed by Richard E. Biddle and associates during the 1970s (Bemis, Belenky, & Soder, 1983), was designed for use when employment discrimination could be charged. The Behavioral Consistency Method was yet another approach to job analysis that was developed by the U.S. Office of Personnel Management (Schmidt et al., 1979).

It was during the 1970s and 1980s that the distinction between inductive and deductive job analysis became important. As described earlier, the inductive approach begins with the collection of information about jobs from subject matter experts. The job analyst then organizes this information to form constructs or categories of job behavior. The inductive approach usually results in specific task and KSAO lists that precisely describe the job and its requirements. As an example, the U.S. Air Force developed the Comprehensive Occupational Data Analysis

Programs (CODAP; Christal, 1974) to analyze jobs. CODAP, a large-scale job analysis system based on the administration of task inventories (each containing as many as 500 tasks), has been used to organize and analyze occupational data for many human resource purposes.

Deductive job analysis, on the other hand, begins with a classification scheme or taxonomy, such as a list of physical abilities in Fleishman's system (Fleishman & Quaintance, 1983) or lists of worker functions in FJA (Fine & Wiley, 1971) or the PAQ (McCormick, Mecham, & Jeanneret, 1972). The O*NET described in the preceding chapter has many different taxonomies included as part of its database (Peterson, Mumford, Borman, Jeanneret, & Fleishman, in press). Jobs are analyzed in terms of those predefined categories. The deductive approach can be particularly useful for comparing various jobs across a number of dimensions. Both inductive and deductive approaches can be combined by including some information that is generated from the job itself, such as a task list, and other information that relies on existing taxonomies.

The job/task inventory method described in this chapter is generic and incorporates ideas and concepts from many of the job analysis systems developed by others.

HOW TO DEFINE THE TARGET POPULATION

At this point it is important to clarify how we use the terms *job* and *position* in this chapter. Widespread agreement about such definitions does not exist among job analysts, but the distinctions are important when describing how a job analysis is conducted. Within a company or organization, employees may hold different positions that have specific titles, such as project manager or foreman. *Position* refers to the location of an employee within the organizational structure and usually has a job title attached to it. Employees in different positions throughout the organization may perform similar functions for the company by doing the same kinds of work. By our definition, such employees are performing the same *job*.

When analyzing a job, or a group of jobs, the positions to be included must be determined. In other words, we need to define the target population. In some cases, the job will be defined by a particular job title, and employees who belong in that job have that job title. For example, on a residential construction site, the electrical workers are called residential wiremen, or residential trainees if they are still serving their apprenticeship. In other cases, defining the jobs to be analyzed may be more ambiguous. For example, if one is analyzing the job of salesperson in a company, one would need to determine if customer service representatives, who take orders by telephone, would be included. Persons in these positions may not actively make sales calls, but they might be able to increase a customer's order by convincing the customer to buy a more expensive product or by persuading a customer to buy additional products from a different line. Following are some questions that might be asked to help define the target population:

- Which job titles are to be included in the job analysis?
- What are the main occupational subgroups included as part of the job title(s)?
- Are there any other groups of employees with different job titles who perform similar work?
- Should any positions be excluded in advance because the work they do is very different from others with that job title?

In the case of the electrician job analysis, three jobs were analyzed: inside wireman, residential wireman, and lineman. Each of these jobs had two different levels, apprentice and journeyman. Although inside wireman is a job by our definition, a particular journeyman on a construction project to build an airline terminal may serve in the position of foreman or estimator. Therefore, the work that the foreman or estimator performs needs to be included in the job analysis of an inside wireman.

HOW TO IDENTIFY DUTIES AND TASKS

Developing a job/task inventory involves breaking job behavior down into relatively small units in a hierarchical fashion. Within a particular job (e.g., inside wireman), duties provide the highest level of description; tasks are relatively small units of work behavior and provide a more detailed level of description. A description of the processes for identifying duties and tasks follows.

IDENTIFYING DUTIES

The highest level of description in the job inventory is the job duty, responsibility, or function. Various authors have preferred one or another of these three terms. For instance, Gael (1983, p. 9) refers to a function as "a broad subdivision of a job composed of a group of tasks that are somewhat related because of the nature of the work or the behavior involved." The *Uniform Guidelines* (EEOC, CSC, DOL, & DOJ, 1978) refer to work behaviors, perhaps to emphasize that a job analysis should focus on observable behavior. Ghorpade (1988, p. 94) suggests that responsibility "can be used to depict the results or objectives for which the worker can be held accountable." We will use the term *duty* as the highest level of classification throughout this chapter. An operational definition of a job duty is a major part of the work that an incumbent performs, comprised of a series of tasks, which together accomplish a job objective.

Duties can be defined a priori, before task statements are written, or information can be collected on tasks and the tasks can later be grouped into duties. This grouping can occur using either an empirical approach, such as a factor analysis or cluster analysis of data from questionnaires, or a judgmental approach in which subject matter experts group the tasks into duties based on similarity of behavior. For an example of the empirical approach, see Sanchez and Fraser (1994), who used factor analysis to group 54 managerial job tasks into seven factors. Each factor (e.g., Evaluate and Supervise Subordinates or Plan Work of Subordinates) can be thought of as a job duty.

The number of duties used to describe jobs can vary widely. Most jobs can be described by between 5 and 15 duties. A job may have more duties if it is very complex. For example, the electrical worker positions were described by many job duties, although not all workers performed all duties. The inside wireman position was described by 19 duties, the outside lineman position was summarized by 18 duties, and the residential wireman position was described by 12 duties (Williams, Peterson, & Bell, 1994). The job duties of an inside wireman are listed in Table 3.1.

Duties are typically described in broad terms and encompass several tasks. They are written at a higher level of generalization than job tasks and each begins with a verb ending in "ing" to suggest a relatively large segment of work. For example, the duty Planning and Initiating Projects, for the inside wireman job, includes the tasks:

- Study blueprints and specifications.
- Load, haul, and unload materials and supplies.
- Assemble tools and equipment.

IDENTIFYING TASKS

When using a job/task inventory approach to analyze jobs, tasks are the basic unit of analysis. Writing clear and concise task statements is very important when collecting information about jobs. A *task* is a discrete

TABLE 3.1   Job Duties of an Inside Wireman

1. Planning and Initiating Project
2. Establishing OSHA and Customer Safety Requirements
3. Establishing Temporary Power During Construction
4. Establishing Grounding System
5. Installing Service to Buildings and Other Structures
6. Establishing Power Distribution Within Project
7. Erecting and Assembling Power Generation Equipment
8. Planning and Installing Raceway Systems
9. Installing New Wiring and Repairing Old Wiring
10. Providing Power and Controls to Motors, HVAC, and Other Equipment
11. Installing Receptacles, Lighting Systems, and Fixtures
12. Installing Instrumentation and Process Control Systems, Including Energy Management Systems
13. Installing Fire Alarm Systems
14. Installing Security Systems
15. Installing and Repairing Telephone and Data Systems
16. Installing, Maintaining, and Repairing Lightning Protection Systems
17. Installing and Repairing Traffic Signals, Outdoor Lighting, and Outdoor Power Feeders
18. Troubleshooting and Repairing Electrical Systems
19. Supervising Journeymen and Apprentices

unit of work performed by an employee that is a logical and necessary step in the performance of a duty and usually has an identifiable beginning and end (Gael, 1983).

Job duties should not be restated in various ways as tasks, but rather should be broken down into logical steps. For example, consider the duty Installing Service to Buildings and Other Structures. A task statement such as "Build an underground system using conduit to bring power in from main line" is not a discrete part of the work, but rather a general restatement of the job duty. In contrast, the task statement "Measure locations for placing conduit before pouring of concrete" is a discrete part of the work.

Writing Task Statements

Task statements have a three-part structure, as shown in Table 3.2. Task statements begin with a verb. The verb should be written in the present tense and should be in the active rather than the passive voice (e.g., "Order materials and supplies," not "Materials and supplies are ordered") (Ghorpade, 1988). The subject is understood; it is the worker. The verbs

TABLE 3.2   Structure of Task Statements

Verb	Object	Qualifier
Splice	high-voltage cables	
Grade and level	trench	
Study	blueprints	to determine location of high-voltage room or electrical closet

TABLE 3.3   Qualifiers to Be Used in Task Statements

How	Establish temporary power requirements *by consulting with other crafts.*
Why	Install batteries in parallel *to provide backup power source.*
Where	Install plates and covers *on receptacles and switches.*
When	Complete "as built" drawings *after work is complete.*
How much	Measure length of wire needed *to pull through conduit and attach to the tugging machine.*

chosen should be as specific as possible and describe behaviors that can be observed. Sometimes a statement may have two verbs. This should happen only if the actions are closely related and are part of the same unit of work (e.g., "Grade and level" as shown in Table 3.2). The second part of the task statement is the object. The object describes on whom or on what the action is performed. The third part of the statement, the qualifier, is included when additional information is needed to modify the statement. A qualifier may be included for a number of reasons to describe how, why, where, when, or how much a task is performed (Gael, 1983). Table 3.3 provides examples of different types of qualifiers that often are used in task statements.

An important issue to be resolved when conducting a job analysis is the level of detail to be used in the task statements. A discrete unit of work is a part of the work that can be defined so that it is relatively self-contained. One way to determine if a task statement is written at the appropriate level of specificity is to identify whether it has a beginning and an end. If one cannot make such a determination, the statement is probably too vague and written at too general a level. On the other hand, it is possible to break a job down into very small steps that would produce thousands of tasks, subtasks, or elements. For example, the task statement "Pull wire through conduit connected to fish tape or rope by hand" could be broken down into the following statements:

Step 1. Pick up wire with left hand,
Step 2. Put right hand on wire and grip it with both hands,
Step 3. Pull the wire back with the right hand and move the left hand forward on the wire,
Step 4. Continue to pull the wire one hand over the other.

Most task statements can be elaborated to this very fine level of detail. These steps may be considered subtasks or task elements and the process of defining them is task analysis rather than job analysis.

The purpose of the job analysis will dictate the level of detail required. If the job analysis is being conducted to support the redesign of a work process, for example, a relatively fine level of detail may be required. On the other hand, if the job analysis is intended to support the development of a selection system, such detail probably is unnecessary. The number of tasks required to describe most jobs typically is between 300 and 500 (Clifford, 1994). To minimize the overlap of task content, it is useful to write task statements so that the level of detail is relatively consistent throughout the task list.

The development of the task statements culminates in a list that is frequently put into a survey format. The characteristics of the respondents to the survey or participants in an interview or focus group should be considered when developing this list. Some guidelines adapted from Melching and Borcher (1973) are:

- The task statement must be written clearly so that it has the same meaning for all workers in the occupational area.
- The task statement must be stated using terminology that is consistent with current usage in the occupational area.
- The task statement should be brief to save reading time of the employee. Short words and expressions are preferable to longer ones (e.g., "Fill out work orders," not "Prepare forms for vehicle repairs to be accomplished by mechanics").
- Abbreviations should be used cautiously, since they may not be understood throughout the occupational area. It is good practice to spell out the term and follow it by the abbreviation in parentheses where it first appears in the inventory. In later usage the abbreviation may stand alone. However, it is best to avoid abbreviations whenever possible.

After the task list has been developed, it should be reviewed by subject matter experts (SMEs). The SMEs can meet as a group and recommend revisions, or the lists can be sent to individual SMEs for review and comment. For the electrician study, the lists were initially reviewed at a meeting of training directors. The training directors were divided into as many groups as there were job duties and each group reviewed the tasks in a particular job duty. The entire list of job duties and tasks was then revised and individually sent to eight senior training directors for final review.

GATHERING INFORMATION ABOUT DUTIES AND TASKS

After duty and task lists have been developed and reviewed and are considered complete, additional information about the tasks usually is gathered. The kinds of information to be collected will depend on the purpose(s) for which the job analysis is being conducted. Following are descriptions of these task attributes. Later in this chapter we discuss methods for collecting the information.

Part of the Job
The most basic kind of information, and the kind that almost always is collected regardless of the purpose of the job analysis, is whether or not a task is performed by job incumbents. When constructing a job analysis questionnaire, this often is the first question following a task statement. The response can then be used as a screening device before other questions about the task are asked. If a respondent does not perform the task, then he or she would not answer further questions about the importance or frequency of task performance. A task may only be performed by certain individuals in a given job. In the electrician job analysis, some of the work with fiber-optic cables was only performed in certain areas of the country.

Time Spent/Frequency
Closely related to the issue of whether a task is performed is how frequently it is performed. This information is important for a number of reasons. Tasks that are performed more frequently may be tasks that should receive greater emphasis during training. For selection purposes, the abilities required to perform such tasks may receive more emphasis when considering the kinds of measures to develop to screen people for jobs.
Queries about the time spent performing a task are couched in terms of frequency of performance (e.g., daily, weekly, monthly) or in terms of

TABLE 3.4   Frequency Scale for Rating Tasks

Frequency—How often do you perform this task?

Rate the task from 0 to 5 using the following scale:

0—*Never perform.* Use this rating for tasks you do not perform.

1—*A few times per year or less.* Use this rating for tasks that are performed less frequently than any other tasks. You may perform these tasks a few times per year (up to 6), or even less.

2—*Once a month.* Use this rating for tasks that you usually perform about once a month, or at least every other month, but not every week.

3—*Once a week.* Use this rating for tasks that you perform several times a month, usually every week, but not every day.

4—*Once a day.* Use this rating for tasks that you usually perform every day.

5—*More than once a day.* Use this rating for the tasks you perform most frequently. On most days, you perform these tasks more than once.

relative amount of time spent performing this task compared to other tasks. An example of a frequency scale, used in the electrician job analysis (Williams et al., 1994), is shown in Table 3.4.

Alternatively, one may ask respondents about the relative amount of time they spend on a task compared to other tasks. An example of such a scale is shown in Table 3.5. Some have called for the elimination of relative time spent ratings due to their high positive correlation with the much simpler rating of whether a task is performed. Wilson and Harvey (1990) obtained correlations in the .80–.90 range between ratings on a relative time spent scale versus a dichotomous scale of whether the task was performed across many different jobs. They concluded that relative time spent ratings should not be automatically included on a task inventory, but that the purpose for obtaining such information should determine their use.

Importance

The importance of a task for performing the job is one of the most frequently collected pieces of information. Many tasks may be performed frequently, but others may determine success or failure on the job. For the job of an airline pilot, the tasks involved in taking off and landing may be rated as the most important. If these are not performed well, disaster can result. On the other hand, whether the pilot banks smoothly while turning may be less important. Table 3.6 shows the task importance scale used in the electrician study.

TABLE 3.5   Relative Time Spent Scale for Rating Tasks

Relative Time Spent—How often do you perform this task compared with other tasks?

Use the time guide shown below to indicate your estimate of the time you spend on each task you perform:

0—I do not perform this task.

1—Relative to other tasks, I spend a lot less time on this task than on other tasks.

2—Relative to other tasks, I spend somewhat less time on this task than on other tasks.

3—Relative to other tasks, I spend as much time on this task as on other tasks.

4—Relative to other tasks, I spend somewhat more time on this task than on other tasks.

5—Relative to other tasks, I spend a lot more time on this task than on other tasks.

TABLE 3.6   Importance Scale for Rating Tasks

Importance—How important is this job task for successfully performing the job?

Rate the task from 0 to 5 using the following scale:

0—*None.* Use this rating for tasks you do not perform.

1—*Of little importance.* Use this rating for tasks that have very little importance in relation to the successful completion of the job.

2—*Of some importance.* Use this rating for tasks that have some importance, but generally are given low priority.

3—*Moderately important.* Use this rating for tasks that are of average importance relative to other tasks, but are not given high priority.

4—*Very important.* Use this rating for tasks that are important for successful completion of the work. These tasks receive higher priority than other tasks, but are not the most important tasks.

5—*Extremely important.* Use this rating for the tasks that are essential for successful job performance. Such a task must be completed and performed correctly in order to have a satisfactory outcome.

TABLE 3.7   Difficulty Scale for Rating Tasks

Difficulty—How difficult is it to become proficient at this task?

Rate the task from 0 to 5 using the following scale:

0—*Never perform.* Use this rating for tasks you do not perform.

1—*Very easy.* Use this rating for tasks that you observe once or have explained once and then you can perform the task correctly, usually on the first try.

2—*Easy.* Use this rating for tasks that you can learn without a lot of practice. After seeing the task demonstrated you can perform it, and after a few tries you can do it correctly.

3—*Moderately difficult.* Use this rating for tasks that you must study and practice to perform well. Such a task may require a few days of practice before full proficiency is reached.

4—*Very difficult.* Use this rating for tasks that cannot be learned in a few days. You must study materials and examples and then try to perform the task. After several weeks of practice and instruction you can perform satisfactorily.

5—*Extremely difficult.* Use this rating for tasks that take a long time to learn how to perform correctly. You need to study how to complete the task, observe others for a long period, and gradually improve your skills over several months, or even years, of practice.

Difficulty

In almost any job, some tasks are more difficult to perform than others. This can be important information if the purpose of the job analysis is to support training development (e.g., more difficult tasks may be given more emphasis in training). Another reason for using a difficulty scale is to determine the degree of physical or mental effort required for various tasks. Tasks requiring greater levels of effort could become the focus of a selection measure or a job redesign effort. Table 3.7 shows a task difficulty scale that can be used to collect such information.

Consequence of Error

For jobs in which errors may have extreme outcomes, a consequence of error scale may be useful. For some parts of a job, it may not matter if a worker is not quite precise; some mistakes are easily corrected. For certain tasks, however, the consequences of error can be significant. Such tasks may receive greater emphasis in selecting or training individuals. An example of this kind of scale is shown in Table 3.8.

TABLE 3.8   Consequence of Error Scale for Rating Tasks

Consequence of Error—What is the probable effect of making an error on this task?

Rate the task from 0 to 5 using the following scale:

1—*Little or no consequence.* Use this rating for tasks for which there is little consequence from error.

2—*Small consequence.* Use this rating for tasks for which there is only a small consequence from error.

3—*Moderate consequence.* Use this rating for tasks for which there is some consequence from error, but not a large amount.

4—*Large consequence.* Use this rating for tasks for which the consequence of error is large and could cause damage to persons or property.

5—*Extreme consequence.* Use this rating for tasks for which the consequence of error is extreme in terms of property damage or personal injury.

HOW TO IDENTIFY KNOWLEDGES, SKILLS, ABILITIES, AND OTHER CHARACTERISTICS

Gael (1983) distinguished between two main types of job analysis information. The first type, information directly related to the job tasks and their characteristics, was described in the preceding section of this chapter. The second main type of job analysis information describes the variety of personal characteristics required to perform a job. This second type of job analysis information is the focus of this section of the chapter.

Identifying a set of knowledges, skills, abilities, and other characteristics is important for many reasons. For selection purposes, one needs to determine which knowledges (e.g., knowledge of Ohm's law), abilities (e.g., ability to lift 50 pounds), skills (e.g., skill at driving a truck), and other characteristics (e.g., willingness to perform job duties in extreme weather conditions) are required to perform a job so that measures can be developed that predict performance. Identifying knowledges also is important for developing training curricula. From such information, one can determine the training content, as well as the sequence of training.

DEFINING THE TERMS

The *Uniform Guidelines* (EEOC, CSC, DOL, & DOJ, 1978) define knowledge as a body of information applied directly to the performance of a function or task. More simply, *knowledges* are specific types of information people need in order to perform a job. Some knowledges are required of workers before they can be hired to perform a job, and other knowledges may be acquired on the job. Examples of knowledges identified for performing the electrician job are:

- Knowledge of National Electrical Code
- Knowledge of building specifications
- Knowledge of blueprint symbols

Skill is typically defined as synonymous with proficiency, to denote the degree of mastery already acquired in an activity (Super & Crites, 1962); for our purposes, it is convenient to think of *skills* as the proficiencies needed to perform a function or task. Skills are usually acquired through practice. They often have physical and motor components, and involve cognitive components (Dunnette, 1976). Two general examples of skills—skill at typing and skill at hang gliding—require all three of these components. To type well, one must develop the finger dexterity necessary to move the fingers independently over keys arranged along a keyboard, and learn where specific keys are located so that the key for each letter can be quickly selected to form each word. Skills sometimes are used to screen job applicants. For example, word processors may be asked to type at a rate faster than a specific number of words per minute when applying for a job. Skills required to perform the electrician job include:

- Skill at splicing aluminum or copper wire
- Skill at welding
- Skill at operating a crane

Abilities are generally defined as relatively enduring attributes of an individual's capability for performing a particular range of different tasks; abilities exhibit some degree of stability over time (Fleishman, Costanza, & Marshall-Mies, 1997). However, abilities may develop over time and with exposure to multiple situations (Snow & Lohman, 1984). In a job analysis context, abilities are the specific patterns of attributes needed to perform a function or task. Individuals are expected to possess specific abilities to perform a job. In a selection context, ability tests are often administered to job applicants to determine if they have some predetermined level of ability (such as cognitive ability) that has been shown to be related to adequate performance on the job. Alternatively, an applicant may be required to obtain a score above a specific cutoff score to be accepted into a training program that prepares applicants for a job.

Examples of abilities for the electrician job are:

- Ability to climb ladders and poles up to 25 feet
- Ability to lift objects weighing up to 50 pounds
- Ability to add, subtract, multiply, and divide and use formulas
- Ability to discriminate between colors
- Ability to hear warning signals
- Ability to picture the way a completed construction project will appear before it is finished

Other characteristics are all other personal characteristics, such as occupational values and interests and work styles (Peterson, Mumford, Borman, Jeanneret, & Fleishman, 1995), personal preferences and interests (Holland, 1973), and individual difference variables (Jackson, 1967) that are required for performing a job. Personality characteristics may be important for specific types of jobs that require individuals to work in teams or, conversely, for jobs that require individuals to work alone with no human contact for long periods of time. Physical characteristics or preferences for certain kinds of environmental characteristics may be important for working under extreme temperature conditions or in high noise or hazardous conditions. Although these other characteristics are job related, they sometimes are subjected to legal challenge, since they may allow for discrimination on the basis of race or sex (Bemis et al., 1983). Examples of other characteristics for the electrician job include:

- Possesses car and valid driver's license for transportation among multiple job sites each day
- Is motivated to work under extreme temperature conditions
- Works with others as a member of a team
- Remains calm in an emergency situation

We note that it is often difficult to make distinctions among knowledges, skills, abilities, and other characteristics. In fact, these terms are occasionally used interchangeably and often are collectively called competencies, attributes, or requirements. In the remainder of this chapter, we will use the term KSAOs to refer to the variety of characteristics required to perform a job.

Writing KSAO Statements

In the previous section of this chapter, we described methods for writing job tasks. In a similar manner, KSAOs may be written to reflect what is required of the worker to perform a specific job. There are several general guidelines to follow in writing KSAO statements (e.g., Bemis et al., 1983):

- Use a standardized format. Begin each statement with the same wording: "Knowledge of," "Skill in," or "Ability to." In the case of other characteristics, try to specify exactly what the proficiency is (e.g., "Exhibits willingness to work in extreme weather conditions;" "Prefers working as a member of a team"). Some researchers determine whether each other characteristic most nearly fits into the knowledge, skill, or ability category, and then phrase it as such.
- Aim for an appropriate degree of specificity of the statement. KSAO statements should be written to match the purpose of the job analysis study. For example, if the purpose is to define the KSAO domain for a specific job in order to determine which of a variety of jobs it is most similar to, the statements would likely be more general than when one anticipates conducting a task analysis.
- Use operational terms to clarify the appropriate type and level of the KSAO that is required to perform the job (e.g., "Ability to read highway traffic signs and labels").
- Emphasize the underlying characteristic, rather than perceived determinants of the characteristic. For example, if knowledge of mathematics is required, it is preferable to mention the kinds of math knowledge required (e.g., algebra), rather than training, education, or experience (e.g., high school diploma).

A logical and systematic approach to writing KSAO statements is first to identify KSAOs using the task statements developed to describe work activities (Bemis et al., 1983). The four-step process described here can be followed to develop a matrix to represent tasks and their associated KSAOs:

Step 1. *Create the matrix shell.* List task statements as matrix rows and make broad column headings for knowledges, skills, abilities, and other characteristics.

Step 2. *Specify KSAOs for each task statement.* Think of the specific KSAOs necessary to perform each task, write each one as a separate column heading in the appropriate section (K, S, A, or O), and make a checkmark in the appropriate cells of the matrix. If task statements need additional KSAOs to completely specify their requirements, but it is difficult to pinpoint what they are, flag those tasks and review them again later.

Step 3. Review the matrix: Is it complete, consistent, concise, and nonoverlapping?
Complete: If components of the job seem to be missing, consider the extremes of conditions encountered when performing the job. Review tasks that were problematic and ask questions of job experts as necessary to clarify the KSAOs.
Consistent: If KSAOs appear to be at very different levels of description, consider combining or splitting KSAOs to make the statements more similar in level of generality.
Concise: If there are so many KSAOs that it will be difficult to collect meaningful data for them, reconsider the level of generality.
Nonoverlapping: If some of the statements under K, S, A, or O sections sound very similar to each other, consider simplification by writing the statement such that it can be included in the most logical place.
Step 4. Evaluate the set of KSAOs in terms of the following criteria:
Use of operational terms: Specify the exact level of competency required with objective terms, (e.g., "sufficient to [achieve a specific outcome]" or "as demonstrated by [outcome]").
Consistency and clarity of terms: Communicate exactly what is meant so that different individuals will interpret each statement the same way.
Include externally imposed "other" requirements for the job: Examples are licenses/board certifications, completing an apprenticeship; include KSAOs related to special equipment.

Job analysts can use this four-step process, but it also is common to have panels of SMEs develop these types of matrices. An example is given in Table 3.9. The row entries specify three electrician tasks; the column entries are KSAOs. Procedures for linking tasks to KSAOs, or determining which KSAOs are required to perform which tasks, are described later in this chapter.

GATHERING INFORMATION ABOUT KSAOS

In addition to listing KSAOs required to perform a job, it often is useful to collect information about KSAOs. The purposes of the job analysis will dictate the types of information to collect. To narrow a complete set of KSAOs to a smaller set of "critical" KSAOs, information is collected about the importance of KSAOs for job performance. A scale that can be used to collect such information is shown in Table 3.10.

TABLE 3.9 Specification of KSAOs for Example Electrician Tasks

	Knowledge of		Skill at			Ability to	
Tasks	National Electrical Code	OSHA requirements	Terminating fiber-optic cable sufficient to meet code	Welding as demonstrated by placement of spot weld	Splicing twisted-pair cable sufficient to meet code	Read and understand text (verbal comprehension)	Work with both hands as demonstrated by use of common tools
Splice wire	✓	✓	✓		✓		✓
Test and calibrate instruments						✓	✓
Attach fixture to pole	✓	✓					✓

TABLE 3.10   Importance Scale for Rating KSAOs for Electrician Tasks

Importance—How important is this knowledge, skill, ability, or other characteristic for performing the job tasks of an electrician?

Rate the KSAOs from 0 to 5 using the following scale:

0—*Of no importance.* Use this rating for knowledge that is unnecessary for performing the job, skills that are unnecessary, or abilities and other characteristics that an electrician does not need.

1—*Of little importance.* Use this rating for knowledge that is nice to have but not really necessary, skills that are rarely used, or abilities and other characteristics that are of little importance in relationship to the job.

2—*Of some importance.* Use this rating for knowledge, skills, or abilities and other characteristics that have some importance, but still would be ranked below average in relation to others.

3—*Moderately important.* Use this rating for knowledge, skills, or abilities and other characteristics that are of average importance in terms of successful completion of the job. These KSAOs are not the most critical, but still are needed to be successful on the job.

4—*Very important.* Use this rating for knowledges, skills, or abilities and other characteristics that are very important for successful job performance. These knowledges, skills, abilities, and other characteristics are essential, but are not the most critical.

5—*Extremely important.* Use this rating for knowledge that is critical for an electrician to have in order to perform safely and correctly, skills that are essential and are used throughout the job, and abilities and other characteristics that all electricians must possess for successful completion of job tasks.

When determining minimum requirements for job applicants or planning the content or sequencing of training, it often is necessary to collect information about KSAOs to develop an understanding of when, during their careers, individuals should be able to demonstrate specific proficiencies. Table 3.11 shows a scale frequently used for collecting such information about KSAOs. Using this scale, if the average rating for a KSAO (e.g., Ability to read and understand written material) is near 1.0, then the KSAO should be considered for use as a screening device for selection. On the other hand, if the average rating for a KSAO (e.g., Knowledge of which materials are good conductors and insulators) is approximately 2.0, then the KSAO should be considered for inclusion in a training curriculum.

TABLE 3.11   Proficiency Scale for Rating KSAOs for Electrician Tasks

Proficiency—When is proficiency needed for this knowledge, skill, ability, or other characteristic? Should applicants be selected based on their proficiency in this area or can they learn it on the job?

Rate the KSAOs as a 0, 1, 2, or 3 using the following criteria:

0—*Not needed*. Use this rating for knowledges, skills, abilities, or other characteristics that you consider unnecessary for performing the job tasks of an electrician.

1—*Before entry into apprenticeship*. Use this rating for KSAOs that you feel should be used for selecting applicants into the program. An entering apprentice should already have some proficiency in these knowledges, skills, abilities, or other characteristics before entering the program.

2—*During the apprenticeship program*. Use this rating for KSAOs that should be taught during the program. The apprentice should master these KSAOs while completing the program.

3—*After working as a journeyman*. Use this rating for KSAOs that are difficult and may require additional instruction or practice even after completion of the apprenticeship program.

If you feel that any important knowledges, skills, abilities, or other characteristics are not on these lists, please add them at the end of each section. Rate them as you did the others.

HOW TO COLLECT JOB ANALYSIS INFORMATION

A variety of methods can be used to collect job analysis information. The purpose of the job analysis often determines the most appropriate method for collecting information needed to understand the job. Purposes for conducting a job analysis may include identifying, developing, and validating selection measures; managing and appraising the performance of job incumbents; classifying and evaluating jobs; designing jobs; and developing training curricula. These purposes will dictate the kinds of information to be collected. Most job analysis efforts use more than one method (e.g., including methods described in this chapter as well as in Chapters 2 and 4) to increase efficiency and to ensure that comprehensive data are collected.

Before discussing the specific methods for collecting job analysis data, it is important to emphasize the use of systematic methods for both practical and legal reasons. A structured data collection process is essential to define the job domain comprehensively. To the extent that data are collected haphazardly, incomplete coverage is likely to result. Also, if there are legal challenges to personnel practices that are based on the job analysis, it will be crucial to have documentation about the procedures for conducting the job analysis, and descriptions of individuals providing information. For a more extensive discussion of job analysis and legal requirements, see Ghorpade (1988).

Methods for collecting job analysis data include: reviewing existing documentation, interviewing incumbents or other job experts, observing employees on the job and participating in job tasks, convening panels of subject matter experts, and administering questionnaires. Each method is explained below, with examples drawn from the electrician study.

REVIEWING EXISTING DOCUMENTATION

The first step in conducting most job analyses is to collect and review written materials containing information about the job. These materials may include position descriptions, training guides, lesson plans, self-paced instruction manuals, and the broad position descriptions available from the *Dictionary of Occupational Titles* (DOT; U.S. Department of Labor, 1991). These documents can provide preliminary information about how the job domain is structured. Job descriptions are also a good starting point, although they often are outdated and more likely to describe expected activities rather than activities actually performed. It also is useful to review job analysis documents from similar jobs in other industries.

As discussed in Chapter 2, KSAO domains often are defined as cognitive, physical, psychomotor, personality, and preferences and interests (e.g., Peterson, et al., 1990; Peterson, et al., 1995). Explicitly referring to such categories helps to ensure that all attribute domains are considered when determining requirements for a job.

The objective of reviewing existing written materials is to develop an understanding of:

1. The variety of tasks involved in the job
2. The KSAOs that may be required to perform the variety of tasks
3. How the task or KSAO domains have been organized (e.g., into categories or into a hierarchy), whether for similar or different purposes

It often is useful to construct a preliminary task and KSAO list before proceeding with other data collection methods. An example of a preliminary list of KSAOs based on our electrician job analysis is shown in Table 3.12.

TABLE 3.12   Preliminary List of KSAOs for the Electrician Job

Knowledges
1. Knowledge of blueprints, including symbols used
2. Knowledge of ladder logic diagrams
3. Knowledge of state and local electrical codes
4. Knowledge of which materials are good conductors and insulators
5. Knowledge of which wire/cable to use in different circumstances
6. Knowledge of the properties of fiber-optic cable
7. Knowledge of how a surge protector or lightning protector works
.
.
.
58. Knowledge of direct and alternating current

Skills
1. Skill at reading a wire table to determine conductor size required
2. Skill at programming programmable logic controllers
3. Skill at splicing aluminum or copper wire
4. Skill at splicing high-voltage cable
.
.
.
47. Skill at working in rubber gloves on high-voltage lines

Abilities
1. Ability to climb ladders and poles up to 25 feet
2. Ability to lift objects above 25 pounds
3. Ability to traverse irregular surfaces while maintaining balance
4. Ability to bend over to get over or under objects while working on top of a pole or tower
5. Ability to work with others on a team to complete a task
.
.
.
54. Ability to operate two-handed power equipment

INTERVIEWING JOB EXPERTS

After reviewing existing documentation, the next step in conducting a job analysis is to interview job experts. Selecting the job experts to be interviewed is an important part of the process.

Selecting Subject Matter Experts (SMEs)
    Job experts are usually incumbents with experience on the job and/or supervisors who are very familiar with the job. The amount of experience needed by subject matter experts often depends on the com-

plexity of the job. Typically, six months to one year on the job is considered adequate. Depending on the nature of the job, experts should be chosen who have worked in the variety of situations required by the job. Physical or geographical settings in which incumbents may work should be represented. In addition, SMEs should be demographically representative of the job incumbent population. Representativeness is important for gathering a variety of viewpoints and also is important from a legal perspective. Finally, SMEs should be competent at the job and they need to be able to respond to written stimuli. An experienced but illiterate job incumbent will not be very helpful as a subject matter expert.

Once all these requirements are met, it may be necessary to draw a sample group of SMEs from the incumbent population. There are two general approaches to sampling incumbents to identify SMEs, as described by Landy and Vasey (1991). The first approach is to sample incumbents randomly based on the expectation that incumbents are interchangeable. The underlying assumption is that they have similar experiences and will report similar information and make similar judgments. However, if there are likely to be systematic factors that influence incumbents' experiences, then a stratified sample may be more appropriate for identifying SMEs. The sample could be stratified on the basis of job level, tenure, geographic location, ethnicity, gender, and education. Then individual SMEs would be randomly selected from within these categories.

Conducting the Interview

An interview protocol may be structured or open-ended, depending on the purpose for conducting the job analysis. If the interviews take place early in the process, interviewees may be asked to talk about their jobs in general terms, and the job analyst will use the information to shape subsequent steps of the job analysis and to inform decisions about the duty areas. Existing structured interview instruments used for similar jobs may be adapted, or new interview protocols may be developed.

Conducting an interview, whether structured or open-ended, requires the ability to listen and put people at ease while directing the conversation and asking questions to probe for job-relevant information. At the beginning of the interview, one should make introductions, describe the purpose of the job analysis, and answer interviewees' questions. A preliminary task list can be used as a starting point for a discussion. The interviewees may be asked to examine the preliminary lists that describe the task/KSAO structure of the job domain. Questions used to query experts might include the following:

Example Questions About the Structure of the Domains
- Are there any tasks missing from this list?
- Are the tasks listed in the appropriate duty areas? (If not, where do they belong?)
- Are there duplicates among the tasks listed?
- Are the tasks at approximately the same level of generality? (If not, which ones are very specific and which others are very general?)
- Are there any tasks that are obsolete?

At a more general level, the interviewees may be asked the following questions:

Example Questions About the Task Domain
- Are there differences in the way tasks are performed due to differences in variables, such as location, industry type, equipment type?
- What accounts for differences in how tasks are performed?

Example Questions About the KSAO Domain
- In general, what KSAOs are needed to perform the work?
- What does the task require in terms of cognitive KSAOs?
- What are the physical requirements of the job?
- What personality characteristics and interests are relevant for successful performance of the job?

OBSERVING JOB PERFORMANCE AND PARTICIPATING IN JOB TASKS

This method of gathering job information is very important for understanding the context or environment of the job. It is especially appropriate for jobs that have a physical component. For example, it may not be very useful to observe a job incumbent whose only tasks involve watching controls and monitoring changes. On the other hand, it would be very useful to observe electricians running conduit, installing wiring, and troubleshooting, to understand how various procedures are incorporated into everyday duties. Job observation also is useful for determining how physical and mental tasks are interrelated and performed.

Common procedures for observing on-the-job performance include:

- Taking notes about what the incumbents do while they are working
- Using a prepared checklist to record information about the variety of tasks performed, the frequency with which they are performed, and the time it takes to complete them

- Asking probing questions while the incumbent works (e.g., "Can you tell me what you are doing now and why?")
- Using devices, such as cameras and physiological equipment, to record performance of tasks or collect information about task performance

Observing incumbents performing parts of the job and interviewing them can be done simultaneously. In some cases, a job analyst may perform some of the tasks to get a firsthand impression of what a task entails (e.g., climbing ladders or bending conduit alongside an electrician). There are some job tasks that would be inappropriate for job analysts to perform (e.g., those with safety requirements or restrictions on who is allowed to perform them). Simulators used for training or testing are useful for a job analyst to perform the job under realistic conditions without risk of injury or damage to equipment.

CONVENING PANELS OF JOB EXPERTS

Convening groups of experts consists of assembling a manageable number of experts (between 10 and 12) who meet at a particular location for a given amount of time to discuss a job. These experts may be incumbents and/or supervisors. Depending on the nature of incumbent/supervisor relationships in the organization, it may be advisable to convene groups of supervisors and incumbents separately. Often, expert panels meet at the beginning of the job analysis process to help define the domain and the job(s) to be studied. Then they may meet periodically throughout the subsequent stages to review the work of the job analysis team and to provide input. The advantages of involving a panel early and meeting with them often include:

- Gaining support from important constituents, since they may be the ones providing people to talk to, to observe, or to give questionnaires to
- Obtaining in-progress reviews from those who know the background and objectives for the study
- Establishing continuity of the oversight and guidance, because the panel is aware of decisions made earlier in the process
- Increasing the likelihood of acceptance of the results, since the panel has been involved from the beginning and since the involvement of "insiders" increases acceptance by others

The job analyst should have a specific agenda to cover and should direct the SME panel meeting. For instance, the panel may be asked to review the structure of the domain based on written documentation and interviews with experts. They may be asked to review a task list for completeness and consistency in level of description. These panel meetings may be very structured, during which the participants create products (such as a revised duty or task list), or they may simply meet to give informal approvals.

RECORDING WORK ACTIVITIES IN A LOG

Having incumbents record their work activities is useful when workers primarily perform cognitive, repetitive tasks. Managers are sometimes asked to complete diaries because a large component of their jobs may not be observable. Job incumbents are asked to keep a log or diary of what they do at set times throughout the workday. For example, workers might record what they are doing at 30-minute intervals. The specific interval and frequency for recording information are determined by a sampling plan devised for the particular study. If a job is expected to change seasonally, then workers might be asked to record everything they do for two days each month for a one-year period. For jobs in which tasks are performed routinely, workers might keep a diary of what they do every 15 minutes for a one-week period.

DEVELOPING AND ADMINISTERING QUESTIONNAIRES

Questionnaires are useful when job analysis data are collected from a large sample of job experts, and especially when the sample is geographically dispersed. Questionnaires have been used more often than any other method for collecting information about managerial-level jobs (Lammlein, 1985). Administration procedures are flexible; questionnaires may be administered in person to individuals or groups, or by mail.

The format of a questionnaire can be either unstructured or structured. Unstructured questionnaires can be developed quickly, but more time may be needed to analyze the resulting data. Open-ended questions require developing content categories for coding and summarizing the variety of written responses. Structured questionnaires, on the other hand, are usually constructed after preliminary information has been gathered from documentation, observation, and/or interviews, and questions are more limited in scope (e.g., ratings of task importance).

The quality of the data is significantly affected by the design of the questionnaire. The format and instructions should be carefully developed so that respondents understand what they are asked to do and can provide complete and accurate data. Examples are helpful, especially for unique types of items or scales.

Typical sections of a questionnaire include:

- Cover page: explains in general terms the purpose and background of the project/study, the role of the questionnaire and the respondents, the use of the data, follow-up steps, and gives the name of a person for respondents to contact in case they have any questions
- Introduction: describes the sections and structure of the questionnaire
- Background information page: requests basic demographic information about the respondent
- Task section and directions: describes the steps to complete the ratings for job tasks, with example scales and items
- KSAO section and directions: describes the steps to complete the KSAO ratings, with example scales and items

Several pages from the job analysis questionnaire developed during the electrician study are included here as examples. Figure 3.1 shows the background information page. Figure 3.2 shows two duty areas and tasks from the task rating section of the questionnaire used to collect Importance, Frequency, and Difficulty ratings. Note that the definitions for the scales and anchor points are abbreviated on this page; the full definitions appeared elsewhere in the questionnaire. Example knowledges and skills from the KSAO rating section, in which Importance and Proficiency are rated, are shown in Figure 3.3.

There are several advantages to administering questionnaires. They are economical to administer to large samples, because less professional staff time is required for data collection. Questionnaires yield data that can be readily analyzed and can permit easy comparison among many different positions in a standardized manner. In addition, questionnaires provide data that represent the job over a period of time, as opposed to a specific time period (e.g., the log and observation methods). This method is useful for many purposes, such as identifying training needs (Dunnette, Hough, & Rosse, 1979), identifying ability requirements for jobs (Bosshardt, Rosse, & Peterson, 1984), and establishing pay grades (Gomez-Mejia, Page, & Tornow, 1982).

1. Name_____

2. Local Union Number_____ City_____ State_____

3. Current Status

❑ Journeyman wireman → Number of years experience_____

    Year apprenticeship completed _____

    Year journeyman status was acquired by means other than
    apprenticeship _____

❑ Apprentice wireman → Year in the program

    ❑ 1st year   ❑ 3rd year   ❑ 5th year

    ❑ 2nd year   ❑ 4th year

    Have you worked in any of the following capacities? (check all that apply)

    ❑ Foreman   ❑ Estimator   ❑ Project Manager

4. Have you worked as an electrician (either as an apprentice or a journey-man) in the past year?

    ❑ Yes   ❑ No

5. Age   _____ years

6. Sex   ❑ Male   ❑ Female

7. Ethnicity

    ❑ Asian or Pacific Islander   ❑ Native American/American Indian

    ❑ Black   ❑ White/Caucasian

    ❑ Hispanic

FIGURE 3.1   Sample of Background Information Form
             Used in Electrician Study

There are several criticisms of the questionnaire method. One is that data collected by questionnaire are based on perceptions of the job, not on actual job behaviors. However, this same criticism can be made of all methods that rely on perceptions of the job. Based on Lammlein's (1985) review of common criticisms of the questionnaire method, the main problem concerns potential misuse of questionnaire data.

HOW TO LINK JOB TASKS AND KSAOS

We have described methods for identifying duties, tasks, and KSAOs as well as collecting information about them. In addition, it often is impor-tant to collect information about the linkage between tasks and KSAOs

Job Duty and Task	*Importance*	*Frequency*	*Difficulty*
	0-None	0-Never	0-Never perform
	1-Little importance	1-A few times a year	1-Very easy
	2-Some importance	2-Once a month	2-Easy
	3-Moderately important	3-Once a week	3-Moderately difficult
	4-Very important	4-Once a day	4-Very difficult
	5-Extremely important	5-More than once a day	5-Extremely difficult

(Circle one number in each column)

I. Planning and Initiating Project

Study blueprints and specifications	0 1 2 3 4 5	0 1 2 3 4 5	0 1 2 3 4 5
Order materials, supplies, and equipment	0 1 2 3 4 5	0 1 2 3 4 5	0 1 2 3 4 5
Load, haul, and unload materials and supplies	0 1 2 3 4 5	0 1 2 3 4 5	0 1 2 3 4 5
Establish work areas	0 1 2 3 4 5	0 1 2 3 4 5	0 1 2 3 4 5
Assemble tools and equipment	0 1 2 3 4 5	0 1 2 3 4 5	0 1 2 3 4 5
Coordinate tool requirements with contractor	0 1 2 3 4 5	0 1 2 3 4 5	0 1 2 3 4 5
Coordinate job schedule with other crafts	0 1 2 3 4 5	0 1 2 3 4 5	0 1 2 3 4 5

II. Establishing OSHA and Customer Safety Requirements

Review applicable OSHA safety standards	0 1 2 3 4 5	0 1 2 3 4 5	0 1 2 3 4 5
Review customer safety requirements	0 1 2 3 4 5	0 1 2 3 4 5	0 1 2 3 4 5

FIGURE 3.2   Example Page: Task Ratings

(e.g., the KSAOs necessary to perform a particular task). Although task statements are often used to generate KSAOs, such linkage information from a small number of SMEs is limited. It is much more useful to collect linkage information from a large sample of subject matter experts. Hence, this step is usually completed after the duty, task, and KSAO information has been collected. When we discussed generating lists of KSAOs, we presented a matrix in Table 3.9. If this matrix were completed, it could show checkmarks or ratings of the importance of the linkage between each task and each of the KSAOs.

Knowledge	*Importance*	*Proficiency*
	0-None	0-Not needed
	1-Little importance	1-Before entry into
	2-Some importance	app'ship
	3-Moderately important	2-During app'ship
	4-Very important	program
	5-Extremely important	3-After working as
		journeyman

(Circle one number in each column)

I. Knowledges

Knowledge of schematic electrical diagrams	0 1 2 3 4 5	0 1 2 3
Knowledge of ladder logic diagrams	0 1 2 3 4 5	0 1 2 3
Knowledge of semiconductor electronics	0 1 2 3 4 5	0 1 2 3
Knowledge of resistance and its effects	0 1 2 3 4 5	0 1 2 3
Knowledge of the functions of capacitors	0 1 2 3 4 5	0 1 2 3
Knowledge of how to perform an emergency rescue	0 1 2 3 4 5	0 1 2 3
Other: _____	0 1 2 3 4 5	0 1 2 3

Skill	*Importance*	*Proficiency*
	0-None	0-Not needed
	1-Little importance	1-Before entry into
	2-Some importance	app'ship
	3-Moderately important	2-During app'ship
	4-Very important	program
	5-Extremely important	3-After working as
		journeyman

(Circle one number in each column)

II. Skills

Skill at reading a wire table to determine conductor size required	0 1 2 3 4 5	0 1 2 3
Skill at programming programmable logic controllers	0 1 2 3 4 5	0 1 2 3
Skill at terminating aluminum or copper cable	0 1 2 3 4 5	0 1 2 3

FIGURE 3.3   Example Page from KSAO Rating Questionnaire

USES OF LINKAGE DATA

Information concerning the linkage between KSAOs and tasks is useful for many human resource applications (e.g., selection and training). For some applications, the task is the unit of analysis (e.g., identifying KSAOs required to perform a particular task). For example, an outside lineman installing a transformer on a neighborhood distribution line may need knowledge of Ohm's law, skill at climbing poles, and the ability to lift objects up to 50 pounds. For other applications, the KSAO may be the unit of analysis. For example, an ability that is linked to many important and frequently performed tasks may be more important to include in selection procedures than one that is linked to only a few important and frequently performed tasks.

Task/KSAO linkage data can also be used to analyze curricula. To prioritize knowledges to be included in classroom instruction, the number of linkages that a particular knowledge has to different tasks may be determined. More weight can be given to knowledges that are linked to more of the tasks rated as frequently performed, important, and difficult to learn.

METHODS FOR COLLECTING LINKAGE DATA

Typically, a panel of subject matter experts (SMEs) is convened to determine which KSAOs are necessary to perform the tasks. Judgments about task/KSAO linkages may be dichotomous (the task either requires the KSAO or it does not) or a scale may be used (the degree to which a KSAO is needed to perform the task). Vinchur, Prien, and Schippmann (1993) present data suggesting that scaling may be useful when more detail is needed, although the results tend to be very similar for both types of response. The procedures discussed in Hughes and Prien (1989) consist of having SMEs make independent judgments. Then they discuss the results as a group and modify them as needed. Alternatively, one could average the ratings without reaching consensus.

The matrix of judgments to be made can be very large. If a job has 250 tasks and 100 KSAOs, each rater must make 25,000 judgments. An alternate method is to have each rater only complete a portion of the matrix. For example, each rater could evaluate 30 tasks for the 100 KSAOs. This strategy is limited by the number of subject matter experts available. A commonly used rule of thumb is that approximately ten raters per cell typically are needed to achieve acceptable reliability.

SUMMARY

In this chapter, we have described an inductive process for specifying and structuring the two domains important to the world of work: the job/task domain and the KSAO domain. The goal of the process is to systematically obtain comprehensive, relevant information appropriate for the purpose(s) of the job analysis. We have also described a variety of methods for collecting information necessary to specify these two domains and a procedure for linking them together. The information obtained by specifying the task and KSAO domains and then collecting a variety of ratings is critical for developing predictor and criterion measures.

At the beginning of this chapter, we described in general terms the purposes for conducting the electrician job analysis. Now that we have described the job analysis process in detail, we can be more specific about the variety of uses of job analysis data. The following list contains examples of "next steps," suggestions for how job analysis data may be used.

1. Once a task list is developed, a job description can be written to capture the variety of tasks performed on the job. This information can be shared with potential job candidates to ensure that they understand what a job entails before they begin the application process.

2. When linkages of tasks to KSAOs are determined, selection tests can be identified or developed. For example, if specific types of cognitive abilities, such as spatial ability and quantitative ability, are identified as important for performing electrician tasks, then appropriate off-the-shelf tests can be identified, or new tests can be developed (see Chapter 6).

3. After ratings of skills, abilities, and other characteristics are collected, then an interview form (see Chapter 7) or biodata inventory (see Chapter 8) can be developed to gather information from candidates about such issues as their related skills and their preferences for working conditions.

4. When knowledges are identified and rated, then training programs can be developed or revised. For example, course training materials can be mapped to knowledge ratings of frequency, difficulty to learn, and importance, to ensure adequacy of content coverage.

5. Task ratings (e.g., time spent, importance) can be used to help determine which tasks are important to include in a work sample

test (see Chapter 12). For example, tasks that are very important and frequently performed might be included to ensure that candidates can perform them without requiring additional training. Such tasks might also be used as criterion measures in test validation studies (see Chapter 13).

While we recognize the need for sound scientific principles to guide job analysis efforts, it is important to recognize that the job analysis process is an art as well as a science. The process requires applying knowledge of sound scientific principles, judgment gained from past experience, and creativity for dealing with new situations.

It is important to view job analysis as a dynamic and evolving process rather than as an unchanging procedure, because job analysis procedures must be tailored to fit a specific context and purpose. In addition, job analysis procedures and the data they yield should be future oriented. Due to rapid changes in technology and the increasingly global nature of work, jobs are rapidly evolving. Examples of changes in the nature of work include decreases in specialization or increases in the occurrences of shared work assignments (Morgan & Smith, 1996), cross-training, job and task rotation, increased responsibility at all organizational levels, and self-managed teams (Sanchez, 1994). These types of changes are likely to cause job analysis information to become obsolete in a relatively short period of time. The commonly used methods for analyzing work (e.g., observations, interviews, questionnaires, and panel meetings) are gradually changing, and must continue to change, to keep pace with changes in work and to provide relevant and useful information. For example, interviews may be conducted with a wider sample of individuals than just incumbents and supervisors, such as the customers, technical experts, or other organizational members with whom incumbents interact. And, increasingly, job analysis data may be collected by having experts interface with a computer rather than with a psychologist or job analyst (Baughman, Sager, & Mumford, 1995).

REFERENCES

Barnes, R. M. (1963). *Motion and time study: Design and measurement of work*. New York: Wiley.

Baughman, W. A., Sager, C. E., & Mumford, M. D. (1995). *Computer-based methods for effective retrieval of human technological knowledge*. Unpublished technical memorandum. Washington, DC: American Institutes for Research.

Bemis, S. E., Belenky, A. H., & Soder, D. A. (1983). *Job analysis*. Washington, DC: Bureau of National Affairs, Inc.

Bosshardt, M. J., Rosse, R. L., & Peterson, N. G. (1984). *Electric power plant study: Analysis of job activities and personal qualifications of maintenance employees in electric power generating plants.* (Institute Report No. 90). Minneapolis: Personnel Decisions Research Institute.

Christal, R. E. (1974). *The United States Air Force Occupational research project.* Lackland Air Force Base, Texas: Occupational Research Division, AFHRL-TR-73-75.

Chruden, H. J., & Sherman, A. W. (1980). *Personnel management: The utilization of human resources.* Cincinnati: South Western.

Clifford, J. P. (1994). Job analysis: why do it, and how should it be done? *Public Personnel Management, 23,* 321–338.

Dunnette, M. D. (1976). Aptitudes, abilities and skills. In M. D. Dunnette (Ed.), *Handbook of Industrial and Organizational Psychology* (pp. 473–520). Chicago: Rand McNally.

Dunnette, M. D., Hough, L. M., & Rosse, R. L. (1979). Task and job taxonomies as the basis for identifying labor supply sources and evaluating employment qualifications. *Human Resources Planning, 2,* 37–51.

Equal Employment Opportunity Commission, Civil Service Commission, Department of Labor, & Department of Justice (1978, August). Uniform guidelines on employee selection procedures. *Federal Register, 43,* (166) 38290-38315.

Fine, S. A., & Wiley, W. W. (1971). *An introduction to functional job analysis.* Kalamazoo, MI: W. E. Upjohn Institute for Employment Research.

Fleishman, E. A., Costanza, D. C., & Marshall-Mies, J. C. (1997). Abilities. In N. G. Peterson, M. D. Mumford, W. C. Borman, P. R. Jeanneret, & E. A. Fleishman (Eds.), *O*NET: An Occupational Information Network.* Washington, DC: American Psychological Association.

Fleishman, E. A., & Mumford, M. D. (1988). Ability requirements scales. In S. Gael (Ed.), *Job analysis handbook for business, industry, and government: Volume II.* New York: Wiley.

Fleishman, E. A., & Quaintance, M. K. (1983). *Taxonomies of human performance: The description of human tasks.* Orlando, FL: Academic.

Gael, S. (1983). *Job analysis: A guide to assessing work activities.* San Francisco: Jossey-Bass.

Ghorpade, J. (1988). *Job analysis: A handbook for the human resource director.* Englewood Cliffs, NJ: Prentice-Hall.

Gilbreth, F. B., & Gilbreth, L. M. (1917). *Applied motion study.* New York: Sturgis and Walton.

Gomez-Mejia, L. R., Page, R. C., & Tornow, W. (1982). A comparison of the practical utility of traditional, statistical, and hybrid job evaluation approaches. *Academy of Management Journal, 24,* 790–809.

Holland, J. L. (1973). *Making vocational choices: A theory of careers.* Englewood Cliffs, NJ: Prentice-Hall.

Hughes, G. L., & Prien, E. P. (1989). Evaluation of task and job skill linkage judgments used to develop test specifications. *Personnel Psychology, 42,* 283–292.

Jackson, D. N. (1967). *Personality research form manual.* Goshen, NY: Research Psychologists Press.

Lammlein, S. E. (1985). *The description of managerial work: A review.* Unpublished manuscript, University of Minnesota, Department of Psychology, Minneapolis.

Landy, F. J., & Vasey, J. (1991). Job analysis: the composition of SME samples. *Personnel Psychology 44,* 27–50.

Lytle, C. W. (1954). *Job evaluation methods.* New York: Ronald Press.

Mayo, E. (1933). *The human problems of an industrial civilization.* New York: Macmillan.

McCormick, E. J., Jeanneret, P. R., & Mecham, R. C. (1972). A study of job characteristics and job dimensions as based on the Position Analysis Questionnaire (PAQ). *Journal of Applied Psychology Monograph 56,* 347–368.

McCormick, E. J., Mecham, R. C., & Jeanneret, P. R. (1972). *Technical manual for the Position Analysis Questionnaire (PAQ).* West Lafayette, IN: PAQ Services.

Melching, W. H., & Borcher, S. D. (1973). *Procedures for constructing and using task inventories.* Center for Vocational and Technical Education, Research and Development Series No. 91. Columbus: The Ohio State University.

Morgan, R. B., & Smith, J. E. (1996). *Staffing the new workplace: Selecting and promoting for quality improvement.* Milwaukee, WI: ASQC Quality Press.

Muensterberg, H. (1913). *Psychology and industrial efficiency.* Boston: Houghton Mifflin.

Peterson, N. G., Hough, L. M., Dunnette, M. D., Rosse, R. L., Houston, J. S., Toquam, J. L., & Wing, H. (1990). Project A: Specification of the predictor domain and development of new selection/classification tests. *Personnel Psychology, 43,* 247–276.

Peterson, N. G., Mumford, M. D., Borman, W. C., Jeanneret, P. R., & Fleishman, E. A. (Eds.). (1995). *Development of prototype Occupational Information Network (O*NET) content model* (Vols. 1–2). Salt Lake City: Utah Department of Employment Security.

Peterson, N. G., Mumford, M. D., Borman, W. C., Jeanneret, P. R., & Fleishman, E. A. (Eds.). (in press). *O*NET: An Occupational Information Network.* Washington, DC: American Psychological Association.

Roethlisberger, F. J., & Dickson, W. J. (1939). *Management and the worker.* Cambridge, MA: Harvard University Press.

Rupe, J. C. (1956). *Research into basic methods and techniques of air force job analysis, IV.* Chanute AFB, IL: Air Force Personnel and Training Research Center.

Sanchez, J. I. (1994). From documentation to innovation: Reshaping job analysis to meet emerging business needs. *Human Resource Management Review, 4* (1), 51–74.

Sanchez, J. I., & Fraser, S. L. (1994). An empirical approach to identify job duty-KSA linkages in managerial jobs: A case example. *Journal of Business and Psychology, 8,* 309–325.

Schmidt, F. L., Caplan, J. R., Bemis, S. E., Decuir, R., Dunn, L., & Antone, L. L. (1979). *The behavioral consistency method of unassembled examining.* Washington, DC: U.S. Office of Personnel Management.

Shartle, C. L. (1959). *Occupational information: Its development and application.* Englewood Cliffs, NJ: Prentice-Hall.

Snow, R. E., & Lohman, D. F. (1984). Toward a theory of cognitive aptitude for learning from instruction. *Journal of Educational Psychology, 76,* 347–375.

Super, D. E., & Crites, J. O. (1962). *Appraising vocational fitness* (Rev. ed.). New York: Harper & Row.

Taylor, F. W. (1911). *Principles of scientific management.* New York: Harper & Row.

U.S. Department of Labor (1939). *Dictionary of occupational titles* (1st ed.). Washington, DC: Author.

U.S. Department of Labor (1991). *Dictionary of occupational titles* (4th ed.). Washington, DC: Author.

U.S. Department of Labor, United States Employment Service (1944). *Training and reference manual.* Washington, DC: U.S. Government Printing Office.

Vinchur, A. J., Prien, E. P., & Schippmann, J. S. (1993). An alternative procedure for analyzing job analysis results for content-oriented test development. *Journal of Business and Psychology, 8,* 215–226.

Williams, K. M., Peterson, N. G., & Bell, J. A. (1994). *Job analysis of three electrical worker positions for the National Joint Apprenticeship and Training Committee.* Washington, DC: American Institutes for Research.

Wilson, M. A., & Harvey R. J. (1990). The value of relative-time-spent ratings in task-oriented job analysis. *Journal of Business and Psychology, 4,* 453–461.

Critical Incident Technique

Lance Anderson
Sandra Wilson

OVERVIEW

The critical incident technique consists of a flexible set of procedures for collecting and analyzing reports of incidents—instances of actual behavior—that constitute job performance at various levels of effectiveness. According to its developer, the critical incident technique is "essentially a procedure for gathering certain important facts concerning behavior in defined situations" (Flanagan, 1954, p. 335). Critical incident reports are obtained from persons who are in a position to observe those performing the activity and who, by training and experience, are qualified to judge the outcome of the activity, in particular the role of the observed behavior in determining that outcome. The term *critical* refers to the fact that the behavior plays an important, or critical, role in determining the outcome.

A critical incident report includes three important pieces of information: (1) a description of the situation that led to the incident, (2) the actions or behaviors of the focal person in the incident, and (3) the results or outcome of those actions. Given these three pieces of information, an interpretation as to the effectiveness of the actions can be made. The description of the situation is important because it helps the

Situation:	A contractor was assigned a project that would involve determinating and removing several hundred wires, removing the conduit from the gear, relocating the gear, reinstalling the conduit and wire, and finally reterminating the wire. The work had to begin at 11:00 P.M. on Thanksgiving, and it had to be completed by 7:00 A.M. the following day, which seemed nearly impossible.
Action:	The foreman chose seven of the best wiremen employed by the company to do the work. Through skillful planning and hard work, the crew worked through the night without stopping for a break and got the job done on time and with no problems.
Outcome:	The customer was extremely impressed that they got such a project completed in such a short amount of time with zero errors. As a result, the customer has chosen this contractor to do almost all of its work.

FIGURE 4.1   Example of a Critical Incident Report

analyst understand the circumstances, anticipate certain actions, and rationalize why certain actions were or were not taken. It may include information such as the type of industry, type of job, specific tasks being performed, environmental conditions, and relationships among others in the situation. Descriptions of the action are important because they describe the behavior of the focal person. Finally, descriptions of the outcome are important because they provide the basis for inferences as to the effectiveness of the behavior and the skills needed to enact the behavior. All three descriptions also allow for verification of the plausibility of the presumed relationship between the actions and the outcomes. An example of a critical incident report is shown in Figure 4.1.

The critical incident technique is used for a variety of purposes, including creating performance measurement instruments such as behavior-based rating scales (described in Chapter 11); developing predictors such as situational judgment tests (described in Chapter 9) and structured interviews (described in Chapter 7); developing instructional objectives; designing curricula; evaluating services, equipment, and system performance (Fitts & Jones, 1947); and establishing performance requirements as a basis for certification and licensure tests (Jacobs, Fivars, & Fitzpatrick, 1982). A recent example of the use of critical incidents is Project A, one of the largest personnel selection projects in the field of industrial psychology. In this project, critical incident reports were used to develop behavior-based rating scales as a criterion measure to evaluate the validity of the U.S. Army's selection and classification tests for military jobs (Campbell, et al., 1990).

The critical incident technique also has been applied outside the realm of personnel research. For example, it has been used to identify competencies needed by children and adults in managing asthma (McNabb, Wilson, & Jacobs, 1986; Wilson et al., 1987; Wilson, Mitchell, Rolnick, & Fish, 1993; Wilson, 1993), to evaluate the impact of a medical information system (Lindbergh, Siegel, Rapp, Wallingford, & Wilson, 1993; Wilson, Starr-Schneidkraut, & Cooper, 1989), and to help reduce the level of risk of anesthesia by identifying corrective actions when mishaps occur (Newbower, Cooper, & Long, 1981).

This chapter will review the history of the technique and describe how to collect incident reports and edit and analyze the resulting data.

BRIEF HISTORY OF THE CRITICAL INCIDENT TECHNIQUE

The critical incident technique, as a formal qualitative methodology, is most widely known through John C. Flanagan's article in the *Psychological Bulletin* (Flanagan, 1954). Earlier descriptions appear in Volume 1 of the report of the Aviation Psychology Program in the U.S. Army Air Forces (Flanagan, 1948a) and in an article in *Personnel Psychology* (Flanagan, 1948b).

The critical incident technique was developed during World War II. In 1941, Dr. Flanagan, then head of the Aviation Psychology Program, was ordered to determine the causes of the high rate of pilot failure during training. He began to focus on factual incidents embedded in reports prepared by the Army Air Force Elimination Board. The detailed observations of human behavior described in the reports appeared to him to be more significant than the many generalizations about the causes of failure and the personality "traits" of good and poor trainees also contained in the reports. He and his colleagues augmented these factual reports of incidents with behavioral observations of aviation cadets, gathered from flight instructors. Analysis of the observations provided the basis for a battery of selection tests that resulted in a substantial reduction in the failure rate for aircrew trainees (pilots, navigators, and bombardiers). The Aviation Psychology Program subsequently went on to gather specific incidents of effective and ineffective behavior in the context of other projects. This led to the gradual refinement of the data collection and analysis procedures and, eventually, their designation as the "critical incident technique."

Following the end of World War II, Dr. Flanagan joined the faculty of the University of Pittsburgh and founded the American Institutes for Research. There, the critical incident technique was further developed. Perhaps the most significant result was the use of the technique to identify knowledges, skills, abilities, and other characteristics (KSAOs) that lead to success or failure on the job, and the development of selection instruments (Flanagan, 1957).

Other researchers have expanded the technique and applied it in different ways (Atkin & Conlon, 1978; Borman, 1979; Borman & Dunnette, 1975; Campbell, Dunnette, Lawler, & Weick, 1970; Campbell, Dunnette, Arvey, & Hellervick, 1973). The technique is widely used today. One testimony to its ubiquitousness is the fact that Flanagan's 1954 article explaining the technique is more frequently cited by industrial and organizational psychologists than any other article over the past 40 years (Sackett, 1994).

In this chapter we describe methods for collecting incident reports, editing and processing them, and analyzing the resulting data. These methods are intended as a set of suggestions based on the experience of the authors. Some variations of these procedures may be warranted based on research needs. In addition, we caution readers that some procedures may compromise the validity and utility of the data. During our discussion of the critical incident technique, we present various examples. Each of these examples is based on a recent study of electrical workers (Williams, Peterson, & Bell, 1994).

HOW TO COLLECT AND EDIT CRITICAL INCIDENTS

COLLECTING CRITICAL INCIDENTS

There are various methods for collecting critical incidents, including face-to-face interviews, telephone interviews, workshops, and systematic record-keeping efforts. The goal of each of these methods is to assist subject matter experts (SMEs) in providing clear and concise examples of behavior that they have observed over time.

Each of the methods has trade-offs. Face-to-face interviews involve a one-to-one exchange between the researcher and a subject matter expert. While this method is fairly costly and time-consuming, the quality of the incidents is likely to be high since the researcher can question the SME at the time incident reports are written. Telephone interviews have several of the same benefits and are less expensive, since no travel is involved. Workshops also are less expensive than face-to-face interviews, but there is less clarification and exchange between the researcher and each SME, and some SMEs in a workshop setting may be unwilling or unable to write reports of incidents that contain sufficient detail. Finally, systematic record-keeping efforts can provide high-quality data, since the SME does not have to recall events that happened months or even years prior to the data collection. However, record-keeping efforts must take place over an extended period of time, requiring the SME to be strongly motivated to continue the effort.

In this chapter, we discuss the workshop method in the context of personnel research. (It is important to note, however, that there are various other methods for collecting data and other purposes for using the critical incident technique.) In general, the workshop method entails assembling SMEs into a small group, training them on how to report critical incidents, and then having them write down critical incidents relevant to the job or issue. A description of the steps follows.

Step 1: Identify SMEs

SMEs are the individuals who will provide the critical incident reports, as well as initial ratings of the effectiveness of the behaviors described. It is important that the researcher selects SMEs who understand the job being analyzed and who have had opportunities to observe recent job performance. For these reasons, job incumbents or supervisors are a good source of SMEs. It also is important that the set of SMEs selected incorporates a diversity of perspectives so that the incidents are comprehensive in their coverage of the job domain. SMEs drawn at random from a population of job incumbents may not provide the needed diversity. Therefore, it may be necessary to overrepresent certain subgroups when selecting SMEs. Important variables to consider to ensure diversity among the SMEs include job title, work site, grade/level, race, and gender. For most purposes, it is important to document the SME characteristics to ensure representation as well as experience with the job being analyzed.

Step 2: Prepare for Critical Incident Workshops

The workshops should be arranged several weeks in advance. Each workshop session should be scheduled to last about three hours, with 30 minutes for training and two and a half hours for writing the incident reports. There should be 10 to 20 individuals per session, with each SME attending only one session. Equipment and facilities that will be needed

TABLE 4.1 Tips for Writing Critical Incident Reports

1. Concisely describe the situation, the action taken, and the outcome. Carefully decide what information is relevant to each event.
2. Describe what the apprentice or journeyman did (or failed to do) in that specific situation. Do not describe "types of things that people do" or general traits of effective or ineffective workers. The emphasis should be on what was observed, not on interpretation of the action.
3. Focus on the actions of a single person rather than those of a team.
4. Write events in the third person (he or she) and do not use personally identifying information. Use terms such as "the apprentice" and "the supervisor." Even if you relate events that are things you did, please write them in the third person.
5. Write about actions you have taken or the actions of others that you have personally observed, not situations reported to you by someone else, because your recollection of these events will be the most vivid and accurate.

include a large room with tables and chairs for participants, critical incident forms, pencils, and various materials to train the participants on how to write critical incident reports.

Step 3: Conduct Critical Incident Workshops

In general, the purpose of the workshops is to have individuals who are knowledgeable about the job write reports of instances of ineffective, average, and effective job performance. Workshop participants are asked to think back over the last six months and relate actual behaviors they have exhibited or observed others exhibit on the job. Participants are asked to record the circumstances leading up to the incident, what actions were taken by the job holder, and the outcome of the actions.

The first 30 minutes of each workshop should be used to train the SMEs on how to write critical incident reports. During this training, the individual conducting the workshop should review the goals of the workshop, explain the format of critical incident reports, explain some tips for writing a usable critical incident report, and provide examples of both usable and unusable critical incident reports. Table 4.1 includes tips for writing critical incident reports. During this review and background discussion of critical incidents, participants should be encouraged to ask questions. When providing examples of incident reports, it may be best to use an example from a different but similar job because a job-relevant example may unduly narrow participants' focus. In other words, if an example incident report for the job of Inside Apprentice Electrician involved reading blueprints, it is likely that a disproportionate number of

Critical Incident Report Form   Participant #_____

1. What was the situation leading up to the event? [Describe the context.]

2. What did the apprentice or journeyman do?

3. What was the outcome or result of the apprentice or journeyman's action?

4. Circle the number below that best reflects the level of performance that this event exemplifies.

1	2	3	4	5	6	7
Highly Ineffective			Moderately Effective			Highly Effective

FIGURE 4.2   Critical Incident Report Form

incidents written in that workshop would involve reading, or not reading, blueprints. This is undesirable because it may cause participants to neglect reporting critical incidents from other important parts of the job.

Some researchers opt to place additional structure on the critical incident workshop by providing dimensions of performance for which the SMEs should write incidents. The idea behind using predefined dimensions is that they appear to help ensure that participants write incidents on all the relevant aspects of the job. At times, this has been done by asking participants to write at least one critical incident for each performance dimension. Note, however, that use of predefined performance dimensions will cause SMEs to focus on those dimensions—perhaps to the exclusion of other important, yet "undiscovered" dimensions. Also, the use of predefined dimensions means that the researcher cannot use the critical incident technique to discover the underlying structure of performance, thus losing a particularly useful outcome of the critical incident method.

After the workshop leader conducts the training, the participants should begin to write their reports. A form that is useful for collecting critical incident reports is shown in Figure 4.2. The form that SMEs use to write incidents should include prompts for the situation, the behavior, the outcome, and a rating of the behavior's effectiveness.

TABLE 4.2   Probes for Stimulating SMEs to Write Critical Incidents

- Think of something you did in the past that you are proud of.
- Think of a time when you learned something the hard way. What did you do and what was the outcome?
- Think of a person whom you admire on the job. Can you recall an incident that convinced you that the person was an outstanding performer?
- Think of a time when you realized too late that you should have done something differently. What did you do and what was the outcome?
- Think about the last six months. Can you recall a day when you were particularly effective? What did you do that made you effective?
- Think of a time when you saw someone do something in a situation and you thought to yourself, "If I were in that same situation, I would handle it differently." What was the scenario you saw?
- Think about mistakes you have seen workers make when they are new at the job.
- Think about actions taken by more experienced workers that help them to avoid making mistakes.

During the workshop, participants may have difficulty thinking of incidents. When this happens, the researcher should probe the participants to stimulate recall. A typical probe is, "Think of a recent situation in which you observed an employee do something that was especially effective or ineffective on the job. What led up to the performance? What did the person do? What happened as a result?" Table 4.2 contains a set of probes that were used in the electrician study.

In the workshop, it should be emphasized that reports should describe actions participants saw a person do, not what the participants inferred from the action about the skills or personal characteristics of the person. For example, rather than write that an individual "displayed loyalty," the reports should describe what the individual did that was so effective (e.g., worked all night to finish a job, or defended the supervisor's position to a group of subordinates).

When participants start writing reports, the analyst conducting the workshop should encourage and reinforce them. The purpose is to shape their behavior so that they write productively. Review the incidents during the workshop and as they are being handed in to ensure compliance with the instructions. If an incident does not contain important information (e.g., describes an individual knowledge, skill, ability, or other characteristic rather than the behavior that occurred), the writer should be prodded for more detail about the behavior. Since many individuals hesitate to write, especially in a group setting, small editorial changes

What were the circumstances leading up to the incident?
During the installation of a new feeder on the exterior of a building, it was decided to carry the cable up a nearby exterior stairway and push the cable down into the conduit.

What actions did the worker take that were effective or ineffective?
The cable easily went into the conduit. However, as it gained momentum all of the cable went through the conduit and out onto the ground.

What were the outcomes of these actions?
The crew had to repeat the job, but this time the cable was tied off on the high end of the conduit.

FIGURE 4.3   An Example of a Critical Incident Report That Is Not Useful

should be ignored during the workshop. These changes can be made by an analyst after the workshop. Although the number of incidents written by each subject matter expert will vary, it is reasonable to expect that an average of 5 to 10 critical incident reports can be generated by each SME in a two-hour workshop.

Figure 4.3 contains a critical incident report written by an inside wireman electrician. This particular report is not very useful because:

- It is written in the passive voice.
- It is unclear who performed the behaviors.
- It does not refer to the actions of a single person.
- An action is not clearly presented; therefore it is unclear what led to the outcome.

Figure 4.4 contains the report as it might have been correctly written. Note that the report shown in Figure 4.4 is improved because:

- It discusses a specific incident in an action–oriented manner
- It describes a complete situation, action, and result
- It refers to the behavior of one individual rather than a team

The number of incidents needed to adequately describe a job's performance requirements will depend on the complexity of the job. For example, it would take fewer critical incident reports to describe thoroughly the effective and ineffective performance of a toll collector than it would to describe the performance of an electrician. For relatively complex professional occupations or positions, 500 to 1,000 or more incidents may be needed. For less complex jobs, 400 to 500 incidents

What were the circumstances leading up to the incident?
A journeyman was to install a new feeder on the exterior of a large 10-story building, and there was no obvious method for getting the cable through the conduit.

What actions did the worker take that were effective or ineffective?
The journeyman decided to run the cable up a nearby stairway and drop the cable in from above. He placed the bottom end of the cable into the conduit and let it go so that gravity would pull the cable through the conduit. He failed to tie off the top end of the cable to keep all of it from falling to the ground. The cable gained momentum as more and more cable went into the conduit, and the journeyman was unable to stop it when it got to the end.

What were the outcomes of these actions?
All of the cable slipped through the conduit and landed on the ground. The journeyman had to repeat the job, but this time the cable was tied off on the high end of the conduit.

FIGURE 4.4   An Example of a Critical Incident Report That Is Useful

may be sufficient. To ensure that enough incidents are generated to fully describe the job domain, the critical incident reports obtained in each workshop session should be reviewed. When fewer than two or three new incidents are gathered at a subsequent workshop, it is likely that a comprehensive set of incident reports has been generated. In addition, it also is usually desirable to have critical incident reports depicting performance that spans the effectiveness range. The effectiveness ratings provided by the SMEs can be used to monitor how well the range of effectiveness is being represented.

EDITING CRITICAL INCIDENTS

After critical incident reports are collected, the information is entered into a database and edited. The purposes of editing are: (1) to place each incident in a standard, readable format; (2) to clarify some of the wording by correcting spelling, grammar, and punctuation; (3) to group redundant or highly similar critical incidents; (4) to ensure a comparable level of detail across incidents; and (5) to rephrase statements as necessary to eliminate jargon that is not widely used in the SME community. This editing is usually done by a researcher familiar with the job being studied. Following are guidelines for editing critical incidents.

- Incidents are written in three parts, but the writer may not have made the correct distinctions about where to record each part. All information about the background leading up to the incident should be part of the situation or context. The middle section on the actions taken should include all of the key steps taken by the actor in the incident. Sometimes writers put some of this information under the outcome. The outcome can usually be summarized in one sentence. The outcome should be as concrete as possible.
- Use the words of the writer as much as possible. Do not make your own interpretations about what happened, but try to describe it clearly and concisely.
- Correct spelling, grammar, and punctuation.
- Make sure that the report is actually about the actor named in the report. Sometimes a person will think he or she is writing a report about a trainee or subordinate, when the report is really about the supervisor. One way to figure this out is to determine whose actions resulted in the outcome. If the supervisor's actions produced the outcome, then the incident is about the supervisor.
- Keep all references to the actors gender-neutral (unless it is somehow important to the incident). Eliminate masculine and feminine pronouns.
- Discard incident reports that provide insufficient information or that do not include a plausible relationship between the person's actions and the outcomes.

HOW TO IDENTIFY, DEFINE, AND TEST PERFORMANCE DIMENSIONS

IDENTIFYING PERFORMANCE DIMENSIONS

In personnel selection research, it is important to understand the performance domain. One way to facilitate understanding of the performance domain is to develop a structure detailing the dimensions that underlie job performance. Performance dimensions provide a breakdown of those factors important to job performance and thus provide us with a structure for researching, measuring, evaluating, and improving job performance. Some performance dimensions that may be relevant to the typical managerial position include problem solving, planning, and supervising. Performance dimensions are typically defined by the job behaviors relevant to them. Understanding the dimensions of job performance can inform the researcher on many issues. A clear set of performance dimensions can be particularly useful in developing predictor and criterion instruments. For example, through examination of performance dimensions, a researcher may be able to infer that quantitative ability and written communication skills are highly important to job performance, but spatial ability and interpersonal skills are not (see Chapter 5 on developing test plans). Therefore, understanding various techniques for identifying and defining performance dimensions is important.

The critical incident technique is one method for identifying and defining performance dimensions. It allows the researcher to gain insight into the dimensional structure of performance without having to ask SMEs to directly provide the dimensions. This is an important advantage because, while SMEs may know good performance when they see it, they may have difficulty identifying the factors that lead to it or the constructs that underlie it. The four steps involved in identifying and defining performance dimensions using critical incidents are detailed as follows.

Step 1: Assemble a Set of Three to Five Analysts
to Review and Categorize the Incidents
After incidents are collected and edited as just described, they need to be reviewed and categorized into dimensions by analysts who are knowledgeable about the psychological factors that underlie performance and who are somewhat familiar with the job being studied. Analysts can develop a dimensional structure by consensus or by independent judgment. In order to achieve the full benefit of the group of analysts, it may be most useful to have the analysts sort the critical incident reports independently from one another. The following activities may be conducted to prepare and conduct this review.

- Place each critical incident report on a separate sheet of paper or card so that it can be easily sorted.
- Make enough copies so that each analyst has a complete set of reports.
- Have analysts review the reports and place similar reports together, according to the behavior performed in the incident.
- Have analysts label each set of similar reports, with a brief abstraction of the behavior.

Step 2: Develop a Common Set of Dimensions Among Analysts
This common set of category labels or dimensions can be derived through negotiation among analysts, where analysts describe their cate-

gories and the behaviors encompassed in each. They then take turns explaining their rationale for forming different categories. After this discussion, the analysts need to negotiate to derive a common set of performance dimensions. A single set of dimensions also can be empirically derived (Rosenberg & Kim, 1975), but a detailed discussion of this method is beyond the scope of this chapter. The number of dimensions identified should be somewhere between 10 and 25, depending on the complexity of the job. This number of dimensions typically provides enough detail and separation among dimensions for describing the job.

Step 3: Develop a Description of Each Performance Dimension
Descriptions of the dimensions should be written with enough detail on the defining characteristics of each dimension so that SMEs are likely to categorize similar incidents into the same dimension. They should describe the behaviors subsumed under each dimension and should distinguish these behaviors from those belonging to other dimensions. Appendix A provides a set of dimensions and descriptions identified as part of the electrician study (Williams et al., 1994).

Step 4. Pilot Test the Performance Structure
A small number of SMEs or analysts should review the definition of each performance dimension for clarity and assign the incidents to the dimensions. If there is low agreement during pilot testing, the structure may need to be refined or some of the dimension definitions may need to be rewritten.

TESTING THE CLASSIFICATION STRUCTURE
OF PERFORMANCE DIMENSIONS

The structure of performance dimensions needs to be tested with an independent group of SMEs. This process also is known as "retranslation" (Smith & Kendall, 1963). Following are steps for conducting this test.

Step 1: Identify SMEs
These SMEs could be incumbents and/or supervisors who are knowledgeable about the job. These SMEs can be the authors of the incidents and/or they can be an independent sample. Identifying an independent sample of SMEs helps accomplish an alternative goal of developing the dimensional structure using information from the broadest possible set of SMEs.

Step 2: Present Dimensions, Their Definitions, and
a Randomly Ordered List of Edited Critical Incidents to the SMEs

This could be done in the context of a workshop or in a mail-out. The task is to sort each incident into one dimension based on its content and then to rate the effectiveness level of that incident. A 7-point scale is often used for these ratings, where 1 = highly ineffective and 7 = highly effective performance.

Step 3: Analyze the Data

Data from this set of experts should be analyzed by calculating the mean and standard deviation of the effectiveness ratings given to each behavioral incident. In addition, the percent of respondents who sorted each incident into each performance dimension should be calculated. Appendix B shows the output of a critical incident retranslation data analysis. The first column shows the dimensions into which the SMEs categorized the incidents; the second column shows the percent of respondents who indicated that the incident should be placed in that category; the third column shows the number of subject matter experts, from among those participating in retranslation, who indicated that the incident should be placed in that category; the fourth column shows the mean effectiveness rating of the incident; the fifth column shows the standard deviation of the effectiveness rating; and the sixth column shows the incident. As shown in Appendix B, the first incident was sorted into Dimension A: Planning, preparing, and organizing work by 76% (16 out of 21) respondents. The mean effectiveness rating is 5.69, which is fairly high on a seven-point scale, and the standard deviation is .85, indicating a relatively high degree of agreement. Conversely, respondents appeared to have trouble categorizing the fourth incident shown in Appendix B. Seven out of 18 (39%) respondents put the incident in Dimension A, whereas 9 out of 18 (50%) put the incident in Dimension H. The incident received fairly high effectiveness ratings in both categories, but the standard deviations of effectiveness also were somewhat high (over 1.50).

Step 4: Use Results to Inform Instrument Development

The results of the data analyses just described will reveal where and how well an incident fits into the performance structure, and where the behavior depicted in the incident lies along a continuum of effectiveness. When there is high agreement among SMEs as to the dimensional placement of an incident, it can clearly be assigned to that dimension. Those incidents with the highest agreement on category placement can be considered most representative of the dimension and thus can be used as examples when discussing and defining performance on the dimensions. Incidents can be chosen to represent effective, moderately effective, or ineffective performance by selecting those incidents that have low variance in effectiveness ratings and that have high, medium, or low mean effectiveness ratings, respectively.

Given this information, the researcher may choose to select incidents for use in training exercises, rating instruments, exemplars of performance, or assessment exercises. The way the incidents will be used will affect which incidents are selected. For example, the researcher may want to select incidents that exhibit different mean levels of effectiveness so that they can be used for behavioral anchors at low, moderate, or high levels of performance on a particular dimension (see Chapter 11 on rating scales). In general, the best incidents tend to be those where there is high agreement among SMEs on category placement and on the effectiveness ratings (as indicated by a low standard deviation).

SUMMARY

The critical incident technique can be used to address many research questions. It is particularly useful for understanding the performance of individuals, systems, and organizations. Various applications arise from this greater understanding of performance, such as training individuals, designing systems and organizations, conducting performance appraisals, developing assessment tools, evaluating systems, and conducting organizational interventions.

The critical incident technique is particularly appropriate for analyzing complex jobs in which the behavior performed depends largely on the situation encountered, as opposed to routine jobs in which the same behaviors are routinely performed. The products of the technique can be used for a variety of purposes. Predictor instruments often are developed using dimensions derived through the critical incident technique. On the criterion side, Chapter 11 discusses the development of rating scales using the critical incident technique.

APPENDIX A
JOB PERFORMANCE DIMENSIONS

A. Planning, Preparing, and Organizing Work
- Thinking through job requirements
- Ordering materials and ensuring sufficient supplies
- Planning for problems that might occur
- Laying out steps and procedures
- Documenting or diagramming the job

B. Working Hard, Taking Initiative, and Being Responsible
- Completing a lot of work in a short time period
- Taking on more responsibility
- Continuing to work in difficult circumstances
- Adhering to job rules, including starting times
- Not using drugs or alcohol on the job

C. Solving Problems
- Finding new methods to complete a task when a problem occurs
- Improvising using available materials
- Finding a better way to do a task

D. Working Safely
- Following correct safety procedures
- Using tools and equipment safely
- Using precautions when working with hot circuits

E. Teamwork
- Communicating clearly with other workers
- Helping other team members
- Following the instructions given for completing a task
- Asking for help if needed
- Warning others of danger

F. Troubleshooting
- Finding the cause of an electrical problem
- Inspecting or testing equipment
- Getting a system or equipment to work

G. Responding to an Emergency
- Preventing a problem from worsening
- Administering first aid
- Keeping the public out of danger

H. Supervising
- Assigning tasks to others and monitoring progress
- Contributing to crew morale
- Disciplining other workers
- Managing project resources
- Working with contractor, inspectors, and other outside people
- Checking working conditions

I. Training
- Providing learning opportunities for others
- Demonstrating proper techniques
- Giving feedback on performance
- Explaining the reasons behind work procedures

J. Following Blueprints, Code, and Installation Instructions
- Checking blueprints to install correctly
- Making sure that an installation meets code
- Reading instructions from kits

K. Using Tools and Equipment
- Using hand tools
- Using machinery, including trucks
- Using ladders

L. Planning and Installing Conduit
- Finding a path for a duct bank or raceway
- Installing a duct bank and securing the conduit
- Building a raceway and supporting the conduit

M. Preparing Conduit for Installation
- Cutting and threading conduit
- Bending conduit

N. Pulling Wire or Cable
- Measuring wire or cable
- Using a fish tape, mouse, or other means to establish a pull line
- Setting up a hand or machine tugger
- Lubricating the pull
- Tagging the wire or cable

O. Installing Panels
- Establishing panel location
- Terminating wires in panel
- Labeling the panel

P. Installing Switches, Receptacles, Lighting, and Other Fixtures
- Establishing correct location for the outlet or fixture
- Making terminations
- Finishing the installation

Q. Installing Buss Ducts and Switchgear
- Moving switchgear into place
- Making terminations
- Installing and securing buss ducts

R. Installing Transformers
- Checking phases
- Marking wires
- Connecting wires to the equipment

EXAMPLE OF RESULTS FROM ANALYSES OF CRITICAL INCIDENTS

Dimension	Percent of Respondents Placing an Incident with a Particular Dimension	Number of Respondents Placing an Incident with a Particular Dimension	Mean Effectiveness Rating of Incidents	Standard Deviation of Effective-ness Ratings	Critical Incident
A: Planning, preparing, and organizing work	76	16/21	5.69	0.85	An electrical apprentice working on the construction of a six-story hospital was responsible for the installation of all underground conduit runs for the parking lot lighting. Before beginning to run the conduit, the apprentice ensured that there would be enough material to finish the project. After gathering all the material that was needed to successfully complete the job and organizing it in a manner that would allow the apprentice to keep easy access to it, the apprentice began the project. The result of the apprentice's organizing was that the project was finished in a short amount of time and was completed correctly and effectively.

EXAMPLE OF RESULTS FROM ANALYSES OF CRITICAL INCIDENTS (continued)

Dimension	Percent of Respondents Placing an Incident with a Particular Dimension	Number of Respondents Placing an Incident with a Particular Dimension	Mean Effectiveness Rating of Incidents	Standard Deviation of Effectiveness Ratings	Critical Incident
F: Trouble-shooting	82	18/22	4.94	1.08	An apprentice was asked to troubleshoot a lighting fixture. The lighting system was a 120/208 system. The apprentice opened up the belly bar on the fixture and found that the voltage rating was 277/480 ballast. It was installed incorrectly by the manufacturer. The apprentice changed the ballast to the correct voltage reading.
B: Working hard, taking initiative, and being responsible	24	5/21	6.40	0.49	A journeyman put an apprentice on a speaker system that was showing no load with a general idea as to the route of the speakers. The apprentice looked up the plans for the speaker system, better understood the job, and started to troubleshoot the system using a meter. The apprentice located and fixed the problem well before the journeyman expected.
F: Trouble-shooting	57	12/21	6.08	0.76	

A: Planning, preparing, and organizing work	39	7/18	5.86	1.67	The foreman of a job gave a print to an apprentice and said, "Lay this whole floor out and pipe it." The apprentice took time to look over the prints and judged what the best way to do the task would be. The apprentice successfully completed the job and felt very proud.
H: Supervising	50	9/18	5.22	1.53	
A: Planning, preparing, and organizing work	60	12/20	2.45	0.66	The job was piping schoolrooms for lighting. An apprentice used shallow boxes for lighting because that was all that was available at the time. The apprentice had a very hard time doing makeup in the boxes, C: which took extra time.
C: Solving problems	15	3/20	3.75	0.43	
N: Pulling wire or cable	20	4/20	3.50	0.50	
A: Planning, preparing, and organizing work	77	17/22	6.06	0.80	Twelve workers were spread over a pharmaceutical plant with approximately 20 buildings on site. The apprentice suggested that the workers turn in material lists a day in advance so that the apprentice could have it ready and organized. Since the apprentice took the initiative to better organize the material and the demand for it, there was minimal downtime for the mechanics.

EXAMPLE OF RESULTS FROM ANALYSES OF CRITICAL INCIDENTS (continued)

Dimension	Percent of Respondents Placing an Incident with a Particular Dimension	Number of Respondents Placing an Incident with a Particular Dimension	Mean Effectiveness Rating of Incidents	Standard Deviation of Effectiveness Ratings	Critical Incident
C: Solving problems	95	19/20	1.16	0.36	While pulling in a "pull line," the rope got hung up in a block. An apprentice took the bucket, set up and tried to free the "p-line" by reaching through an open wire secondary without gloves and sleeves on. The apprentice was electrocuted and died.
A: Planning, preparing, and organizing work	80	16/20	2.25	0.83	The apprentice was told to load material on the trucks before going home. The apprentice went home before finishing loading the trucks. The apprentice forgot some material the next day, which delayed the job.
A: Planning, preparing, and organizing work	52	11/21	3.00	1.13	A job was to run pipe starting from an MCC to a trough 80 feet away, using the best path to run with the least amount of bends. Instead of waiting to see where the the pipe would line up, the apprentice mounted the trough and knocked out the top before the pipe was run to it. The result was the pipe had to be offset to reach the knockout.
J: Following blueprints, code, and installation instructions	48	10/21	2.70	0.78	

REFERENCES

Atkin, R. S., & Conlon, E. J. (1978). Behaviorally-anchored rating scales: Some theoretical issues. *Academy of Management Review, 3,* 119–128.

Borman, W. C. (1979). Format and training effects on rating accuracy and rater errors. *Journal of Applied Psychology, 64,* 410–421.

Borman, W. C., & Dunnette, M. D. (1975). Behavior-based versus trait-oriented performance ratings: An empirical study. *Journal of Applied Psychology, 60,* 561–565.

Campbell, C. H., Ford, P., Rumsey, M. G., Pulakos, E. D., Borman, W. C., Felker, D. B., DeVera, M.V., & Riegelhaupt, B. J. (1990). Development of multiple job performance measures in a representative sample of jobs. *Personnel Psychology, 43,* 277–300.

Campbell, J. P., Dunnette, M. D., Arvey, R. D., & Hellervik, L.V. (1973). The development and evaluation of behaviorally based rating scales. *Journal of Applied Psychology, 57,* 15–22.

Campbell, J. P., Dunnette, M. D., Lawler, E. E., & Weick, K. E. (1970). *Managerial behavior, performance, and effectiveness.* New York: McGraw-Hill.

Fitts, P. M., & Jones, R. E. (1947). *Psychological aspects of instrument display.* Dayton, OH: US Air Force, Air Materiel Command, Wright-Patterson Air Force Base.

Flanagan, J. C. (Ed.) (1948a). *The aviation psychology program in the Army Air Forces* (Army Air Forces Aviation Psychology Program Research Report No. 1). Washington, DC: U.S. Government Printing Office.

Flanagan, J. C. (1948b). Contributions of research in the Armed Forces to personnel psychology. *Personnel Psychology, 1,* 52–53.

Flanagan, J. C. (1954). The critical incident technique. *Psychological Bulletin, 41,* 237–358.

Flanagan, J. C. (1957). *Research on the selection of aircrew personnel.* American Institutes for Research, Research Notes. No. 13, 1–4.

Jacobs, A. M., Fivars, G., & Fitzpatrick, R. (1982). What the new test will test. *American Journal of Nursing, 82,* 625–628.

Lindbergh, D. A. B., Siegel, E. R., Rapp, B. A., Wallingford, K. T., & Wilson, S. R. (1993). Use of MEDLINE by physicians for clinical problem solving. *Journal of American Medical Association, 269,* 3124–3129.

McNabb, W. L., Wilson, S. R., & Jacobs, A. M. (1986). Critical self-management competencies for children with asthma. *Journal of Pediatric Psychology, 11,* 103–117.

Newbower, R. S., Cooper, J. B., & Long, C. D. (1981). Learning from anesthesia mishaps: Analysis of critical incidents in anesthesia helps reduce patient risk. *Quality Review Bulletin,* 10–16.

Rosenberg, S., & Kim, M. J. (1975). The method of sorting as a data-gathering procedure in multivariate research. *Multivariate Behavioral Research, 10,* 489–502.

Sackett, P. (1994, April). *The content and process of the research enterprise within industrial and organizational psychology.* Presidential Address delivered at the annual meeting of the Society of Industrial and Organizational Psychology, Inc., Nashville, TN.

Smith, P. C., & Kendall, L. M. (1963). Retranslation of expectations: An approach to the construction of unambiguous anchors for rating scales. *Journal of Applied Psychology, 47,* 149–155.

Williams, K. M., Peterson, N. G., & Bell, J. A. (1994). *Job analysis of three electrical worker positions for the National Joint Apprenticeship and Training Committee.* Washington DC: American Institutes for Research.

Wilson, S. R. (1993). Patient and physician behavior models related to asthma care. *Journal of Medical Care, 31,* MS49–MS60.

Wilson, S. R., Mitchell, J.H., Rolnick, S., & Fish, L. (1993). Effective and ineffective management behaviors of parents of infants and young children with asthma. *Journal of Pediatric Psychology, 48,* 63–81.

Wilson, S. R., Scamagas, P., Arsham, G. M., Chardon, L., Coss, S., German, D. F., & Hughes, G. W. (1987). An evaluation of approaches to asthma self-management education for adults: The AIR/Kaiser-Permanente study. *Health Education Quarterly, 14,* 333–343.

Wilson, S. R., Starr-Schneidkraut, N., & Cooper, M. (1989). *Use of the critical incident technique to evaluate the impact of MEDLINE, Final Report.* Bethesda, MD: National Library of Medicine (Contract No. N01-LM-8-3529).

DEVELOPING
A TEST PLAN

The Test Plan

Teresa L. Russell
Norman G. Peterson

OVERVIEW

Organizations use employment tests and other assessment tools to select workers who are likely to perform well in their new jobs. In doing so, organizations hope to become more competitive by employing well-qualified staff and to save money that would otherwise be lost through poor employee performance. Even so, the validity of the selection procedure for identifying well-qualified workers, while it might be the paramount objective, is not the organization's only concern. When designing employee selection procedures, organizations attempt to balance three goals:

1. Maximize validity
2. Minimize adverse impact (i.e., test score differences between legally or societally significant subgroups)
3. Enhance the efficiency of the procedures

Maximizing test validity increases the likelihood that organizations will select applicants who will perform well on the job. Evidence of validity can come from correlations between employee test scores and job performance, linkages between the content of the job and the content of tests, and linkages between job-relevant worker characteristics and the tests that measure them, as well as documentation of the validity of a test for similar jobs.

Minimizing adverse impact against minorities and women is important for enhancing the diversity of the organization's workforce and for meeting professional and legal standards for employee testing (AERA, APA, & NCME, 1985; SIOP, 1987). The *Uniform Guidelines on Employee Selection Procedures* (EEOC, CSC, DOL, & DOJ, 1978) recommends that employers seek valid alternatives to cognitive ability tests when such tests are found to produce substantial adverse impact. Minimizing adverse impact enhances the legal defensibility of the selection procedures.

No matter how it is done, employee selection costs time and money. Tests of underlying personnel characteristics must be selected or developed, and then administered and scored. Interview questions must be developed, interviewers must be trained, and the sessions must be conducted. Biodata instruments and situational inventories also may be constructed, administered, and scored. The amount of time and money an organization is willing to spend developing, maintaining, and operating an employee selection program will depend on the type of job under consideration as well as available organizational resources.

This chapter describes methods that we have used to develop test plans that, on balance, satisfy the three objectives of employee selection. A test plan summarizes information from a thorough job analysis and literature review. It provides a rationale for tests and assessment methods that are chosen as part of the selection procedure and for those that are not chosen. It documents the hypothesized relationships between measurement methods and worker characteristics. A test plan is a blueprint for development and validation of selection procedures.

THE WORKER CHARACTERISTIC AND METHOD OF MEASUREMENT MATRIX

The centerpiece of a test plan is a matrix, shown in Table 5.1, that compares worker characteristics or KSAOs to be measured against possible measurement methods. Worker characteristics to be measured are listed along the rows; those worker characteristics should be ones resulting from either a deductive or inductive job analysis, as described in Chapters 2, 3, and 4. Possible measurement methods, derived from review of the research literature, are listed in the columns. Several alternative measurement methods are described in Chapters 6, 7, 8, 9, and 10.

TABLE 5.1 Worker Characteristics and Methods of Measurement Matrix

MEASUREMENT METHODS

WORKER CHARACTERISTICS	Aptitude or Achievement Tests	Interview	Self-Report	Simulation
Ability to add, subtract, multiply, and divide and use formulas				
Ability to understand verbal instructions and warnings				
Ability to communicate orally with others				
Ability to read and understand graphs, charts, and diagrams				
Ability to develop alternative olutions to a problem and choose the best alternative				
Ability to work in a noisy environment				
Ability to work at heights				
....				

Judgments about the quality with which different measurement methods are likely to measure the worker characteristics appear in the cells of the matrix.

There are three primary steps for completing the matrix. The first is to identify the job-relevant worker characteristics that should be measured through a thorough job analysis. Once the job analysis is complete, the second step is to identify methods of measuring the worker characteristics—methods that are likely to prove useful given organizational constraints on resources and a desire to maximize validity and minimize adverse impact. The third step is to complete the matrix—making judgments about the quality of a measurement method for assessing the constructs at hand and weighing in concerns about adverse impact and costs.

HOW TO IDENTIFY WORKER CHARACTERISTICS

Worker characteristics—knowledges, skills, abilities, and other characteristics (KSAOs)—must be derived from a thorough job analysis. Chapters 2, 3, and 4 explain job analysis methodologies that yield job-relevant worker characteristics. Generally, all job analysis methods involve soliciting job information from subject matter experts (SMEs), who may be supervisors, job incumbents, trainers, or job analysts. Regardless of the job analysis methodology, professional standards and legal guidelines (AERA, APA, & NCME, 1985; EEOC, CSC, DOL, & DOJ, 1978; SIOP, 1987) suggest that worker characteristics selected for measurement should be:

1. Job relevant
2. Before-hire requirements
3. Supported by prior research

Job relevance means that the worker characteristic is needed to perform job activities. Evidence of job relevance can come from several sources. Two of the most frequently used ones are: (1) the overall importance of the worker characteristics for performing the job, and (2) the importance of the worker characteristic for performing critical job tasks, duties, or activities. The first judgment often is obtained from a questionnaire or focus group in which SMEs are asked to judge the importance of various worker characteristics. The second judgment is usually obtained from a second exercise in which SMEs are asked to rate the importance of each of many worker characteristics for performing job activities. Both of these procedures are described in greater detail in Chapters 2 and 3.

Worker characteristics used for selection into entry-level jobs should be ones that are required before hire. Worker characteristics that can be learned in a brief orientation period after job entry are candidates for training programs, not selection methods (EEOC, CSC, DOL, & DOJ, 1978). Evidence that the worker characteristic is one that employees should bring with them to the job is typically collected during a job analysis as described in Chapters 2 and 3. This "before-hire" requirement may be particularly subject to differences across organizations. Some organizations may choose, as a matter of philosophy, to provide their own training for many characteristics; others may provide training for only a very few characteristics unique to the organization.

Another factor to consider in selecting worker characteristics for measurement is prior research support. Characteristics that have demonstrated validity in previous studies of similar jobs are good candidates for inclusion.

HOW TO IDENTIFY METHODS FOR MEASURING WORKER CHARACTERISTICS

Test designers must carefully consider different types of measurement methods, their properties, and the test administration medium that is most likely to prove useful to the organization. Measurement methods can be broadly clustered into four categories—achievement or aptitude tests, interviews, self-report measures, or simulations. Each type of method offers some advantages and disadvantages as noted in Table 5.2.

APTITUDE OR ACHIEVEMENT TESTS

Aptitude or achievement tests include measures of cognitive ability (which are discussed in greater detail in Chapter 6) and knowledge. Relative to other tests, aptitude and achievement measures are usually inexpensive to administer and score.

The chief advantage of aptitude or achievement tests lies in their excellent psychometric quality. Aptitude and achievement tests typically are highly reliable (with observed reliabilities commonly in the .80-.90 range), and there is strong evidence of their validity for most occupations (Hunter & Hunter, 1984; Schmitt, Gooding, Noe, & Kirsch, 1984).

TABLE 5.2   Characteristics of Several Types of Measurement Methods

Measurement Method	Advantages	Disadvantages/Concerns
Achievement or Aptitude Tests		
General cognitive ability Specific cognitive ability Knowledge or achievement	Operational costs are relatively low. There is strong evidence of the validity of cognitive tests for many occupations. Reliability usually is high.	Racial/ethnic subgroup differences tend to be large.
Interviews		
	Interviews are appealing to organizations. Interviews have proven to be valid selection tools for some jobs, but the magnitude of the validity typically is not large.	Operational costs are relatively high. Interviewers and raters must be trained.
Self-Report		
Biographical Data Personality Inventories	Operational costs are relatively low. Can predict contextual performance. Can provide incremental validity over cognitive tests.	All self-report measures can be susceptible to response distortion. Content validation usually is not an option. Applicants may find some items offensive.
Simulations		
Situational Judgment Tests Work Sample Tests Assessment Center Exercises	Simulations can have content and face validity. There is some evidence of criterion-related validity.	Operational costs are high for high-fidelity simulations. Assessors must be trained.

Aptitude and achievement tests are particularly useful for predicting task performance (Borman & Motowidlo, 1993; Campbell, McCloy, Oppler, & Sager, 1993) and training performance or grades (Schmitt, et al., 1984).

There are average differences among racial/ethnic groups and between the sexes on cognitive abilities. Those differences can lead to adverse impact on aptitude and achievement tests. Differences between Whites and African Americans are relatively uniform across a wide variety of cognitive abilities (e.g., verbal, math, spatial); there typically is about one standard deviation difference between Whites' and African Americans' scores (U.S. Department of Defense, 1982; Jensen, 1980; National Center for Education Statistics, 1994). Hispanic and Asian-American differences are more difficult to estimate because sample sizes are too small in most studies. Large-scale studies of nationally administered tests, such as the Scholastic Aptitude Test (NCES, 1994), suggest that mean score differences between Hispanics and Whites are about two-thirds of a standard deviation for most cognitive tests and that Asians typically score higher than Whites on mathematical ability tests by almost half a standard deviation.

Sex differences vary with the cognitive ability construct being measured. Males typically score higher than females on tests of mathematical ability by almost half a standard deviation (Hyde, Fennema, & Lamon, 1990). Females have a small advantage, about one-tenth of a standard deviation, on measures of verbal ability (Hyde & Linn, 1988). Sex differences in spatial ability vary widely with the type of spatial measure (Voyer, Voyer, & Bryden, 1995). Measures that require three-dimensional mental rotation of objects yield the largest differences, and measures that require spatial reasoning or fitting pieces of objects together yield the smallest differences.

INTERVIEWS

Interviews are very appealing to organizations. Interview questions can be developed to tap a range of cognitive and noncognitive skills and abilities. They often focus on communication skills, interpersonal skills, decision making, and substantive (i.e., declarative) knowledge. Chapter 7 provides additional information on types of interviews.

Interviews have proven to be valid selection tools, with validities of about .44 for job-related, structured interviews designed to predict job performance (McDaniel, Whetzel, Schmidt, & Maurer, 1994). Interviews correlate with cognitive ability measures, and interview ratings that correlate higher with cognitive ability tend to be better predictors of job performance (Huffcutt, Roth, & McDaniel, 1996). But interviews have also been shown to provide some incremental validity over and above that obtained by cognitive tests (Pulakos & Schmitt, 1995).

On average, the reliability of interviews where two or more raters evaluate the applicants ranges from about .53 to .77 depending on the interview setting (Conway, Jako, & Goodman, 1995)—notably lower than that obtained by aptitude and achievement tests.

Research on the magnitude of subgroup differences in interview ratings is mixed, sometimes yielding higher scores for the majority group (e.g., Parsons & Linden, 1984), higher results for the minority group (e.g., Mullins, 1982), very small differences (Pulakos & Schmitt, 1995), or no differences among subgroups (e.g., Motowidlo, et al., 1992). When comparing levels of subgroup differences observed across different measurement methods, it is important to note the relationship between reliability and estimates of subgroup differences. Less reliable measures yield smaller subgroup differences as a consequence of their poorer measurement qualities (Russell & Oppler, 1996). Therefore, the lower level of subgroup differences observed for interview ratings compared to achievement and aptitude tests could be due at least in part to lower interview reliability.

Finally, interviews are relatively expensive compared to other measurement methods. Interviewers must be trained; applicants must be interviewed one at a time, often for an hour or more. For that reason, many organizations place interviews at the end of their selection process—interviewing only those applicants who have performed successfully on preceding components of the selection process.

SELF-REPORT MEASURES

Self-report measures include instruments that job applicants use to describe their experiences and personal characteristics. Such measures can typically be completed on scannable forms, making their operational costs relatively low.

Recent research suggests that biographical and personality variables, two commonly used self-report measures, are important predictors of contextual performance factors such as work effort and motivation (Borman & Motowidlo, 1993; Campbell et al., 1993). Although personality variables are not particularly good predictors of training or task performance, they have been shown to provide additional validity over and above that of cognitive tests in predicting overall job performance (McHenry, Hough, Toquam, Hanson, & Ashworth, 1990). Biographical data and personality measures differ somewhat in their patterns of prediction because biographical data can tap cognitive constructs as well as noncognitive ones. Chapter 8 discusses biographical data in more detail.

Self-report personality measures often yield little or no differences among racial/ethnic groups (Kamp & Hough, 1986); however, they do yield small to moderate differences between men and women (Feingold, 1994; Maccoby & Jacklin, 1974; Peterson, Russell, et al., 1990). Males tend to score higher than females on assertiveness and self-esteem; females score higher than males on extraversion, anxiety, trust, and nurturance (Feingold, 1994).

Unfortunately, all self-report measures can be susceptible to distortion by the job applicant. A number of studies have documented the tendency for applicants to respond in a socially desirable way (e.g., Oppler, Peterson, & Russell, 1993). Socially desirable responding reduces the variance in a measure because responses become skewed and can result in a ceiling effect. Even so, it is unclear how severely socially desirable responding affects validity; the results across studies are mixed (Reynolds, 1994). For example, Barrick and Mount (1996) found that applicants for truck driver jobs (n = 286) distorted their responses to a personality questionnaire, but the distortion did not attenuate the predictive validities of the personality constructs. On the other hand, Oppler et al. (1993) found that new Army recruits (n > 40,000) were much more likely to respond to a personality questionnaire in a socially desirable way than incumbents (n > 9,000). Criterion-related validities were also substantially lower for the new recruit sample. While other factors such as differences between the samples could have affected the validities, it is possible that response distortion had an attenuating effect.

One other drawback regarding most self-report measures is that they may lack face validity and can be difficult to justify based on content validity alone. Applicants are likely to question the relevance of background and personality items, and in some cases applicants view the items as intrusive (Mael, Connerly, & Morath, 1996).

SIMULATIONS

Simulations are exercises intended to faithfully represent work situations. They vary greatly in terms of their fidelity—how realistically the work situation is represented. Paper-and-pencil situational judgment tests that are described further in Chapter 9 are low-fidelity simulations; work samples, discussed in Chapter 12, anchor the high-fidelity end of the simulation fidelity continuum.

Simulations also vary greatly in their costs. Paper-and-pencil measures can be relatively inexpensive to develop and administer, while assessment centers require one-on-one contact over a period of several hours and can be quite expensive. Also, assessors must be trained; that adds to the cost. Consequently, assessment centers, like interviews, are typically placed near the end of a hiring process to minimize the number of applicants to be assessed. To complicate the cost issue, simulations that are high in fidelity generally cover less of the job performance domain than do lower-fidelity measures. A multiple-choice paper-and-pencil instrument can cover dozens of relevant job situations in an hour or two; work samples using actual equipment and realistic contexts would require days, if they could be administered at all, to cover the same number of situations.

A primary advantage of simulations is that they can have substantial face and content validity. They reflect the job, and if they are developed through solid content validation procedures, their relevance to the job is obvious. For the same reasons, though, they may not meet the "before-hire" requirement.

Simulations provide moderate criterion-related validity. On average, assessment center validities corrected for range restriction are about .37 (Gaugler, Rosenthal, Thornton, & Bentson, 1987). Work sample tests also yield validities in the mid-.30s (Schmitt et al., 1984), as do situational judgment tests (Motowidlo, Dunnette, & Carter, 1990; Pulakos, Schmitt, & Keenan, 1994). Information about reliability and subgroup differences in performance on simulations is not systematically reported and is thus difficult to summarize (Gaugler et al., 1987).

THE MODE OF ADMINISTRATION

Technology is rapidly changing the world of work and will probably continue to do so for a few more decades ("Hitchhiker's Guide to Cybernomics," 1996). Many organizations are contemplating or have begun to use computer-based or video-based testing. Some organizations are considering other technological devices on the horizon such as touch screens and pen-based computers.

To date, most of the research in computer-based testing has focused on assessing the construct equivalence of computer-administered and paper-and-pencil test batteries. For cognitive tests, results differ depending on the degree of speededness of the test. For power tests, paper-and-pencil versions of tests and their computer-administered counterparts appear to measure the same construct (Mead & Dragsow, 1993). Computerization of a speeded test, however, may change the nature of the construct being measured; correlations between computer-administered and paper-and-pencil speeded tests are relatively low. Only one published study has assessed construct equivalence of noncognitive measures across paper-and-pencil and computer media; the mode of administration had no effect (King & Miles, 1995).

Several video-based situational judgment tests have been developed in recent years. Some are administered on video to a room full of examinees, and others make use of CD-ROM technology. So far, validities for video-administered situational judgment tests appear to range from .08 to .27 (Dragsow, 1995; Barbera, Ryan, Desmarais, & Dyer, 1995)—slightly lower than those obtained for paper-and-pencil versions. Proponents of video-based assessment argue that video-based situational judgment tests are purer measures of their intended constructs since the need to read items is eliminated; thus, video-based tests may have more incremental validity over cognitive ability (Dragsow, 1995). But no reported studies have directly assessed the construct equivalence of paper-and-pencil and video-based situational tests or their correlations with reading ability.

Multimedia testing is a rapidly evolving area. It holds the promise of making reliable work sample assessment administratively cost effective, in that many applicants could complete work samples at computer stations, with little monitoring by the examiner.

HOW TO COMPLETE THE TEST PLAN MATRIX

When complete, the worker characteristics and methods of measurement matrix illustrated in Table 5.1 provides a solid basis for the test plan. The rows of the matrix list job-relevant worker characteristics that are not likely to be learned in a brief job orientation period—characteristics that the worker should bring to the job. The measurement methods defining the columns of the matrix should be based on a literature review identifying possible methods for measuring the worker characteristics. The cells of the matrix contain judgments about the quality of the various methods for measuring each worker characteristic.

SPECIFYING MEASUREMENT METHODS
IN THE COLUMNS

A thorough literature review of the methods of measuring each of the worker characteristics resulting from the job analysis is an important step for identifying measurement methods for consideration. The literature review should yield several pieces of information about each measurement method under consideration, including:

- A short description of the test, scale, or measurement method
- A description of psychometric properties:
  - Scoring
  - Correlations with other constructs and measures
  - Reliability
  - Subgroup differences
  - Proneness to socially desirable responding
  - Proneness to practice effects
  - Validity evidence
- Cost information

Short summaries of two different measures, situational judgment tests and a test of spatial ability used in a study by Russell et al.(1995), appear in Figures 5.1 and 5.2.

As the literature review proceeds, measurement methods, tests, and scales will emerge as viable candidates for test development/validation. The level of detail specified in the columns of the matrix will vary depending on the purposes of the selection test battery and the needs of the organization. For example, if the organization wishes to use published test batteries in its selection system, it is best to review the merits of each published test specifically under consideration—such as the *Wonderlic* (Schmidt, 1985) and the *Bennett Mechanical Comprehension Test* (Ghiselli, 1966; Guilford & Lacey, 1947)—against the worker characteristics. Even if the organization plans to develop its own tests, it is a good idea to include some published tests in the matrix as "markers" for the new tests to be developed. Also, if the measurement methods include scales from tests that have subscales—for example, Emotional Stability from the *Guilford-Zimmerman Temperament Survey* (Guilford, 1959; Guilford & Zimmerman, 1956) or Work Orientation from the *California Personality Inventory* (Gough, 1985; Megargee, 1972)—each scale should be listed separately in a column. An example page from a worker characteristics and measurement methods matrix completed in this fashion appears in Table 5.3.

Situational Judgment Tests (SJTs) have also been called low-fidelity simulations, social intelligence tests, and tacit knowledge tests. SJTs measure effectiveness in social functioning, including: conflict resolution, negotiation skills, interpersonal problem solving, communication, rewarding and disciplining, facilitating team-work and unit cohesion, motivating others, and working with culture and or gender differences. SJTs are useful in assessing managerial and leadership abilities (Motowidlo, Dunnette, & Carter, 1990; Pulakos, Schmitt, & Keenan, 1994).

SJTs provide a verbal description of a scenario and a list of potential plans of action. The respondent is to read the situation and to indicate which plan of action he/she believes to be the most effective and to indicate which plan of action he/she believes to be the least effective. A sample item appears below:

You volunteered to serve on the computer committee. The person in charge of the committee frequently arrives late for meetings and shows little interest in the work to be done. You would:

A. Take the problem to his boss.
B. Resign from the committee.
C. Talk to him and encourage him to have a positive attitude.
D. Tell him you would be willing to take over the chairmanship.
E. Discuss the problem with the other committee members to get their ideas.

Scoring: Test questions are generally based on critical incidents. Alternatives are generated by incumbents and supervisors. Scores are based on subject matter experts' ratings of the best and worst alternatives.

Correlations with other constructs: In Motowidlo et al. (1990); ($N = 120$), aptitude test measures did not correlate with the SJT, except for GPA in major ($r = .30$, $p<.05$). However, SJT ratings did correlate significantly with interview ratings of interpersonal skills ($r = .21$), communication skills ($r = .16$), and negotiation ratings ($r = .50$).

Subgroup Differences: Subgroup differences are often not reported. Motowidlo et al. (1990) reported higher scores for women than men.

Reliability: Motowidlo et al. (1990) reported an internal consistency estimate of .56, although they suggest that test-retest statistics might be a more appropriate measure of reliability because situational judgment tests are not expect-ed to be unidimensional or homogeneous.

Validity Evidence: Motowidlo et al. (1990) reported validity estimates of .30 ($p<.01$) for overall effectiveness ratings for managers ($N = 120-140$). The SJT was one of the best predictors of FBI agent performance in the Pulakos et al. (1994) study.

Motowidlo, S. J., Dunnette, M. D., & Carter, G. W. (1990). An alternative selection procedure: The low-fidelity simulation. *Journal of Applied Psychology, 75,* 640–647.

Pulakos, E. D., Schmitt, N., & Keenan, P. (1994). *Validity and implications of the FBI special agent entry level selection system* (Technical Report No. 94–20). Alexandria, VA: Human Resources Research Organization.

FIGURE 5.1   Example Literature Summary on Situational Judgment Tests

Assembling Objects Test (AO)

Construct Measured: General Spatial Ability—Spatial Visualization

Short Description of Test:

Subjects visualize how an object will look when its parts are put together or assembled according to instructions. In part one, the items in the picture are labeled with letters and the subject must visually put the parts together according to the letters. In part two, pieces in the pictures fit together like a puzzle. Subjects must determine which figure from 4 alternatives is the correct shape when the parts are all put together.

Number of Items: 36   *Time Limit:* 18 minutes

Psychometrics:

Scoring: The score is the total number of correct answers.

Correlations with other constructs: Assembling Objects correlates with Object Rotation r = .41, .46; MAZE r = .51, .51; Orientation r = .46, .50; Reasoning r = .56, .56; Map test r = .50; .52; all N's = 9332, 6941, respectively (Peterson, Russell et al., 1990). Factor analytic research suggests that Assembling Objects is a good marker test for general spatial ability (Russell, Humphreys, Rosse & Peterson, 1992).

Subgroup Differences: Gender differences tend to be rather small with effect sizes ranging from -.02 to .08 in large samples (Peterson, Russell et al. 1990). Whites tend to score higher than African Americans, with effect sizes ranging from .78 to .83. Whites tend to score higher than Hispanics, with effect sizes .15, .24, and .25 (Peterson, Russell, et al. 1990).

Reliability: Cronbach alphas of .88 (N = 6754); .90 (N = 9332); .92 (N =290). Test-Retest Reliability: .70 (N = 499); .74 (N = 97) (Peterson, Russell, et al., 1990).

FIGURE 5.2   Sample Literature Summary for a Spatial Ability Test

COMPLETING THE CELLS OF THE MATRIX

The cells of the matrix indicate which measurement methods are likely to be valid measures of the worker characteristics. The matrix can be completed by one psychologist in an organization or by many psychologists or testing professionals as part of a research team. The entries can be checkmarks, qualitative descriptions (e.g., high, low), or numeric ratings. The level of formality needed for a given situation depends on the degree of novelty and complexity of the worker characteristics and measurement methods. If there is little research information on which to base decisions, if the measurement method is a newly emerging tech-

Practice and Coaching Effects: Test performance on spatial ability tests is to some degree malleable; test scores improve with practice (Lohman, 1988). However, the gains are not substantially larger than those observed for tests of other abilities (Russell et al., 1994). There also is some evidence that gains from practice are larger for speeded tests than for power tests (Dunnette, Corpe, & Toquam, 1987). Gains from practice on the Assembling Objects test have been low in two studies. With a one-week interval between testing sessions (N = 100), subjects' scores went up .08 sd from testing 1 to testing 2 (Peterson, 1987). With one month between testing sessions (N = 473) subjects' scores again went up .06 sd from testing 1 to testing 2 (Toquam, Peterson, Rosse, Ashworth, Hanson, & Hallam, 1986). Busciglio and Palmer (1992) studied the effects of practice and coaching on three spatial tests, one of which was Assembling Objects. Practice effects were significant for all three tests. The effects of coaching on Assembling Objects were negligible.

Validity Evidence: In Project A, McHenry et al. (1990) combined six Project A spatial tests to form one composite score. The spatial score yielded modest incremental validity (beyond that afforded by the ASVAB) for predicting technical proficiency in Army enlisted MOS and hands-on performance. Similar results were obtained for a longitudinal validation sample.

Mayberry and Hiatt (1990) found that Assembling Objects was the best new predictor of the job knowledge criterion; corrected incremental validities were .02 for four military jobs. Carey (1992) examined incremental validities (over the ASVAB) for several tests. Assembling Objects added the most incremental validity to the cognitive test for predicting the hands-on performance criterion in automotive and helicopter mechanic samples.

FIGURE 5.2 Sample Literature Summary for a Spatial Ability Test (continued)

nology, or if the worker characteristics are of a clinical nature (e.g., resistance to stress and anxiety), it often is desirable to carry out more formal expert judgments to link constructs to methods. Prior research suggests that psychologists can reliably make these judgments (e.g., Russell et al., 1995). Studies typically report reliabilities in the .80–.90 range for experts' judgments of relationships among constructs (Peterson & Bownas, 1982; Wing, Peterson, & Hoffman, 1984; Peterson, Owens-Kurtz, Hoffman, Arabian, & Whetzel, 1990). Indeed, experts can make reasonably accurate estimates of empirical validities for tests (Schmidt, Hunter, Croll, & McKenzie, 1983).

Expert judgment exercises have used a variety of scales—asking experts for judgments of such issues as validity and measurement efficiency (Peterson & Bownas, 1982). The most important judgment to obtain is a judgment about the extent to which the test, scale, or measurement method measures the worker characteristic. An example of an extent-of-

TABLE 5.3   Example Page of a Worker Characteristics and Methods of Measurement Matrix

MEASUREMENT METHODS

WORKER CHARACTERISTICS	Aptitude or Achievement Tests		Interview	Self-Report	Simulation	
	Basic Math Test	Test of Verbal Compre-hension	Skilled Trades Selection Interview	Environmental Reactions Biographical Inventory	Situational Judgment Test	Work Sample
Ability to add, subtract, multiply, and divide and use formulas						
Ability to understand verbal instructions and warnings						
Ability to communicate orally with others						
Ability to develop alternative solutions to a problem and choose the best alternative						
Ability to work in a noisy environment						
Ability to work at heights						
....						

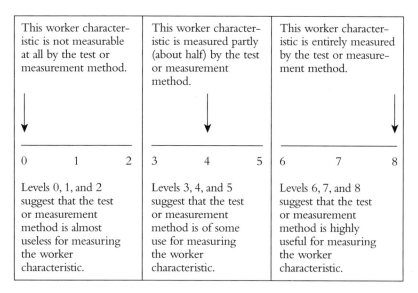

This worker character-istic is not measurable at all by the test or measurement method.	This worker character-istic is measured partly (about half) by the test or measurement method.	This worker character-istic is entirely measured by the test or measure-ment method.
0 1 2	3 4 5	6 7 8
Levels 0, 1, and 2 suggest that the test or measurement method is almost useless for measuring the worker characteristic.	Levels 3, 4, and 5 suggest that the test or measurement method is of some use for measuring the worker characteristic.	Levels 6, 7, and 8 suggest that the test or measurement method is highly useful for measuring the worker characteristic.

FIGURE 5.3   Example of an Extent-of-Measurement Rating Scale

measurement rating scale that has been used in a number of studies (Peterson & Bownas, 1982, Russell et al., 1995) appears in Figure 5.3.

WEIGHING DIFFERENT MEASUREMENT METHODS

Table 5.4 shows a completed matrix after judgments have been made. Entries (*X*s in this example) in different cells of the matrix represent instances in which experts have judged that the measurement method is likely to be a valid measure of the worker characteristic. Thus, the Basic Math Test is unlikely to predict Ability to understand verbal instructions and warnings; however, it is more likely to predict Ability to add, sub-tract, multiply, and divide and use formulas.

Recall that validity is not the only consideration in test planning. Developing the test plan is a balancing act. The test designer must try to maximize validity and minimize adverse impact while keeping costs under control. To facilitate this weighing procedure, it often is useful to add sum-mary rows to the worker characteristics and methods of measurement matrix as shown in Table 5.4. One row summarizes the adverse impact information for the test, scale, or method; other rows summarize the antic-ipated development and operational costs of the test, scale, or method.

When selecting tests for an experimental battery, it is wise to err on the side of inclusiveness. Even well-thought-out and conscientiously developed tests do not always yield adequate validity. To the extent possible, therefore, the experimental battery should include a couple of measures of some of the most important worker characteristics. If the battery includes highly experimental measures with little research support, then it would be prudent to include fall-back measures anticipated to have high validity.

A host of other practical questions also enter the equation. How many tests/measures can the organization afford to develop? How will the tests be validated and how long (in time) can an experimental test battery be before it becomes burdensome? What types of facilities and equipment will be available for testing? Which tests require special settings? Will the testing, interviewing, or assessing take place at a few locations or many? How many interviewers, test administrators, or assessors will have to be trained?

Two mechanisms for organizing and designing a test battery help establish balance among the competing concerns. One involves organizing the selection tests or measurement methods into a series of hurdles. Multiple-hurdle approaches can reduce costs by placing more expensive selection procedures near the end of the selection process. Multiple-hurdle approaches can also be used to reduce the overall level of adverse impact in a selection system or to maximize validity (Sackett & Roth, 1996).

The other mechanism is the "whole job" measurement approach. That is, most jobs require a wide range of worker characteristics, including, for example, cognitive abilities and interpersonal skills. The whole job measurement approach concentrates on predicting the entire range of job performance by assessing a wide array of relevant worker characteristics. The intent is to maximize the validity of the entire selection procedure by using a variety of measures, each contributing validity over and above that provided by the other measures. It can also mitigate the effects of large subgroup differences on some tests through inclusion of other measures with little or no subgroup differences.

As an example, if we were to use the matrix shown in Table 5.4 to select a set of predictors for the job of apprentice electrician, we would probably consider each of the predictors listed in the columns. The Basic Math Test is the only predictor listed here that measures Ability to add, subtract, multiply, and divide and use formulas. There are no development costs, since it can be purchased off the shelf; there are low operational costs, since individual responses can be optically scanned;

TABLE 5.4   Example Page of a Completed Worker Characteristics and Methods of Measurement Matrix

| | MEASUREMENT METHODS | | | | | |
| | Aptitude or Achievement Tests | | Interview | Self-Report | Simulation | |
WORKER CHARACTERISTICS	Basic Math Test	Test of Verbal Comprehension	Skilled Trades Selection Interview	Environmental Reactions Biographical Inventory	Situational Judgment Test	Work Sample
Ability to add, subtract, multiply, and divide and use formulas	X					
Ability to understand verbal instructions and warnings		X	X	X		X
Ability to communicate orally with others		X	X	X		
Ability to develop alternative solutions to a problem and choose the best alternative			X	X	X	X
Ability to work in a noisy environment				X		
Ability to work at heights				X		
OTHER FACTORS						
Anticipated Adverse Impact	High	High	Low	Low	Moderate	Moderate
Anticipated Development Cost	None	None	Moderate	None	Moderate	Moderate
Anticipated Operational Cost	Low	Low	High	Low	Low	High

however, it may have a high degree of adverse impact. Experts indicated that the Test of Verbal Comprehension measures two worker characteristics: Ability to understand verbal instructions and warnings, and Ability to communicate orally with others. Like the Basic Math Test, there are no development costs since it can be purchased off the shelf; there are low operational costs, since responses are optically scanned; and it may have high adverse impact.

According to the experts, the selection interview measures Ability to understand verbal instructions and warnings, Ability to communicate orally with others, and Ability to develop alternative solutions to a problem and choose the best alternative. Even though the development cost is moderate and the operational cost is high, the interview could be an attractive predictor because the anticipated adverse impact of this method is low. Use of this predictor could help offset the adverse impact of the first two predictors, but it is important to remember that the interview is likely to be less reliable and valid than the other two tests. Also, interviewers must be trained in order to make an interview process work validly; if the organization is highly decentralized and has little control over interviewer training, the interview may not be advantageous.

Self-reports, often measured using background data questionnaires, are useful because they measure constructs that are difficult to measure otherwise (i.e., Ability to Work in a Noisy Environment; and Ability to Work at Heights). This is a good alternative predictor because it may have low adverse impact and because development and operational costs would be low. In spite of these advantages, one must be concerned with face validity and user acceptance of the questions asked.

Simulations also are useful predictors. The Situational Judgment Test measures Ability to develop alternative solutions to a problem and choose the best alternative. The adverse impact of this measure is likely to be moderate, the cost of development is moderate, and the cost of using the method is low since it typically is administered using pencil and paper. The work sample kind of simulation also measures Ability to develop alternative solutions to a problem and choose the best alternative, as well as Ability to understand verbal instructions and warnings. Similar to the Situational Judgment Test, the adverse impact is moderate and the development costs are moderate. However, the operating costs of work samples are high because tests typically are administered individually and scorers need to be trained. If one were to eliminate a predictor due to testing time or costs, the work sample predictor may be viewed as one that could be omitted from the battery, since the constructs it measures are assessed by other predictors at lower cost.

In sum, the final test plan describes the tests to be developed, their hypothesized relationships with worker characteristics derived from the job analysis, and the mode of administration to be used. It is a blueprint for development and validation of personnel selection procedures.

SUMMARY

A test plan helps measurement specialists identify tests and other assessment tools that, on balance, maximize validity, minimize adverse impact, and use resources efficiently. It summarizes information from a thorough job analysis and literature review, and forms a blueprint for test development and validation. It provides a rationale for tests and assessment methods that are chosen for a selection test battery and for those that are not chosen.

A test plan can be conceptualized as a matrix where the rows are worker characteristics derived from a job analysis and the columns list measurement methods. The cells of the matrix document the hypothesized relationships between measurement methods and worker characteristics.

While the matrix facilitates decision making about tests to be developed or validated, a host of other concerns must also be considered in creating the final test plan. Minimizing adverse impact and making efficient use of resources are two of those concerns. Many other practical constraints will also affect the organization's final test plan.

REFERENCES

American Educational Research Association, American Psychological Association, & National Council on Measurement in Education (1985). *Standards for Educational and Psychological Testing*. Washington, DC: American Psychological Association.

Barbera, K. M., Ryan, A. M., Desmarais, L. B., & Dyer, P. J. (1995, April). *Multimedia employment tests: Effects of attitudes and experiences on validity*. Paper presented at the annual Conference of the Society for Industrial and Organizational Psychology, Inc., Orlando, FL.

Barrick, M. R., & Mount, M. K. (1996). Effects of impression management and self-deception on the predictive validity of personality constructs. *Journal of Applied Psychology, 81* (3), 261–272.

Borman, W. C., & Motowidlo, S. J. (1993). Expanding the criterion domain to include elements of contextual performance. In N. Schmitt & W. C. Borman (Eds.), *Personnel selection in organizations*. San Francisco: Jossey-Bass.

Busciglio, H. H., & Palmer, D. R. (1992, August). *An empirical assessment of coaching and practice effects on three army tests of spatial aptitude.* Paper presented at the annual meeting of the American Psychological Association, Washington, DC.

Campbell, J. P., McCloy, R. A., Oppler, S. H., & Sager, C. E. (1993). A theory of performance. In N. Schmitt & W. C. Borman (Eds.), *Personnel selection in organizations.* San Francisco: Jossey-Bass.

Carey, N. B. (1992, August). *New predictors of mechanics' job performance: Marine Corps findings.* Paper presented at the annual meeting of the American Psychological Association, Washington, DC.

Conway, J. M., Jako, R. A., & Goodman, D. F. (1995). A meta-analysis of interrater and internal consistency reliability of selection interviews. *Journal of Applied Psychology, 80* (5), 565–579.

Dragow, F. (1995). *Computer versus paper-and-pencil assessment.* A workshop for the Personnel Testing Council of Metropolitan Washington.

Dunnette, M. D., Corpe, V. A., & Toquam, J. L. (1987). Cognitive paper-and-pencil measures: Field test. In N. G. Peterson (Ed.), *Development and field test of the trial battery for Project A* (ARI TR-739). Alexandria, VA: U.S. Army Research Institute for the Behavioral and Social Sciences.

Equal Employment Opportunity Commission, Civil Service Commission, Department of Labor, & Department of Justice (1978, August). Uniform Guidelines on Employee Selection Procedures. *Federal Register, 43* (166), 38290–38315.

Feingold, A. (1994). Gender differences in personality: A meta-analysis. *Psychological Bulletin, 116* (3), 429–456.

Gaugler, B. B., Rosenthal, D. B., Thornton, G. C., & Bentson, C. (1987). Journal of Applied Psychology Monograph: Meta-analysis of assessment center validity. *Journal of Applied Psychology, 72* (3), 493–511.

Ghiselli, E. E. (1966). *The validity of occupational aptitude tests.* New York: Wiley.

Gough, H. G. (1985). A work orientation scale for the California Psychological Inventory. *Journal of Applied Psychology, 69,* 233–240.

Guilford, J. P. (1959). *Personality.* New York: McGraw-Hill.

Guilford, J. P., & Lacey, J. I. (Eds.). (1947). *Printed classification tests* (AAF Aviation Psychology Program, Research Reports, Rep. No. 5). Washington, DC: U.S. Government Printing Office.

Guilford, J. P., & Zimmerman, W. S. (1956). Fourteen dimensions of temperament. *Psychological Monographs, 70* (10, Whole No. 417).

Hitchhiker's guide to cybernomics. (1996, September 28). *The Economist,* pp. 33–46.

Huffcutt, A. I., Roth, P. L., & McDaniel, M. A. (1996). A meta-analytic investigation of cognitive ability in employment interview evaluations: Moderating characteristics and implications for incremental validity. *Journal of Applied Psychology, 81* (5), 459–473.

Hunter, J. E., & Hunter, R. F. (1984). Validity and utility of alternative predictors of job performance. *Psychological Bulletin, 96* (1), 72–98.

Hyde, J. S., Fennema, E., & Lamon, S. J. (1990). Gender differences in mathematics performance: A meta-analysis. *Psychological Bulletin, 107* (2), 139–155.

Hyde, J. S., & Linn, M. C. (1988). Gender differences in verbal ability: A meta-analysis. *Psychological Bulletin, 104* (1), 53–69.

Jensen, A. R. (1980). *Bias in mental testing.* New York: Free Press.

Kamp, J. D., & Hough, L. M. (1986). Utility of temperament for predicting job performance. In L. M. Hough, J. D. Kamp, & B. N. Barge (Eds.), *Utility of temperament, biodata, and interest assessment for predicting job performance: A review and integration of the literature.* Minneapolis, MN: Personnel Decisions Research Institute.

King, W. C., & Miles, E. W. (1995). A quasi-experimental assessment of the effect of computerizing noncognitive paper-and-pencil measurements: A test of measurement equivalence. *Journal of Applied Psychology, 80,* 643–651.

Lohman, D. F. (1988). Spatial abilities as traits, processes, and knowledge. In R. J. Sternberg (Ed.), *Advances in the psychology of human intelligence* (Vol. 4, pp. 181–248). Hillsdale, NJ: Lawrence Erlbaum.

Maccoby, E. E., & Jacklin, C. N. (1974). *The psychology of sex differences.* Stanford, CA: Stanford University Press.

Mael, F. A., Connerly, M., & Morath, R. A., (1996). None of your business: Parameters of biodata invasiveness. *Personnel Psychology, 49* (3), 613–650.

Mayberry, P. W., & Hiatt, C. M. (1990). *Incremental validity of new tests in prediction of infantry performance* (CRM 90-110). Alexandria, VA: Center for Naval Analyses.

McDaniel, M. A., Whetzel, D. L., Schmidt, F. L., & Maurer, S. D. (1994). The validity of employment interviews: A comprehensive review and meta-analysis. *Journal of Applied Psychology, 79* (4), 599–616.

McHenry, J. J., Hough, L. M., Toquam, J. L., Hanson, M. A., & Ashworth, S. (1990). Project A validity results: The relationship between predictor and criterion domains. *Personnel Psychology, 43,* 335–354.

Mead, A. D., & Drasgow, F. (1993). Equivalence of computerized and paper-and-pencil cognitive ability tests: A meta-analysis. *Psychological Bulletin, 114* (3), 449–458.

Megargee, E. I. (1972). *The California Psychological Inventory handbook.* San Francisco: Jossey-Bass.

Motowidlo, S. J., Carter, G. W., Dunnette, M D., Tippins, N., Werner, S., Burnett, R. Jr., & Vaughan, M. J. (1992). Studies of the structured behavioral interview. *Journal of Applied Psychology, 77* (5), 571–587.

Motowidlo, S. J., Dunnette, M. D., & Carter, G. W. (1990). An alternative selection procedure: The low-fidelity simulation. *Journal of Applied Psychology, 75,* 640–647.

Mullins, T. W. (1982). Interviewer decisions as a function of applicant race, applicant quality, and interviewer prejudice. *Personnel Psychology, 35,* 161–174.

National Center for Education Statistics (1994). *Condition of education 1993.* Washington, DC: Author.

Oppler, S. H., Peterson, N. G., & Russell, T. L. (1993). Basic LVI validation results. In J. P. Campbell & L. Zook (Eds.), *Building and retaining the career force: FY 1991 annual report.* Alexandria, VA: U.S. Army Research Institute for the Behavioral and Social Sciences.

Parsons, C. K., & Linden, R. C. (1984). Interviewer perceptions of applicant qualification: A multivariate field study of demographic characteristics and nonverbal cues. *Journal of Applied Psychology, 69* (4), 557–568.

Peterson, N. G. (Ed.). (1987). *Development and field test of the trial battery for Project A* (ARI Technical Report 739). Alexandria, VA: U.S. Army Research Institute for the Behavioral and Social Sciences.

Peterson, N. G., & Bownas, D. A. (1982). Skill, task structure, and performance acquisition. In M. D. Dunnette, & E. A. Fleishman (Eds.), *Human performance and productivity* (Vol. 1). Hillsdale, NJ: Erlbaum.

Peterson, N. G., Owens-Kurtz, C., Hoffman, R. G., Arabian, J. M., & Whetzel, D.L. (1990). *Army synthetic validity project: Report of Phase II Results: Volume I* (TR No. 892). Alexandria, VA: U.S. Army Research Institute for the Behavioral and Social Sciences.

Peterson, N. G., Russell, T. L., Hallam, G., Hough, L. M., Owens-Kurtz, C., Gialluca, K., & Kerwin, K. (1990). Analysis of the experimental predictor battery: LV sample. In J. P. Campbell & L. Zook (Eds.), *Building and retaining the career force: FY 1990 annual report* (ARI-FR-PRD-90-6). Alexandria, VA: U.S. Army Research Institute for the Behavioral and Social Sciences.

Pulakos, E. D., & Schmitt, N. (1995). Experience-based and situational interview questions: Studies of validity. *Personnel Psychology, 48* (2), 289–308.

Pulakos, E. D., Schmitt, N., & Keenan, P. (1994). *Validity and implications of the FBI special agent entry level selection system* (Technical Report No. 94-20). Alexandria, VA: Human Resources Research Organization.

Reynolds, D. (1994). Personality, interest, and biographical attribute measures. In T. L. Russell, D. H. Reynolds, & J. P. Campbell (Eds.), *Building a joint-service classification research roadmap: Individual differences measurement* (AL/HR-TP-1994-0009). Brooks Air Force Base, TX: Armstrong Laboratory.

Russell, T. L., Crafts, J. L., Peterson, N. G., Rohrback, M. R., Nee, M. T., & Mael, F. (1995). *Development of a roadmap for Special Forces selection and classification research.* Alexandria, VA: U.S. Army Research Institute for the Behavioral and Social Sciences.

Russell, T. L., Humphreys, L., Rosse, R. L., & Peterson, N. G. (1992, October). *The factor structure of a spatial test battery.* Paper presented at the 34th annual conference of the Military Testing Association (MTA), San Diego, CA.

Russell, T. L., & Oppler, S. H. (1996). *Psychometric considerations in the estimation of subgroup differences and differential prediction.* A workshop presented for the Personnel Testing Council of Metropolitan Washington.

Russell, T. L., Reynolds, D.H., & Campbell, J. P. (Eds.) (1994). *Building a joint service classification research roadmap: Individual differences measurement* (AL/HRTP1994 0009). Brooks AFB, TX: Armstrong Laboratory.

Sackett, P. R., & Roth, L. (1996). Multi-stage selection strategies: A monte carlo investigation of effects on performance and minority hiring. *Personnel Psychology, 49* (3), 549–572.

Schmidt, F. L. (1985). Review of Wonderlic Personnel Test. In J. V. Mitchell (Ed.), *Ninth mental measurements yearbook* (Vol. 2; pp. 1755–1757). Lincoln: University of Nebraska Press.

Schmidt, F. L., Hunter, J. E., Croll, P. R., & McKenzie, R. C. (1983). Estimation of employment test validities by expert judgment. *Journal of Applied Psychology, 47,* 590–601.

Schmitt, N., Gooding, R. Z., Noe, R. A., & Kirsch, M. (1984). Meta-analyses of validity studies published between 1964 and 1982 and the investigation of study characteristics. *Personnel Psychology, 37,* 407–423.

Society of Industrial and Organizational Psychology, Inc. (1987). *Principles for the validation and use of personnel selection procedures* (3rd ed.). College Park, MD: Author.

Toquam, J., Peterson, N. G., Rosse, R. L., Ashworth, S., Hanson, M. A., & Hallam, G. (1986). *Concurrent validity data analyses: Cognitive paper-and-pencil and computer-administered predictors.* Presentation to the Project A Scientific Advisory Group, Minneapolis, MN.

U.S. Department of Defense (1982). *Profile of American Youth: 1980 nationwide administration of the Armed Services Vocational Aptitude Battery.* Washington, DC: Office of the Assistant Secretary of Defense.

Voyer, D., Voyer, S., & Bryden, M. P. (1995). Magnitude of sex differences in spatial abilities: A meta-analysis and consideration of critical variables. *Psychological Bulletin, 117* (2), 20–270.

Wing, H., Peterson, N. G., & Hoffman, R. G. (1984, August). *Expert judgments of predictor-criterion validity relationships.* Paper presented at the annual American Psychological Association Convention, Toronto, Ontario.

Wise, L. L., Peterson, N. G., Hoffman, R. G., Campbell, J. P., & Arabian, J. M. (1990). *Army synthetic validation project: Phase III results* (RS-WP-90). Alexandria, VA: U.S. Army Research Institute for the Behavioral and Social Sciences.

DEVELOPING MEASURES TO PREDICT JOB PERFORMANCE

Tests of Cognitive Ability

Ruth A. Childs
Wayne A. Baughman
Charles T. Keil, Jr.

OVERVIEW

Think of several assessments used in employment contexts. Probably the examples that come to mind are tests of cognitive ability. These might include a vocabulary test for a proofreading job; a basic math skills test for promotion to a job as a cashier; or a battery of tests, such as the *Armed Services Vocational Aptitude Battery* (ASVAB), which includes such diverse subtests as Auto and Shop Information and Word Knowledge, and is used by the U.S. military to select recruits and place them into occupational specialties. Cognitive ability tests are among the most economical and easily administered of the job selection and assessment tools, and can be especially useful when measuring abilities that have been identified through job analysis as necessary for successful job performance.

Common as they are in industry, tests of cognitive ability are even more common in education. From kindergarten through the end of graduate school, students take ability tests for placement in special education programs or accelerated classes, as well as district- or state-mandated tests of general academic aptitude and tests for admission into competitive institutions.

In both educational and employment contexts, tests of cognitive ability are often the bases for making comparisons among and decisions regarding individuals—for example, deciding which students should be admitted to an honors program or which applicants should be hired. This chapter describes the history of cognitive ability testing and the advantages and possible pitfalls of using such tests. In addition, it explains how to select or develop appropriate cognitive ability tests for use in employment settings, based on the results of job/task analyses.

We urge the reader to keep three principles in mind when using cognitive ability tests. First, when discussing ability tests, the precise use of language is essential. For example, the term *ability* is often used colloquially to refer to any individual characteristic that contributes to learning or performance (in other words, "aptitude"). As our later discussion of different theories of ability illustrates, there is no single definition of ability. Therefore, the researcher is responsible for defining such terms clearly.

Second, any cognitive ability test is linked to one or more theories of cognitive abilities. Later in this chapter, we survey several theories and discuss their implications for test development and use. Test constructors should carefully consider the theoretical implications of their test construction choices. Third, those constructing cognitive ability tests can expect to be held to extremely high technical standards. This is because cognitive ability tests often have high stakes for examinees or institutions such as schools or training programs. By high stakes we mean that test results can have significant consequences for decisions involving hiring, promotion, or admission to training programs. Because of these consequences, the test developer is responsible for providing theoretical and empirical support for the use of a cognitive ability test to the psychological, educational, business, and legal communities.

In this chapter, we first describe highlights from the history of cognitive ability testing and summarize several theories of cognitive ability. We then discuss measurement issues in cognitive ability testing and the psychometric characteristics of cognitive ability tests. Finally, we present a step-by-step approach for selecting or developing a cognitive ability test.

HISTORY AND THEORIES
OF COGNITIVE ABILITY

A Brief History of Cognitive
Ability Measurement

The first recorded example of formal employment testing was a series of examinations used as early as 2200 B.C. by the Chinese emperor to select officials for his government (DuBois, 1970; Wing, 1980). By A.D. 200, these examinations included written tests in five areas: civil law, military affairs, agriculture, revenue, and the geography of the Chinese empire. The Chinese examination system was advocated during the late eighteenth and nineteenth centuries by various European and American politicians as a model for civil service testing. The system survived for more than 4,000 years, until 1905, when it was abolished to make way for modern university training and testing.

The earliest recorded formal educational examinations were orally administered tests used to certify teachers in Europe during the thirteenth century A.D. (DuBois, 1970). Both the early employment exams in China and the early educational exams in Europe emphasized measuring acquired knowledge. It was not until the nineteenth century that scientists began investigating differences among individuals in more fundamental attributes. For example, Wilhelm Wundt (1862) in Germany and Francis Galton (1883) in Britain investigated individual differences in reaction time and auditory acuity. Although early efforts of Wundt's student American James McKeen Cattell to establish a relationship between these fundamental attributes and academic performance (e.g., Cattell & Farrand, 1896) were largely unsuccessful, the idea that it might be useful to measure individual attributes apart from a particular context or particular subject matter took hold.

In 1904, Alfred Binet (Binet & Simon, 1905), in France, developed a test of attributes that correlated with academic performance but were not specific to the material that particular students had been taught. The test contained more complex mental tasks and was intended to help school authorities identify students who might benefit from remedial classes. Binet's test is generally considered the first individual intelligence test. It might also be considered the first modern cognitive ability test.

The first large-scale cognitive ability testing program was the U.S. Army's program for testing recruits during World War I, headed by

Harvard psychologist Robert M. Yerkes (1921). The Army tests were intended to screen out recruits who were unfit for service and to place recruits in jobs according to their cognitive abilities. Two examinations were developed based on educational testing work by Arthur Otis. These two examinations were administered to approximately 1.75 million recruits (DuBois, 1970; Gregory, 1992). One, the *Army Alpha,* was intended for literate recruits. The second, the *Army Beta,* was intended for recruits with limited English proficiency or limited reading skills. Both examinations tested the abilities to follow oral directions, solve simple mathematical problems, and recognize patterns. Both the *Army Alpha* and the *Army Beta* had some of the characteristics associated with modern tests, such as group testing, standardized administration, and multiple-choice items. The *Army Alpha* consisted of the following eight subtests, some of which became prototypes for modern ability tests: Following Oral Directions, Arithmetic Reasoning, Practical Judgment, Synonym-Antonym Pairs, Disarranged Sentences, Number Series Completion, Analogies, and Information. The *Army Beta* consisted of seven subtests covering maze tracing, cube counting, series completion, digit symbols, number checking, picture completion, and geometrical construction. The Army testing program was widely considered a success and served as a model for later large-scale educational and employment testing programs.

Although tests such as the *Army Alpha* and *Army Beta* were very successful from a practical standpoint, the underlying concept of cognitive ability is even today still evolving. The concept of cognitive ability in general—and the identification of specific abilities that might comprise cognitive ability—has been refined in part through explorations of the statistical attributes of cognitive ability tests. British psychologist Charles Spearman (1904), in particular, used factor analytic techniques to demonstrate that individuals' scores on diverse cognitive ability tests, such as mathematical computation and verbal reasoning, were quite highly correlated. Spearman argued, therefore, that a single factor could account for much of the variance in test scores. Spearman called this factor *g,* or general intelligence, and concluded that one general cognitive ability could account for most individual differences on diverse cognitive ability tests. Later work, pioneered by American L. L. Thurstone, focused on identifying factors that corresponded more closely to particular types of tests. Thurstone's (1938) "primary mental abilities," which were also identified through factor analyses, included Verbal Relations, Word Fluency, Number Facility, Space, Memory, Perceptual Speed, and Induction. Spearman also postulated *s,* specific factors, to supplement *g* in accounting for the variance he found in cognitive ability tests. However, unlike Thurstone's primary mental abilities, Spearman's specific factors were only used to account for residual variance not accounted for by g.

More recently, Carroll (1993) re-factor analyzed more than 450 data sets containing test results from thousands of cognitive ability tests. Based on these analyses, Carroll constructed a comprehensive, hierarchical taxonomy of cognitive abilities that includes both relatively general and more specific constructs. This taxonomy and a variety of other theories about or perspectives on cognitive ability testing are described in the next section.

A DEFINITION OF COGNITIVE ABILITY

From the beginning, cognitive ability testing has been accompanied by a debate about the nature of cognitive abilities. The debate is about whether cognitive abilities are inherited ("ability as aptitude"; e.g., Burt, 1940; Goddard, 1912; Herrnstein & Murray, 1994; Jensen, 1969; Spearman, 1927) or trainable ("ability as achievement"; e.g., Eysenck & Kamin, 1981; Gould, 1981). Testing cognitive capacities has flourished despite the continuing disagreement among experts as to the source and stability of cognitive abilities. Cognitive ability tests clearly measure individual attributes that contribute to performance on a wide variety of tasks in different situations. We follow Carroll (1993) in using a definition of cognitive abilities that acknowledges both their heritable and their learned aspects. Specifically, we define *cognitive abilities* as "variations in individuals' potentials for *present* performance on a defined class of tasks" (Carroll, 1993, p. 16, emphasis added).

THEORIES OF COGNITIVE ABILITY

We have already mentioned some of the many schools of thought concerning cognitive abilities, their structure, and their relationship to other abilities. In general, we might think of the theories as lying on a continuum. At one end is Spearman's (1904) postulation of a single overall cognitive factor g, or general intelligence. At the other end is Guilford's (1985) Structure-of-Intellect theory, which ultimately included 156 distinct cognitive abilities. In between are many other theories concerning the nature and structure of cognitive abilities. Spearman's g and

Thurstone's (1938) primary mental abilities have already been described. In this section, we describe several other prominent theories, with the purpose of illustrating their diversity. Note that Carroll (1993) and Ceci (1990) provide excellent surveys of many cognitive ability theories.

Raymond B. Cattell (1943) suggested the existence of two general types of cognitive ability—fluid intelligence, roughly corresponding to aptitude, and crystallized intelligence, corresponding to achievement. Based on factor analytic research, his model was later expanded to include other aspects of cognitive ability. However, the original dichotomy between fluid and crystallized intelligences is still influential in current thinking about cognitive ability testing (e.g., Carroll, 1993).

Guilford (1985; Guilford & Hoepfner, 1971) developed an intricate model of cognitive ability called the Structure-of-Intellect model. The early model is often represented graphically by a cube—four types of content are crossed with five types of operations and six types of products, yielding a three-dimensional matrix with 120 cells. Later models had as many as 156 cells. Through a large number of factor analytic studies, Guilford was able to identify factors corresponding to many of these cells.

Sternberg's triarchic theory of intelligence (1988) divided cognitive ability into three parts: componential, which involves abstract reasoning and includes what is traditionally thought of as academic ability; experiential, which involves the ability to understand and relate to novel stimuli; and contextual, which involves coping with real-world experiences and might be called "street smarts." Sternberg maintained that experiential and contextual aspects of intelligence should be included along with the componential aspects in intelligence testing (e.g., Sternberg, Wagner, Williams, & Horvath, 1995). The *Sternberg Multidimensional Abilities Test,* for example, produces a profile of an individual's performance on these three aspects of intelligence.

Carroll's (1993) extensive factor analytic study of cognitive abilities, described briefly in the previous section, is the basis for the most comprehensive taxonomy of cognitive abilities to date. Carroll's taxonomy is hierarchical, with general intelligence, the single third-order factor, subdivided into eight second-order factors: fluid intelligence, crystallized intelligence, general memory and learning, broad visual perception, broad auditory perception, broad retrieval ability, broad cognitive speededness, and processing speed. Each of these second-order factors is subdivided into between three and sixteen first-order factors. Carroll's empirically based taxonomy combines elements of several of the theories of cognitive ability described earlier. In particular, the hierarchical organization of the taxonomy permits the inclusion of both a general factor, similar to Spearman's *g*, and factors specific to different types of tests, including Cattell's fluid and crystallized intelligences and several of Thurstone's primary mental abilities.

Other theories of cognitive ability are based on concepts from cognitive psychology. Snow and Lohman (1989) have described how recent advances in cognitive psychology's understanding of human problem solving might guide the development of cognitive ability tests. Work in this area was stimulated in part by an earlier article by Carroll (1976), which showed that an information-processing model of cognition could be used to characterize items on cognitive ability tests.

In addition to the many theories of cognitive abilities, there have been a number of important procedures developed for applying the various cognitive ability theories, particularly in personnel assessment. For example, Fleishman and Reilly (1992) have, building on the work of Ekstrom and colleagues at the Educational Testing Service (e.g., Ekstrom, French, Harman, & Dermen, 1976) and earlier work by Fleishman (e.g., Fleishman, 1956, 1964), described a comprehensive taxonomy of abilities that includes cognitive abilities, psychomotor abilities, physical abilities, and sensory/perceptual abilities. Fleishman and Reilly's taxonomy has been operationalized in a deductive job analysis questionnaire, the *Fleishman Job Analysis Survey* (F-JAS; Fleishman, 1992), which includes 52 abilities across the four areas. It also serves as the basis for the abilities component of the U.S. Department of Labor's Occupational Information Network (O*NET; Peterson, Mumford, Borman, Jeanneret, & Fleishman, in press), where it is being used to describe the abilities required for jobs previously described in the *Dictionary of Occupational Titles* (*DOT;* U.S. Department of Labor, 1991). Because the F-JAS describes jobs, not individuals, Fleishman and Reilly (1992) have identified commercially available tests that can be used to assess individuals on each ability.

MEASUREMENT OF COGNITIVE ABILITY

In the first part of this chapter, we sketched a brief history of cognitive ability testing and described several prominent theories of cognitive ability. In this section, we describe three test features to consider when developing cognitive ability tests: (1) types of test scores, (2) types of items, and (3) test administration methods.

TYPES OF TEST SCORES

One of the assumptions of cognitive ability testing is that we are measuring an attribute that is independent of the particular items included on a test—the items simply provide opportunities for the examinee to demonstrate that attribute. For example, we probably are not concerned about whether an examinee can compute the product of 34 and 57, but we are concerned about what the examinee's performance on that item suggests about his or her mathematical ability. Therefore, in scoring a cognitive ability test, we summarize the examinee's performance in relation to the underlying ability. Usually a test yields a numerical score for the individual. Traditionally, this score is the number of questions or tasks on the test that the individual correctly completes. An alternative to "number right" scoring is item response theory (IRT) scoring, which, instead of assigning equal weight to all test items, incorporates information about each item's difficulty and relatedness to the underlying ability being measured when computing scores. With IRT scoring, missing a difficult item will have less of an impact on an individual's score than missing an easy item, and correctly answering a difficult item will count more than correctly answering an easy item. IRT scoring is computationally complex but is becoming more widespread, especially in large-scale testing programs, due to the availability of powerful computers. Van der Linden and Hambleton's (1997) *Handbook of Modern Item Response Theory* presents an excellent overview of IRT methodology and applications.

When scoring a cognitive ability test, whether using traditional scoring or IRT scoring, it is important to consider how the test score will be used. For instance, is the primary purpose of the test to differentiate among individuals—and probably to rank them—or is the test intended to determine whether the individual possesses a certain level of ability, or both? If the test is only intended to rank individuals, then a ranking or a percentile score may be appropriate. Such a test would be classified as a norm-referenced test. For example, an intelligence test such as the *Wechsler Adult Intelligence Scale-Revised* (WAIS-R; Wechsler, 1981) provides intelligence quotient (IQ) scores in relation to a population distribution of scores. If the test is intended to determine competency, then a rating in relation to predefined levels of competency may be appropriate. Such a test would be considered a criterion-referenced test, since individuals' scores are compared to a predefined criterion. For example, a promotion test to determine whether candidates possess the abilities to perform tasks at the next level of the job might be a criterion-referenced test. Sometimes a single test can yield both norm-referenced and criterion-referenced scores.

When scoring a cognitive ability test, it also is important to consider the level of aggregation. For example, if a cognitive ability test consists of distinct subtests that measure different aspects of ability, it usually makes sense to compute a score for each subtest separately. A test such as the U.S. Department of Labor's *General Aptitude Test Battery* (GATB; Hartigan & Wigdor, 1989), for example, contains multiple subtests providing nine scores and would yield not a single score, but a score profile. Score profiles can be particularly useful in determining an individual examinee's relative strengths and weaknesses and are often used in occupational counseling. Score profiles should be interpreted with caution, however, with care taken not to overemphasize small differences between scores. For example, a high school student who scores very high on the General Science subtest of the *Armed Services Vocational Aptitude Battery* (ASVAB) may be counseled to pursue a career in a scientific field, although his or her score on the Paragraph Comprehension subtest may also be high and suggest possible success in a literary career. The tendency to focus on differences among subtest scores is particularly problematic when the test scores are not very reliable. (Test reliability is discussed later in this chapter.) In such cases, a second test administration could yield a different profile and prompt very different advice.

Sometimes subtest scores are combined to yield a summary index of cognitive ability—for example, scores on four of the ten subtests on the ASVAB are combined to form the *Armed Forces Qualification Test* (AFQT) score, a summary index that is the basis for deciding whether to accept a recruit into military training. Sometimes tests that do not include previously defined subtests can be analyzed so as to provide profiles of scores. The goal in scoring cognitive ability tests is to determine a level of aggregation that provides detailed information about the ability or abilities being measured, but also is sufficiently summarized to be useful—for pass-fail or hire-reject decisions, for example. Of course, the decision to produce a profile of scores on particular cognitive abilities versus a single composite score may also depend on the cognitive ability theory to which one subscribes.

Occasionally, the purpose of cognitive ability testing will be to screen for abilities with very low rates of occurrence. For example, perfect pitch, the ability to identify a heard pitch precisely, is a rare individual attribute. A test for perfect pitch would probably include a short screening test that could be administered quickly and inexpensively to a large number of people. Only if an individual passed the initial screening test would that individual be administered a more comprehensive test to determine whether he or she actually possessed perfect pitch. This strategy could, if carefully implemented, increase the test's efficiency by decreasing the number of individuals taking the second, more expensive test, without decreasing the test's ability to identify individuals with perfect pitch.

TYPES OF ITEMS

Cognitive ability tests usually consist of tasks that the examinee must complete. For example, examinees may be required to write an essay, draw a diagram, interpret a graph, or recall particular facts. These tasks may be presented in many different formats. Multiple-choice items have the advantage of being easily and objectively scorable—it is much easier to determine whether an individual selected the correct response from among options than whether he or she constructed a sufficiently correct response. True-false items also share this advantage. Consequently, multiple-choice items, especially, are common in large-scale group-administered tests. However, both multiple-choice and true-false items have been widely criticized (e.g., Darling-Hammond & Lieberman, 1992; National Commission on Testing and Public Policy, 1990; Wigdor & Garner, 1982) as being susceptible to guessing and as measuring only limited aspects of complex abilities. Some innovative modifications to the multiple-choice item, such as the multiple selection item, in which examinees select a response to each item from the same lengthy list of response options, preserve the advantages of easy and objective scoring, while being less susceptible to guessing (Anderson & Hyers, 1991; Fry, 1990). Multiple selection items might be suitable for a test on human anatomy, for example, that includes items about parts of the body and has as response options a list of those parts, but cannot be used in tests with more heterogeneous response options, such as a test of verbal ability that includes vocabulary, grammar, and reading comprehension items.

Criticisms of multiple-choice items have prompted a recent movement to return to more "authentic" presentation of tasks (e.g., Camara & Brown, 1995; Miller & Legg, 1993). In educational testing, in particular, a suspicion of multiple-choice tests as promoting the "wrong" kinds of learning has caused a resurgence of constructed response tests (containing, for example, essay or short-answer items) and performance tests. Unfortunately, educational test users often have been unprepared for the increase in scoring cost, decrease in relative reliability, and change in relevant validity that accompany this move to "authentic assessment" (Baker, O'Neil, & Linn, 1993). In employment testing, multiple-choice and performance tests have had fairly stable roles, even in recent years. Many, if not most, tests of cognitive ability that are widely administered in employment settings are multiple-choice tests. However, the cognitive ability testing principles presented in this chapter generally apply across tests with different item types.

TEST ADMINISTRATION METHODS

Our discussion of cognitive ability testing up to this point has assumed that the cognitive abilities are being tested independently of speed of performance. In actual practice this rarely is the case. While few tests explicitly reward speed—the exception being tests of perceptual speed, such as the ASVAB's Coding Speed subtest—almost all tests (especially group-administered tests) have an enforced time limit for completing the test. Therefore, while in theory the distinction can be made between speeded and power tests—with power tests measuring performance independent of speed—most power tests in actuality have some element of speededness. Carroll (1993) explored the impact of test speededness on the measurement of cognitive abilities and concluded that speed and level of performance were logically distinguishable aspects of performance and should be carefully distinguished when determining what a test is measuring. Carroll recommends, for example, that researchers make use of the response time records for individual test items that are available from computerized tests, in addition to response accuracy, when judging an examinee's ability using such tests. Other researchers have also examined the impact of speededness on ability tests (e.g., Donlon, 1980; Peterson, 1993; Rindler, 1979).

A common rule-of-thumb method for assessing the speededness of a test is to draw a graph of the distribution of items that examinees finish. If a test is not speeded, we would expect that about 80% of the examinees would attempt all the items on the test and all of the examinees would attempt at least 80% of the items (Peterson, 1993, adapted from Donlon, 1973). Figure 6.1 shows the percent of examinees attempting and reaching the items in a Verbal Comprehension test. The 80-80 rule is shown as a dark diagonal line on the figure, and two lines are plotted. One line represents the number of items examinees attempted; the other line represents the number of items examinees reached on the test. The

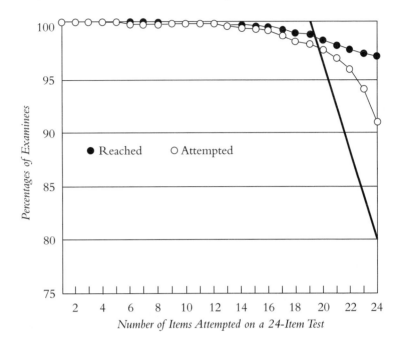

FIGURE 6.1   Percentages of Examinees Reaching and Attempting Items
on a Test of Verbal Comprehension

number of items reached is higher than the number of items attempted, because examinees were allowed to skip items that they could not answer. This graph shows that 91% of examinees attempted all of the items and that 98% of the examinees attempted at least 80% of the items. Thus, this test comes very close to satisfying the 80-80 rule, and by this criterion would probably not be considered a speeded test.

Another important aspect of test administration is the standardization of administration conditions across examinees. Typically, test developers take great pains to develop detailed instructions for administering a test, including time limits, lighting and noise levels, and verbal instructions to be given to all examinees. Standardization is particularly important if the test results are to be the basis for comparisons across individuals. The guiding principle in test administration should be that all examinees receive an equal opportunity to demonstrate their abilities. Additionally, the rights of examinees with physical or mental disabilities to equitable opportunities to demonstrate their abilities on cognitive ability tests are protected by the Americans with Disabilities Act (ADA, 1990). Ensuring that an examinee with a disability is not prevented by the disability from demonstrating his or her cognitive abilities may require testing accommodations, such as Braille editions of tests, longer time limits, or word processing devices.

PSYCHOMETRIC CHARACTERISTICS OF MEASURES OF COGNITIVE ABILITY

Because the results of cognitive ability tests often have important implications for individuals, the reliability, validity, and adverse impact of cognitive ability measures have been extensively studied. Reliability is concerned with the precision and consistency of test scores. Validity is concerned with evidence that the test measures what it purports to measure. Adverse impact concerns the extent to which there are subgroup differences in test scores and the effects these differences have on outcomes associated with testing. The following discussion addresses reliability, validity, and adverse impact as they specifically relate to cognitive ability testing.

RELIABILITY

Reliability refers to the stability of test scores over time, to test score consistency over different forms of the same test, to the similarity of different raters' ratings of the same test responses, and to the degree to which items within a test or subtest are correlated. A test does not have a single reliability—reliability coefficients can be computed that reflect each of these types of consistency. Therefore, when talking about reliability it is important to specify which aspect of reliability is meant and how it was computed. For in-depth discussions of this topic, see Feldt and Brennan (1989) or Shavelson and Webb (1991).

In this section, we describe general trends in reliability. When using or developing a cognitive ability test, it is important to consider whether characteristics of the test will tend to increase or decrease reliability. This is important because if there is evidence that the test scores are relatively unreliable, it may be difficult to justify actions taken on the basis of the test scores—for example, excluding a candidate for an electrician apprenticeship program who scores just below the cutoff on a cognitive ability test used for selection purposes.

One characteristic of a test that affects reliability is the type of items included in the test. Multiple-choice items have two main advantages here: (1) They can be objectively scored, so consistency across judges is not a concern; and (2) response time for a multiple-choice item is usually fairly short, so many such items can be administered in a single test. The fact that a test can contain many multiple-choice items means that examinees will have many more opportunities to demonstrate their ability, usually on items that target different aspects of an ability. A test that consists of essay items, in contrast, would not contain as many items for the same testing time. Consequently, the smaller number of items on the test might be less representative of the ability domain being examined—especially if examinees were allowed to choose among essay topics. Across different forms of an essay test, each containing different essay questions, scores might be less reliable. However, as noted earlier, constructed response and performance tests also have some advantages over multiple-choice tests in that they may be able to test different, more complex aspects of an ability. Many tests, including many individually administered intelligence tests, such as the WAIS-R, use a combination of item types. In this way, they try to test different aspects of ability while maintaining adequate score reliability.

When a test includes items that are subjectively scored by raters—for example, essays or performance tests—it is important to determine whether the raters are assigning the same scores for the same quality of response. Providing uniform training to the raters using a set of sample responses can help ensure that all raters are interpreting the rating scale in the same way. However, it should be understood that even the best training is unlikely to yield complete uniformity among raters. A study of interrater reliability will usually involve having multiple raters score each response, then determining how much the ratings vary. One way to improve the reliability of scores is to increase the number of raters of each response and then assign the final score as an average of the ratings. However, increasing the number of raters (for example, having three judges score a single essay) can dramatically increase the cost of scoring.

Test administration procedures can also affect the reliability of scores across time and across different test forms. Standardization of testing conditions, including enforcement of time limits, noise control, and presentation of instructions, is essential for consistency of test results across administrations. Even physical features of the test, such as formatting of items or the way examinees are required to mark their answers on an answer sheet, can introduce unwanted variation in test scores (Cizek, 1994; Bloxom et al., 1993). These features should be made as consistent as possible across test forms and test administrations.

VALIDITY

Validity has traditionally referred to whether a test measures a particular ability and, if it does, whether results from the test are appropriate for particular uses. Like evidence for reliability, evidence for validity can be of many different types. For example, validity evidence has often been divided into three categories (e.g., *Uniform Guidelines on Employee Selection Procedures;* EEOC, CSC, DOL, & DOJ, 1978). The first of these is content validity. A test is *content valid* when the test items are representative of the content of the job. Evidence for establishing content validity often is accumulated by having subject matter experts indicate the extent to which job incumbents need to know the answers to test items in order to perform the tasks required by their jobs. For instance, in Table 3.9, verbal comprehension ability is shown to be linked to the task Test and calibrate instruments because that task requires being able to read and follow instructions. The second type of validity evidence is construct validity. A test is *construct valid* when it correlates meaningfully with a variety of different tests. In applied settings, a test is construct valid when it can be shown to measure an ability that has, in turn, been shown to be important for success on the job. Evidence for establishing construct validity often is accumulated by assessing the relationship between the ability test in question and a well-established measure of the same ability. The last type of validity evidence is criterion-related validity. A test has *criterion-related validity* when scores on the test are related to measures of performance on the job. Evidence for assessing the criterion-related validity of cognitive ability tests often is collected by administering the test to applicants or job incumbents and correlating their performance on the test with their performance on the job. Methods for conducting criterion-related validity studies are described in detail in Chapter 13.

Alternatively, and controversially, Messick (1989, 1995) has proposed six categories of validity: content—whether the test items are relevant and representative; substantive—whether response patterns correspond to those predicted by theories about the targeted ability; structural—whether test scoring is designed to be consistent with theories about the ability; generalizability—whether score interpretations are appropriate across populations and for different test forms; external—whether test scores are related in expected ways to scores on tests of similar and different abilities; and consequential—whether test scores are interpreted and used in ways that may be harmful to individuals or groups. Messick's inclusion of possible social consequences of testing as an aspect of validity has been widely disputed (e.g., Tenopyr, 1996).

Traditionally, establishing validity for a test's use with a particular job has required collecting evidence about the relationship between scores on that specific test and performance on that specific job, even perhaps at a specific job site or location. Schmidt and Hunter (1977, 1981), however, have argued that validity evidence can apply to multiple jobs. Their work on validity generalization theory has demonstrated that much of the between-study variance in validity coefficients of cognitive ability tests for predicting job performance may be due to statistical artifacts, such as sampling error. Hunter (1980) showed that the average validity of cognitive ability tests—in particular, the GATB—was .53 (with a standard deviation of .15) when cumulated over 425 studies including 32,124 examinees. Validity generalization, however, has been controversial (e.g., Cronbach, 1984; Hartigan & Wigdor, 1989; Schmidt, Pearlman, Hunter, & Hirsh, 1985; Zedeck & Cascio, 1984). Validity generalization has been criticized as encouraging an overreliance on inadequate validity evidence. Nevertheless, it has been widely promoted, particularly in supporting the use of the GATB in jobs where traditional validity studies were not or could not be carried out. In studies such as Hunter's 1980 meta-analysis, validity generalization has provided substantial support for the validity of cognitive ability tests for predicting job and training performance across a wide variety of jobs.

Among other evidence that corroborates the validity of cognitive ability tests as predictors of job performance is a very large-scale effort sponsored by the U.S. military and described by McHenry, Hough, Toquam, Hanson, and Ashworth (1990) and Peterson et al. (1990). The purpose of this project, the Army's Project A, was to validate the ASVAB and a variety of supplemental predictors. As part of Project A, thousands of enlisted soldiers in selected combat and noncombat jobs (including infantryman, military police, medical specialist, administrative clerk, and motor transport operator) were administered a large battery of tests (including the ASVAB, tests of spatial ability, and tests of perceptual/psychomotor ability). Criterion data were collected from job knowledge tests, work sample tests, job-specific and overall ratings of performance, and personnel file information related to performance (including promotion rate and number of medals earned). The cognitive ability composite score, computed based on ASVAB subtests, was found to correlate most highly (> 0.60) with composite scores based on the measures of performance both on specific jobs and on general soldiering tasks (McHenry et al., 1990).

In sum, cognitive ability has been shown to have a high degree of validity for predicting performance in a wide variety of jobs and a wide variety of settings. However, because there are differences between various groups in mean scores on tests of cognitive ability (Gottfredson & Crouse, 1986; Herrnstein & Murray, 1994; Jensen, 1986), the possibility of adverse impact is an important concern. This is the next issue to be discussed.

ADVERSE IMPACT

Adverse impact occurs when test results have a differential and negative effect on particular groups of examinees—usually women or racial or ethnic minorities. For example, a test of spatial ability used to screen applicants for an electrician apprenticeship program might have adverse impact if a disproportionate number of women failed the test. Similarly, a test of verbal ability might have adverse impact if a higher proportion of members of a protected ethnic minority group failed to pass the test than members of the majority group.

To determine if a test has adverse impact, the *Uniform Guidelines* (EEOC, CSC, DOL, & DOJ, 1978) advocate applying the "four-fifths rule"—if the percentage of examinees in a particular group who are selected using a test is less than four-fifths of the percentage of examinees in the group with the highest selection rate who are selected using the same test, then the test is considered to have an adverse impact. For example, let's assume that only 15% of women pass a mechanical ability test, while 25% of men pass the same test. In this case, the question is whether 15% is less than four-fifths of 25%. Since it is, the test would be considered to have adverse impact. It is important to note that the computation uses percentages, not absolute numbers—in fact, the absolute numbers of men and women who apply for the mechanic job are irrelevant. Under the *Uniform Guidelines,* a finding of adverse impact does not preclude the use of the test, but does make it necessary for the test user to demonstrate that the test measures an ability that is necessary for the job (i.e., that it possesses content, construct, and/or criterion-related validity) and measures it sufficiently accurately (i.e., that it has an adequate level of reliability) that the differences in results between groups reflect real differences. The examination of adverse impact illustrates the importance of collecting and considering a wide variety of validity evidence when deciding whether or not to use a test.

Concerning the adverse impact of cognitive ability tests, research has shown that some racial or ethnic minorities tend to obtain lower scores on valid and unbiased selection procedures, particularly on tests of cognitive ability (Gottfredson & Sharf, 1988). These differences in scores can have significant impact on the employment and educational opportunities available to members of these groups. Consequently, a variety of scoring and/or hiring practices have attempted to reduce the effects of the differences in test scores (Brown, 1994; Geisinger, 1992; Gottfredson, 1994; Hartigan and Wigdor, 1989; Sackett & Wilk, 1994). Two examples of such practices are hiring quotas and within-group norming. Within-group norming, in particular, involves reporting examinees' test scores in relation to norms for a subgroup of examinees, not norms for the entire group (i.e., a minority applicant's score percentile or rank may be computed by comparing his or her score only with the scores of other minority applicants, while a majority applicant's score would be compared to the scores of majority applicants).

Research has documented the trade-offs between use of minority hiring quotas and similar practices, and productivity and individual fairness (Gottfredson & Sharf, 1988; Hunter, Schmidt, & Rauschenberger, 1977). This research has shown that to the extent such race-conscious practices are enforced, the overall utility of cognitive ability tests to employers is reduced. After the recent controversy surrounding within-group scoring of the GATB (Hartigan & Wigdor, 1989), the Civil Rights Act of 1991 was enacted, which prohibits race-conscious practices, including within-group scoring (Civil Rights Act of 1991).

This issue, however, is far from resolved. Cascio, Outtz, Zedeck, and Goldstein (1991), for example, recommend score-banding procedures, in which all the scores within a statistically-determined range are considered equivalent for selection purposes. Using this technique, if a cognitive ability test is scored from 0 to 100 and the standard error of measurement (SEM) for the test is 3.0, then the standard error of the difference (SED) between scores is SEM $\times \sqrt{2} = 3.0 \times \sqrt{2} = 4.24$, and the width of the band would be calculated as SED $\times 1.96 = 8.32$ (for a 95% confidence band; i.e., 95% confidence that scores differing by that amount reflect true score differences). Therefore, scores of 92 to 100 on the test might then be considered equivalent in making employment selections. Often, banding is used with some form of minority preference, so that, for example, within the band of 92 to 100, all minority applicants would be selected first. Alternatively, applicants could be selected at random from within the band, with all employees within the band being selected before employees in the next band (in this example, scores of 83 to 91). Banding has proven to be very controversial, although some studies do seem to support its ability to reduce adverse impact without greatly reducing utility (e.g., Cascio et al., 1991). Schmidt (1991), in particular, has argued that the rationale used to justify this procedure is logically contradictory.

Another approach to decreasing adverse impact has also been proposed: using more or different tests to predict job performance. This approach is based on the assumption that predictors can be discovered and used that demonstrate smaller subgroup differences than traditionally used tests, but are still predictive of job performance. In an effort to test this hypothesis, Peterson, Oppler, Sager, and Rosse (1995) investigated the impact on subgroup differences of adding measures of specific cognitive abilities (e.g., mental spatial manipulation, counting, memory) to the ASVAB's measures of general cognitive ability. The results of that study indicated that some combinations of tests (i.e., test batteries) minimized score differences between African Americans and Whites or between Hispanics and Whites, while other combinations minimized score differences between males and females. These results illustrate the difficulty of trying to minimize adverse impact on all groups with a single test battery. Additionally, it was found that the tests that made the greatest contributions to minimizing subgroup differences did not necessarily make the greatest contributions to indices of validity.

HOW TO SELECT OR DEVELOP MEASURES OF COGNITIVE ABILITY

In the previous sections, we discussed many of the issues that should be considered when using a cognitive ability test in an employment setting. However, we have not yet addressed the obvious question: Where does the test come from? There are two ways to secure a cognitive ability test: (1) locate an already developed cognitive ability test that is appropriate for the intended use and obtain permission from its author to use it; or (2) develop a new test. Therefore, in this section, we describe both how to select a cognitive ability test and how to develop one. First, however, we discuss some general principles that apply both to selecting cognitive ability tests and to developing them.

There are two important factors that influence the selection or development of cognitive ability tests. First, an assumption underlying our understanding of the contribution of cognitive abilities to human performance is that a small set of precisely defined attributes can account for performance on many different kinds of tasks. Well-designed cognitive ability tests should provide a good deal of economy and efficiency in assessing people. Thus, often only a few tests are needed to predict which individuals will perform well on a particular job.

Second, cognitive abilities and their corresponding measures have the longest history of development of common individual difference attributes. This means that there are many well-designed tests from which to select. This also means there are many good examples of tests that may serve as models for designing new ones.

The decision to use a cognitive ability test in an employment setting is usually based on knowledge of the content of the job. The job analysis methods described in Chapters 2, 3, and 4 should be used to determine which abilities are required for competent job performance. In particular, the knowledges, skills, abilities, and other characteristics (KSAOs) identified using the job analysis procedures described in Chapter 3 can provide the crucial links between job tasks and duties on the one hand and the requisite abilities on the other. Furthermore, job analysis data may provide information to guide the development of specific test content and the structure of the items and tests, including such elements as test item difficulty, reading level, response format, and whether the test should be speeded.

In the following sections, we describe how to select or develop a cognitive ability test. We use as an example a test of Verbal Comprehension intended to be used in selecting candidates for an electrician apprenticeship program. Verbal Comprehension, defined as the ability to read and understand written text, was identified through an extensive job analysis as necessary for success in the apprenticeship training program.

Of course, we cannot provide the level of detail in one section of one chapter that a text dedicated to this topic would provide. We encourage the reader to refer to other sources for detailed information about the methods for constructing ability tests and measuring individual differences. Excellent discussions of these topics are included in texts by Nunnally (1978); Ghiselli, Campbell, and Zedeck (1981); Millman and Greene (1989); and Roid and Haladyna (1982).

SELECTING A COGNITIVE ABILITY TEST

Assuming that a job analysis has been conducted and it has been determined that particular cognitive abilities are required for competent job performance (e.g., as shown in Table 3.9), the next step will be to either find or create an appropriate test or tests measuring those abilities. In this section, we describe how to select a test. In the next section, we describe how to develop a test.

Finding Information About Tests

The first step in selecting a cognitive ability test is to locate candidate tests. A number of resources may be helpful for this purpose. Probably the primary resource for test information is the collection of publications from the Buros Institute of Mental Measurements. These include the *Mental Measurements Yearbooks* (*MMYs*; e.g., Conoley & Impara, 1995) and *Tests in Print* (*TIP*; Murphy, Conoley, & Impara, 1994). The *MMYs*, a series of now 12 volumes published at about five-year intervals since 1938, list thousands of commercially published tests, with descriptive information, references, and critical reviews. Each *MMY* includes only tests that are new, revised, or have been widely used since a previous edition. *TIP*, now in its fourth edition, lists all commercially available tests that are currently in print but does not include critical reviews. Both publications contain descriptions of tests in a variety of subject categories, including Achievement Batteries, Intelligence and Scholastic Aptitude, Reading, Mathematics, Science, Personality, Social Studies, and Multi-Aptitude Batteries.

A second source of information about tests is the *Test Critiques* volumes (e.g., Keyser & Sweetland, 1994), published by Pro-Ed beginning in 1984. The *Test Critiques* volumes, now numbering 10 in all, contain critical reviews of commercially available tests used in psychology, education, and business. *Tests* (Sweetland & Keyser, 1991), also published by Pro-Ed, is a listing of several thousand commercially available tests; it does not include reviews of the tests. *The ETS Test Collection Catalog,* periodically produced by the Educational Testing Service (ETS), includes only very brief citations for tests that are included in ETS's yearly *Tests in Microfiche* release. The tests included in the ETS products are research instruments, not commercially available tests. In addition to these general references, Fleishman and Reilly (1992) provide descriptions of commercially available tests for abilities included in the *Fleishman Job Analysis Survey.*

Recently, the World Wide Web has become another important source of information about tests. The American Psychological Association (1995), for example, posts a document entitled "Frequently Asked Questions (FAQ) on Psychological Tests," which contains suggestions for finding information about tests. The Educational Resources Information Clearinghouse on Assessment and Evaluation (ERIC/AE, 1996) maintains a test locator search facility that searches for tests in the Buros Institute of Mental Measurements and ETS Test Collection databases; however, the test locator does not provide the full test reviews. In addition, many test publishers now have Web sites describing their products, and numerous university libraries have posted listings of their reference books that describe tests and advice on how to use them.

Evaluating the Information

When reviewing tests to be used in employment settings, it is essential to consider a variety of issues, including reliability, validity, standard errors of measurement, administration issues, cost, and the usefulness of the technical and administration manuals. Fortunately, most of these issues are addressed in the critical reviews contained in the *MMY*s or in *Test Critiques*. Of course, only a guess can be made as to an instrument's appropriateness based solely on a review; a final decision about a test's usefulness must wait until the test has been obtained, the manuals studied, and the test tried out with the targeted population.

To continue with our example concerning the selection of applicants to an electrician apprenticeship program, the first step in developing a cognitive test battery would be to consult the test plan, the development of which is described in Chapter 5. After determining that Verbal Comprehension (at a sixth- or eighth-grade level) ability was linked to important tasks involved in the electrician job and therefore was included in the test plan, one might consult the *MMY*s, *TIP, Test Critiques,* or *Tests* to find out what Reading Comprehension tests already exist. Reviewing the subject index in the *Ninth Mental Measurements Yearbook* (Mitchell, 1985), for example, one will discover listings for several Reading tests. By reviewing their titles, one can immediately rule out some tests (e.g., the *Dyslexia Determination Test* or the *Test of Early Reading Ability*).

From among the Reading tests listed in the *Ninth Mental Measurements Yearbook* (Mitchell, 1985), two tests appear worthy of further examination. One is the Industrial Reading Test. It tests reading levels of "grade 9 and over for vocational students and applicants or trainees in technical or vocational training programs" (Sabers, 1985, p. 684). According to the *MMY*, it tests the ability to comprehend written technical materials. Pricing information is provided, as is the name of the publisher. The review of the test (Sabers, 1985) states that although there are adequate reliability data—and many tables of information on criterion-related validity—there are some problems. Essentially, the reviewer found that the items do not require the examinee to read the passages before answering them. The reviewer administered the 38 items, without the passages, to 10 individuals and found that their scores ranged from 18 to 29. In summary, the reviewer recommended that those in need of a Reading Comprehension test should look elsewhere.

Another possible option is the *Nelson-Denny Reading Test*. According to the *Ninth Mental Measurements Yearbook* (Mitchell, 1985), it purports to test grades 9–12 and adults and yields four scores: vocabulary, comprehension, total, and rate. The two parts to the test are vocabulary and comprehension; a total score is calculated from these subtest scores and the rate score is the number of words in the first passage read in the first minute. In a review of the *Nelson-Denny Reading Test,* Tierney (1985) noted that a great deal of useful information is provided regarding: the selection of items based on item difficulty levels, item discrimination, and item–test correlations; the subsamples used for establishing norms; and passage dependency of the reading comprehension questions. On the negative side, however, this reviewer questioned whether the test has the precision or generalizability necessary to sustain the types of interpretations suggested by the authors. In a second review of the *Nelson-Denny Reading Test,* Ysseldyke (1985) indicated that the test produces consistent reliability results (test-retest reliabilities ranged from .89 to .95 for the Vocabulary test and .75 to .82 for the Comprehension test), but that evidence of validity for its intended uses is limited. After examining these reviews, one would be faced with the choices of further exploring the possibility of using this test, looking for other possible tests, or developing a test.

Obtaining the Test

After reviewing critiques of a number of tests and identifying one or more for possible use as a measure of Verbal Comprehension for the electrician apprenticeship program, the next step would be to obtain copies of the test and test manuals and permission to use the test. Different test publishers have different requirements for the purchase and use of tests (Eyde et al., 1993). For example, some publishers require the purchaser to possess an advanced degree in psychology or a related field, have received training in testing methodology and use, and hold a professional license in order to purchase certain tests. The major sources of information about tests, such as the *MMY* and *TIP,* include publisher contact and cost information. Some publishers will allow potential users to purchase only the test manual in order to further evaluate the appropriateness of the test for the intended use.

Trying Out the Test

Finally, once a potentially useful test has been identified and obtained, it must be tried out with the intended population and its reliability and validity with that population assessed. The steps to be followed in evaluating the appropriateness of the test for the intended use are described in Chapter 13. Some of the relevant concerns overlap with those described in this chapter for developing a test, particularly those discussed in the section on conducting tryouts of items.

DEVELOPING A COGNITIVE ABILITY TEST

While there are many widely available off-the-shelf tests of cognitive abilities, there are several reasons for developing new ones. For example, developing a new test would be necessary when (1) alternate forms of existing tests are required, (2) tests become outdated, (3) a client wants a proprietary test, or (4) a test is needed for a newly hypothesized or highly specialized ability.

The steps for developing a cognitive ability test include:

1. Developing test specifications
2. Creating items
3. Conducting technical reviews
4. Conducting sensitivity reviews
5. Creating test administration instructions
6. Conducting tryouts of items
7. Analyzing item data
8. Assembling the test
9. Writing documentation

A description of each of these steps follows.

Developing Test Specifications

Before developing test items, a set of test specifications should be prepared. The test specifications for the electrician apprenticeship program Verbal Comprehension test, for example, might include the reading level at which the verbal items would be written and the relative numbers of items of each format (e.g., multiple choice, true-false, or short answer) and in each content area (e.g., social sciences, physical sciences, technical information). In the following sections we describe several variables to be considered when developing test specifications.

CONSTRUCT DEFINITION: Before we can develop items for any test, we must have a clear definition of the ability we intend to measure. The definition should include a label, a brief narrative description (the definition), and other information to distinguish it from related abilities. Figure 6.2 presents Fleishman's (1992) definition of Written Comprehension, which is analogous to the Verbal Comprehension ability measured by the test in our example.

ITEM DIFFICULTY: Another consideration is the level of difficulty of the items on the test. The level of item difficulty should be identified

Written Comprehension	This is the ability to read and understand written sentences and paragraphs.

How Written Comprehension Is Different from Other Abilities

Written Comprehension: Involves **reading** and **understanding written** words and sentences.	vs.	*Oral Comprehension:* Involves **listening to** and **understanding** words and sentences spoken by others.
		Oral Expression and Written Expression: Involve **speaking** or **writing** words and sentences so others will understand.

Note. From *Fleishman Job Analysis Survey* (Fleishman, 1992). Adapted with permission.

FIGURE 6.2 Written Comprehension Definition

during the job analysis, prior to item development. The level of difficulty of items on a cognitive ability test will depend on two things: (1) the population for which the test is being developed, and (2) the capacity of the items to discriminate among examinees. For example, if our Verbal Comprehension test is to be administered to examinees with high school diplomas but not post–high school training, a tenth-grade reading level may be appropriate. For a test of an ability other than Verbal Comprehension intended for the general population—arithmetic reasoning, for example—a lower reading level might be appropriate (a commonly accepted target level is sixth grade); otherwise, differences in the targeted ability might be obscured by differences in reading ability.

ITEM HOMOGENEITY: In general, the more narrowly defined the ability, the more homogeneous the items comprising the measure should be. Since cognitive ability tests represent narrowly defined attributes, the items comprising the test are homogeneous, or similar, in two important ways. First, the items contain elements that make them appropriate indicators of the ability they are intended to measure. For example, the passages on a test of Verbal Comprehension usually contain material that requires people to simply read and identify information. Complex passages that require information synthesis and abstraction would not be appropriate for a test of Verbal Comprehension ability, but would be appropriate for a test of Reasoning ability. The types of items that are most appropriate are dictated by the definition of the ability that was derived from the job analysis information that singles out particular knowledges, skills, abilities, and other characteristics (KSAOs), as described in Chapter 3.

Second, the items should not contain elements that confound measurement. That is, performance on the test should reflect the intended ability, and not other KSAOs. For example, questions relating to a passage of text should not require knowledge of a particular content area (e.g., Verbal Comprehension test questions referring to a passage about thermodynamics should not require knowledge of thermodynamics apart from the information provided in the passage). Additionally, one should guard against extreme stylistic or structural elements, in which obtaining a correct answer is not a function of comprehension at all, but of being well-read or having the ability to avoid being distracted by unusual vocabulary. Thus, items should be written so that all examinees will have an equal opportunity to display the ability being measured, not alternative KSAOs.

NUMBER OF ITEMS: Finally, in developing specifications for a test, we must decide how many items of each type should be included on the test. For example, we might decide that our test of Verbal Comprehension should include vocabulary and grammar items, in addition to reading passages with comprehension questions. Before beginning to write the items for the test, we would need to decide how many items of each type to include on the test. In addition, we might decide that particular types of reading passages were needed and that particular types of items should accompany the passages. For example, we might decide that the test used to select apprentice electricians should include one passage addressing social sciences subject matter and two passages about electronics or construction, with two items for each passage assessing general understanding of the passage's main argument and two items tapping understanding of more subtle points. Specifying in detail the numbers and types of items that will comprise a test not only makes test construction easier, but also helps to ensure that multiple forms of a test are comparable, since all the forms will be developed based on the same detailed specifications.

In the next section, we describe specific methods for developing test passages and multiple-choice items.

Creating Multiple-Choice Items
Item development techniques vary depending on the ability being measured and the item format that is selected. In this section we describe

methods for developing a multiple-choice measure of Verbal Comprehension, consisting of several prose passages each followed by a set of multiple-choice items. We discuss passages, item formats, and rationales, and illustrate the principles with an example. Many of the methods described in this section apply to other item types and abilities as well.

PASSAGES: Six guidelines are useful when developing passages:

- *Passage source*—When using material from external sources, permission should be obtained from the author and appropriate citations should be provided.

- *Topic*—Topics may be selected that have some face validity but do not require knowledge of a particular topic. For example, for electrician apprentices, the test might include a passage about Ohm's law; however, it would be important that all technical terms in the passage be clearly defined, because the purpose of the Verbal Comprehension test is to measure verbal ability, not knowledge about electricity.

- *Readability*—An appropriate reading level should be used, and the vocabulary, style, and organization of the passages should be suitable for the examinee population.

- *Length*—Passages can be as short as a single paragraph or as long as 500 to 600 words. The length of the passage should depend on the construct being measured and the time available for test administration.

- *Familiarity*—Passages should not deal with commonly known information. Thus, topics that have received recent media attention, for example, should be avoided.

- *Timeliness of information*—Passages should be relevant for at least a decade.

ITEM FORMAT: The passages and items included in our test of Verbal Comprehension should test the level that each applicant possesses of the required ability (i.e., the ability to identify information in a passage and recall simple relationships among variables described in the passage). When developing items to go with a passage, the variety of items should be linked to the cognitive operations that underlie performance on ability tests or other relevant taxonomies (e.g., Bejar, Chaffin, & Embretson's, 1991, taxonomy of semantic relations). Besides ensuring the substantive variety of the set of items that go with a passage, developing items with explicit links to cognitive operations also contributes to their construct validity.

Each passage with its set of questions is a unit. Each question accompanying a passage has a stem and a set of responses. The correct response to the item stem is called the item key. All other responses are distractors. In this section, we describe issues to consider when developing item stems and response alternatives.

- *Organization*—The question asked in a stem should immediately precede the responses. Explanatory information should introduce the question. This may require writing the stem as several short sentences, ending with a sentence such as, "According to the passage how would the two measurements compare?"
- *Clarity*—Item stems should be direct, brief, and as clear as possible. Able examinees should be able to answer items correctly without doubt. Stems should be constructed from familiar words with simple syntax and should not repeat information in the passage.
- *Completeness*—Item stems should be complete. That is, item stems should provide enough information to clarify the question. Examinees should not need to read the responses to find out the question. For example, a stem such as "The author asserts that solar electricity generation:" places the burden of asking the question on the subsequent responses. A much better stem would be, "The author asserts that solar electricity generation utilizes sunlight through the mechanism of:" With this stem, it is easy to construct a uniform set of simple responses.
- *Consistency*—The responses must be grammatically and logically consistent with the stem and with other responses. All responses must be addressed to a question asked in the stem.
- *Single key*—Each item must have one and only one response that is demonstrably better than any of the others. This means that the key should be the only response that finds support in the stimulus material—in this case, the passage. No distractor should be so similar in meaning to the correct answer that it can justifiably be defended as correct.
- *Plausibility of distractors*—The effectiveness of distractors in the set of responses also depends on their plausibility and discreteness. Since distractors are meant to attract examinees who read superficially, they must appear superficially plausible. With respect to discreteness, all responses must be mutually exclusive. This means that no response can logically contain another.
- *Independence*—Finally, each item in a unit must be independent of all other items; neither the stem nor any response of an item may

contain information that suggests the key to another item. An example would be one item that asked "What was the source of Thomas Edison's fame?" followed by another that includes a reference to the "Edison Electric Light Company."

RATIONALES: When developing test units, it is important to justify the key for each item. For each item, the writer should record the reason that each key is correct and why each distractor is incorrect. When developing items as a group activity, writers typically will provide impromptu rationales for evaluation and feedback by the group. Developing rationales provides an important control on the quality of the items. Items with sound rationales will be more likely to survive pilot testing and less likely to be successfully challenged by examinees.

When tests measure relatively complex abilities and the correct answers are quite difficult to discern (e.g., in a test of reasoning), or when the consequences of testing involve high-stake decisions or the potential for legal challenges, formal procedures for developing item rationales are virtually mandatory. As previously mentioned, item rationales are often used to justify the key to examinees who question it.

Item rationales should be both precise and convincing. As appropriate, rationales for Verbal Comprehension items should include corroborative quotations from the passage, citing the paragraph in which each quotation occurs. Item writers may be given a style sheet for item rationales specifying rationale order, format, and style. However structured, the format of rationales should simplify the validation of keys and distractors.

AN EXAMPLE: Figure 6.3 contains an example of a passage and items developed for the electrician apprenticeship program test of Verbal Comprehension. The example was developed following the above guidelines for passage and item development.

More detailed item writing guidelines are available elsewhere. In particular, we encourage the reader to refer to discussions by Millman and Greene (1989) and Roid and Haladyna (1982).

Conducting Technical Reviews
A technical review is a formal procedure in which test materials are reviewed by subject matter experts and by testing experts before field testing. The purpose of the subject matter expert review is to ensure the technical accuracy of the items (e.g., that the keyed answer is correct and that the distractors are incorrect). The purpose of the test expert review is to ensure that the items assess the appropriate level of the ability and

The timing of New Year's Day has changed with customs and calendars. In the Middle Ages in Europe, Christians shifted the marking of the new year from January, where it had been since Roman times, to March 25, when the conception of Christ was commemorated. Contracts were often negotiated to start on this "Lady Day," referring to the mother of Christ. During the fifteenth century A.D., the Renaissance encompassed a renewed attention to ancient customs, and the Roman calendar was reinstituted, with the year beginning in January.

The Mayan civilization, on what is now called the Yucatán Peninsula of Mexico, used a different criterion to mark the new year. There is strong evidence that these people celebrated the new year on one of the two days when the noonday sun is directly overhead. In the equatorial regions of the earth, between the Tropics of Cancer and Capricorn, the sun is in this position twice a year, once on its passage southward, and once on its passage northward. At the early Mayan city of Izapa in the southern Yucatán, the overhead date for the sun on its southward passage was August 13. The Mayans celebrated this as the date for the beginning of the world. At a later, more northerly Mayan site at Edzna, the corresponding overhead date is July 26. Analyses of Mayan pictorial calendars indicate that they celebrated the new year on August 13 prior to A.D. 150, and on July 26 after that year. This change has been explained by archaeological dating showing that A.D. 150 was the time that the Mayans moved the hub of their civilization from the southern to the northern site.

Among the ruins at Edzna are several pyramids, the largest of which apparently served as the marker for New Year's Day. At the front of this pyramid is a stone pillar that is tapered, being thicker at the bottom. At the top of this pillar is a mounted disk whose circumference is exactly the same as the bottom of the pillar. When the noonday sun is not directly overhead but at an angle, this arrangement results in a stripe of light on the pillar. When the sun is precisely overhead, however, the pillar is completely in the shadow of the disk. This occurs, as the Mayans had no doubt determined, on July 26.

It is interesting to note that the Mayans at Edzna did not forget the new year date previously commemorated when they were in the south. A main doorway of the pyramid is aligned with an opening on a platform at the main plaza of the site. The axis of the alignment, when projected to the horizon, points precisely in the direction where the sun sets on August 13. Still another axis at the site was used by the Mayans to predict eclipses of the moon.

1. According to the passage, the main doorway of the large pyramid at Edzna was used to
   A. memorialize the Mayan ancestors at Edzna.
   B. create a shadow used to determine solar position.
   C. determine the date for celebration of New Year's Day at Edzna.
   D. indicate solar position at sunset on the New Year's Day previously celebrated at Izapa.

FIGURE 6.3   An Example Passage and Items for a
Verbal Comprehension Test

2. Why did the Mayans move their capital city from Izapa to Edzna?
   A. The climate at Edzna was more temperate.
   B. Lunar eclipses were more visible at Edzna.
   C. The terrain at Edzna was more suitable for agriculture.
   D. Cannot be determined from the information given.

3. If the Mayans had moved their civilization's center south of Izapa, their new date for celebration of the new year would probably have been closest to which of the following dates?
   A. January 1
   B. February 20
   C. March 25
   D. September 15

4. The passage indicates that a reason for the shift during the European Renaissance to celebrating January 1 as the new year was that
   A. contracts began on that date.
   B. the sun was directly overhead on that date.
   C. some Roman traditions had returned to prominence in European culture.
   D. Christ was believed to have been conceived on that date.

5. According to the passage, the sun at Edzna was directly overhead at noon on
   A. July 26 only.
   B. August 13 only.
   C. July 26 and one other date.
   D. August 13 and one other date.

6. The passage states that the Mayans concluded that the sun was directly overhead by the use of
   A. telescopes.
   B. locations of shadows.
   C. alignment of trees.
   D. documented observations of the stars.

7. Lunar eclipses were predicted at Edzna by
   A. direct observation only.
   B. the date the sun was overhead at noon.
   C. the arrangement of certain architectural markers.
   D. the position of the shadows created by the main pyramid.

8. Based on the information in the passage, the Europeans and the Mayans based their observance of New Year's Day on
   A. solar position in both societies.
   B. religious customs in both societies.
   C. cultural traditions and solar position, respectively.
   D. business conventions and seasonal markers, respectively.

FIGURE 6.3   An Example Passage and Items for a Verbal
             Comprehension Test (continued)

the correct content, as identified in the job analysis. Technical experts also ensure that the items follow the format guidelines described earlier. The technical review may occur concurrently with the sensitivity review.

Conducting Sensitivity Reviews

A sensitivity review is a formal procedure in which representatives of various demographic groups review test materials. The purpose of this review is to provide feedback concerning the potential offensiveness of test materials. Sensitivity reviews typically focus on three issues. The first issue is determining whether test materials avoid assumptions about ethnic, socioeconomic, geographic, or religious subgroups, or knowledge of stereotypes, and avoid characterizing groups in demeaning or objectionable terms.

A second issue is identifying irrelevant characteristics of items that might give one examinee group an advantage. Examples of such irrelevant characteristics might include:

- Regional history or geography that would be unknown to examinees outside the region
- "Country club sports" (e.g., yachting, polo, golf) that are less accessible to economically disadvantaged individuals
- Subjects typically more familiar to males or to females (e.g., sports and fashion)

A third issue is identifying items that deal with potentially sensitive topics. In general, religious and sexual topics should be avoided altogether, and items should not contain offensive language.

Creating Test Administration Instructions

Test administration procedures must ensure that all examinees take the test under as similar conditions as possible. Standard test administration instructions represent an important way of controlling conditions to ensure that examinees' scores on the test are comparable across administrations.

Test administration instructions should be explicit with regard to physical testing conditions—for example, noise levels, room temperature, and lighting. They should also include instructions on how to respond to examinees' questions, perhaps including answers to common questions to be read verbatim. Typical test administration protocols provide explicit instructions on handling secure test materials, setting up the testing room, submitting completed materials for scoring, and timing the test. Test administration instructions should also specify whether test administrators need any special training or certification before administering the test.

Conducting Tryouts of Items

Prior to operational administration (when tests are scored for decision making), it is important to finalize test administration procedures for newly developed tests and to determine the statistical characteristics (e.g., difficulty level and homogeneity) of the items. To do this, items typically are administered to a sample of examinees as part of a pilot test. During the pilot test, examinees are administered newly developed items under conditions similar to an operational administration.

For newly developed tests, administration procedures such as the timing of the test can be refined during a pilot test. For example, if the time allotted for our Verbal Comprehension test is 60 minutes and nearly all examinees are finished after 40 minutes, we might consider reducing the time required for administering the test.

If the items are to be used as part of an ongoing testing program, it may be possible to administer new items (unscored) along with scored items as part of a routine test administration. The new items can either be embedded in a test form or administered in a separate section added to the test. The new items do not contribute to examinees' scores, but examinees' responses to the new items are analyzed to determine the item characteristics.

If it is impossible to administer new items to applicants, it may be necessary to administer them to job incumbents. If job incumbents are used to evaluate items for a selection test, the probable differences between incumbents and applicants must be considered. In particular, it is likely that the incumbents will have a higher level of ability than would many of the applicants—for example, scores for incumbents might range from 45 to 95, while scores for applicants range from 20 to 95. This problem is referred to as range restriction and may cause an underestimate of the correlations of test scores with other measures. Also, because the pilot test has no stakes for the job incumbents, possible motivational differences must be considered.

Analyzing Item Data

A variety of statistical analyses may be performed on data from a pilot study. The purpose of these analyses is to determine the difficulty level and discrimination of the test items, to guide construction of the test forms. The traditional measure of item difficulty is p, the proportion of examinees who answer an item correctly. Consider two ability tests. On one, the items are so difficult that no examinee can answer any item correctly ($p = .00$). On the other, the items are so easy that all examinees can answer all of them correctly ($p = 1.00$). Most people would agree that both tests are useless, since examinees taking either test will obtain identical scores: a zero on the difficult test or a perfect score on the easy one. When examinees obtain the same score on a test, we have no information that can allow us either to compare them to each other or to predict performance on some criterion.

From a psychometric standpoint, an item will best differentiate among examinees when approximately half the examinees taking the test answer the item correctly. If we only wanted to maximize the discrimination among examinees with respect to the relative amount of the ability they possessed, the best test would be one in which the average proportion correct is about .50 across a range of difficulty levels for all test items.* If, however, we wanted to increase our chances of screening for a particular proportion of the population, the best test would be one in which the average proportion of correct items corresponded to the selection ratio—that is, the ratio of the number of openings to the number of applicants. For example, if we had 20 openings for an apprenticeship program and 100 applicants, the best test would be one that identified the top 20 examinees. Our best test, then, would be one in which the average p value of the items comprising the test is .20. Such a test would be so difficult that only about 20% of the examinees taking the test would likely obtain a high score (Ghiselli, Campbell, & Zedeck, 1981).

A traditional measure of item discrimination is a point biserial correlation (Crocker & Algina, 1986). This indicates the extent to which performance on a test item is correlated with performance on the test. To the extent that examinees who answer the item correctly also obtain high scores on the test, one can say that the item discriminates between good and poor performers on the test. One rule of thumb is to retain items for which the correct response option (key) biserial is greater than or equal to 0.20; the biserials on incorrect options (distractors) should be

---

*It is easy to demonstrate that this is true by considering that the item variance for an item scored as right or wrong is pq, where p is defined as above and q is $1 - p$. The maximum value for pq is 0.25, when $p = 0.5$. If $p = 0.45$ or $p = 0.55$, for example, then $pq = 0.2475 < 0.25$. If $p = 0.1$ or 0.9, then $pq = 0.09$. Greater item variance contributes to greater test score variance, which is related to the test's ability to discriminate among individuals at different levels of ability.

negative (i.e., individuals choosing the incorrect option should obtain lower scores on the test as a whole). Items with a positive point biserial on an incorrect response option should be carefully reviewed for ambiguity before being judged acceptable.

Indices of item bias can also be computed (Holland & Wainer, 1993). For example, differential item functioning (DIF) indices indicate whether examinees from different groups, such as different ethnicities or genders, who are matched on overall test performance, perform differently on individual items. IRT analyses can also yield estimates of item difficulty, discrimination, and potential bias. Items that appear problematic from a statistical point of view should be carefully reviewed for possible content-related and structural reasons for the problems (e.g., inadvertent cues to the right answer or distractors that are too close to correct).

Assembling the Test

Item analysis results determine, in large part, the items that will appear on an operational test. When assembling a test, point biserial correlations should be considered in order to achieve internal consistency, and item difficulty should be considered in order to achieve a range of overall test difficulty. Other information about the test items should be considered, such as their similarity in content to other items; items that are redundant or that give clues to the correct answers on other items should not be included. Additionally, the test specifications, which stipulated the target numbers, types, and content of items in the final test, should be consulted.

Although the item analysis results from the pilot tests are needed to assemble tests, it is important to realize that these results are only estimates of how the items will perform in the operational test. Items may perform differently in an operational administration—because of motivational differences, differences in examinee ability level, administration conditions, or even the items' relative positions in the tests, for example. Consequently, items should be reanalyzed after they are administered in an operational test.

Writing Documentation

Final documentation for the test should include a summary of the pilot test results. This summary should indicate the number of items with statistics meeting the predefined standards for inclusion in an operational test. Distributions of surviving items by difficulty level and point biserial correlation should also be provided. A description of each pilot test should be included, indicating areas of needed improvement (e.g., if the instructions or time limits needed to be changed) and the results of such changes.

SUMMARY

Because cognitive ability tests are among the most economical and easily administered of the job selection and assessment tools, they are widely used in employment contexts, with applications including selection, placement, and promotion. However, determining when it is appropriate to use a cognitive ability test, what type of test to use, and how to score it and report the results are complicated matters.

Throughout this chapter, we have emphasized the practical aspects of selecting, developing, and using cognitive ability tests. Even in the brief overview of the history of cognitive ability testing and the variety of ability testing theories, we have emphasized the practical applications of ability testing. Selecting, developing, and using cognitive ability tests, however, requires an awareness of and respect for relevant theory and the complexity of these tests. Our discussions of the psychometric and measurement characteristics of ability tests and our descriptions of how to select and develop cognitive ability tests highlighted the complexity—and creativity—involved in developing and using these instruments. As noted earlier, Carroll (1993) and Ceci (1990) provide excellent reviews of the domain of cognitive ability testing. These works provide a good starting point for becoming familiar with the classic works in the area, as well as more important recent studies.

At the beginning of the chapter, we urged readers to remember three principles when using cognitive ability tests: (1) define terms precisely and use them carefully, (2) consider the theoretical basis of a test before using it, and (3) be ready to provide evidence supporting the proposed uses of a test. Of course, these principles describe the responsibilities of any test user. Although many of the other techniques described in this book have the potential to impact the lives and livelihoods of individual applicants or employees, cognitive ability testing can do so directly, and often permanently. This is because cognitive ability tests capture performance-related capacities that are relatively stable. Thus, examinees cannot remedy their shortcomings vis-à-vis their abilities. If individuals are screened out of consideration for hiring or promotion because of low scores on a cognitive ability test, they have little recourse. Worse, neither will they have the opportunity to demonstrate other performance-related capacities (e.g., skills, knowledges, and other abilities) that could compensate for low scores on an ability test.

REFERENCES

American Psychological Association (1995). *Frequently asked questions (FAQ) on psychological tests.* Washington, DC: Author. Retrieved June 12, 1997, from the World Wide Web: http://www.apa.org/science/test.html

Americans with Disabilities Act of 1990, 42 U.S.C. §12101 et seq., as amended by the Civil Rights Act of 1991, as passed by Congress November 7, 1991.

Anderson, P. S., & Hyers, A. D. (1991). *Quantitative comparisons of difficulty, discrimination and reliability of machine-scored completion items and tests (in the MDT un-cued answer-bank format) in contrast with statistics from comparable multiple choice questions: The first round of answers.* Unpublished manuscript. (ERIC Document Reproduction Service No. ED 349 319)

Baker, E. L., O'Neil, H. F., & Linn, R. L. (1993). Policy and validity prospects for performance-based assessment. *American Psychologist, 48,* 1210–1218.

Bejar, I. I., Chaffin, R., & Embretson, S. (1991). *Cognitive and psychometric analysis of analogical problem solving.* New York: Springer-Verlag.

Binet, A., & Simon, T. (1905). Methodes nouvelles pour le diagnostic du niveau intellectuel des anormaux. *Annee Psychologique, 11,* 191–244. (Cited by DuBois, 1970)

Bloxom, B., McCully, R., Branch, R., Waters, B. K., Barnes, J., & Gribben, M. (1993). *Operational calibration of the circular-response optical-mark-reader answer sheets for the Armed Services Vocational Aptitude Battery (ASVAB)* (DMDC Technical Report No. 93-009). Monterey, CA: Defense Manpower Data Center.

Brown, D. C. (1994). Subgroup norming: Legitimate testing practice or reverse discrimination? *American Psychologist, 49,* 927–928.

Burt, C. (1940). *The factors of the mind: An introduction to factor-analysis in psychology.* London: University of London Press. (New York: Macmillan, 1941.)

Camara, W. J., & Brown, D.C. (1995). Educational and employment testing: Changing concepts in measurement and policy. *Educational Measurement: Issues and Practice, 14,* 5–11.

Carroll, J. B. (1976). Psychometric tests as cognitive tasks: A new "Structure of Intellect." In L. Resnick (Ed.), *The nature of intelligence* (pp. 27–56). Hillsdale, NJ: Erlbaum.

Carroll, J. B. (1993). *Human cognitive abilities: A survey of factor-analytic studies.* New York: Cambridge University Press.

Cascio, W. F., Outtz, J., Zedeck, S., & Goldstein, I. L. (1991). Statistical implications of six methods of test score use in personnel selection. *Human Performance, 4,* 233–264.

Cattell, J. M., & Farrand, L. (1896). Physical and mental measurements of the students of Columbia University. *Psychological Review, 3,* 618–648.

Cattell, R. B. (1943). The measurement of adult intelligence. *Psychological Bulletin, 40,* 153-193.

Ceci, S. J. (1990). *On intelligence . . . more or less: A bio-ecological treatise on intellectual development.* Englewood Cliffs, NJ: Prentice Hall.

Cizek, G. J. (1994). The effect of altering the position of options in a multiple-choice examination. *Educational and Psychological Measurement, 54,* 8–20.

Conoley, J. C., & Impara, J. C. (Eds.). (1995). *Twelfth mental measurements yearbook.* Lincoln: University of Nebraska Press.

Crocker, L., & Algina, J. (1986). *Introduction to classical and modern test theory.* Fort Worth, TX: Harcourt Brace Jovanovich.

Cronbach, L. J. (1984). *Essentials of psychological testing* (4th ed.). New York: Harper & Row.

Darling-Hammond, L., & Lieberman, A. (1992, January 29). The shortcomings of standardized tests. *Chronicle of Higher Education,* pp. B1–B2.

Donlon, T. F. (1973). *Establishing time limits for tests.* Paper presented at the annual meeting of the Northeast Educational Research Association, Ellenville, NY.

Donlon, T. F. (1980). *An exploratory study of the implications of test speededness* (GREB No. 76-9P). Princeton, NJ: Educational Testing Service.

DuBois, P. H. (1970). *A history of psychological testing.* Boston: Allyn and Bacon.

Ekstrom, R. B., French, J. W., & Harman, H. H. with Dermen, D. (1976). *Manual for kit of factor-referenced cognitive tests* (3rd ed.). Princeton, NJ: Educational Testing Service.

Equal Employment Opportunity Commission, Civil Service Commission, Department of Labor, & Department of Justice (1978, August). Uniform guidelines on employee selection procedures. *Federal Register, 43* (166), 38290–38315.

ERIC/AE test locator [Electronic search facility] (1996). Wasshington, DC: Educational Resources Information Center Clearinghouse on Assessment and Evaluation. Assessed on June 12, 1997, on the World Wide Web: http://eri-cae2.educ.cua.edu/testcol.htm

Eyde, L. E., Robertson, G. J., Krug, S. E., Moreland, K. L., Robertson, A. G., Shewan, C. M., Harrison, P. L., Porch, B. E., Hammer, A. L., & Primoff, E. S. (1993). *Responsible test use: Case studies for assessing human behavior.* Washington, DC: American Psychological Association.

Eysenck, H. J., & Kamin, L. (1981). *The intelligence controversy.* New York: Wiley-Interscience.

Feldt, L. S., & Brennan, R. L. (1989). Reliability. In R. L. Linn (Ed.), *Educational measurement* (3rd ed.; pp. 105–146). Washington, DC: American Council on Education.

Fleishman, E. A. (1956). Factorial analysis of complex psychomotor performance and related skills. *Journal of Applied Psychology, 40,* 96–104.

Fleishman, E. A. (1964). *The structure and measurement of physical fitness.* Englewood Cliffs, NJ: Prentice-Hall.

Fleishman, E. A. (1992). *Fleishman Job Analysis Survey* (F-JAS). Bethesda, MD: Management Research Institute.

Fleishman, E. A., & Reilly, M. E. (1992). *Handbook of human abilities: Definitions, measurements, and job task requirements.* Palo Alto, CA: Consulting Psychologists Press.

TESTS OF COGNITIVE ABILITY | 181

Fry, D. J. (1990). The database format question: An alternative to multiple choice and free format for computer based testing. *Computers and Education, 14,* 395–401.

Galton, F. (1883). *Inquiries into human faculty and its development.* New York: Macmillan.

Geisinger, K. F. (1992). Fairness and selected psychometric issues in the psychological testing of Hispanics. In K. F. Geisinger (Ed.), *Psychological testing of Hispanics* (pp. 17–42). Washington, DC: American Psychological Association.

Ghiselli, E. E., Campbell, J. P., & Zedeck, S. (1981). *Measurement theory for the behavioral sciences.* San Francisco: Freeman.

Goddard, H. H. (1912). *The Kallikak family: A study in the heredity of feeble-mindedness.* New York: Macmillan.

Gottfredson, L. S. (1994). The science and politics of race norming. *American Psychologist, 49,* 955–963.

Gottfredson, L. S., & Crouse, J. (1986). Validity versus utility of mental tests: Example of the SAT. *Journal of Vocational Behavior, 9,* 363–378.

Gottfredson, L. S., & Sharf, J. C. (Eds.). (1988). Fairness in employment testing [Special issue]. *Journal of Vocational Behavior, 33* (3).

Gould, S. J. (1981). *The mismeasure of man.* New York: Norton.

Gregory, R. J. (1992). *Psychological testing: History, principles, and applications.* Boston: Allyn & Bacon.

Guilford, J. P. (1985). The structure-of-intellect model. In B. B. Wolman (Ed.), *Handbook of intelligence: Theories, measurements, and applications* (pp. 225–266). New York: Wiley.

Guilford, J. P., & Hoepfner, R. (1971). *The analysis of intelligence.* New York: McGraw-Hill.

Hartigan, J. A., & Wigdor, A. K. (1989). *Fairness in employment testing: Validity generalization, minority issues, and the General Aptitude Test Battery.* Washington, DC: National Academy Press.

Herrnstein, R. J., & Murray, C. (1994). *The bell curve.* New York: Free Press.

Holland, P. W., & Wainer, H. (Eds.). (1993). *Differential item functioning.* Hillsdale, NJ: Erlbaum.

Hunter, J. E. (1980). *Validity generalization for 12,000 jobs: An application of synthetic validity and validity generalization to the General Aptitude Test Battery (GATB).* Washington, DC: U.S. Employment Service, Department of Labor.

Hunter, J. E., Schmidt, F. L., & Rauschenberger, J. M. (1977). Fairness of psychological tests: Implications of four definitions for selection utility and minority hiring. *Journal of Applied Psychology, 62,* 245–260.

Jensen, A. R. (1969). How much can we boost IQ and scholastic achievement? *Harvard Educational Review, 39,* 1–123.

Jensen, A. R. (1986). g: Artifact or reality? *Journal of Vocational Behavior, 9,* 301–331.

Keyser, D. J., & Sweetland, R. C. (Eds.). (1994). *Test Critiques* (Vol. 10). Austin, TX: Pro-Ed.

McHenry, J. J., Hough, L. M., Toquam, J. L., Hanson, M. A., & Ashworth, S. (1990). Project A validity results: The relationship between predictor and criterion domains. *Personnel Psychology, 43,* 335–354.

Messick, S. (1989). Validity. In R.L. Linn (Ed.), *Educational measurement* (3rd ed.; pp. 13–103). New York: Macmillan.

Messick, S. (1995). Validity of psychological assessment: Validation of inferences from persons' responses and performances as scientific inquiry into score meaning. *American Psychologist, 50,* 741–749.

Miller, M. D., & Legg, S. M. (1993). Alternative assessment in a high-stakes environment. *Educational Measurement: Issues and Practice, 12,* 9–15.

Millman, J., & Greene, J. (1989). The specification and development of tests of achievement and ability. In R. L. Linn (Ed.), *Educational measurement* (3rd ed.; pp. 335–366). Washington, DC: American Council on Education.

Mitchell, J.V. (Ed.). (1985). *Ninth mental measurements yearbook.* Lincoln: University of Nebraska Press.

Murphy, L. L., Conoley, J. C., & Impara, J. C. (Eds.). (1994). *Tests in print IV.* Lincoln: University of Nebraska Press.

National Commission on Testing and Public Policy (1990). *From gatekeeper to gateway: Transforming testing in America.* Chestnut Hill, MA: Author.

Nunnally, J. C. (1978). *Psychometric theory* (2nd ed.). New York: McGraw-Hill.

Peterson, N. G. (1993). *Review of issues associated with speededness of GATB tests.* Washington, DC: American Institutes for Research.

Peterson, N. G., Hough, L. M., Dunnette, M. D., Rosse, R. L., Houston, J. S., Toquam, J. L., & Wing, H. (1990). Project A: Specification of the predictor domain and development of new selection/classification tests. *Personnel Psychology, 43,* 247–276.

Peterson, N. G., Mumford, M. D., Borman, W. C., Jeanneret, P. R., & Fleishman, E. A. (Eds.). (in press). *O*NET: An Occupational Information Network.* Washington, DC: American Psychological Association.

Peterson, N. G., Oppler, S. H., Sager, C. E., & Rosse, R. L. (1995). *Analysis of the Enhanced Computer Administered Test battery: An evaluation of potential revisions and additions to the Armed Services Vocational Aptitude Battery.* Washington, DC: American Institutes for Research.

Rindler, S. E. (1979). Pitfalls in assessing test speededness. *Journal of Educational Measurement, 16,* 261–270.

Roid, G. H., & Haladyna, T. M. (1982). *A technology for test-item writing.* Orlando, FL: Academic Press.

Sabers, D. L. (1985). Review of the Industrial Reading Test. In J.V. Mitchell (Ed.), *Ninth mental measurements yearbook* (pp. 684–685). Lincoln: University of Nebraska Press.

Sackett, P. R., & Wilk, S. L. (1994). Within-group norming and other forms of score adjustment in preemployment testing. *American Psychologist, 49,* 929–954.

Schmidt, F. L. (1991). Why all banding procedures in personnel selection are logically flawed. *Human Performance, 4,* 265–277.

Schmidt, F. L., & Hunter, J. E. (1977). Development of a general solution to the problem of validity generalization. *Journal of Applied Psychology, 62,* 529–540.

Schmidt, F. L., & Hunter, J. E. (1981). Employment testing: Old theories and new research. *American Psychologist, 36,* 1128–1137.

Schmidt, F. L., Pearlman,K., Hunter, J. E., & Hirsh, H. R. (1985). Forty questions about validity generalization and meta-analysis. *Personnel Psychology, 38,* 697–798.

Shavelson, R., & Webb, N. (1991). *Generalizability theory: A primer.* Newbury Park, CA: Sage.

Snow, R. E., & Lohman, D. F. (1989). Implications of cognitive psychology for educational measurement. In R. L. Linn (Ed.), *Educational measurement* (3rd ed.; pp. 263–331). New York: Macmillan.

Spearman, C. (1904). General intelligence objectively determined and measured. *American Journal of Psychology, 15,* 201–293.

Spearman, C. (1927). *The abilities of man: Their nature and measurement.* London: Macmillan.

Sternberg, R. J. (1988). *The triarchic mind.* New York: Viking.

Sternberg, R. J.,Wagner, R. K.,Williams,W. M., & Horvath,J.A. (1995).Testing common sense. *American Psychologist, 50,* 912–927.

Sweetland, R.C., & Keyser, D. J. (Eds.). (1991). *Tests* (3rd ed.). Austin,TX: Pro-Ed.

Tenopyr, M. L. (1996, April). *Construct-consequence confusion.* Paper presented at the annual meeting of the Society for Industrial and Organizational Psychology, San Diego, CA.

Thurstone, L. L. (1938). Primary mental abilities. *Psychometric monographs* (No. 1).

Tierney, R. J. (1985). Review of the Nelson-Denny Reading Test, Forms E and F. In J. V. Mitchell (Ed.), *Ninth mental measurements yearbook* (pp. 1035–1037). Lincoln: University of Nebraska Press.

U.S. Department of Labor (1991). *Dictionary of Occupational Titles* (4th ed.). Washington, DC: Author.

van der Linden, W. J., & Hambleton, R. K. (Eds.). (1997). *Handbook of modern item response theory.* New York: Springer.

Wechsler, D. (1981). *Manual for the Wecsler Adult Intelligence Scale–revised.* San Antonio, TX: Psychological Corporation.

Wigdor,A. K., & Garner,W. R. (Eds.). (1982). *Ability testing: Uses, consequences, and controversies. Part 1: Report of the committee.* Washington, DC: National Academy of Sciences, National Research Council.

Wing, C. W., Jr. (1980). *Three thousand years of talent searching.* Invited presentation for the meeting of the National Association of Schools of Music, Philadelphia, PA. (ERIC Document Reproduction Service No. ED 322 209)

Wundt, W. (1862). Die Geschwindigkeit des Gedankens. *Gartenlaube,* 263–265. (Cited by Gregory, 1992)

Yerkes, R. M. (Ed.). (1921). Psychological examining in the United States army. *Memoirs of the National Academy of Sciences* (Vol. 15).

Ysseldyke, J. E. (1985). Review of the Nelson-Denny Reading Test, Forms E and F. In J. V. Mitchell (Ed.), *Ninth mental measurements yearbook* (p. 1038). Lincoln: University of Nebraska Press.

Zedeck, S., & Cascio,W. F. (1984). Psychological issues in personnel decisions. *Annual Review of Psychology, 35,* 461–518.

Employment Interviews

Deborah L. Whetzel
Michael A. McDaniel

OVERVIEW

Interviews are face-to-face interactions between an interviewer and an interviewee. An interview typically is initiated to achieve one or more objectives (e.g., obtaining data in response to a survey, disciplining employees, providing feedback as part of performance appraisal, career counseling, and selecting employees from a pool of applicants) and occurs as part of a sequence of activities (e.g., reviewing résumés, interviewing a subset of candidates, and administering cognitive ability tests for the purpose of selecting applicants; or reviewing training curricula and interviewing employees to assess training needs). The interview's objectives and the sequence of activities in which the interview takes place are known as the *context* of the interview. In this chapter, we discuss interviews in the context of selection, that is, interviews used to select employees from a pool of applicants. In this setting, interviews typically focus on past, present, or future behavior, beliefs, opinions, attitudes, or convictions of applicants. Information about individuals' previous experience, education, and vocational aspirations reported during the interview, and behavior observed during the interview, are considered the *content* of the interview. Interviewers are required to interpret information and draw inferences about traits, attributes, attitudes, and skills that the applicant possesses. These inferences often take the form of ratings on dimensions of personal attributes or rankings of applicants.

In spite of conflicting evidence regarding its reliability and validity (Arvey & Campion, 1982; Mayfield, 1964; Reilly & Chao, 1982; Wagner, 1949; Wright, 1969), the interview is one of the most widely used methods of selecting employees. Ulrich and Trumbo (1965) surveyed 852 organizations and found that 99% of them used interviews as a selection tool. This likely is due to its intuitive appeal to human resource professionals and hiring authorities. Because of its widespread use, techniques for developing the interview that enhance its reliability and validity are of great importance in selection. This chapter describes various types of interviews, their reliability and validity, and how to create questions for two kinds of interviews.

TYPES OF INTERVIEWS

Interviews typically vary according to content of the interview (i.e., what is measured), degree of structure provided for interviewers (i.e., specification of questions and effectiveness of various responses prior to the interview), and number of interviewers. Following are descriptions of various types of interviews.

CONTENT OF THE INTERVIEW

In a review of the literature on interviews, McDaniel, Whetzel, Schmidt, and Maurer (1994) found that interviews could be divided into three content areas: (1) situational interviews, (2) job-related interviews, and (3) psychological interviews. Situational interviews (Latham, Saari, Pursell, & Campion, 1980) present the interviewee with a situation and ask for a description of the actions he or she would take in that scenario. These interviews focus on the individual's ability to project what his or her behavior would be in a given situation that might occur on the job in the future. In contrast, job-related interviews focus on past behaviors and job-related experience. The underlying assumption of such interviews is that future behavior is predicted by past behavior and to the extent that individuals have relevant experience in an area, they will be able to perform the duties of the job for which they are interviewing. These interviews often are conducted by personnel officers or hiring authorities. Examples of job-related interviews are the patterned behavior description interview (Janz, 1982; 1989), the experience-based interview (Pulakos & Schmitt, 1995), and the structured behavioral interview (Motowidlo et al., 1992). Psychological interviews are conducted by a psychologist and the content of questions is intended to assess personal traits such as dependability. These interviews are often included in individual assessments (Ryan & Sackett, 1989) of personnel conducted by consulting psychologists or management consultants.

LEVEL OF STRUCTURE

Interviews can be differentiated by their level of structure. Huffcutt (1992) defined structure as the reduction in procedural variability across applicants, which can translate into the degree of discretion an interviewer is allowed when conducting the interview. In unstructured interviews, the interviewer typically asks the interviewee to "tell me about yourself" and the interviewee can describe a wide range of behavior ranging from hobbies to experience performing duties similar to those likely performed on the job. In these kinds of interviews, the interviewer can ask follow-up questions but is not required to do so. The interviewer has a great deal of discretion in terms of what questions are asked.

In structured interviews, on the other hand, there are predetermined rules for eliciting, observing, and evaluating responses. This often includes specifying the questions in advance and rating the responses for appropriateness of content. The structured interview limits interviewers' discretion by stipulating the kinds of issues they are to ask about when questioning applicants about their behavior.

Huffcutt (1992) reviewed the literature on interview structure and described four progressively higher levels of structure. Level 1 was the typical unstructured interview characterized by no constraints on the questions and a global evaluation of responses. Level 2 imposed limited constraints by specifying the topics to be covered by the questions and some degree of structure on response evaluation. Level 3 required the prespecification of questions, although applicants were not asked precisely the same questions because different interview forms were used or interviewers were allowed to choose among alternative questions and to probe responses to the specified questions (e.g., Janz, 1982). Responses were evaluated using some degree of structured response evaluation.

Level 4 involved asking applicants precisely the same questions with no deviation or follow-up probes and responses were scored according to benchmark answers (e.g., Latham et al., 1980).

NUMBER OF INTERVIEWERS

Interview information can be collected using different numbers of interviewers. One can interview candidates using a single interviewer. On the other hand, candidates may be interviewed using a board or panel technique in which multiple raters, independently or consensually, provide ratings. These interviews often require an applicant to answer questions before a group of interviewers who ask the questions and record and score the responses.

PSYCHOMETRIC CHARACTERISTICS OF THE INTERVIEW

RELIABILITY

One of the most prevalent criticisms of the interview is its lack of reliability. That is, different interviewers independently interviewing the same candidate often disagree about the candidate's suitability for employment (Valenzi & Andrews, 1973). There are several likely causes for the lack of reliability among interviewers. First, the unstructured interview does not guide the interviewing procedure in any way to ensure that common questions are asked and that the interviewers are thereby provided with a common basis for assessment (Webster, 1962). Another problem with unstructured interviews is that they fail to standardize the way in which the information obtained is to be interpreted or weighted. For example, one interviewer may value interpersonal skills more than past experience while another interviewer may think past experience is more important than interpersonal skills. Still another interviewer may think that the way an applicant dresses is important. Differences in how interviewers weight relevant variables and whether they consider potentially irrelevant variables are likely to result in different overall evaluations of the same applicant.

Several early reviews of the literature on employment interviews suggested that this method of selecting applicants for jobs was unreliable and therefore lacking in validity (Mayfield, 1964; Ulrich & Trumbo, 1965;

Wagner, 1949). Mayfield suggested that typical unstructured interviews with no prior data on interviewees were inconsistent in their coverage. He indicated that interview validities were low even in studies that reported moderate reliabilities. He reasoned that while interviewers may be consistent in their approach to interviewees, they are inconsistent in their interpretation of data. Several researchers have made suggestions about methods for improving the reliability of employment interviews, thereby increasing their potential validity. After reviewing the literature, Landy (1985) stated that higher degrees of structure appear to increase interviewers' agreement on their overall evaluations or predictions. In addition, asking questions that tap specific job requirements increases interrater agreement.

The effect on reliability of interview structure and of using job analysis to determine interview content was addressed by Conway, Jako, and Goodman (1995). They conducted a meta-analysis using 111 interrater reliability coefficients and found that the overall mean and variance were .70 and .035, respectively, and that the 90% confidence interval for the mean was .39 to 1.00. Since the interval did not include zero, the reliability of interviews was considered to generalize across situations. However, they uncovered a number of variables that moderated interview reliability. Conway et al. (1995) found that standardization of questions, standardization of response evaluation, use of job analysis to determine interview content, and interviewer training moderated (increased) reliability. Given the levels of reliability they found, the authors estimated that the upper limits of validity were .67 for highly structured interviews and .34 for unstructured interviews.

In sum, contrary to previous reviews, recent research on the reliability of employment interviews suggests that the interview can be a reliable tool for assessment and prediction. Its reliability can be enhanced by: (1) using job analysis to define the content of the interview, (2) using a structured set of questions for all applicants, and (3) standardizing response evaluation.

VALIDITY

There have been several quantitative reviews of the validity of interviews (in which the mean validity was calculated) that appear to substantiate Mayfield's (1964) pessimistic findings. Hunter and Hunter's (1984) analysis, including 27 coefficients, found that the validity of the interview for predicting supervisor ratings was low (.14). Reilly and Chao

(1982) obtained a higher validity (.19) for predicting training and job performance, but they only had 12 coefficients available. Dunnette, Arvey, and Arnold's (1971) analysis used 30 coefficients in which the criterion was supervisor ratings, and they obtained an average validity of .16.

However, four relatively recent meta-analytic reviews suggest that, contrary to previous results, the interview method has at least moderate validity (Huffcutt & Arthur, 1994; McDaniel et al., 1994; Wiesner & Cronshaw, 1988; Wright, Lichtenfels, & Pursell, 1989).

Wright et al. (1989) found that after correcting for criterion unreliability, the mean validity of the interview, using 13 coefficients, was .37. Placing the 95% confidence interval around this mean suggested that the true validity fell between -0.07 and 0.77. Since this interval included zero, they could not conclude that the interview was valid for all jobs. However, after eliminating one study that reported a negative validity coefficient (-.22; Kennedy, 1986) with a very large sample size, the mean corrected validity was .39, with a 95% confidence interval of .27 to .49.

Wiesner and Cronshaw (1988) investigated interview validity using 150 coefficients in which 15,459 individuals were studied. They investigated validity as a function of interview format (individual vs. board) and degree of structure (structured vs. unstructured). They found that structured interviews, in which the questions and various levels of response were specified in advance, yielded a much higher mean corrected validity than unstructured interviews (.63 vs. .20) and that structured board interviews using consensus ratings had the highest corrected validity (.64). They also found that validity increased as a function of whether a job analysis was conducted. However, because their analysis pooled such criteria as job performance, training performance, and tenure, additional investigation was warranted.

Huffcutt and Arthur (1994) conducted a meta-analysis using 114 validity coefficients, in which 18,652 individuals were studied. They examined the level of interview structure as a moderating variable. They classified interviews in terms of standardization of interview questions and response scoring procedures. They found that: (1) structure moderated interview validity; (2) interviews, particularly when structured, can reach levels of validity that are comparable to those of mental ability tests (.37); and (3) although validity does increase through much of the range of structure, there is a point at which additional structure essentially yields no incremental validity, thus suggesting a ceiling effect for structure.

McDaniel et al. (1994) cumulated 245 validity coefficients in which 86,311 individuals were studied. They compared different kinds of inter-

TABLE 7.1   Summary of Previous Research on the Validity
            of the Interview for Predicting Performance

Researcher	Criterion	Number of Validity Coefficients	Mean Validity
Dunnette, Arvey, & Arnold (1971)	Supervisor ratings	30	.16
Reilly & Chao (1982)	Mixture of training and performance	12	.19
Hunter & Hunter (1984)	Supervisor ratings	10	.14
	Promotion	5	.08
	Training performance	9	.10
	Tenure	3	.03
Wiesner & Cronshaw (1988)	Performance (primarily supervisor ratings)	150	.26
Wright, Lichtenfels, & Pursell (1989)	Supervisor ratings	13	.26
Huffcutt & Arthur (1994)	Supervisor ratings	114	.37
McDaniel, Whetzel, Schmidt, & Maurer (1994)	Job Performance	160	.37
	Training performance	75	.36
	Tenure	10	.20

view content (situational, job-related, and psychological), different methods for conducting interviews (structured and unstructured; board and individual), and used different criteria (job performance, training performance, and tenure) collected for different purposes (research criteria, administrative criteria). For the prediction of job performance criteria, situational interviews had a higher mean validity (.50) than job-related interviews (.39), which had a higher mean validity than psychological interviews (.29). They found that if the interview was structured, it was more valid than previously believed (.44). In fact, even unstructured interviews appeared to be more valid than previously believed (.33). When all interviews were considered together, individual interviews were more valid than board interviews (.43 vs. .32). When interviews were differentiated by structure, the results were similar. Individual interviews were more valid than board interviews when they were structured (.46 vs. .38) and slightly more valid when they were unstructured (.34 vs. .33). Table 7.1 summarizes the results of these meta-analytic reviews.

Whereas these meta-analytic reviews combined several kinds of structured interviews, Pulakos and Schmitt (1995) reviewed the validity of experience-based questions (asking individuals how they had handled situations in the past requiring skills and abilities necessary for effective performance) and situational questions (asking individuals how they would respond if they were confronted with particular problems in the future). They found that experience-based interview questions yielded higher levels of validity than situational questions (.32 vs. -.02).

In sum, although previous quantitative reviews have suggested that the employment interview is not a good predictor of job performance, relatively recent meta-analytic studies, with greater numbers of coefficients, show that the interview does predict job performance, especially if the interview is structured and the questions and response rating scales are based on job analysis results. Later in this chapter, we describe how to create structured interview questions using job analysis data of the type described in Chapter 4.

ADVERSE IMPACT

Several researchers have studied the degree of adverse impact on interview ratings. Mullins (1982) used videotaped stimulus materials to examine interviewer ratings of high- and low-quality candidates role-played by African Americans and Whites. Results showed that while applicant quality was the most important variable influencing ratings, African American applicants were significantly favored over White applicants. On the other hand, in a field study examining actual interviewer ratings of candidates, Parsons and Linden (1984) found lower ratings for African American applicants compared to White applicants on several rating dimensions. Motowidlo et al. (1992) compared interview scores by race (Whites, African Americans, Hispanics) and by gender, and found no significant effects of race or gender. They concluded that their results offer no reason to believe that the interview is likely to have an adverse impact on African Americans, Hispanics, or women. Pulakos and Schmitt (1995) found small differences in scores on the interview as well as in job performance ratings between different subgroups (White, African American, Hispanic, male, and female); however, the interview was equally valid for all subgroups. In sum, the evidence suggests that in spite of slight differences in interview ratings, there is little reason to believe that interviews are differentially valid for various subgroups.

INCREMENTAL VALIDITY BEYOND COGNITIVE ABILITY

There is considerable research showing that the best predictor of job performance is cognitive ability (Hunter & Hunter, 1984). However, given the relatively large differences between minorities' and nonminorities' scores on such tests (Gottfredson, 1986), identifying valid predictors to supplement prediction beyond cognitive ability and reduce subgroup differences is an important concern. Results from several studies (e.g., Campion, Pursell, & Brown, 1988) have led to the conclusion that the interview operates like an "orally administered cognitive ability test." However, in the Campion et al. (1988) study, the interview included questions about reading, math, and mechanical knowledge. In a later study, Campion, Campion, and Hudson (1994) used the interview to predict constructs such as teamwork, self-management, commitment, and other social attributes not typically viewed as cognitive ability. They found that the interview showed substantial correlations with the cognitive ability tests, but still had meaningful incremental validity for predicting both cognitive and noncognitive performance criteria. Pulakos and Schmitt (1995) examined the incremental validity of experience-based interviews over cognitive ability tests (the Air Force Officer Qualification Test). The correlation between the interview and a composite performance rating was .38; the correlation between cognitive ability and performance was .17. The correlation between the interview and cognitive ability was very low (.09). Concerning incremental validity, they found that the interview explained additional variance in the performance measure beyond that explained by the cognitive test. Huffcutt, Roth, and McDaniel (1996) investigated the extent to which cognitive ability is assessed in employment interviews. Their meta-analysis of 49 studies showed that the average correlation between interview ratings and cognitive ability test scores was .25, which increased to .40 after correction for artifacts. They also looked at potential moderating variables and found that the correlation between interview scores and ability tended to decrease as the level of structure increased and that the correlation was higher for low-complexity jobs.

These studies suggest that the correlation between cognitive ability and interview ratings is low (.09; Pulakos & Schmitt, 1995) or moderate (.40; Huffcutt et al., 1996). However, since the interview has some incremental validity over cognitive ability, it should be considered for use during selection in addition to tests of cognitive ability.

SUMMARY

This review of the recent literature regarding the psychometric characteristics of employment interviews suggests that the interview indeed is
a valid predictor of job and training performance. While there are variables that influence interviewers' ratings, such as preinterview impression
effects (Dipboye, 1982), contrast effects with other applicants (Landy &
Bates, 1973; Hakel, Ohnesorge, & Dunnette, 1970), interviewer experience (Carlson, 1967), and interviewers' stereotypes (Hakel, Hollemann,
& Dunnette, 1970), interviewers can make judgments that are related to
performance in job and training situations. Two major factors appear to
increase reliability and therefore potential validity. First, interviews
should be structured such that all interviewers receive similar information from the applicant. Second, interviews should be job-related,
whether they focus on past experience (Janz, 1982; Pulakos & Schmitt,
1995) or on what individuals may do in a specified situation in the
future (Latham et al., 1980). We now turn to procedures for creating
structured interview questions for two kinds of interviews: situational
interviews and structured behavioral interviews.

HOW TO CREATE STRUCTURED INTERVIEW QUESTIONS

This section describes methods for developing different kinds of interview questions for use in employee selection. The number of questions
used as part of the interview will depend on the complexity of the job
and the amount of time to be spent on the interview. The scoring of
questions and the cumulation of scores across questions will depend on
the relative importance of the knowledges, skills, abilities, and other
characteristics (KSAOs) being measured.

Structured interview questions are usually based on some knowledge of
job content. Job analysis methods, described in Chapters 2, 3 and 4, are often
used to determine job requirements on which interview questions are
based. Field and Gatewood (1989) gave two reasons for using job analysis
data for developing a structured interview for selection: (1) The use of job
analysis results serves to enhance the effectiveness of the interview as a selection tool, and (2) the use of a content-related development strategy aids in
compliance with legal guidelines for measures used in personnel selection.

Critical incident job analysis (Flanagan, 1954), described in Chapter
4, often is used to define behavioral dimensions around which to orga-

nize interview questions. Large numbers (i.e., hundreds or thousands) of critical incidents that describe effective and ineffective performance are collected. They are sorted, by similarity of behavior, into categories that define the dimensions of performance. One potential problem with solely using critical incidents is that only a fraction of them is used as actual interview questions. By developing and including additional interview questions using other kinds of job analysis information (e.g., KSAOs or tasks), the interview can be structured to cover the job domain more adequately. Job analysis procedures for identifying tasks, for determining required KSAOs, and for linking these domains are described in Chapter 3.

Field and Gatewood (1989) suggested a Job Content Method that combines the use of KSAOs with critical incidents to ensure adequate coverage of job requirements. In their approach, once tasks and KSAOs are defined (see Chapter 3), KSAOs are selected according to three criteria. Each KSAO must be: (1) rated by subject matter experts (SMEs) as important for job performance; (2) acknowledged by a majority of SMEs as essential for a newly hired employee upon job entry; and (3) linked to the performance of at least one critical job task. KSAOs meeting all of these criteria are used to define the content of the interview. Critical incidents are then collected in the context of the KSAOs meeting the three criteria just described.

Field and Gatewood (1989) suggest a four-step method for generating critical incidents that can, in turn, be used to develop structured employment interviews. First, a panel of SMEs, who have had opportunities to observe individuals performing the job is assembled. The SMEs review the KSAOs (those that meet the criteria just described) to be assessed during the interview as well as the tasks associated with those KSAOs. Then they describe, in writing, incidents of effective and ineffective job behaviors they have seen that reflect the KSAOs and associated tasks. The second step consists of having a second group of SMEs read each incident and allocate it to the one KSAO they believe the incident best illustrates. Incidents that are not allocated to the same KSAO by a certain percentage of the SMEs (e.g., 75%) are eliminated. This process of "retranslation," or testing a performance structure, is described in Chapter 4. The third step consists of writing questions from the incidents retained from the second step. In the situational interview, these questions are descriptions of situations concerning an important behavior on the job; the interviewee is to describe what he or she would do in that situation. In the structured behavioral interview, these questions ask interviewees to describe events that have occurred in their lives that are similar to those that might occur on the job. The fourth and last step consists of having SMEs think of persons whose performance on the job they would rate as outstanding, average, and poor, and provide written narratives describing how those persons would respond to each question. SMEs then rate the simulated responses, and those responses on which there is a high degree of rater agreement are retained as anchors for a rating scale. Assuming job analysis information (critical incidents) has been collected and prepared, the questions can be created. Following are descriptions of the methods for creating questions for two different kinds of interviews.

SITUATIONAL INTERVIEWS

Latham et al. (1980) and Latham (1989) described the situational interview in which the underlying assumption is that intentions are related to behavior (Locke, 1968). The purpose of the situational interview is to identify a potential employee's intentions by presenting that person with a series of job-related incidents and asking what he or she would do in each situation. Six steps for developing a situational interview are:

1. Conduct a job analysis using the critical incident technique and group the incidents into clusters (or dimensions) based on similarity of behavior (Flanagan, 1954). Methods for collecting and analyzing critical incidents are described in Chapter 4.
2. Select one or more incidents from each cluster or dimension that exemplify performance in that cluster.
3. Turn each critical incident into a "What would you do if . . ." question.
4. Review the questions for comprehensiveness in terms of covering the material identified in the job analysis.
5. Develop a scoring guide to facilitate agreement among interviewers on what constitutes a good, acceptable, or unacceptable response to each question.
6. Conduct a pilot study to eliminate questions to which applicants/interviewees give the same answers (i.e., the questions do not differentiate among applicants), or where interviewers cannot agree on the scoring.

To develop questions for situational interviews (Steps 2, 3, and 4), a subject matter expert panel is created. SME panels often consist of job incumbents/supervisors with six months to one year of experience or with some knowledge of the job requirements. The SME panel examines critical incidents collected in a job analysis. Then, for each dimension, each SME chooses an incident that he or she believes best represents the behavior identified in that dimension (Step 2) and turns the incident into a question (Step 3). The amount of time allocated for the interview may dictate the number of questions actually used. Typically, this is done by selecting the best question(s) for each dimension. For jobs with large numbers of dimensions, the most important dimensions may need to be identified prior to generating questions.

The five critical incidents in the list that follows were collected as part of a job analysis for the job of apprentice electrician. The percentage of SMEs who sorted each incident into the Working hard, taking initiative, and being responsible dimension are shown after each incident.

1. An apprentice was working on site lighting. The journeyman did not show up for work that day, so the foreman did not have anyone to help the apprentice. The apprentice said there was enough work to do that day and that no one needed to provide help. The apprentice had a very productive day and got a lot done. The foreman thanked the apprentice for the effort and said it was a great job. 82%

2. The wiring of a department store was in the beginning stages. During the winter, the temperature was between zero and 20 degrees below zero for about two weeks. The apprentice was running feeders out of the main distributor in a building that had no roof. The apprentice worked each day wearing weather-protective clothing and was able to keep a respectable pace and the job was finished one week early. 89%

3. An apprentice was hired by a foreman and told to be on time for work every day. The apprentice showed up for work late three days in a row and always had an excuse. The foreman did not say anything, but docked the apprentice on the next paycheck. The apprentice was never late again. 70%

4. An apprentice was busy working one day and several journeymen decided to start pitching quarters to a wall (gambling). They invited the apprentice to join them. The apprentice gave in and decided to pitch quarters with them. The apprentice lost over six dollars in quarters, but still got paid for a full day. The employer lost almost a half day of work. 84%

5. A ditch was being trenched to supply power for a new building. It was a hot summer with frequent showers adding to the delay in the work that was already running behind schedule. Two apprentices were piping six parallel runs of four-inch PVC under the supervision of a journeyman. While in the ditch, one of the apprentices constantly encouraged co-workers by having a positive attitude and remaining upbeat. The project was moved closer to completion through the apprentice's attitude benefiting the project by encouraging the others to remain constantly at work. 92%

Since critical incident No. 4 was allocated to the Working hard, taking initiative, and being responsible dimension by more than 75% of the SMEs, it was available for use as an interview question. A question that might be developed using this incident is shown below:

You have been assigned to a job with several journeymen. While still on the job, you notice several of them goofing off. You know that you are falling behind on the schedule to complete the project. What would you do?

After several questions are created for each cluster or dimension of behavior, the questions are read aloud to the SME panel to ensure that the SMEs agree that the questions fit the dimension and will elicit responses that differentiate among applicants. Through group consensus, one or at most two interview questions are selected for each dimension to ensure comprehensiveness of coverage (Step 4).

To create a scoring guide for each question (Step 5), each member of the SME group is independently asked to benchmark a "5" answer—that is, "things you have actually heard said in an interview by employees who subsequently were considered outstanding on the job"; a "1" answer—that is, "things that you have actually heard said in an interview by people who were hired, but who turned out to be very poor performers"; and a "3" answer—that is, "things that you have actually heard said in an interview by people who were hired and who turned out to be average performers." For SMEs who do not have much experience interviewing, the instructions can be changed to, "Think of people you know who are outstanding, very poor, and average on the job. How do you think they would respond to this question if they were being interviewed?" The SMEs then answer each question the way they think outstanding, average, and very poor performers would. Their simulated answers potentially serve as benchmarks against which applicants' answers are to be rated. Each SME then reads his or her answers to the other SMEs. After group discussion, consensus is reached on the answers

LOW	MEDIUM	HIGH
Interviewee indicated that he or she would join the journeymen because they have been around longer and know the "ins and outs" of how to get the job done in a hurry and if it's okay for the journeymen to goof off occasionally, then it should be okay for apprentices.	Interviewee said that he or she would watch the journeymen and see if they got in trouble. He or she would continue to work on the job and probably would not tell the foreman about the situation later.	Interviewee said that he or she would not join the journeymen and would tell the foreman about the situation later. They were clearly losing money due to lower productivity and he or she did not want to be part of it.
1	2 3 4	5

FIGURE 7.1   Example Rating Scale for Scoring Situational Interviews on the Dimension "Working Hard, Taking Initiative, and Being Responsible"

to be used as benchmarks. Rating scales are then constructed (see Chapter 11 for methods for developing rating scales). Figure 7.1 shows a rating scale in which SMEs described how employees at various levels of competence might answer the question posed above using critical incident No. 4 to assess the dimension Working hard, taking initiative, and being responsible.

After the questions and rating scales are developed, a pilot study (Step 6) is conducted to ensure that the questions yield useful responses. SMEs who have a lot of job experience may develop questions that an applicant could not answer without some amount of job knowledge. Therefore, questions need to be tried out on people who have characteristics similar to the applicant pool (e.g., similar amounts of job experience).

STRUCTURED BEHAVIORAL INTERVIEWS

The structured formats of the situational interview and the patterned behavior description interview (Janz, 1982, 1989) form the basis for the structured behavioral interview (Motowidlo et al., 1992). Structured behavioral interviews essentially ask interviewees for critical incidents that relate to a stimulus question. The interview protocol requires interviewers to ask each standard question and then probe with follow-up questions until they are satisfied that they have all the information they need about the situational context, what the applicant did in the situation, and the outcome of the behavior. Motowidlo et al. (1992) described the structured behavioral interview as having several characteristics:

1. Stimulus questions are based on the results of a critical incident job analysis.
2. The interview is organized around behavioral dimensions defined from analysis of the critical incidents.
3. The interview consists of a set of standard questions about how interviewees handled past situations that are like situations that could happen on the job and that might elicit behavior representing one or more of the interview dimensions. Questions take the form of "Tell me about a time when. . ." or "What did you do in that situation?"
4. The interviewer asks discretionary probing questions for details of the situation, the interviewee's behavior in it, and the outcome (e.g., "What happened when you did that?").
5. The interviewer takes notes as the applicant talks.
6. After asking all standard questions and discretionary probes, the interviewer reviews his or her notes and rates the interviewee using scales anchored with behavioral illustrations.
7. The ratings are then mathematically combined (as an unweighted sum) to yield a total interview score that is used to guide selection decisions.

A critical incident written by a SME during job analysis follows. The incident was sorted by 85% of SMEs into a dimension called Ability to Plan and Organize Tasks to Meet Deadlines.

An experienced journeyman and apprentice were given a job to terminate about 32 500 kc mil cables in the back of a 2000 amp switchgear. The foreman was pushing the workers to get as much work done as possible in the least amount of time. Before beginning the job, the journeyman planned what to do and explained to the apprentice how to lay the cables efficiently. The journeyman terminated the cables first, working carefully and taking time to be neat, then supervised the apprentice. The job was done in enough time to satisfy the foreman and ensure that the finished product was electrically safe. The apprentice also learned the importance of having a good plan before jumping into a big project.

A structured behavioral interview question using this critical incident might be:

Tell me about a time when you were given a tight deadline for a project you were working on. What did you do?

If an interviewee provides insufficient information about an incident in response to this question, interview probes might be:

What did you do then? (This probe is designed to solicit the action, if the applicant only describes the situation.)

What was the result of what you did? (This probe is designed to solicit the outcome, if the applicant describes the situation and the action but does not describe the result.)

Scales used with this kind of interview are behaviorally defined and anchored with general behavioral descriptions at high, medium, and low points on the scale. Methods for developing behaviorally based rating scales are described in Chapter 11. After each applicant is rated on all dimensions, the ratings are summed to form a total interview score that determines whether applicants are sent to the next stage of the hiring process. A rating scale that could be used for rating responses on the dimension Ability to Plan and Organize Tasks to Meet Deadlines for the stimulus question just given and its associated probes is shown in Figure 7.2.

Motowidlo et al. (1992) stated that the structured behavioral format limits interviewers' discretion by defining specific behavioral dimensions about which they are to collect information and along which they are to evaluate applicants. The format further restricts them to a standard set of questions for all applicants. The structured behavioral format allows interviewers discretion in deciding whether and how to probe for additional information and in interpreting the implications of applicants' answers for their standing on the behavioral dimensions.

SUMMARY

There has been a great deal of research regarding the reliability and validity of interviews for selecting individuals for jobs. Some of the earlier reviews suggested that interviews were not reliable methods for collecting information about individuals since interviewers often do not agree on decisions as a result of the interview. Due to their low reliability, the validity of interviews also was brought into question. However, several recent meta-analytic reviews of interview validity suggest that the

LOW	MEDIUM	HIGH
Responses showed limited use of potential human and material resources. Answers suggested that repondent may work harder, but that work may not be completed to specifications and would involve little cooperation with other employees to complete the job more efficiently.	Responses suggested some use of human and material resources, but the work may have been somewhat inefficient. Responses involved some limited cooperation with others. Work was of average quality.	Responses indicated a great deal of resourcefulness in terms of both human and material resources. The respondent cooperated with supervisors and peers to accomplish work in an efficient, timely manner. Work was of high quality.
1	2 3 4	5

FIGURE 7.2   Example Rating Scale for Scoring Structured Behavioral Interviews on the Dimension "Ability to Plan and Organize Tasks to Meet Deadlines"

interview is more valid than previously believed. This is particularly so if one follows these guidelines:

- To the extent that the interview is structured, it is likely to be reliable and valid. That is, the information obtained from a set of applicants is more likely to be based on similar kinds of content.
- To the extent that the interview is job related (i.e., based on a job analysis), it is likely to be more valid. Information that applicants provide is likely to be more relevant to the job if the questions (whether focusing on past or future behavior) are based on a job analysis.

There are certain contexts in which one interview method may be more appropriate than others. For example, interviews that focus on actions one might take in the future may be more useful when selecting entry-level employees who are not expected to have much job-related experience. These kinds of interviews may also be useful when diagnosing training needs of junior employees. Determining what such individuals would do in a given situation might help identify areas for future development.

In contrast, interviews that focus on past experiences may be more useful for making promotion decisions when one wishes to use past behavior to predict future behavior. Interviews that focus on the past may also be useful for career counseling when the focus is on current strengths and weaknesses and how they may be useful in new jobs or careers. Remedial counseling, when the goal is to correct past performance, also is a good use of interviews that focus on past behavior.

The main difference between situational interviews and structured behavioral interviews is that situational interviews focus on questions requiring an applicant to project what his or her behavior might be in a given situation. Structured behavioral interviews focus on questions about what applicants did in past situations resembling those that could occur on the job (Motowidlo et al., 1992). Both the situational and structured behavioral interviews are structured because all interviewers ask the same questions of all interviewees. Both methods rely on a critical incident job analysis for the development of interview questions. Both techniques include behavioral rating scales, developed from results of a job analysis, that interviewers use to record their evaluations of applicants' responses.

REFERENCES

Arvey, R. D., & Campion, J. E. (1982). The employment interview: A summary and review of recent research. *Personnel Psychology, 35,* 281–322.

Campion, M. A., Campion, J. E., & Hudson, J. P., Jr. (1994). Structured interviewing: A note on incremental validity and alternative question types. *Journal of Applied Psychology, 79,* 998–1002.

Campion, M. A., Pursell, E. D., & Brown, B. K. (1988). Structured interviewing: Raising the psychometric properties of the employment interview. *Personnel Psychology, 41,* 25–42.

Carlson, R. E. (1967). Selection interview decisions: The effect of interviewer experience, relative quota situation, and applicant sample on interviewer decisions. *Personnel Psychology, 20,* 259–290.

Conway, J. M., Jako, R. A., & Goodman, D. F. (1995). A meta-analysis of interrater and internal consistency reliability of selection interviews. *Journal of Applied Psychology, 80,* 565–579.

Dipboye, R. L. (1982). Self-fulfilling prophecies in the selection interview. *Academy of Management Review, 7,* 579–586.

Dunnette, M. D., Arvey, R. D., & Arnold, J. A. (1971). *Validity study results for jobs relevant to the petroleum refining industry.* Minneapolis: Personnel Decisions. (Also published as American Petroleum Institute Report No. 754)

Field, H. S., & Gatewood, R. D. (1989). Development of a selection interview: A job content strategy. In R. W. Eder & G. R. Ferris (Eds.), *The employment interview: Theory, research and practice* (pp. 143–157). Newbury Park, CA: Sage.

Flanagan, J. C. (1954). The critical incident technique. *Psychological Bulletin, 51,* 327–358.

Gottfredson, L. S. (1986). The *g* factor in employment [Special issue]. *Journal of Vocational Behavior, 29*(3).

Hakel, M. D., Hollemann, T. D., & Dunnette, M. D. (1970). Accuracy of interviewers, certified public accountants, and students in identifying the interests of accountants. *Journal of Applied Psychology, 54,* 115–119.

Hakel, M. D., Ohnesorge, J. P., & Dunnette, M. D. (1970). Interviewer evaluations of job applicants' résumés as a function of the qualifications of the immediately preceding applicants: An examination of contrast effects. *Journal of Applied Psychology, 54,* 27–30.

Huffcutt, A. I. (1992). *An empirical investigation of the relationship between multidimensional degree of structure and the validity of the employment interview.* Unpublished doctoral dissertation, Texas A&M University, College Station.

Huffcutt, A. I., & Arthur, W. (1994). Hunter and Hunter (1984) revisited: Interview validity for entry-level jobs. *Journal of Applied Psychology, 79,* 184–190.

Huffcutt, A. I., Roth, P. L., & McDaniel, M. A. (1996). A meta-analytic investigation of cognitive ability in employment interview evaluations: Moderating characteristics and implications for incremental validity. *Journal of Applied Psychology, 81,* 459–473.

Hunter, J. E., & Hunter, R. F. (1984). The validity and utility of alternative predictors of job performance. *Psychological Bulletin, 96,* 72–98.

Janz, T. (1982). Initial comparisons of patterned behavior description interviews versus unstructured interviews. *Journal of Applied Psychology, 67,* 577–580.

Janz, T. (1989). The patterned behavior description interview: The best prophet of the future is the past. In R. W. Eder & G. R. Ferris (Eds.), *The employment interview: Theory, research and practice* (pp. 158–168). Newbury Park, CA: Sage.

Kennedy, R. (1986). An investigation of criterion-related validity for the structured interview. Master's thesis, East Carolina University.

Landy, F. J. (1985). The psychology of work behavior. Homewood, IL: Dorsey Press.

Landy, F. J., & Bates, F. (1973). Another look at contrast effects in the employment interview. *Journal of Applied Psychology, 57,* 23–27.

Latham, G. P. (1989). The reliability, validity and practicality of the situational interview. In R. W. Eder & G. R. Ferris (Eds.), *The employment interview: Theory, research and practice* (pp. 169–182). Newbury Park, CA: Sage.

Latham, G. P., Saari, L. M., Pursell, E. D., & Campion, M. A. (1980). The situational interview. *Journal of Applied Psychology, 65,* 422–427.

Locke, E. A. (1968). Toward a theory of task motivation and incentives. *Organizational Behavior and Human Performance, 3,* 157–189.

Mayfield, E. C. (1964). The selection interview: A re-evaluation of published research. *Personnel Psychology, 17,* 239–260.

McDaniel, M. A., Whetzel, D. L., Schmidt, F. L., & Maurer, S. (1994). The validity of employment interviews: A comprehensive review and meta-analysis. *Journal of Applied Psychology, 79,* 599–616.

Motowidlo, S. J., Carter, G. W., Dunnette, M. D., Tippins, N., Werner, S., Burnett, J. R., & Vaughan, M. J. (1992). Studies of the structured behavioral interview. *Journal of Applied Psychology, 77,* 571–587.

Mullins, T. W. (1982). Interviewer decisions as a function of applicant race, applicant quality, and interviewer prejudice. *Personnel Psychology, 35,* 161–174.

Parsons, C. K, & Linden, R. C. (1984). Interviewer perceptions of applicant qualification: A multivariate field study of demographic characteristics and nonverbal cues. *Journal of Applied Psychology, 69,* 557–568.

Pulakos, E. D., & Schmitt, N. (1995). Experience-based and situational interview questions: Studies of validity. *Personnel Psychology, 48,* 289–308.

Reilly, R. A., & Chao, G. T. (1982). Validity and fairness of some alternative employee selection procedures. *Personnel Psychology, 35,* 1–62.

Ryan, A. M., & Sackett, P. R. (1989). Exploratory study of individual assessment practices: Interrater reliability and judgments of assessor effectiveness. *Journal of Applied Psychology, 74,* 568–579.

Ulrich, L., & Trumbo, D. (1965). The selection interview since 1949. *Psychological Bulletin, 63,* 100–116.

Valenzi, E., & Andrews, I. R. (1973). Individual differences in the decision processes of employment interviewers. *Journal of Applied Psychology, 58,* 49–53.

Wagner, R. (1949). The employment interview: A critical review. *Personnel Psychology, 2,* 17–46.

Webster, E. C. (1962). *Decision making in the employment interview.* Montreal: Industrial Relations Center, McGill University.

Wiesner, W. H., & Cronshaw, S. F. (1988). The moderating impact of interview format and degree of structure on the validity of the employment interview. *Journal of Occupational Psychology, 61,* 275–290.

Wright, O. R. (1969). Summary of research on the selection interview since 1964. *Personnel Psychology, 22,* 391–413.

Wright, P. M., Lichtenfels, P. A., & Pursell, E. D. (1989). The structured interview: Additional studies and a meta-analysis. *Journal of Occupational Psychology, 62,* 191–199.

Background Data

Michael D. Mumford
Deborah L. Whetzel

OVERVIEW

Background data items, in which individuals are asked to recall and report their typical behaviors or experiences in a referent situation likely to have occurred earlier in their lives (Mumford & Owens, 1987), represent a standardized paper-and-pencil technique for collecting life history information (Nickels, 1994). An item might ask "How many books have you read in the last year?" or "How often have you fixed broken appliances?" To answer these questions, people choose the answer from a predefined list of alternatives that provides the best description of their past behavior and experiences.

Background data questions have been extensively used in personnel selection (Owens, 1976). Reviews by Ghiselli (1973), Hunter and Hunter (1984), Mumford and Owens (1987), and Reilly and Chao (1982) indicate that background data measures are effective predictors of job performance, typically yielding criterion-related validity coefficients in the .40–.50 range. In addition, as Mitchell (1994) points out, background data scales appear to have incremental validity over traditional aptitude and ability measures.

Background data items often are used for purposes other than personnel selection. For example, Gessner, O'Connor, Clifton, Connelly, and Mumford (1993) and Gessner, O'Connor, Mumford, Clifton, and Smith (1995) have shown how background data items can be used to identify developmental events that lead to destructive tendencies and life situations likely to provoke expression of these tendencies. Other studies by Schaefer and Anastasi (1969) and Mumford, O'Connor, Clifton, Connelly, and Zaccaro (1993) indicated that these items can also be used to examine the development of leadership and creativity.

In this chapter, we describe the development and use of background data items in the context of personnel selection. In the first section, we discuss personnel selection issues and describe different types of item content, the kinds of questions that stimulate accurate recall, and different methods of scaling items. The next section of this chapter discusses the psychometric characteristics of background data items. Finally, we explain how to generate background data items and how to scale items after pretesting.

PERSONNEL SELECTION ISSUES

ITEM RELEVANCE

When background data items are used for personnel selection, a variety of issues needs to be considered. Background data items should be developed that describe situations to which all groups of applicants have had potential exposure (Stone, Stone-Romero, & Eddy, 1995). Restrictive situations, to which only a privileged few would have been exposed, create the perception of bias and are of little use in comparing applicants (e.g., questions about yacht clubs). Further, items should be written in a way that minimizes social stereotyping. For example, questions such as "To what extent do you enjoy knitting?" or "To what extent do you enjoy football?" are inappropriate. In personnel selection, the concern is the individual, not the individual's environment (Guion, 1966). Therefore, it is common practice to focus on behavior and experiences that are under the individual's control (e.g., things a person did rather than things done to the person; Gandy, Dye, & McLane, 1994).

FAKING

When applying for a job, there is a tendency to present oneself in the best way possible. Thus, applicants may respond to questions in a way that they think an employer would consider favorable to obtain a higher score (i.e., faking). Although the extent to which faking affects the validity of background data measures is unclear, the need to obtain an accurate appraisal of life histories has led to a number of attempts to minimize faking (Lautenschlager, 1994; Kluger & Colella, 1993). One way to control for the effects of faking is through the use of statistical techniques. For example, Norman (1963) showed how items can be weighted to control for faking, which results in deceptive answers being assigned mean scores.

Another method of controlling faking concerns the items themselves. For example, including impossible life event items (e.g., "Did you ever win a [nonexistent] award?") is a strategy used to control for faking. Kilcullen, White, Mumford, and Mack (1995) found that background data items are less likely to be subject to faking than personality items requiring projections about future behavior. Klein and Owens (1965) found that applicants were likely to fake when they had an accurate picture of the job and items could readily be mapped onto this idealized picture. In a study of foreign service applicants, Mumford (1994) found that faking was reduced when applicants could not find obvious "right" and "wrong" answers to background data items. Faking on background data items might be minimized by avoiding the use of "loaded" items— items that are linked to stereotypic ideas of the job. A related issue concerns minimizing the use of items that are likely to elicit socially desirable responses. Appropriate and inappropriate items that address these issues are shown in Table 8.1.

The type of faking controls just described are appropriate when the construct being measured requires subjective judgment. In many cases, background data items can be written to capture verifiable, factual aspects of life history. Asher (1972) and Mael and Hirsch (1993) stated that objective and potentially verifiable items are less likely to be faked when applicants believe that their responses might be verified. An example of a verifiable item would be, "What was your grade-point average in high school?"

ITEM CONTENT

Background data measures represent an assessment technique in which items are defined by the nature and structure of people's lives as they unfold over time (Mumford, Reiter-Palmon, & Snell, 1994). Most theorists suggest that people's life histories unfold as a dynamic interaction between characteristics of the individual and the situations to which

TABLE 8.1   Examples of Appropriate and Inappropriate Items
That Address Faking Issues

Faking Issues	Appropriate Items	Inappropriate Items
Restrictive	How many of the following activities have you participated in during the past year? 1. Sky diving 2. Scuba diving/ snorkeling 3. Hiking 4. Camping	How often have you been scuba diving in the past year?
Social Stereotyping	How important has it been for you to have co-workers who showed an interest in your projects?	How often have you enjoyed working with women who were very nurturing?
Controllability	When choosing houses or apartments, how likely are you to look in uncrowded suburbs or in the country?	What was the size of the town in which you grew up?
Job Relevance	How many days per week do you typically stay late to finish something at work?	How many times per month do you go to church?
Verifiable	What was your average pay raise over the last five years?	Are you typically seen as a better performer than your peers?
Social Desirability	How often have you gone out of your way to spend time with unpopular colleagues?	How important has it been for you to be friends with your co-workers?
Loaded	How often have you continued to put in extra time on a project to compensate for mistakes made by management?	How hard have you worked on assignments?

the individual has been exposed (Caspi, 1987; Lerner & Tubman, 1989; Magnusson, 1988; Schooler, 1990). Thus, individual characteristics influence perceptions of the environment, the kinds of situations encountered, behavior in these situations, and the outcomes of situa-

TABLE 8.2   Six Types of Background Data Item Content

Item Type	Openness to Experience	Achievement Motivation
Situational Exposure	How many times did your family move while you were in grade school and high school?	How much encouragement did your parents give you when you were trying to do something new?
Situational Choice	How often have you taken a class simply to learn something new?	How many difficult classes did you take in high school?
Behavior in Situation	How often have you looked for a new way to complete an assignment?	How often have you put aside other tasks to complete a difficult assignment?
Reactions to a Situation	How much have you enjoyed meeting new people at parties?	To what extent have you felt proud after completing a difficult assignment?
Others' Reactions to a Situation	How often have people described your approach to problems as different or unusual?	How often has your supervisor thanked you for putting in extra time on a project?
Outcomes Associated with Situational Exposure	How many times has a project you worked on resulted in a patent or publication?	How often have you been asked to step in when someone else was having difficulty finishing a piece of work?

tional exposure. The outcomes of this interaction, through mechanisms such as learning, memory, and cognition, lead to changes in individual development. These changes, however, often tend to be self-reinforcing as people seek out situations where existing characteristics will contribute to performance.

Background data items specify situations likely to have occurred in a person's life, and then ask about that person's typical behavior in the situation (Mumford & Owens, 1982). Six types of questions are typically asked: (1) Situational Exposure, (2) Situational Choice, (3) Behavior in a Situation, (4) Reactions to a Situation, (5) Other People's Reactions to a Situation, and (6) Outcomes of Situational Exposure. Examples of these six types of item content that assess the constructs of Openness to Experience and Achievement Motivation are shown in Table 8.2.

Because people's lives are complex and varied, one could develop thousands of background data items to predict performance for any given job. To develop a manageable number of items, background data items are typically generated that tap specific predictor constructs thought to underlie performance. Such constructs usually are identified through job analysis, as described in Chapters 2, 3, and 4, by having subject matter experts brainstorm lists of knowledges, skills, abilities, and other characteristics (KSAOs). Thus, items may be generated to assess Openness to experience if we are interested in predicting the performance of behavioral scientists; items examining Attention to detail may be useful for predicting performance in clerical jobs; and items examining Willingness to work in extreme weather conditions may be useful for predicting performance in outdoor jobs, such as apprentice electrician.

Background data items do not directly ask individuals to evaluate their relative standing on a particular construct. Instead, such items ask how a construct might have manifested itself in different situations. Since people behave differently from one situation to the next, the situational bounding of background data items is a critical consideration in developing reliable and valid background data measures. Questions typically examine how the variable manifests itself across a range of situations (e.g., work, school, leisure activities, family, and friends; Epstein & O'Brien, 1985). Responses to a particular background data item are of little use; it is the pattern of responses across different situations that enables valid and reliable prediction. Thus, most background data inventories contain between 10 and 30 questions to assess any given construct. The number of constructs measured using background data items depends on the testing time allowed, as well as other measures in a battery that assess similar constructs. Chapter 5 describes the development of test plans, in which the measurement methods for assessing various constructs are specified.

To interpret responses to background data items, relevant questions must be asked about life situations. Since the situations individuals are exposed to change over time, and since people from different backgrounds may be exposed to different types of situations (Ferguson, 1967; Revo, 1976), different items may need to be written to measure a construct (e.g., achievement motivation) for different age groups and organization levels (e.g., apprentice electricians vs. journeymen electricians). It is essential to tailor item content to the situations to which members of the applicant pool are likely to have been exposed. Two sets of example items measuring Conscientiousness follow. In the first set, the construct is assessed for two different age groups; in the second set, the construct is assessed for two different kinds of jobs. All four questions are of the item type Behavior in a Situation (see Figure 8.2).

Age groups:

> Adolescence: How important was it for you to get A's and B's in your high school classes?
>
> Adulthood: How important has it been for you to get ratings of "excellent" on your performance evaluations?

Different kinds of jobs:

> Apprentice electrician: How important has it been for you to inventory your tools at the end of the day?
>
> Journeyman electrician: How frequently have you been able to complete construction projects on time and within budget?

RECALL OF LIFE EXPERIENCES

Since responding to background data items relies on individual memory, it is important to consider what people remember about their lives and how those memories are retrieved (Asher, 1972). A number of studies have examined the nature and structure of autobiographical recall (Barsalou, 1988; Conway, 1990; Kolodner, 1984; Reiser, Black, & Abelson, 1985; Robinson & Swanson, 1990). These studies indicate that autobiographical memory is organized and recalled in terms of categories reflecting different types of goal-relevant events (e.g., taking a vacation). These event categories provide summary information about key actions and relevant goals and include information about participants, locations, outcomes, and affect. Both temporal sequencing and event similarity may be used to organize the event summaries that provide the working raw material for autobiographical memory.

Several studies have documented the ability to recall prior behavior and experiences using background data items. In one study, Shaffer, Saunders, and Owens (1986) asked undergraduates to complete 118 background data items. The undergraduates' parents were also asked to describe their children using the same items. Generally, a high level of agreement was observed between the undergraduates' and parents' responses, although somewhat greater agreement was found when people were asked to report about observable behavior rather than subjective feelings. Other studies by McCrae and Costa (1988) and Roberts, Block, and Block (1978) also provide evidence for the surprising accuracy of autobiographical recall, at least when there is no motive for faking.

TABLE 8.3   Examples of Background Data Items
That Encourage Good and Poor Levels of Recall

Item Types	Good Recall	Poor Recall
Event Summaries	How often were you able to improve your grades in a class when you did poorly on the first test?	How much did you improve your grade on your algebra test?
Goal Relevant	How often have you been angry with someone who took advantage of a co-worker?	How often have you been angry?
Event Organizers	When meeting new people, how easy is it for you to introduce yourself?	How easy is it for you to introduce yourself?
Relevant Events	How difficult was it for you to learn calculus in college?	How difficult was it for you to learn addition in elementary school?

Accurate recall is facilitated when background data items are structured to be consistent with the nature of autobiographical memory. Clifton (1994) found that more accurate recall was observed on background data items written to capture summaries of past behavior than on items written to capture summaries of discrete, somewhat atypical events. He found that background data items linked to the goals and outcomes of people's actions were associated with better recall than items that asked people to report past behavior out of context.

Several conclusions can be drawn about the nature of effective background data items from research on the nature of autobiographical memory. First, good items should seek to assess event summaries, not narrowly defined behaviors. Second, items should reflect goal-relevant behavior and experiences, rather than behavior and experiences taken out of context. Third, it may be useful to provide temporal or event organizers (e.g., in high school). Fourth, items should focus on salient, developmentally significant events, rather than on routine events. Fifth, items should focus on recent events (i.e., those occurring in the last few years), rather than on events that occurred some time ago. Examples of background data items that encourage good and poor levels of recall are shown in Table 8.3.

SCALING METHODS

After items are pretested on a sample of examinees, the item data are used to group items into categories or scales. The psychometric characteristics of four methods for scaling items are described in the next section, and methods for actually scaling items are described later in this chapter. We provide a brief description here to introduce each method.

Empirical scaling procedures typically are used to select and weight items on the basis of their ability to differentiate membership in higher- and lower-performing criterion groups (Hogan, 1994). Rather than understanding constructs that account for prediction, predictive efficiency is established through demonstrated prediction of criterion performance. In the *rational scaling* approach to scaling, the test developer identifies and defines an individual difference variable (based on job analysis, as described in Chapters 2, 3, and 4) and writes questions to elicit information regarding the manifestation of the characteristic (Hough & Paullin, 1994). Item inclusion is based on the test developer's judgment of the relevance of the item to the characteristic or construct. The *factorial scaling* approach assumes that some basic structure of individual differences exists and that this structure can be discovered through factor or cluster analysis (Burisch, 1984). As such, the internal structure of the item pool determines the placement of an item with a particular scale and its direction of keying. *Subgrouping* procedures identify groups of individuals whose prior behavior and experiences are similar enough to be summarized with little loss in information about individual group members (Hein & Wesley, 1994). Subgroups are defined by the items through the application of profile similarity measures (e.g., distances and correlations) and clustering algorithms.

PSYCHOMETRIC CHARACTERISTICS OF BACKGROUND DATA ITEMS

Background data measures have a number of psychometric characteristics that make them useful for predicting job performance. First, background data measures are highly reliable (Shaffer et al., 1986). Second, background data measures have acceptable levels of validity (Brown, 1994). Third, background data measures have less adverse impact against minority groups than many other types of measures commonly used to predict performance (Mumford & Owens, 1987). Following are discussions of these three characteristics.

RELIABILITY

Empirical Scales

For empirical scales, in which items are weighted to the extent that they differentiate between desirable and undesirable criterion groups, test-retest is an important measure of reliability. The few studies that report test-retest reliability describe values ranging from .60 to .96, with the level being partially determined by time between testing sessions and by item type (Brush, 1974; Chaney, 1964; McManus & Mitchell, 1987).

Rational Scales

Internal consistency reliability is a major concern when developing rationally based or homogeneous scales. Research shows that rational scaling procedures yield reliable background data scales. Mumford, Costanza, Connelly, and Johnson (1996) found that scales developed using these procedures produce internal consistency coefficients in the low .70s. Stricker's (1989) final five biodata-based personality scales yielded coefficient alpha reliability estimates of .66 to .78. Goldberg (1972) found internal consistency reliability values for 22 homogeneously developed scales ranging from .48 to .88, with a mean of .74.

Factorial Scales

In factorial approaches, in which dimensions are discovered empirically through factor analysis, it is important that the resulting dimensions be internally consistent. Results of internal consistency analyses by Baehr and Williams (1967) and Owens (1976) suggest that typical dimension reliabilities are in the .70s range. A concern related to reliability is the consistency of factor structures when applied to new samples. Research suggests that different factor structures are likely for men and women (Owens, 1976) and for different age groups (Mumford et al., 1983). Given such differences, one might expect there to be different factor structures for different racial and ethnic groups, which can be problematic for applied selection purposes.

Subgrouping

This approach to biodata keying is based on the belief that people grouped on the basis of the pattern of their prior experiences will behave similarly in the future (Brown, 1994). The purpose of this method is to identify coherent groups of people based on responses to biodata items. Concerning reliability, cluster analysis results will only be stable if the measures that are clustered are reliable. A concern with this approach involves the reproducibility of the subgroups in a new setting. Research reported by Mumford and Owens (1987) suggests relatively positive results for the subgrouping approach evaluated in their large-scale biodata research program.

VALIDITY

Empirical Scales

This approach to scaling biodata items tends to yield validity estimates that are often higher than other approaches (Asher, 1972; Henry, 1966; Mumford & Owens, 1987; Owens, 1976; Reilly & Chao, 1982; Schuh, 1967). For selection into the U.S. civil service, Gandy, Outerbridge, Sharf, and Dye (1990) report the cross-validity (the predictor-criterion correlations that resulted from application of the scoring keys developed on each sample half to the independent half) of the Individual Achievement Record (IAR) to be .33 and .32. Little shrinkage occurred in the validity coefficients in the cross-validities, providing strong support for the robustness of the empirical keys developed on large samples ($N = 13,000$).

A question regarding the validity of biodata concerns the extent to which validity is generalizable across situations, or whether validity estimates for an instrument are only applicable for the population being studied. Many researchers have suggested that the validity of such instruments is situation specific. However, Schmidt and Rothstein (1994) conducted a meta-analysis using 79 validity coefficients and found a mean true validity of .36 with ratings on "Ability to perform," and .34 with ratings on "Performance of duties." The standard deviations of true validities were .082 and .104, respectively; and the 90% credibility values were .26 and .20, respectively. These findings show that valid biodata scales can be developed for multiple settings. Results of a study by Rothstein, Schmidt, Erwin, Owens, and Sparks (1990) suggest that biodata validity may not be specific to a particular organization and that validity may not be moderated by age, sex, race, education, tenure, or previous experience. They caution that their results do not indicate that the level of generalizability they found can always be expected from biodata, and that given conventional methods of biodata instrument construction, these results likely represent the exception rather than the rule.

Rational Scales

Mumford et al. (1996) found that when rationally developed background data scales were used to predict performance, they yielded initial validities in the low .40s, which, when cross-validated, shrank by roughly .05 to .10 points. Mumford and his colleagues indicate that the resulting scales showed construct validity, yielding theoretically meaningful patterns of relationships with external reference measures (Kilcullen et al., 1995; Mumford, Baughman, Threlfall, Costanza, & Uhlman, 1993). These validity coefficients are comparable to those obtained from empirical keys, and support the idea that rational scales and empirical keys are equally effective predictors of job performance (Hough & Paullin, 1994). As Mumford and his colleagues point out, however, rational scales maintain the constructs underlying initial item generation. As a result, it becomes possible to accrue a wider range of construct validation evidence for rational scales, using techniques such as convergent and discriminant validation.

Factorial Scales

A concern when validating factorial scales is the likely difference between applicant and incumbent samples. Basing development efforts on an employee sample could yield scales that only are appropriate for current employees. Research suggests that validities can be substantial, though typically lower than those associated with empirical approaches (Fuentes, Sawyer, & Greener, 1989; Mitchell & Klimoski, 1982; Mumford & Owens, 1987). Because items are scaled in terms of empirically identified constructs, a variety of construct validation analyses can be conducted that often are useful for theory development.

Subgrouping

Research reported by Mumford and Owens (1987) has shown subgroup status to be a valid predictor in 80 to 90% of the studies conducted. Areas of performance included academic achievement, vocational interests, drug use, personality, social behavior, and motivation.

ADVERSE IMPACT

Mumford and Owens (1987) indicate that background data measures have less adverse impact on minority groups than do many other types of measures commonly used to predict performance. Reilly and Chao (1982) reviewed 11 background data studies that reported ethnic subgroup data and found significant mean differences in three cases. They concluded that for empirically keyed forms, a relationship exists between criterion mean differences and background data mean differences. When criterion differences are large, adverse impact will exist. However, background mean differences will be smaller where criterion mean differences are smaller. This means that when there are relatively large differences in criterion (e.g., job) performance, there will be greater adverse impact than when there are smaller differences in criterion performance.

Research on the IAR (Gandy et al., 1990) indicated that females averaged slightly higher scores than males. In addition, Whites averaged higher scores than African Americans and Hispanics; however, these differences in score levels between Whites and minority groups were small relative to those typically found on ability tests. No statistically significant differences in subgroup validities were found and comparisons of subgroup standard errors, regression slopes, and intercepts (Cleary, 1968) failed to indicate any unfairness to minorities and gender groups.

HOW TO GENERATE BACKGROUND DATA ITEMS

To develop background data items that provide a fair and accurate portrayal of an individual's life history, one must identify how various characteristics of the individual, particularly those differential characteristics likely to affect job performance, have manifested themselves in the individual's daily life. To do this, two key steps are required (Mumford et al., 1996). First, one must identify constructs that predict job performance. In Chapter 3, we described how to identify KSAOs. After a list of KSAOs is developed, one must determine the appropriate method for measurement, as described in Chapter 5. Second, hypotheses must be developed about why a given behavior or experience in a situation might serve as an appropriate marker of the target construct using our understanding of the construct and available psychological theory (Messick, 1995).

There are two broad frameworks for identifying constructs leading to the development of background data items. In the person-oriented approach, constructs such as spatial ability and reading skills are used to develop background data items. For example, one might try to assess mechanical ability by asking, "Did you ever build a model airplane that flew?" This item, along with a number of other items intended to assess mechanical ability, might then be used to predict performance on a variety of jobs (e.g., electrician, engineering, computer programming, automotive repair) in which mechanical ability is known to be an important determinant of performance. Illustrations of this approach may be found in Mumford, O'Connor et al. (1993) and DuBois, Loevinger, and Gleser (1952).

In contrast, the job-oriented approach leads to the creation of items that focus on prior behavior similar to that found on the job. These questions center on the performance of duties and their associated tasks. Methods for identifying duties and tasks were described in Chapter 3. Illustrations of the job-oriented approach to item development may be found in Hough (1984) and Pannone (1984). For example, to assess Organizational Skills for journeyman electricians, one might ask, "To what extent do you take extra time to order enough materials to ensure sufficient supplies are on hand for a job?" Although this job-oriented approach typically yields items that have face validity, it may not be useful for entry-level positions in which most applicants lack relevant job experience. Because behaviorally oriented items tend to be highly loaded, care must be taken to minimize faking. Despite these concerns, the job-oriented approach, like the person-oriented approach, requires explicit hypotheses to generate background data measures likely to result in good prediction. The remainder of this section describes four methods for generating background data items. We then describe item response formats and suggest methods for assembling a background data questionnaire. These procedures reflect practices that have resulted in demonstrably valid background data measures. Other methods may be feasible, depending on the purpose for which such measures are developed.

CONSTRUCT-BASED ITEM GENERATION

Once a set of constructs has been identified and defined, background data items can be developed. A procedure frequently used to develop items is described by Mumford et al. (1996) and Mumford and Stokes (1992). The procedure begins by assembling a group of five or six psychologists, drawn from diverse backgrounds, who have some formal training and experience in developing background data measures. Typically, multiple sessions are needed to generate items. During the course of a two-hour session, panel members usually can generate items for two or three constructs. Prior to starting item generation, panel members are asked to review the job analysis, in which the constructs are identified. In addition, available research that describes the nature of the constructs, their development, and the ways in which these characteristics influence performance in various situations should be reviewed. For example, for the construct Achievement Motivation, one might review McClelland (1975) and Atkinson and Raynor (1974). Additionally, panel members are given a description of the population to which these measures will be applied and are asked to think about job-relevant situations that most individuals in the population would have encountered.

At the beginning of an item generation session, panel members are given a definition of a relevant construct and are asked to discuss its importance for predicting performance in the population. Panel members are then given about 15 to 20 minutes to write items that they think reflect how the construct might manifest itself in people's interactions with situations they are likely to have encountered. Although no constraints are placed on item content, panel members are asked to generate items of the types described previously: (a) Situational Exposure, (b) Situational Choice, (c) Behavior in the Situation, (d) Reactions to the Situation, (e) Others' Reactions, and (f) the Outcomes of Behavior in this Situation. In addition, panel members are asked to keep in mind the nature of autobiographical memory.

After writing the items for a particular construct, panel members are asked to read their items aloud. If the hypothesis underlying an item is not immediately apparent to other panel members, the panel member reading an item will be asked to state the hypothesis underlying the item. The other panel members are asked to review the proposed item for its appropriateness for the construct and for the population, the feasibility of developing an objective scoring system for the item, and the appropriateness of the item for use in personnel selection. Items that lack adequate construct relevance, are not under the individual's personal control, are highly loaded, or appear to be unfair with respect to situational exposure and stereotypes are eliminated. Other problems pointed out by panel members, such as social desirability, are noted and an attempt is made to rewrite the item. These procedures typically yield 50 to 60 candidate items that might be used to measure a construct.

Once the candidate items have been generated, psychologists familiar with the job should review the items to ensure that a full range of potential item content is covered. During this review, the psychologists edit items for clarity and develop response options for each item consistent with the question being asked. The questions are then presented to job incumbents, who assess item clarity and relevance and identify any potentially sensitive items for the target population. Table 8.4 shows examples of items resulting from this procedure for the constructs Initiative and Integrity. They were created for the job of apprentice electrician.

TABLE 8.4   Examples of Construct-Based Items for
the Constructs "Initiative" and "Integrity"

Initiative	Integrity
How often have you worked late to finish a construction project?	How important is it to you that your fellow electricians play by the rules?
How often have you suggested to someone that he or she should try a different way to solve a problem?	How often have you become angry with people who took advantage of their position?
How often have you been the one who had to deliver the "bad news" to a journeyman or foreman?	How often have you pulled someone aside who was "taking things out" on someone you know?
How many times have you volunteered to help someone finish a project?	To what extent have you been embarrassed when someone has praised your work, but not the work of your co-workers?
How much do you enjoy discussing new material that you had to learn on your own?	How likely are you to report that someone has taken credit for work that really was done by someone else?

BEHAVIORAL CONSISTENCY ITEM GENERATION

One alternative to construct-based item generation is the behavioral consistency approach advocated by Fine and Cronshaw (1994), Hough (1984), Pannone (1984), and Schmidt et al. (1979). The behavioral consistency approach assumes that past performance is the best predictor of future performance. Thus, this approach is often used to predict performance in populations in which people have prior experience working on tasks similar to those that they will confront on the job.

As with the construct-based approach, it is essential that a thorough and comprehensive job analysis be available for describing the work itself and the conditions under which the work is performed. This job information may be collected using a variety of techniques, including task analysis and critical incidents, described in Chapters 3 and 4, respectively. Job analysis results are provided to a panel of three or four psychologists who have some familiarity with the job. Each panel member is asked to identify prior behaviors and experiences that reflect good performance in situations similar to those found on the job. For example, if the electrician job is found to require Organizational Skills, then panel members would be asked to write background data items that reflect prior performance in organizing activities. Thus, one might develop background data items asking "How often did you set goals/milestones for construction projects?" or "How frequently did you complete projects on time?" or "Did you ever receive a raise or bonus that was based on the quality of the project you completed?"

Items written by one panel member should be reviewed by other panel members and necessary revisions should be made. Unlike construct-based item generation, however, the behavioral consistency approach assumes prior performance opportunities. As a result, all items should be reviewed to ensure that: (a) most applicants would have had opportunities to engage in the situations suggested in the item(s), and (b) the questions have a clear relationship to job performance. Following are examples of job-oriented behavioral consistency items developed to predict performance of electrician apprentices:

1. How difficult has it been for you to work outside on a cold day?
2. How difficult has it been for you to install electrical appliances (e.g., dishwashers)?
3. How many times have you repaired electrical appliances around your home?
4. Relative to other people you know, how much do you enjoy working outdoors?
5. How frequently have you assembled pieces of electrical equipment (e.g., radios)?

Although the behavioral consistency approach is most appropriate for predicting the performance of applicants who have prior job experience, this approach can be extended to settings where such experience is lacking. One strategy, described by Fine and Cronshaw (1994) and illustrated by Keinan, Friedland, Yitzhaky, and Moran (1981), involves identifying life situations in the past that have similar performance demands to the construct of interest. Thus, for the construct Organizational Skills, one might ask, "To what extent do you prepare to go on a long trip?"

In contrast to construct-based item generation, the behavioral consistency approach yields items with greater job relevance, thereby minimizing negative applicant reactions. However, these items are somewhat transparent, making it easier for applicants to fake good responses. As a result, when the behavioral consistency approach is used, it is necessary to develop items that can be verified.

TABLE 8.5   Examples of Career History Items Developed to
Predict the Performance of Apprentice Electricians

- How many jobs have you had where you had to work with people who did not share your goals?
- How much have you enjoyed getting a new idea into shape so someone could work with it?
- How important has it been for you to be able to learn from more experienced persons?
- To what extent have you learned from projects that were not completed on time?
- How often have you collaborated with people on two or three different projects at the same time?
- How often have disagreements with other co-workers improved the quality of your work?
- How much have you enjoyed working with people who had a clear idea of what they wanted to do?

CAREER HISTORY ITEM GENERATION

A third approach to developing background data items is the career history approach. This is similar to the behavioral consistency approach because it focuses on performance in a particular setting. However, generating these items involves identifying the experiences and behaviors that contribute to the development of performance capabilities, rather than past performance.

One method for developing career history items relies on the performance of successful individuals who are asked to write essays describing their lives, or incidents that were key events in shaping their careers (Russell, Mattson, Devlin, & Atwater, 1990). The essays, typically drawn from at least 20 to 40 successful individuals, are reviewed by psychologists who identify: (1) key themes or dimensions in the essays, and (2) the prior behaviors and experiences related to performance. For example, based on information from the essays, it might be found that successful journeyman electricians were mentored and were given challenging construction projects. Thus, items might be written asking "In the course of your career, have you worked closely with senior-level journeyman electricians?" or "How often have you been asked to take over a project that had run into problems?" Table 8.5 provides examples of career history questions developed to predict performance of apprentice electricians.

There are several possible variations of this approach. For example, one might obtain essay or interview information from both successful and unsuccessful individuals and then use the content differences observed between these groups as a basis for item generation. Alternatively, prior research may be used to specify key developmental issues (Russell & Domm, 1990; Russell & Kuhnert, 1992). Regardless of the method for developing career history items, an item content review should be conducted if the items are used in making selection or promotion decisions.

There are practical issues that should be considered when using this approach for generating items. First, career history items often reflect things done to the individual and limited personal control may make it difficult to justify using such items. Second, items typically are generated to predict performance in a career field rather than performance on a particular job, so evidence will be needed to ensure job relevance.

ARCHIVAL ITEM GENERATION

The three item generation approaches just described require a substantial amount of time and energy to develop an adequate item pool. This has led many investigators to consider using previously developed, or archived, background data items. As such, this actually is an item selection rather than an item development strategy.

The archival approach begins with a literature review to identify existing background data items used to predict performance. This review focuses on studies in which background data items were used to predict performance in the target job, or in a similar job. Items are selected that yield high correlations with the criterion and/or are found to measure constructs that predict performance.

When using an archival approach, it is important to remember that background data items developed for one population may not apply to other populations. Thus, items must be reviewed for a given population by a panel of psychologists familiar with that population. Inappropriate items should be eliminated or rewritten to increase relevance to the target population. Because substantial revisions may be required if archival items are used, revised items should be reviewed by a new panel of psychologists to ensure the appropriateness of item content. To the extent that item content is revised, it may be necessary to consider the impact of such revisions on item validity and internal consistency estimates. Examples of items that were developed for a civilian population and then edited to make them appropriate for a military population are shown in Table 8.6.

TABLE 8.6   Examples of Items Developed for a Civilian Population
and Edited to Be Made Appropriate for a Military Population

Civilian	Military
How much have you enjoyed having a job that let you do things your own way?	How important has it been for you to have supervisors who would listen to your suggestions?
How important has it been for you to be friends with the people working for you?	How important has it been for you to know when subordinates are having personal problems?
How successful have you been persuading people to see things differently?	To what extent have you been able to avoid giving orders?

ITEM RESPONSE FORMATS

It is crucial that response formats be consistent with item content and the nature of the target population. Item response options using a five-point ordinal scale (e.g., 1 = Strongly Disagree; 5 = Strongly Agree) are recommended for several reasons. First, the findings reviewed by Owens (1976) indicate that items using such response options are more reliable than items using other kinds of response options. Second, scoring items on an underlying continuum enables a wider range of analyses to be conducted. Third, although 400 subjects are sufficient for scaling and validating continuum type items, larger sample sizes of up to 2,000 subjects are required when non-continuous items are used because each response option is treated as an item (Mumford & Owens, 1987).

ASSEMBLING A QUESTIONNAIRE

After the items and item response options have been developed, one may assemble the background data questionnaire for pretesting. Typically, the questionnaire begins with a few verifiable, job-related items. This presentation strategy helps induce an honesty set and minimizes negative applicant reactions. After the first 10 to 15 items, however, items should be presented in random order. Use of random ordering is necessary because it is easier for people to guess at the scoring protocol if all items for a given construct are presented together. People can answer three or four background data items per minute; thus, questionnaires typically contain 300 to 400 items. After all the data are collected from the pretest sample, item characteristics are assessed. Some items may require minor revision in wording to make them more understandable. If the revisions are substantial (i.e., likely to result in changed statistical characteristics), the items will need to be pretested again prior to operational use. Following is a description of methods for analyzing item characteristics and developing scales consisting of appropriate items.

HOW TO SCALE AND VALIDATE BACKGROUND DATA ITEMS

The purpose of scaling is to identify items to be incorporated in the final version of a background data questionnaire because they measure the constructs of interest and/or they predict job performance. Usually only one-third of the items administered to a pretest sample are retained in the final version of a background data questionnaire. Four general strategies are commonly used for scaling background items: (1) empirical keying, (2) rational scaling, (3) factorial scaling, and (4) subgrouping (Mumford & Owens, 1987). These strategies are described below. These four scaling methods were introduced in our earlier discussion of biodata issues that arise in the course of personnel selection.

EMPIRICAL KEYING

Three methods frequently used for empirical keying of background data measures are the correlational method (Lecznar & Dailey, 1950), the differential regression method (Malone, 1978), and the weighted application blank (England, 1971). The first two methods are most appropriate when continuous response options (e.g., five-point Likert scales, where 5 = Strongly Agree and 1 = Strongly Disagree) are used. The correlational method involves using the magnitude and direction of the correlation between the item and the criterion to determine the item's weight. Item weights may be the actual correlation coefficients or unit weights, depending on the statistical significance of the item correlation (e.g., plus or minus 1 for $p < .05$). As a general rule of thumb, a minimum correlation of .10 to .15 has been suggested for inclusion of items on a scale (Mumford & Owens, 1987). The differential regression method uses least squares regression analysis to develop a model that maximizes explained criterion variance. Items are selected based on the increment in criterion variance accounted for over and above that which is explained by items already in the equation. It is important to note that variance maximizing procedures are likely to capitalize heavily on chance, making cross-validation (using weights from one sample to predict performance for a different sample, and vice versa) very important. The weighted application blank method involves weighting alternative response options on the basis of differences in option selection for different criterion groups. Criterion groups that are well differentiated are needed to produce differential weights and these groups need to be large enough to produce stable weights. There are several studies that suggest that unit weights produce scales with validities that are nearly equal to those produced with differential weights (Dawes, 1971).

In sum, the empirical keying approach requires that items be retained for the final version of the questionnaire based solely on their ability to predict performance on a criterion (Mumford & Owens, 1987). To develop empirical keys, scores of a criterion group (people who are good performers on the criterion) are compared to the scores of a reference group (population of job applicants). Mean differences (when items are scored on a continuum) or percent response differences (when response options are scored) are obtained reflecting the differences between these groups. Items are retained if they discriminate between criterion group and reference group members; items that fail to distinguish between these groups are eliminated. Retained items are weighted based on the magnitude of the differences observed between the groups (Hogan, 1994).

An empirical keying strategy maximizes the ability of background data items to predict performance on the criterion of interest. In addition, evidence suggests that empirical keys may be less sensitive to faking than other alternative scaling procedures (Russell & Kuhnert, 1992). However, empirical keys suffer from a number of limitations. As Wernimont (1962) pointed out, empirical keys tend to be unstable, requiring cross-validation studies if one is to obtain an adequate estimate of their predictive validity. Moreover, the reliability or construct validity of empirical keys is difficult to assess because of the heterogeneity of items.

The most important problem associated with empirical keys is that scaling is based on a single criterion measure. As a result, the empirical key can be no better than the criterion used to define performance. If the criterion measure is biased or contaminated, these deficiencies may also appear in the resulting background data measures (Mumford & Owens, 1987). Thus, whenever an empirical keying strategy is used to develop background data scales, evidence must be provided that the criterion measure is a valid, reliable, and unbiased measure of performance.

RATIONAL SCALING

Rational scaling is another technique for scaling background data items. Using this approach, items are scaled according to the constructs the items are intended to measure. Scores on construct-oriented scales are then used to predict performance on various criteria of interest. Thus, constructs, rather than items, serve as predictors in the rational scaling approach.

One clear advantage of rational scaling is that the problems associated with poor criterion measures do not contaminate the background data items. Another advantage of this approach is that the scales can be used to predict performance of different criteria in different settings (Hough & Paullin, 1994), assuming there is reason to believe that the constructs are relevant as indicated by a job analysis. The ability to generalize to different settings and criteria, however, is not the most important characteristic of rational scales. Rational scales preserve the substantive framework underlying initial item generation. As a result, rational scales allow a greater range of validation tests, particularly the kind of theoretically driven construct validation tests that provide the best evidence for the meaningfulness of the measures (Lawshe, 1985; Messick, 1995). When background data measures are developed using this approach, they often provide a vehicle for theory development as well as serve as a selection tool (Mumford, Baughman, Uhlman, Costanza, & Threlfall, 1993; Mumford, Gessner, Connelly, O'Connor, & Clifton, 1993).

The procedures used to develop rational scales are straightforward (Mumford & Owens, 1987; Mumford & Stokes, 1992; Mumford, Uhlman, & Kilcullen, 1992). Initially, all items that measure a construct are identified and a total construct score is obtained by summing scores for each construct. Individual items are then correlated with total construct scores and the reliability of each scale is established by examining the internal consistency of the items included in the scale.

Variations on this procedure include assigning items to multiple scales if the initial hypothesis underlying item development suggests that the item is complex, in the sense that it marks multiple constructs and the resulting item-total correlations justify inclusion in multiple scales. Another variation on the approach, suggested by Mael (1991), Mumford et al. (1992), and Mumford and Owens (1982), involves examining item-criterion correlations as well as inter-item correlations when forming scales. This approach involves some elements of empirical keying and rational scaling, and is useful when there is some ambiguity about the way constructs manifest themselves in performance. However, problems with generalizability and construct measurement may arise if an adequate criterion is not available.

FACTORIAL SCALING

The approach used to develop factorial scales is similar to the approach used to develop rational scales inasmuch as items are retained to form construct scales based on observed correlations. In factor analytic scaling, however, items are not assumed to measure a particular construct. Instead, constructs are induced from the data using factor analysis to group items together that yield similar patterns of responses. Typically, items are retained if they yield correlations above .30 with a particular factor. Factor scores are obtained by summing scores on the items assigned to a factor.

Factor analysis is used when there is no theory about a set of constructs that provide the basis for scaling. This does not mean that one should factor analyze any collection of background data items. Items should be systematically developed and factoring should be used to articulate the kind of constructs accounting for item responses (Schoenfeldt & Mendoza, 1994). Factoring is most frequently used when a theory does not define the constructs of concern, as is often the case when the career history approach has been used to develop background data items (Mumford, Stokes, & Owens, 1990). An extended discussion of factor analysis, as applied to background data items, is beyond the scope of this chapter. Interested readers should consult Schoenfeldt and Mendoza (1994).

SUBGROUPING

The fourth major scaling technique used to develop background data measures is subgrouping (Owens, 1968, 1971; Owens & Schoenfeldt, 1979). Subgrouping is more closely related to empirical keying than to rational or factorial scaling. Like empirical keying, in which scaling is based on the identification of groups of people who are high performers, subgrouping strategies attempt to identify naturally occurring groups of people. Rather than defining groups based on performance on a particular criterion measure, groups are defined by clustering together people who have similar responses on a number of background data items. Subgrouping attempts to identify types of people who have similar life histories. Responses are scaled by assigning respondents to the group that is most similar to their pattern of item responses. Group membership—defined by the type of life history on the background data items—then provides the basis for making predictive statements about a person.

Subgrouping techniques are still in their initial stage of development and, with a few notable exceptions (e.g., Brush & Owens, 1979), are not commonly applied in performance prediction. Over the years, a systematic research program conducted by Owens and his colleagues (Mumford & Owens, 1984; Mumford et al., 1990; Stokes, Mumford, & Owens, 1989; Owens & Schoenfeldt, 1979; Mumford, Snell, & Reiter-Palmon, 1994) has provided some understanding of the nature of subgrouping. Subgroups appear to capture people's models of themselves and their world that guide their behavior in a variety of situations. Because subgroups appear to capture these broad organizing structures, they are more useful in predicting long-term outcomes and making classification or placement decisions than in predicting performance for a particular job (Gustafson & Mumford, 1995; Katzell, 1994). For the purpose of personnel selection, care must be taken that the subgrouping strategy does not result in different keys or clusters for protected groups. For legal reasons, different keys may be viewed as providing an advantage to subgroups, even if that is not the intention of background item developers.

SUMMARY

In this chapter, several issues concerning the development and scaling of background data items for predicting job performance have been discussed. However, little effort has been made to describe many other potential applications of background data measures. For example, we only briefly touched on the application of background data measures to the study of adult development (Gessner et al., 1993; Morrison, 1994) and the classification and assessment of qualitative individual differences (Gustafson & Mumford, 1995; Mumford, Snell, & Hein, 1993).

There are several important conclusions about the development of background data measures, as related to personnel selection, that need to be emphasized. First, the development of background data items is a difficult and time-consuming task. One must have an understanding of adult development and its implications for appropriate item content, and items must be written in such a way that they permit accurate recall of past experiences. Further, items must be appropriate for use in personnel selection (i.e., they cannot refer to issues regarding marital status or gender- and race-related issues). Further, item development requires an understanding of the nature of the constructs of interest and the ways in which they influence people's behavior and experiences.

Second, item writers need to understand both the job, which requires a thorough job analysis, and the ways in which relevant constructs manifest themselves in people's lives. Scoring strategies and validation procedures must be carefully planned, taking into account both the nature of the items and the intended applications of the measure. Indeed, one should expect to devote substantial resources to item development as well as to scaling and validation efforts.

Third, gains in validity are only one reason for applying background data measures. The use of background data items inherently is a contextual assessment technique in which performance is examined in the context of the situations to which people have been exposed. As such, background data measures evidence less adverse impact than other types of measures.

Fourth, because of the contextual nature of biodata items, it is important to revalidate them every five to seven years. Revalidation is essential because the life history characteristics of job applicants may change, resulting in the need for new kinds of background data items. In addition, scoring keys may be compromised, resulting in the need for new selection measures. In fact, whenever possible, it is desirable to develop two or three alternative forms of a background data inventory and carefully monitor changes in applicants' mean scores to ensure that the test has not been compromised.

As is the case with any assessment, the value of the resulting inferences about performance can be no better than the kinds of questions asked. This chapter has provided some initial guidelines for framing these questions and developing background data measures that can be used to predict performance in a number of different settings.

REFERENCES

Asher, E. J. (1972). The biographical item: Can it be improved? *Personnel Psychology, 25,* 251–264.

Atkinson, J. W., & Raynor, J. O. (1974). *Motivation and achievement.* Washington, DC: Winston.

Baehr, M. E., & Williams, G. B. (1967). Underlying dimensions of personal background data and their relationship to occupational classification. *Journal of Applied Psychology, 51,* 481–490.

Barsalou, L. W. (1988). The content and organization of autobiographical memories. In V. Reisser & E. Winograd (Eds.), *Remembering reconsidered: Ecological and traditional approaches to the study of memory* (pp. 143–243). Cambridge, England: Cambridge University Press.

Brown, S. H. (1994). Validating biodata. In G. S. Stokes, M. D. Mumford, & W. A. Owens (Eds.), *Biodata handbook: Theory, research and use of biographical information in selection and performance prediction* (pp. 199–236). Palo Alto, CA: Consulting Psychologists Press.

Brush, D. (1974). *Predicting major field of college concentration with biographical and vocational interest data: A longitudinal study.* Unpublished master's thesis, University of Georgia, Athens.

Brush, D. H., & Owens, W. A. (1979). Implementation and evaluation of an assessment and classification model for manpower utilization. *Personnel Psychology, 32,* 369–383.

Burisch, M. (1984). Approaches to personality inventory construction: A comparison of merits. *American Psychologist, 39,* 214–227.

Caspi, A. (1987). Personality in the life course. *Journal of Personality and Social Psychology, 53,* 1203-1213.

Chaney, F. B. (1964). *The life history antecedents of selected vocational interests.* Unpublished doctoral dissertation, Purdue University, West Lafayette, IN.

Cleary, T. A. (1968). Test bias: Prediction of grades of negro and white students in integrated colleges. *Journal of Educational Measurement, 5,* 155-124.

Clifton, T. C. (1994). *Background data and autobiographical memory: Effects of item types and task characteristics.* Unpublished doctoral dissertation, George Mason University, Fairfax, VA.

Conway, M. A. (1990). Associations between autobiographical memory and concepts. *Journal of Experimental Psychology: Learning, Memory and Cognition, 16,* 749–812.

Dawes, R. (1971). The robust beauty of improper linear models in decision making. *American Psychologist, 37,* 571–582.

DuBois, P. H., Loevinger, J., & Gleser, G. C. (1952). *The construction of homogeneous keys for a biographical inventory.* Lackland AFB, TX: Air Force Human Resources Laboratory.

England, G. W. (1971). *Development and use of weighted application blanks* (Bulletin No. 55). Minneapolis: University of Minnesota, Industrial Relations Center.

Epstein, S., & O'Brien, E. J. (1985). The person-situation debate in historical and current perspective. *Psychological Bulletin, 48,* 513–537.

Ferguson, L. W. (1967). Economic maturity. *Personnel Journal, 46,* 22–26.

Fine, S. A., & Cronshaw, S. (1994). The role of job analysis in establishing the validity of biodata. In G. S. Stokes, M. D. Mumford, & W. A. Owens (Eds.), *Biodata handbook: Theory, research and use of biographical information in selection and performance prediction* (pp. 39–64). Palo Alto, CA: Consulting Psychologists Press.

Fuentes, R. R., Sawyer, J. E., & Greener, J. M. (1989). *Comparison of the predictive characteristics of three biodata scaling methods.* Paper presented at the annual meeting of the American Psychological Association, New Orleans.

Gandy, J. A., Dye, D. A., & McLane, D. N. (1994). Federal government selection: The Individual Achievement Record. In G. S. Stokes, M. D. Mumford, & W. A. Owens (Eds.), *Biodata handbook: Theory, research and use of biographical information in selection and performance prediction* (pp. 275–310). Palo Alto, CA: Consulting Psychologists Press.

Gandy, J. A., Outerbridge, A. N., Sharf, J. C., & Dye, D. A. (1990). *Development and initial validation of the Individual Achievement Record (IAR).* Washington, DC: U.S. Office of Personnel Management.

Gessner, T. E., O'Connor, J. A., Clifton, T. C., Connelly, M. S., & Mumford, M. D. (1993). The development of moral beliefs: A retrospective study. *Current Psychology, 12,* 236–254.

Gessner, T. E., O'Connor, J. A., Mumford, M. D., Clifton, T. C., & Smith, J. A. (1995). Situational variables influencing the propensity for destructive acts: Taxonomy development and validation. *Current Psychology, 13,* 303–325.

Ghiselli, E. E. (1973). The validity of aptitude tests in personnel selection. *Personnel Psychology, 26,* 461–477.

Goldberg, L. R. (1972). Parameters of personality inventory construction and utilization: A comparison of prediction strategies and tactics. *Multivariate Behavior Research Monograph* (No. 72-2).

Guion, R. M. (1966). *Personnel selection.* New York: McGraw-Hill.

Gustafson, S. B., & Mumford, M. D. (1995). Personal style and person-environment fit: A pattern approach. *Journal of Vocational Behavior, 46,* 163–188.

Hein, M., & Wesley, S. (1994). Scaling biodata through subgrouping. In G. S. Stokes, M. D. Mumford, & W. A. Owens (Eds.), *Biodata handbook: Theory, research and use of biographical information in selection and performance prediction* (pp. 171–198). Palo Alto, CA: Consulting Psychologists Press.

Henry, E. R., (1966). *Research conference on the use of autobiographical data as psychological predictors.* Greensboro, NC: Creativity Research Institute, Richardson Foundation.

Hogan, J. B. (1994). Empirical keying of background data measures. In G.S. Stokes, M. D. Mumford, & W. A. Owens (Eds.), *Biodata handbook: Theory, research and use of biographical information in selection and performance prediction* (pp. 69–108). Palo Alto, CA: Consulting Psychologists Press.

Hough, L. M. (1984). Development and evaluation of the "accomplishment record" method of selecting and promoting professionals. *Journal of Applied Psychology, 69,* 135–146.

Hough, L. M., & Paullin, C. (1994). Construct-oriented scale construction: The rational approach. In G. S. Stokes, M. D. Mumford, & W. A. Owens (Eds.), *Biodata handbook: Theory, research and use of biographical information in selection and performance prediction* (pp. 109–146). Palo Alto, CA: Consulting Psychologists Press.

Hunter, J. E., & Hunter, R. F. (1984). Validity and utility of alternative predictors of job performance. *Psychological Bulletin, 96,* 72–98.

Katzell, R. A. (1994). Contemporary meta-trends in industrial and organizational psychology. In H. C. Triandis, M. D. Dunnette, & L. M. Hough (Eds.), *Handbook of industrial and organizational psychology* (Vol. 4, pp. 1–89). Palo Alto, CA: Consulting Psychologists Press.

Keinan, G., Friedland, N., Yitzhaky, J., & Moran, A. (1981). Biographical, physiological, and personality variables as predictors of performance under sickness-inducing motion. *Journal of Applied Psychology, 66,* 233–241.

Kilcullen, R. N., White, L., Mumford, J. D., & Mack, H. (1995). Assessing the construct validity of rational biodata scales. *Military Psychology, 7,* 17–28.

Klein, S. P., & Owens, W. A. (1965). Faking of a scored life history blank as a function of criterion objectivity. *Journal of Applied Psychology, 49,* 452–454.

Kluger, A. N., & Colella, A. (1993). Beyond the mean bias: The effect of warning against faking on biodata item variances. *Personnel Psychology, 46,* 763–780.

Kolodner, J. L. (1984). *Retrieval and organizational strategies in conceptual memory.* Hillsdale, NJ: Erlbaum.

Lautenschlager, G. J. (1994). Accuracy and faking of background data. In G. S. Stokes, M. D. Mumford, & W. A. Owens (Eds.), *Biodata handbook: Theory, research and use of biographical information in selection and performance prediction* (pp. 341–420). Palo Alto, CA: Consulting Psychologists Press.

Lawshe, C. H. (1985). Inference from personnel tests and their validity. *Journal of Applied Psychology, 70,* 237–238.

Lecznar, W. B., & Dailey, J. T. (1950). Keying biographical inventories in classification test batteries. *American Psychologist, 5,* 279.

Lerner, R. M. & Tubman, J. G. (1989). Conceptual issues in studying continuity and discontinuity in personality development across life. *Journal of Personality, 57,* 343–374.

Mael, F. A. (1991). A conceptual rationale for the domain and attributes of biodata items. *Personnel Psychology, 44,* 763–792.

Mael, F. A., & Hirsch, A. C. (1993). Rainforest empiricism and quasi-rationality: Two approaches to objective biodata. *Personnel Psychology, 46,* 719–738.

Magnusson, D. (1988). Individual development from an interactional perspective. In D. Magnusson (Ed.), *Paths through life* (pp. 1–18). Hillsdale, NJ: Erlbaum.

Malone, M. P. (1978). *Predictive efficiency and discriminatory impact of verifiable biographical data as a function of data analysis procedure.* Unpublished doctoral dissertation, University of Minnesota, Minneapolis.

McClelland, D. C. (1975). *Power: The inner experience.* New York: Irvington.

McCrae, R. R., & Costa, P. T. (1988). Recalled parent-child relations and adult personality. *Journal of Personality, 56,* 417–433.

McManus, M. A., & Mitchell, T. W. (1987). *Test and retest reliability of the Career Profile.* Hartford, CT: Life Insurance Marketing and Research Association.

Messick, S. (1995). Validity of psychological assessment: Validation of inferences from persons' responses and performance as scientific inquiry into score meaning. *American Psychologist, 50,* 741–744.

Mitchell, T. W. (1994). The utility of biodata. In G. S. Stokes, M. D. Mumford, & W. A. Owens (Eds.), *Biodata handbook: Theory, research and use of biographical information in selection and performance prediction* (pp. 485–516). Palo Alto, CA: Consulting Psychologists Press.

Mitchell, T. W., & Klimoski, R. J. (1982). Estimating the validity of cross-validity estimation. *Journal of Applied Psychology, 71,* 311–317.

Morrison, R. F. (1994). Biodata applications in career development research and practice. In G. S. Stokes, M. D. Mumford, & W. A. Owens (Eds.), *Biodata handbook: Theory, research and use of biographical information in selection and performance prediction* (pp. 451–484). Palo Alto, CA: Consulting Psychologists Press.

Mumford, M. D. (1994). *Report on the 1993 foreign service exam: The stability of background data measures.* Fairfax, VA: Author.

Mumford, M. D., Baughman, W. A., Threlfall, K. V., Costanza, D. P., & Uhlman, C. E., (1993). Personality, adaptability and performance: Performance on well-defined and ill-defined problem solving tasks. *Human Performance, 5,* 241–285.

Mumford, M. D., Baughman, W. A., Uhlman, C. E., Costanza, D. P., & Threlfall, K. V. (1993). Personality variables and skill acquisition: Performance at different stages of practice on a complex task. *Human Performance, 6,* 345–381.

Mumford, M. D., Costanza, D. P., Connelly, M. S., & Johnson, J. F. (1996). Item generation procedures and background data scales: Implications for construct and criterion-related validity. *Personnel Psychology, 49,* 361–398.

Mumford, M. D., Gessner, T. E., Connelly, M. S., O'Connor, J. A., & Clifton, T. C. (1993). Leadership and destructive acts: Individual and situational influences. *Leadership Quarterly, 4,* 115–148.

Mumford, M. D., O'Connor, J. A., Clifton, T. C., Connelly, M. S., & Zaccaro, S. J. (1993). Background data constructs as predictors of leadership behavior. *Human Performance, 5,* 241–285.

Mumford, M. D., & Owens, W. A. (1982). Life history and vocational interests. *Journal of Vocational Behavior, 21,* 330–348.

Mumford, M. D., & Owens, W. A. (1984). Individuality in a developmental context: Some empirical and theoretical considerations. *Human Development, 27,* 84–108.

Mumford, M. D., & Owens, W. A. (1987). Methodology review: Principles, procedures, and findings in the application of background data measures. *Applied Psychological Measurement, 11,* 1–31.

Mumford, M. D., Reiter-Palmon, R., & Snell, A. M. (1994). Background data and development: Structural issues in the application of life history measures. In

G. S. Stokes, M. D. Mumford, & W. A. Owens (Eds.), *Biodata handbook: Theory, research and use of biographical information in selection and performance prediction* (pp. 555–584). Palo Alto, CA: Consulting Psychologists Press.

Mumford, M. D., Shaffer, G. S., Jackson, K. E., Neiner, A., Denning, D., & Owens, W. A. (1983). *Male-female differences in the structure of background data measures.* Athens, GA: Institute for Behavioral Research.

Mumford, M. D., Snell, A. N., & Hein, M. A. (1993). Varieties of religious experience: Continuity and change in religious involvement. *Journal of Personality, 61,* 69–88.

Mumford, M. D., Snell, R. M., & Reiter-Palmon, R. (1994). Personality and background data: Life history and self-concepts in an ecological system. In G. S. Stokes, M. D. Mumford, & W. A. Owens (Eds.), *Biodata handbook: Theory, research and use of biographical information in selection and performance prediction* (pp. 553–625). Palo Alto, CA: Consulting Psychologists Press.

Mumford, M. D., & Stokes, G. S. (1992). Developmental determinants of individual action: Theory and practice in applying background data measures. In M. D. Dunnette & L. E. Hough (Eds.), *Handbook of industrial and organizational psychology* (Vol III, pp. 62–138) Palo Alto, CA: Consulting Psychologists Press.

Mumford, M. D., Stokes, G. S., & Owens, W. A. (1990). *Patterns of life adaptation: The ecology of human individuality.* Hillsdale, NJ: Erlbaum.

Mumford, M. D., Uhlman, C. E., & Kilcullen, R. N. (1992). The structure of life history: Implications for the construct validity of background data scales. *Human Performance, 5,* 104–137.

Nickels, B. J. (1994). The nature of biodata. In G. S. Stokes, M. D. Mumford, & W. A. Owens (Eds.), *Biodata handbook: Theory, research and use of biographical information in selection and performance prediction* (pp. 1–16). Palo Alto, CA: Consulting Psychologists Press.

Norman, W. T. (1963). Personality measurement, faking and detection: An assessment of a method for use in personnel selection. *Journal of Applied Psychology, 47,* 317–324.

Owens, W. A. (1968). Toward one discipline of scientific psychology. *American Psychologist, 23,* 782–785.

Owens, W. A. (1971). A quasi actuarial basis of individual assessment. *American Psychologist, 26,* 992–999.

Owens, W. A. (1976). Background data. In M. D. Dunnette (Ed.), *Handbook of industrial and organizational psychology* (pp. 609-643). Chicago: Rand McNally.

Owens, W. A., & Schoenfeldt. L. F. (1979). Toward a classification of persons. *Journal of Applied Psychology, 64,* 569–607.

Pannone, R. D. (1984). Predicting test performance: A content valid approach to screening applicants. *Personnel Psychology, 37,* 507–514.

Reilly, R. A., & Chao, G. T. (1982). Validity and fairness of some alternative employee selection procedures. *Personnel Psychology, 35,* 1–62.

Reiser, B. J., Black, J. B., & Abelson, R. P. (1985). Knowledge structures in the retrieval and organization of autobiographical memories. *Cognitive Psychology, 17,* 89–137.

Revo, B. (1976). Using biographical information to predict the success of men and women in the Army. *Journal of Applied Psychology, 61,* 106–118.

Roberts, K. V., Block, J., & Block, J. E. (1978). Relationship between personality and life history. *Journal of Personality, 46,* 223–242.

Robinson, J. A., & Swanson, L. (1990). Autobiographical memory: The next phase. *Applied Cognitive Psychology, 4,* 321–335.

Rothstein, H. R., Schmidt, F. L., Erwin, F. W., Owens, W. A., & Sparks, C. P. (1990). Biographical data in employee selection: Can validities be made more generalizable? *Journal of Applied Psychology, 75,* 175–184.

Russell, C. J., & Domm, D. R. (1990, April). *On the construct validity of biographical information: Evaluation of a theory-based measure of item generation.* Paper presented at the annual meeting of the Society for Industrial and Organizational Psychology, Inc., Miami Beach, FL.

Russell, C. J., & Kuhnert, K. W. (1992). New frontiers in management selection systems: Where measurement technologies and theory collide. *Leadership Quarterly, 3,* 109–135.

Russell, C. J., Mattson, J., Devlin, S. E., & Atwater, D. (1990). Predictive validity of biodata items generated from retrospective life experience essays. *Journal of Applied Psychology, 75,* 569–580.

Schaefer, C. E., & Anastasi, A. (1969). A biographical inventory for identifying creativity in adolescent boys. *Journal of Applied Psychology, 52,* 42–48.

Schmidt, F. L., Caplan, J. R., Bemis, S. E., Decuir, R., Dunn, C., & Antone, L. (1979). *The behavioral consistency method for unassembled examining.* Washington, DC: U.S. Office of Personnel Management.

Schmidt, F. L., & Rothstein, H. R. (1994). Application of validity generalization to biodata scales in employment selection. In G. S. Stokes, M. D. Mumford, & W. A. Owens (Eds.), *Biodata handbook: Theory, research and use of biographical information in selection and performance prediction* (pp. 237–260). Palo Alto, CA: Consulting Psychologists Press.

Schoenfeldt, L. F., & Mendoza, G. C. (1994). Developing and using factorially derived biographical scales. In G. S. Stokes, M. D. Mumford, & W. A. Owens (Eds.), *Biodata handbook: Theory, research and use of biographical information in selection and performance prediction* (pp. 147–170). Palo Alto, CA: Consulting Psychologists Press.

Schooler, C. (1990). Psychological effects of complex environments during the life span: A review and theory. *Intelligence, 8,* 254–281.

Schuh, A. L. (1967). The predictability of employee tenure: A review of the literature. *Personnel Psychology, 20,* 133–152.

Shaffer, G. S., Saunders, V., & Owens, W. A. (1986). Additional evidence for the accuracy of biographical information: Long-term retest and observation ratings. *Personnel Psychology, 39,* 791–809.

Stokes, G. S., Mumford, M. D., & Owens, W. A. (1989). Life history prototypes in the study of human individuality. *Journal of Personality, 57,* 509–545.

Stone, D. L., Stone-Romero, E. F., & Eddy, E. (1995, April). *Factors that influence the perceived invasiveness of biographical data.* Paper presented at the annual conference of the Society for Industrial and Organizational Psychology, Inc., Orlando, FL.

Stricker, L. J. (1989). *Assessing leadership potential at the naval academy with a biographical measure* (Research Report No. RR 89-14). Princeton, NJ: Educational Testing Service.

Wernimont, P. F. (1962). Reevaluation of a weighted application blank for office personnel. *Journal of Applied Psychology, 46,* 417–419.

CHAPTER

9

Low–Fidelity Simulations

Stephan J. Motowidlo
Mary Ann Hanson
Jennifer L. Crafts

OVERVIEW

In addition to paper-and-pencil tests of cognitive ability (Chapter 6), employment interviews (Chapter 7), and background data (Chapter 8), job simulations are another important type of predictor. Job simulations rely on the principle that a person's behavior in certain kinds of situations in the past can predict how he or she is likely to behave in similar situations in the future. This means that one way to predict how effectively job applicants will perform on the job when they become employees is to measure how effectively they perform in a simulation of the job when they are applicants. Some simulations are more realistic than others. Although very realistic simulations might be expected to have an advantage in their predictive potential, they can be so expensive to develop and administer that less realistic simulations often are an attractive alternative.

This chapter discusses the potential usefulness of less realistic (low-fidelity) simulations for predicting job performance. It describes different forms that such simulations might take, summarizes research evidence about their reliability and validity, and describes procedures for developing them.

WHAT IS A LOW-FIDELITY SIMULATION?

A simulation is an abstracted representation of the job. It can be more or less realistic depending on how closely it mirrors the job. We can distinguish four levels of realism, or fidelity, for job simulations.

The most realistic level is a job tryout. For instance, applicants for the job of apprentice electrician would be hired on a temporary basis, their performance would be observed over a trial period, and the decision whether to hire them permanently would be made on the basis of their performance during the trial period. The job tryout is a simulation with such a high degree of fidelity that it is virtually identical to the job itself. The only difference is that applicants performing during the trial period would know that their employment is temporary and that a decision about their continued employment depends on how they perform during the tryout.

Work sample tests represent the next highest level of fidelity. They are less realistic than job tryouts because they present applicants with carefully developed samples of work-related problems and require the applicants to solve the problems as if they were on the job, but without putting them on the job (Asher & Sciarrino, 1974). For instance, applicants for the job of apprentice electrician would be shown an electrical system that has something wrong with the circuitry and they would be asked to repair it. Their performance would be observed and evaluated as they tried to repair the system. Chapter 12 describes methods for developing work sample tests.

Instead of actually having applicants perform the tasks in a job sample, another possibility is to have them describe how they would handle the tasks in a work sample as though they were on the job. This makes the simulation even less realistic; at this third level of fidelity are simulations that present applicants with samples of work problems and require them to describe what they would do instead of actually having them do it (e.g., Hedge & Teachout, 1992). For instance, applicants for the job of apprentice electrician would be shown an electrical system with something wrong in the circuitry and they would be instructed to describe the steps they would take in trying to repair it.

Finally, at the lowest level of fidelity are simulations that present applicants with only a description of the work problem and require them to describe how they would deal with it. The point here is that neither the work sample nor the applicant's response to it is real. Both are hypothetical. Motowidlo, Dunnette, and Carter (1990) used the term *low-fidelity simulation* to describe a simulation that presents a written or oral description of the work situation and then requires applicants to give a written or oral description of how they would respond to it. As an example of a low-fidelity simulation, applicants for the job of apprentice electrician might be told something like this: "Imagine that a customer has a problem with an electrical system in which something is wrong with the circuitry. When turned to a certain voltage, the system cuts off. What steps would you take to repair it?"

Because high-fidelity simulations correspond very closely to features of the task and responses on the job, they might be better predictors of job performance than low-fidelity simulations. However, it often is prohibitively expensive to develop and use highly realistic simulations. Furthermore, it is not clear that any gains in validity from using them as predictors are sufficient to offset such costs. For these reasons, low-fidelity simulations are a promising alternative.

Several low-fidelity simulations have been developed to predict job performance in managerial and supervisory positions (e.g., Anderson et al., 1996; Bruce & Lerner, 1958; Forehand & Guetzkow, 1961; Mandell, 1950; Motowidlo et al., 1990; Mowry, 1957; Rosen, 1961). They have also been developed to predict success in police and corrections work (DuBois & Watson, 1950; Pine, 1994), insurance agent turnover (Dalessio, 1992), success in insurance claim positions (Ashworth & McHenry, 1992), success in telephone sales and collection positions (Phillips, 1992, 1993), and skill in managing conflict (Olson-Buchanan, Drasgow, Moberg, Mead, & Keenan, 1994). Thus, low-fidelity simulations are quite flexible and can be developed for use in a variety of jobs.

THE STRUCTURE AND FORMAT OF LOW-FIDELITY SIMULATIONS

STRUCTURE

There are several alternative structures for presenting the situations and collecting responses in low-fidelity simulations. Some simulations present a situation and then ask respondents to answer several different questions about that situation (e.g., Mowry, 1957). Other simulations present a new situation for each question (e.g., Mandell, 1950). For the responses, the options have included asking respondents:

- What they would do in each situation (e.g., Bruce & Learner, 1958)
- What they would be most and least likely to do in each situation (e.g., Motowidlo et al., 1990)
- To choose the best response (e.g., Phillips, 1992, 1993)
- To choose the best and the second-best responses (e.g., Richardson, Bellows, Henry and Co., 1981)
- What would most likely occur next in a certain problem situation or as the result of a particular administrative decision (Mandell, 1950)

In addition, low-fidelity simulations can either be structured linearly, in which all respondents are presented with the same series of situations regardless of the responses they choose, or they can use a branching format. In the branching format, examinees respond to an initial situation. That response leads to more information about the situation (i.e., a new situation), and respondents are then asked to choose from a new set of response options. The information and response options presented in the later portions of each problem depend on the responses chosen for the initial situation. In other words, respondents are required to make a series of sequential, interdependent decisions.

FORMAT

Low-fidelity simulations have been developed in written formats, interview formats, and video formats. Following is a description of each format.

Written Format

In the written format, individuals are typically provided with a written description of a situation and a set of written response options. They are asked to choose the option (in a multiple-choice format) that best indicates what they would do in that specific situation. Written low-fidelity simulations that use a simple linear structure are typically referred to as situational inventories or situational judgment tests. The term *written simulation* has often been used to describe written, low-fidelity simulations that use a branching format (e.g., Smith, 1985), although these tests are now often administered using computers (e.g., Melnick, 1990).

Interview Format

An alternative to the written format is to present situational information orally as part of an interview. In a linear type of presentation, the interviewee is provided with a job-relevant scenario and asked how he or she would handle the situation (Latham, 1989). The response can take one of several different forms. Structured response options can be provided (e.g., in a multiple-choice format) so that the interviewee must select one option. An alternative is to allow interviewees to use their own words to describe how they would handle the situations in the scenarios. This latter type of response must be coded or scored against a set of criteria, either in real time or later, if responses are captured on audio- or videotape or in interviewer notes. If each scenario is a stand-alone item, then this scoring can take place after the interview. However, if a branching structure is used, then judgments may be required of the interviewer during the interview. For instance, the response to an initial situation may determine the follow-up scenarios that are presented to an interviewee.

The situational interview is a structured interview that incorporates the richness of a job context into the interview questions. Structured interviews and their psychometric properties are described in Chapter 7. Therefore, we will not go into more detail on interview forms of low-fidelity simulations in this chapter.

Video Format

With the growing availability of technology and the flexibility that this offers in test administration, video-based assessment is becoming more commonly used (Dalessio, 1992; Frank, 1993; Jones & DeCotiis, 1986; Pine, 1994; Olson-Buchanan et al., 1994). In a video format, examinees are presented with a series of realistic scenarios based on a job analysis, and they select from among the given response options the one they believe should be taken in each situation presented. In this case, the fidelity of the stimulus (scenario) is relatively high, but response fidelity is still low, because the examinee selects an alternative from those provided rather than generating and carrying out a solution. It is worth noting that although video-based simulations improve the fidelity of low-fidelity simulations, they may actually be *more* expensive to develop than high-fidelity simulations. Development involves not only identifying and enacting work-related situations, but also capturing these situations on video and editing the video to create the final test. Administration, on the other hand, will likely be much more cost efficient than for high-fidelity simulations.

An example of a video-based simulation is the Workplace Situations Test, developed by IBM (Desmarais et al., 1992; Desmarais, Masi, Olson, Barbera, & Dyer, 1994; Dyer, Desmarais, Midkiff, Colihan, & Olson, 1992). Thirty brief scenarios depicting training, workload, interpersonal conflict, and work performance problem situations are presented in video scenes. After each scene, the examinee selects from among several response options.

A few researchers have incorporated a branching structure within the video format to further enhance the realism of these measures. These interactive low-fidelity simulations have been used to measure skills that are difficult to assess through more traditional paper-and-pencil formats. For example, the Allstate Multimedia In-Basket was developed to select claims processors and is designed to assess skills such as problem solving and prioritizing (Ashworth & McHenry, 1992). Olson-Buchanan and colleagues have developed a video simulation to assess conflict resolution skills (Olson-Buchanan et al., 1994; Olson-Buchanan, Drasgow, Moberg, Mead, & Keenan, 1995). For each item, a brief conflict scene is presented; the scene stops at a critical point in the conflict and the examinee is asked to choose one of four possible actions (i.e., response options). Based on the examinee's choice, the scene branches to show the subsequent actions, the conflict escalates again, and the examinee is asked to make another decision about how to handle the conflict.

WHAT DO LOW-FIDELITY SIMULATIONS MEASURE?

Low-fidelity simulations are a method of measurement that can be used to assess many psychological constructs. Therefore, if scores on two different low-fidelity simulations are not highly correlated with each other, it is likely that they are measuring different constructs, even if they were developed to predict performance on the same job. For example, some questions might be developed to measure initiative and effort, while others might be developed to measure attention to detail.

Although low-fidelity simulations might be developed to measure specific personality or ability variables, their unique format (presenting a hypothetical work situation and eliciting a hypothetical response to that situation) lends itself especially well to measuring various forms of job knowledge. As mentioned, the predictive principle behind all simulations, including low-fidelity simulations, is that how people have behaved in certain situations in the past can predict how they will behave in similar situations in the future.

One reason people behave somewhat consistently in similar situations is that through experience they develop beliefs about the best thing to do in certain situations in order to achieve desired results. But some people have better opportunities to have these experiences and some people are better able to take advantage of their experiences and learn from them. As a result, people who have acquired this situational knowledge over time should know better how to deal with certain situations and should be consistently more effective in those situations than people who, for whatever reason, have not acquired that knowledge.

Wagner and Sternberg (1985) developed low-fidelity simulations to measure a construct they called "tacit knowledge," which is knowledge that is not acquired through formal or directed learning, but that is gained as a result of experience and learned informally after exposure to various situations and the consequences of different actions in those situations. Wagner and Sternberg's tests describe work-related situations and goals and ask respondents to rate the importance of various possible actions that might be taken in each situation for reaching the described goals (Wagner & Sternberg, 1985; Jagmin, Wagner, & Sternberg, 1989). Although they do not claim to measure tacit knowledge as defined by Wagner and Sternberg (1985), most low-fidelity simulations used to predict job performance appear to measure job knowledge important for effectively handling various kinds of situations at work, especially interpersonal situations.

PSYCHOMETRIC CHARACTERISTICS OF LOW-FIDELITY SIMULATIONS

RELIABILITY OF LOW-FIDELITY SIMULATIONS

Written Format

Most researchers report that written low-fidelity simulations have at least moderate reliability. Internal consistency reliabilities have ranged from the high .50s to the low .90s (Bruce & Learner, 1958; Mandell, 1950; Motowidlo et al., 1990; Mowry, 1957; Richardson et al., 1981), but it is important to note that some of these tests have been designed to measure multiple constructs, so high internal consistency reliability is not always expected. Test–retest reliabilities have been reported in the .77 to .89 range, depending on the retest interval (Bruce & Learner, 1958; Richardson et al., 1981).

Video Format

Because low-fidelity simulations in video form have only recently been used in personnel selection, very little is known about their reliability. In addition, assessing the reliability of video simulations that use a branching format is problematic, since respondents typically do not complete the same sets of items. Smiderle, Perry, and Cronshaw (1994) assessed the psychometric properties of a widely used video-based transit operator selection test (Municipality of Metropolitan Seattle, 1983). The test developers reported internal consistency reliabilities from .59 to .65 across four samples, but Smiderle et al. (1994) found an alpha coefficient of .47 ($N = 366$) and concluded that its reliability was too low to support its operational use.

VALIDITY OF LOW-FIDELITY SIMULATIONS

Written Format

To assess the validity of low-fidelity simulations in written form, researchers have investigated relations between written situational judgment test scores and scores on measures of job performance, such as performance ratings by supervisors or peers, salary, promotion rate, and success in training.

Researchers generally report significant relationships between written situational judgment test scores and ratings of job performance, with correlations ranging from about .20 to about .50. For example, Phillips (1992) obtained correlations of .18 and .24 ($p < .01$) between scores on her Sales Skills Inventory and two performance rating composites. She obtained correlations ranging from .41 to .45 ($p < .001$) between scores on her Negotiation Skills Inventory and supervisory performance ratings (Phillips, 1993).

Tenopyr (1969) obtained a correlation of .25 ($p < .05$) between scores on the Leadership Evaluation and Development Scale (LEADS) and performance ratings made by labor relations staff for a sample of production managers. Motowidlo et al. (1990) obtained correlations ranging from .28 to .37 ($p < .01$) between scores on their Situational Judgment Inventory and ratings of managers' performance collected using behavior-based rating scales. Forehand and Guetzkow (1961) obtained a correlation of .53 ($p < .01$) between Administrative Judgment Test scores and a composite of 39 dimensional performance ratings made by supervisors. Bruce and Learner (1958) obtained a correlation of .62 ($p < .05$) between Supervisory Practices Test scores and supervisors' rankings of overall performance. Bruce and Learner also compared scores obtained by a large sample of supervisors on their Supervisory Practices Test with those obtained by a large sample of nonsupervisors and report that the supervisors scored significantly higher ($p < .01$).

Scores on situational judgment tests also have been shown to be related to other important organizational criteria such as salary, promotion rate, and tenure. Tenopyr (1969) found that scores on LEADS correlated .36 ($p < .01$), with salary corrected for age and length of service, but LEADS scores were not significantly correlated with seniority. Mandell (1950) reported that correlations between Administrative Judgment Test scores and pay grade ranged from .28 (ns) to .56 ($p < .01$) across the three samples studied, with a median of .52 ($p < .01$). For two other samples, Mandell (1956) reported that correlations between Administrative Judgment Test scores and salary level were .48 ($p < .01$) and .54 ($p < .01$) respectively, and in yet another sample Administrative Judgment Test scores correlated .32 ($p < .01$) with the number of promotions received in a four-year period.

The validity of two additional situational judgment tests—How Supervise? and the Supervisory Profile Record—has been studied more extensively than others. How Supervise? has been administered to a total of over 750,000 individuals (Rosen, 1961), and a great deal of research is available concerning the validity of this test in a wide variety of different organizations (e.g., File & Remmer, 1971; Millard, 1952; Weitz & Nuckols, 1953). Rosen (1961) summarized the available validity data for this test and included comparisons between test scores obtained by more and less effective or experienced supervisors, as well as correlations between How Supervise? scores and several criteria, including supervisor ratings and turnover. The results are somewhat mixed, but Rosen concluded that, in general, the published literature revealed more positive than negative evidence for the validity of this test for predicting managerial success.

The Supervisory Profile Record contains both situational judgment and biodata items. Richardson et al. (1981) described a research program to evaluate this test that involved dozens of samples and a total of over 10,000 examinees. They reported correlations ranging from .22 to .40 ($p < .01$) between Supervisory Profile Record scores and performance ratings made using graphic rating scales that tapped duty elements (e.g., planning employee work), and correlations with "ability" ratings (e.g., ability to train others) ranging from .26 to .48 ($p < .01$). In general, the Supervisory Profile Record shows a more consistent pattern of validities than does the How Supervise? test.

Scores on tacit knowledge measures have been shown to correlate significantly with certain measures of occupational success as well. For example, Wagner and Sternberg (1985) developed two tacit knowledge measures: one for business managers and one for academic professors. For the professors, total tacit knowledge scores correlated significantly with number of publications, number of conferences attended, quality of academic program, and percentage of time spent in research, but not with academic rank or year of degree. They interpreted this pattern of relationships to mean that experience per se does not lead to tacit knowledge. Rather, tacit knowledge is what people learn from experience. For graduate students, scores on the measure of academic tacit knowledge correlated significantly with years of school completed, quality of psychology program, number of research projects, and number of publications, but not with amount of teaching experience. For business managers, scores on a measure of tacit knowledge related to business were correlated with level of company (defined as whether or not the company was included among the top companies in the Fortune 500 list), years of schooling beyond high school, and salary; but not with years of management experience, level of title, or number of employees supervised. Wagner (1987) replicated and extended this research and obtained almost identical results.

Video Format

Less information is available concerning the validity of video low-fidelity simulations, but the validity results available to date are encouraging. Jones and DeCotiis (1986) conducted a concurrent validity study in developing a selection system for hotel employees ($N = 362$) and reported a correlation of .38 with supervisory ratings. Dalessio (1992) found that three empirical keys developed to predict attrition based on a video situational judgment test had low but significant correlations with attrition in cross-validation samples (average $r = .12$; $p < .05$). In a predictive study of bank tellers and customer service representatives, Jones and Youngblood (1993) found that scores on a video-based test of financial services skills correlated significantly ($r = .20$) with supervisor ratings. Conflict resolution skill scores were significantly related to job-related conflict management performance (cross-validated $r = .26$, $p < .01$; Olson-Buchanan et al., 1994). Scores on a video-based situational judgment test for corrections officers were significantly correlated with both performance and attitudinal criteria (Pine, 1994). However, Smiderle et al. (1994) reported that scores on the video-based transit operator test were significantly related to only one of three criterion measures, and that correlation was of limited practical significance.

Limitations

In summary, most of the research has shown scores on low-fidelity simulations to be significantly correlated with a variety of criteria. However, it should be noted that with only a few exceptions (Dalessio, 1992; Jones & Youngblood, 1993), all of the available research has involved concurrent validation designs. Some researchers have argued that, in general, results obtained using concurrent and predictive validation studies do not differ systematically in the overall level of validity obtained (e.g., Barrett, Phillips, & Alexander, 1981), but there is reason to expect that this may not hold true for low-fidelity simulations. If these simulations measure knowledge concerning effective interpersonal behaviors and supervisory practices and if this knowledge is, at least to some extent, learned on the job, predictive and concurrent validities for these simulations would be expected to differ systematically.

HOW TO DEVELOP A LOW-FIDELITY SIMULATION

Although low-fidelity simulations come in a variety of formats, they all have the common feature that they present a description of a situation representing a problem or challenge that might be encountered at work and ask applicants how they would respond to the situation. Situations can be presented in either a written, interview, or video format and responses can be either an oral or written description of the action the applicant might take. Applicants' responses can be in either an open-ended format, in which they describe how they would handle the problem situation in their own words, or a multiple-choice format, in which they select a response from a set of alternatives.

Each format has its own advantages and disadvantages. Video formats, for instance, are appealing for the same reason that many people would rather see a movie than read the book upon which the movie is based— the video format presents problem situations in a way that is easy for applicants to assimilate without having to read descriptions. It is possible that the video format can also include subtleties of the situation that are not easily incorporated in a paper-and-pencil description. However, video formats are more difficult and much more costly to develop than written formats.

Interview formats are appealing because many applicants might prefer to talk to someone than take a paper-and-pencil test and because the interviewer is in a position to probe for additional information if the applicant's first response to a situational question does not include enough detail. But an interviewer can only interview one applicant at a time, while written formats can simultaneously be administered to groups of applicants.

Open-ended response formats are appealing because they allow applicants to describe exactly what they would do instead of having to choose a response option that comes closest to what they would do. They also are easier to develop. In addition, generating the correct solution may involve skills (e.g., writing skill) that are not tapped when respondents are simply asked to identify the correct solution in a multiple-choice format. However, open-ended formats are not as standardized as multiple-choice formats and have to be scored subjectively, a process that can introduce error if scorers use idiosyncratic rules for scoring them.

Multiple-choice formats require more work in the beginning to develop, but once they are developed with appropriate scoring keys, scoring them is a simple matter that can be relegated to a computer.

The rest of this chapter offers a recipe for making a low-fidelity simulation in a written format with multiple-choice response alternatives. For convenience, we will call this type of low-fidelity simulation a *situational inventory*. It has also been called a situational judgment test. Once developed, a situational inventory is easy to administer either individually or to groups of applicants and easy to score either by hand or using a computer. What we offer here is a developmental strategy that combines practices that have been successfully followed in the past to develop demonstrably valid situational inventories. However, other ways to do this also are possible, and they might be as good or even better than the approach we describe.

Figure 9. 1 provides an example of an item that might be included in a situational inventory developed for applicants for a journeyman electrician position. Notice that this item presents a short description of a problem situation that might happen in the job for which the applicant is being considered. It lists five alternative ways to handle the situation and asks the applicant to indicate which one he or she would most likely take and which he or she would least likely take. The item can be scored by giving the applicant one point if the alternative selected as most likely is actually one of the best alternatives for that situation and another point if the alternative selected as least likely is actually one of the worst alternatives.

There are three general stages for developing a situational inventory. First, descriptions of problem situations that might occur at work are developed. Second, a set of multiple-choice response alternatives for

You and another journeyman electrician from another crew are jointly responsible for coordinating a project involving both crews. This other person is not carrying out his share of the responsibilities. You would . . .

Most Likely _____   Least Likely _____

a. Discuss the situation with your foreman and ask him to take it up with the other person's foreman.

b. Remind him that you need his help and that the project won't be completed effectively without a full team effort from both of you.

c. Tell him that he is not doing his share of the work, that you will not do it all yourself, and that if he doesn't start doing more, you'll be forced to take the matter to his foreman.

d. Try to find out why he is not doing his share and explain to him that this creates more work for you and makes it harder to finish the project.

e. Get someone else from his crew to help with the project.

FIGURE 9.1   Sample Item from a Situational Inventory

each problem situation is developed. Third, the best and worst responses in each set are determined in order to develop a scoring key. The key will indicate how to assign points to applicants according to the response alternatives they selected.

DEVELOP DESCRIPTIONS OF PROBLEM SITUATIONS

Problem situations should represent classes of events that actually happen on the job. They should represent classes of problems or challenges that people have to handle effectively or their job performance will suffer. They do not have to reflect matters of critical or monumental importance, but they should not be so minor or trivial that it does not matter how people handle them. Further, they should be difficult enough that there are meaningful differences in how effectively different people handle them.

They should be described in enough detail to provide the cues necessary to distinguish more effective from less effective ways of dealing with them, but not in so much detail that the cues point to a single correct response that will be obvious to everyone. These cues should be general enough that they can be correctly interpreted even by people who have never encountered the situation, as long as they have encountered similar situations in different contexts.

The first step in developing descriptions of problem situations is to do a job analysis. The critical incident approach (described in Chapter 4) is especially useful for this purpose. It involves collecting critical incidents that portray especially effective or ineffective behavior on the job. For instance, to develop a situational inventory for electricians, groups of subject matter experts (experienced electricians) would be assembled and they would be asked to think about occasions when they saw an electrician do something that struck them as especially effective or ineffective. Using special forms designed for this purpose, as described in Chapter 4, they would be asked to write about each critical incident by: (a) briefly noting the background or situation in which the electrician being described did something especially effective or ineffective, (b) describing in some detail exactly what the electrician did that was so effective or ineffective, and (c) briefly noting the outcome of that action. After collecting several hundred of these behavioral critical incidents, the incidents would be grouped into categories according to their behavioral content. In this example, three categories that could emerge from this process might be Planning, Preparing, and Organizing Work; Troubleshooting; and Supervising.

These performance categories would thoroughly describe behavioral patterns that differentiate effective from ineffective electricians, but they would not provide much detailed information about situations or problems that electricians have to confront. For that information, other critical incidents that focus more on situational details would be collected.

Consequently, the second step is to assemble other groups of subject matter experts and ask them to write situational critical incidents. In the electrician example, groups of experienced electricians would be assembled and the set of performance dimensions that emerged from the behavioral critical incidents (e.g., Planning, Preparing, and Organizing Work; Troubleshooting; and Supervising) would be provided. They would then be asked to think about occasions when they, or someone they knew, encountered a special problem in a situation that involved one of the performance dimensions. Again using special forms for this purpose, they would be asked to write about each situational critical incident by: (a) describing the problem in full detail, (b) briefly noting how the electrician in the incident dealt with it, and (c) noting which performance dimension it evoked. Subject matter experts would be asked to write several situational incidents for each of the different performance areas so that there are examples of a wide variety of situational challenges electricians might have to face.

The next step is to group the situational incidents according to content of the scenarios or problems that electricians must handle. One way to do this is to ask several judges (about 10 to 20) to sort them into groups such that if someone can handle one of the situations in a group effectively, chances are he or she could also handle other situations in the same group effectively. Combining judgments of the different judges would show which situations tend to be grouped together most often and this would lead to definitions of situational categories. For instance, in the electrician example, three categories that could emerge might be Reading Blueprints, Customers Who Demand More Than Can Be Delivered, and Completing Jobs on Time. These categories are likely to be more specific than the performance dimensions (which are more broadly defined to cover the whole job) used to elicit the descriptions. The situational categories are based directly on the content of challenges facing the electrician.

With these situational categories in hand, the next step is to select representative situational problems from each one and edit them to a standard form that describes the problem clearly in just a few sentences. Selecting situations from each category helps to ensure that the final situational inventory will include examples of all the important kinds of situational problems that occur on the job. Normally, the final version will also contain multiple situations per situational category. The exact number of situations selected per category will be based on some rational procedure. For example, job experts may be asked to rate the importance of the situational categories, and situations from the more important categories will be more heavily represented on the inventory. Alternatively, individual situations may be mapped to the job performance categories, and importance ratings for these categories can be used to define a rule for selecting scenarios for the inventory.

From a technical standpoint, the larger the number of situational items in the final inventory, the better, but practical considerations limit the number of items that can be included. Situational items like the example shown earlier in Figure 9.1 ("You and another journeyman electrician from another crew are jointly responsible . . . ") take about 90 seconds each to answer. So if the final test is to be no longer than an hour or so, it can include no more than about 40 situational items. To be sure that at least 40 good situational items will be available for the final instrument, at least 50 to 60 problem situations should be prepared at this stage in the development process.

DEVELOP RESPONSE ALTERNATIVES

Response alternatives should represent classes of broadly different strategies for handling each situation. The alternatives should all seem reasonable, but some have to be more correct for the situation than others. The more correct alternatives should be more attractive to applicants with the best potential for success on the job.

One way to develop response alternatives with these characteristics is to collect open-ended responses to the situational problems from job incumbents. This can be done by assembling the situational problems into a questionnaire with about two inches of space below each problem. The questionnaire should be administered to relatively new and inexperienced people on the job (apprentice electricians, in our example), who would be asked to complete the questionnaire by writing a short description of how they would handle each problem in the space provided. If there are too many problems for people to answer all of them, the problems can be divided into two or more shorter questionnaires, but at least 30 or so people should answer each problem to help make sure all the potentially different kinds of responses will be collected.

Taking one situational problem at a time, the responses should be reviewed to identify about five different strategies, without worrying at this point about which are the best and worst responses to the problem.

DEVELOP A SCORING KEY

Finally, a scoring key is developed by collecting judgments from subject matter experts about the effectiveness of the alternative response options for handling each problem situation. The test developer prepares a questionnaire asking subject matter experts to make two kinds of judgments about the response alternatives for each problem situation. First, they judge the effectiveness of each alternative response by rating each response on a scale ranging from very ineffective to very effective. Then they identify the best alternative and the worst alternative for each problem situation. The questionnaire should be completed by about 30 to 50 people who are very experienced and knowledgeable about the job. In our example, they would be experienced electricians.

Using these expert judgments, the test developer computes: (a) the proportion of experts who endorsed each alternative as the most effective, (b) the proportion who endorsed each alternative as least effective,

(c) the mean rating of effectiveness given to each item, (d) the standard deviation around that mean rating, and (e) the intraclass correlation or a similar statistic to show how much the experts agree on their ratings for each set of alternatives.

Situational items for which there is little agreement among experts on the relative effectiveness of alternatives should be dropped. For remaining items, the experts' judgments would be used to identify the best and worst response alternatives for each problem situation.

SUMMARY

Low-fidelity simulations are tests that present descriptions of work situations that might occur on the job and ask applicants how they would handle them. Situational inventories (or situational judgment tests) are low-fidelity simulations in a written format that use a multiple-choice response format. They are based on the idea that people have different levels of knowledge about how best to handle various work situations. By measuring this knowledge, situational inventories have the potential to predict job performance, and results of several studies support their validity in this respect. Developing a situational inventory involves three general stages: (1) preparing descriptions of problem situations, (2) preparing multiple response alternatives for each problem, and (3) identifying the best and worst alternatives for each problem. We concluded this chapter by describing a set of procedures that could be followed to develop a situational inventory according to these three stages.

REFERENCES

Anderson, L. E., Crafts, J. L., Motowidlo, S. J., Peterson, N. G., Reynolds, D. H., Rohrback, M. R., Rosse, R. L., & Smith, D. A. (1996). *Expanding the concept of quality in personnel: Development of predictor and criterion measures.* Alexandria, VA: U.S. Army Research Institute for the Behavioral and Social Sciences.

Asher, J. J., & Sciarrino, J. A. (1974). Realistic work sample tests: A review. *Personnel Psychology, 27,* 519–533.

Ashworth, S. D., & McHenry, J. J. (1992, September). *Development of a computerized in-basket to measure critical job skills.* Paper presented at the fall meeting of the Personnel Testing Council of Southern California, Newport Beach.

Ashworth, S. D., & McHenry, J. J. (1993, April). *Developing a multimedia in-basket: Lessons learned.* Paper presented at the Eighth Annual Conference of the Society for Industrial and Organizational Psychology, Inc., San Francisco.

Barrett, G. V., Phillips, J. S., & Alexander, R. A. (1981). Concurrent and predictive validity designs: A critical reanalysis. *Journal of Applied Psychology, 66,* 1–6.

Bruce, M. M., & Learner, D. B. (1958). A supervisory practices test. *Personnel Psychology, 11,* 207–216.

Dalessio, A. T. (1992, May). *Predicting insurance agent turnover using a video-based situational judgment test.* Paper presented at the Seventh Annual Conference of the Society for Industrial and Organizational Psychology, Inc., Montreal, Quebec.

Desmarais, L. B., Dyer, P. J., Midkiff, K. R., Barbera, K. M., Curtis, J. R., Esrig, F. H., & Masi, D. L. (1992, May). *Scientific uncertainties in the development of a multimedia test: Tradeoffs and decisions.* Paper presented at the Seventh Annual Conference of the Society for Industrial and Organizational Psychology, Inc., Montreal, Quebec.

Desmarais, L. B., Masi, D. L., Olson, M. J., Barbera, K. M., & Dyer, P. J. (1994, April). *Scoring a multimedia situational judgment test: IBM's experience.* Paper presented at the Ninth Annual Conference of the Society for Industrial and Organizational Psychology, Inc., Nashville, TN.

DuBois, P. H., & Watson, R. I. (1950). The selection of patrolmen. *Journal of Applied Psychology, 34,* 90–95.

Dyer, P. J., Desmarais, L. B., Midkiff, K. R., Colihan, J. P., & Olson, J. B. (1992, May). *Designing a multimedia test: Understanding the organizational charge, building the team, and making the basic research commitments.* Paper presented at the Seventh Annual Conference of the Society for Industrial and Organizational Psychology, Inc., Montreal, Quebec.

File, Q. W., & Remmer, H. H. (1971). *How Supervise?* (Manual Rev. ed.). New York: Psychological Corporation.

Forehand G. A., & Guetzkow, H. (1961). The administrative judgment test as related to descriptions of executive judgment behaviors. *Journal of Applied Psychology, 45,* 257–261.

Frank, F. D. (1993, April). *Video-based assessment.* Paper presented at the Eighth Annual Conference of the Society for Industrial and Organizational Psychology, Inc., San Francisco.

Hedge, J. W., & Teachout, M. S. (1992). An interview approach to work sample criterion measurement. *Journal of Applied Psychology, 77,* 453–461.

Jagmin, N., Wagner, R. K., & Sternberg, R. J. (1989, April). The development of a generalized measure of tacit knowledge for managers. In W. C. Borman (Chair), *Evaluating "Practical IQ": Measurement issues and research applications in personnel selection and performance assessment.* Symposium conducted at the Fourth Annual Conference of the Society for Industrial and Organizational Psychology, Inc., Atlanta.

Jones, C., & DeCotiis, T. A. (1986). Video-based selection of hospitality employees. *The Cornell H.R.A. Quarterly,* 68-73.

Jones, J. W., & Youngblood, L. K. (1993, April). *Effect of a video-based test on the performance and retention of bank employees.* Paper presented at the Eighth Annual Conference of the Society for Industrial and Organizational Psychology, Inc., San Francisco.

Latham, G. P. (1989). The reliability, validity, and practicality of the situational interview. In R. W. Eder & G. R. Ferris (Eds.), *The employment interview: Theory, research, and practice* (pp. 169–182). Newbury Park, CA: Sage.

Mandell, M. M. (1950). The administrative judgment test. *Journal of Applied Psychology, 34,* 145–147.

Mandell, M. M. (1956). Validity information exchange, No. 9-2. *Personnel Psychology, 9,* 105.

Melnick, D. E. (1990). Computer-based clinical simulation: State of the art. *Evaluation & the Health Professions, 13*(1), 104–120.

Millard, K. A. (1952). Is *How Supervise?* an intelligence test? *Journal of Applied Psychology, 36,* 221–224.

Motowidlo, S. J., Dunnette, M. D., & Carter, G. W. (1990). An alternative selection procedure: The low-fidelity simulation. *Journal of Applied Psychology, 75,* 640–647.

Mowry, H. W. (1957). A measure of supervisory quality. *Journal of Applied Psychology, 41,* 405–408.

Municipality of Metropolitan Seattle. (1983). *Measurement of transit operator applicant human relations skills by video test: Background, test development, and validation.* Seattle, WA: Author.

Olson-Buchanan, J. B., Drasgow, F., Moberg, P. J., Mead, A. D., & Keenan, P. A. (1994). *The conflict resolution skills assessment: Model-based, multimedia measurement.* Paper presented at the Ninth Annual Conference of the Society for Industrial and Organizational Psychology, Inc., Nashville, TN.

Olson-Buchanan, J. B., Drasgow, F., Moberg, P. J., Mead, A. D., & Keenan, P. A. (1995). *Conflict resolution skills assessment: A model-based, multimedia approach.* Champaign, IL: Author.

Phillips, J. F. (1992). Predicting sales skills. *Journal of Business and Psychology, 7,* 151–160.

Phillips, J. F. (1993). Predicting negotiation skills. *Journal of Business and Psychology, 7,* 403–411.

Pine, D. E. (1994, April). *The development and validation of a video-based situational response test.* Paper presented at the Ninth Annual Conference of the Society for Industrial and Organizational Psychology, Inc., Nashville, TN.

Richardson, Bellows, Henry & Co. (1981). *Technical reports supervisory profile record.* Author.

Rosen, N. A. (1961). How Supervise?—1943–1960. *Personnel Psychology, 14,* 87–99.

Smiderle, D., Perry, B. A., & Cronshaw, S. F. (1994). Evaluation of video-based assessment in transit operator selection. *Journal of Business and Psychology, 1,* 3–22.

Smith, I. L. (1985). Issues in the development and scoring of written simulations for credentialing applications. *Professional Practice of Psychology, 6,* 156–193.

Tenopyr, M. L. (1969). The comparative validity of selected leadership scales relative to success in production management. *Personnel Psychology, 22,* 77-85.

Wagner, R. K. (1987). Tacit knowledge in everyday intelligent behavior. *Journal of Personality and Social Psychology, 52,* 1236–1247.

Wagner, R. K., & Sternberg, R. J. (1985). Practical intelligence in real world pursuits: The role of tacit knowledge. *Journal of Personality and Social Psychology, 49,* 436–458.

Weitz, J., & Nuckols, R. (1953). A validation study of *"How Supervise?" Journal of Applied Psychology, 37,* 7–8.

Measuring Complex Skills

Wayne A. Baughman
Michael D. Mumford
Christopher E. Sager

OVERVIEW

It is increasingly necessary for applied researchers to understand the theories and methodologies used to develop measures of complex cognitive skills. Broadly speaking, complex skills are developed capacities of the individual that contribute to learning and performance (Mumford, Peterson, & Childs, 1997). More specifically, they are high-level information-processing capacities that develop with experience and are subject to introspection (i.e., awareness). Complex, high-level cognitive skills require the use of prior knowledge, and include such activities as problem solving and monitoring of complex systems (Snow & Lohman, 1989).

In general, we need to understand measures of complex cognitive skills for two reasons. First, we are increasingly relied on to define and measure constructs representing complex, knowledge-dependent performance (e.g., under the rubrics of "skills-based" or "competency-based" systems), but there are many different and often contradictory ways to define these constructs (e.g., Gagne, 1985; Prien, 1977). The methodologies developed for measuring complex cognitive skills can be used to develop measures of complex workplace skills that overcome these definitional problems. Second, the pace of technological and economic change requires workers to continually develop new skills (Perkins, Jay, & Tishman, 1994). More adaptive organizations will use worker remediation and development as a strategy for buffering the effects of change. Methodologies for measuring complex cognitive skills can be used to obtain information for individualized performance feedback and to inform decisions about worker development.

Educational measurement researchers have taken the lead in developing measures of complex cognitive skills. New educational assessments explicitly link test design and validation with cognitive theory and research (Bejar, Chaffin, & Embretson, 1991; Carroll, 1976; Embretson, 1985; Frederiksen, Mislevy, & Bejar, 1993; Sizer, 1985). New methodologies currently used for the design of many educational assessments not only provide information about where an individual ranks relative to others; but these methodologies also provide information (to instructional design professionals, teachers, and learners) about an individual's relative strengths and weaknesses on attributes that contribute to performance. Thus, properly designed measures of complex skills provide information about the many different strategies and processes that people use in performance. This information can be used to develop a wide variety of interventions for individual remediation and development.

In this chapter we review the nature of current assessments of complex cognitive skills. In addition, we apply design principles derived from these assessments to describe how to develop a construct-based measure of a complex skill for the inside wireman occupation. Measures of complex skills are themselves complex. However, all of the fundamentals of good design that apply to other kinds of measures apply as well to measures of complex skills.

A BRIEF HISTORY:
MEASURES OF COMPLEX
COGNITIVE SKILLS

Formal, objective assessment of people has not always been necessary. Early rural and town life was not technologically complex, people knew each other, and political and social systems enforced a relatively rigid social order. Under these conditions, it was easy to identify the most suitable people to carry out particular production, social, or political functions. People assessed each other implicitly; that is, individual assessment was more informal and subjective, based on opportunities to observe others directly in a variety of social, school, and work settings.

At the turn of the twentieth century, however, the rise of democratic political systems and industrial mass production created conditions that required more formal objective assessments of people. Democratic ideals made it easier for people to cross the boundaries defined by traditional social orders. Factories in major cities, stimulated by technological innovation, created a market both for people with increasingly specialized performance-related capacities and for higher levels of those capacities. Moreover, the migration of people to cities created large populations where much less was known about the individual. Under these conditions, it became increasingly difficult to identify those people most suitable for particular functions. There were few opportunities to observe job candidates directly in common social, school, and work settings.

To satisfy the demand for predicting performance and classifying people, psychologists developed methods for measuring people's intellectual and workplace skills. These methods formed the basis of today's familiar educational and psychological measures, many of which are described in other chapters of this book.

INDIVIDUAL ASSESSMENT OF COMPLEX SKILLS

Initially, psychologists attempted to assess complex cognitive skill by measuring discrete components believed to underlie performance. It seemed reasonable at the time that complex cognitive skills were related to the efficiency of basic physiological processes, since physiological deficits were associated with mental retardation. For example, the late nineteenth century saw the development of many assessments of potential for academic performance that included physiological measures, such as muscular strength and visual acuity (Anastasi, 1988). These indirect physiological measures, however, did not predict intellectual performance. With the increasing demand for effective predictors, psychologists began using more direct measurement approaches.

In France, Binet and his colleagues (Binet & Henri, 1895; Binet & Simon, 1905) believed that predicting intellectual performance would be more effective if people were assessed on their capacity to carry out

complex tasks. Complex intellectual tasks were those requiring comprehension, reasoning, and judgment.

Of course, Binet's approach led to the first widely known measure
of complex cognitive skills strongly related to real-world performance—
the individually administered *Binet-Simon Scale* (Binet & Simon, 1905).
This test was effective at identifying schoolchildren who could not benefit from public education in the Parisian schools of the day. Children
could be ranked with respect to their capacity to complete tasks typical
of their peer age-group. While individual assessment was inefficient and
costly, the *Binet-Simon Scale* predicted performance on complex cognitive tasks.

It is important to note that the success of the *Binet-Simon Scale* taught
us an important lesson about designing measures of complex skills: The
performance requirements of the tasks on the test should correspond to
the performance requirements of the targeted real-world performance as
closely as possible. Thus, the *Binet-Simon Scale* used a variety of reasoning, judgment, and other similar tasks to predict school performance, a
domain requiring those same capacities.

GROUP ASSESSMENT OF COMPLEX SKILLS

During World War I, psychologists in the United States solved the problem of assessing the intellectual skills of large numbers of people by
developing systematic, economical methods for group test administration and scoring. The first examples of tests of complex cognitive skills
using the methodology of group testing were the U.S. Army's *Alpha* and
Beta, used to classify recruits near the end of World War I (Yerkes, 1921;
see Chapter 6). In addition to providing valid prediction, group testing
was efficient and cost-effective. Modern examples of these kinds of
tests include familiar group-administered tests such as the *Scholastic
Aptitude Test* (SAT) and the *Armed Services Vocational Aptitude Battery*
(ASVAB).

THE TRAIT MODEL

Much of the efficiency and economy of traditional mass testing relies on
assumptions about human individuality represented in the "trait model"
of behavior. The term *trait* describes an enduring characteristic of a person that is relatively consistent across time and situations (e.g., honesty).

The trait model of human individuality posits that people can be described by comparing them on a few relatively stable dimensions, or constructs, that summarize many related behaviors. For example, we apply measurements based on the assumptions of the trait model when we predict overall school or job performance for a group of individuals based only on their ranking on measures of general cognitive ability and vocational aptitude.

Despite some important shortcomings (see Mumford, Stokes, & Owens, 1990, for a review), the predictive utility and construct validity of traditional measures of complex skills (e.g., the *General Aptitude Test Battery* [GATB] and the *Scholastic Aptitude Test* [SAT]) based on the trait model taught psychologists that it is possible to predict complex performance indirectly. In developing these measures, psychologists defined constructs related to skilled performance and then developed tasks that assessed individual levels of those constructs. The use of constructs to summarize related behaviors provides a way to predict performance from individual differences less directly linked to specific situations.

GOALS OF ASSESSMENT

Most tests of individual differences used in applied settings are intended either to predict or explain performance. The early examples of individual- and group-administered assessments just described were designed to predict real-world performance. At the same time, however, researchers (including educators and training specialists) continued to pursue the goal of analyzing complex performance into performance-relevant components. The goal of assessment from the perspective of educators and training system design personnel was more complex and no less important. For effective education and training, it is important to analyze skilled performance to understand how, why, and under what conditions performance is enhanced or diminished. This kind of information is crucial for designing interventions intended to enhance learning and performance.

NEW ASSESSMENTS OF COMPLEX SKILLS

Today's assessments of complex skills are designed to capture the strategies or processes that people use during the course of different types of performance. This is not a characteristic of traditional, trait-based measures. For example, comparing people on measures like the GATB and SAT is an effective way to select and classify people because traditional, trait-based measures are primarily designed to rank people according to their levels of specific stable attributes, abilities, skills, or performance (Carroll, 1976; Embretson, 1985; Nunnally, 1978; Sternberg, 1977). However, no traditional measure is designed to assess the strategies or processes that people use during performance.

Newer measures of complex cognitive skills, like more traditional measures, can compare people with respect to levels of performance on some specific attribute. In addition, new measures of complex cognitive skills assess *how* people know what they know and do what they do, and provide information about the ways people can increase these capacities (Carroll, 1976; Mislevy, 1993; Sternberg, 1977).

It is intuitively obvious that qualitative, process-oriented information is crucial for education and training system design, but less obvious that the same qualitative information can be important in other ways. In selection, for example, poor performance on a job sample test because of poor hand–eye coordination is quite different from equally poor performance based on a lack of relevant knowledge. An individual with poor hand–eye coordination might be encouraged to apply for a different position, whereas an individual lacking relevant knowledge might be hired, but might first be sent to a remedial course. Thus, assessments providing diagnostic information in addition to an overall performance score are more flexible. They provide more ways to meet individual and organizational objectives.

The new approaches to the measurement of complex cognitive skills stem from the work of cognitive psychologists who have attempted to assess the mind's operations, or processes. Work in this area has focused both on developing measures of lower-level, biologically linked, automatic ("fast") mental operations and higher-level, learned ("slow") mental operations. In this chapter we are interested in measures of higher-level slow operations. It is useful, however, to contrast briefly how researchers have investigated fast and slow cognitive processes to clarify the nature of complex cognitive skills.

Fast Cognitive Processes

Fast cognitive processes operate automatically, beneath the level of awareness, and are generally measured by response latencies to task components, error rates, or direct measures of people's eye movements and neurophysiology (Massaro & Cowan, 1993; Snow & Lohman, 1989;

Sternberg, 1977). The operation of fast, automatic cognitive processes (e.g., information encoding) is believed to be independent of domain-specific knowledge and skills. Fast processes are measured in the laboratory with simple cognitive tasks such as analogies or spatial visualization items drawn from perceptual ability tests. Examples include the stimulus encoding, memory search-and-mapping, and information evaluation operations comprising components of various problem-solving models (for a review, see Bejar, Chaffin, & Embretson, 1991).

Applied researchers often are called on to understand how measures that relate performance to information-processing models can be used in applied settings. The most obvious example is the use of cognitive task analyses to augment traditional task analysis on complex jobs (e.g., Means & Gott, 1988; Gordon, Schmierer, & Gill, 1993). Cognitive task analysis is an extension of traditional task analysis that uses tasks, together with a variety of data gathering and representational methodologies, to obtain such information as a job's concepts, procedures, and occupation- or position-specific skills. As with measures of fast cognitive processes, the methodologies used in cognitive task analysis emphasize links between behaviors and processes that are hypothesized to underlie or are related to performance (e.g., information encoding).

Slow Cognitive Processes

Measurement approaches for complex cognitive skills have reflected the finding that these skills are conscious control processes (Snow & Lohman, 1989). Researchers have generally measured such complex cognitive skills by presenting people with tasks intended to elicit their application. For example, an assessment of planning skill is based on responses to a planning task. This is identical to common performance assessment practices in education and industry (e.g., work samples, assessment centers, and leaderless group discussions), where the goal of assessment is to measure an individual's level of knowledge and skill with respect to a known absolute standard (Glaser, 1984).

As with the *Binet-Simon Scale,* the design of the tasks used to elicit complex cognitive skills may only reflect a simple consensus of expert opinion as to their appropriateness and power to elicit the skill (Feltovich, Spiro, & Coulson, 1993). That is, these tasks need only be face valid. In responding to these tasks, people provide open-ended verbal and behavioral records. Alternatively, verbal protocol analyses are often used to record observations (Baker, O'Neil, & Linn, 1993; Ericsson & Simon, 1993). Applied researchers will increasingly need to understand how to assess the constructs underlying performance on complex tasks.

The following section discusses important aspects of tasks designed to elicit and measure complex skills.

TASK DESIGN

Tasks designed to measure complex cognitive skills share much in common with other assessments. Broadly speaking, tasks that are appropriate for assessing cognitive skills in general include any task designed to investigate how people perceive, understand, acquire, and use knowledge (Snow & Lohman, 1989). Examples of cognitive tasks range from school learning tasks to educational and psychological tests. What is crucial is that the tasks be designed so that the inferential statements resulting from the observations are strong and speak to the validity of the assessment. That is, performance on the assessment should call forth the intended cognitive skill and be related in the expected way to real-world performance (Baker, O'Neil, & Linn, 1993).

The difference between tasks designed to measure complex cognitive skills and other assessments is that the theory underlying the assessment design must specify which cognitive operations contribute to performance, and the sequence of those operations. For example, research has shown that different items comprising a traditional test of spatial visualization can be solved by applying different abilities, even verbal abilities (Lohman & Kyllonen, 1983). This is not a great problem for traditional tests, since a person is only assessed by a single total score (primarily a quantitative measure) that represents the sum or mean of the items. Thus, individual differences in cognitive strategy or process used to obtain answers (a primarily qualitative measure) are not assessed at all. Contributions of abilities other than spatial ability to performance are treated as error when the items are summed or averaged to compute a total score. An assessment of complex skills would not treat individual differences in cognitive strategy or process as error. Instead, the assessment would be explicitly designed to capture this information.

To assess individual strategies and processes, the features incorporated into each stage of the design of the assessment tasks (e.g., stimulus materials, response options, and presentation format) must reflect links to components of the specified theoretical model. This kind and level of explicit integration of theory into the assessment design provide the basis for establishing the construct validity of the mental operations hypothesized to underlie performance and, by extension, the validity of the assessment itself (Embretson, 1983, 1985; Lohman & Ippel, 1993; Snow & Lohman, 1989; Sternberg, 1977, 1985).

EXAMPLES OF COMPLEX SKILL MEASURES

Today, there are many ways to assess complex cognitive skills. These different approaches reflect the fact that such assessments should be tailored to fit the nature of the skills and the theoretical model(s) posited to underlie performance. Thus, there is no specific format that is used across the board when measuring complex skills.

For example, Baker (1989) used a "text-faulting" procedure to investigate metacognitive performance (i.e., self-awareness of performance) of adults while reading. The specific skill investigated was how well people monitored their own reading comprehension. People were asked to detect faults in written material that could be any one of seven different kinds. These faults ranged from the superficial, such as spelling errors, to the more abstract, such as incongruent semantic relationships.

Lesgold, Lajoie, Logan, and Eggan (1990) used a "think aloud" methodology for assessing planning in electronic troubleshooting tasks. Novice and expert troubleshooters were presented with a problem and asked to suggest hypotheses, state plans, and specify the steps they expected to take in solving the problem. These protocols were mapped onto the replaceable electronic components people selected. This mapping revealed that experts only used relevant electronic components and their plans showed a systematic and linked transition in making these choices. In contrast, the mappings of novices tended to show that they used irrelevant components in a series of unsystematic and unrelated action steps. Note that this experimental task could be adapted to create an assessment instrument.

Gerace and Mestre (1990; as described by Royer, Cisero, & Carlo, 1993) developed an assessment of metacognitive skill (i.e., awareness of one's own cognition) within a specific domain. They decomposed physics problems into a solution plan and an executed plan, each of which could be further decomposed into subactivities of identifying a concept or procedure and justifying its selection. After identifying relevant principles and giving justifications for their application, the individual could then execute the plan and solve the problem. Gerace and Mestre's (1990) assessment approach incorporated response option formats ranging from completely open-ended to fixed choice.

TASK DESIGN CHARACTERISTICS

While there are no specific formats for designing tasks for assessing complex skills, it is useful to note several characteristics common to the tasks that are typical of most measures of complex cognitive skill. Design of a cognitive assessment's items, structure, and response format represents what Lohman and Ippel (1993) call the "observational design." The purpose of the observational design for any measure is to structure the task so that defensible inferences about the nature of the targeted skill can be made from the scores representing the observations.

Complexity

First, most measures of complex skill use complex tasks. As Binet found, complex tasks are required to adequately assess complex performance (Feltovich, Spiro, & Coulson, 1993; Snow & Peterson, 1985). Complex tasks are distinguished from simple tasks by their requirement for integration of diverse knowledge and skills. Cognitive psychologists classify many tasks requiring the integration of diverse knowledge and skills as unstructured, ill-defined tasks (Greeno & Simon, 1987). The bulk of the research in assessing complex knowledge and skills incorporates complex exercises (Baker, 1989; Hershey, Walsh, Read, & Chulef, 1990; Lesgold, Lajoie, Logan, & Eggan, 1990).

Of course, complex cognition, such as introspection, may occur during the performance of simple tasks. Simple tasks, however, do not allow people the opportunity to express the complex cognitive skill in a sufficient variety of ways. Lohman and Ippel (1993) noted, for example, that typical items from standard ability tests do not make informative cognitive tasks because years of item and factor analyses have produced items on standard ability tests that do not capture qualitative differences in performance. That is, they do not capture information about individual differences in the strategies or processes used. This, of course, is precisely the intent of test developers who are trying to measure a specific construct. Thus, the most useful information that may be obtained from cognitive assessment is detecting the important differences in *how* people complete the assessments.

Feltovich, Spiro, and Coulson (1993) summarize the usefulness of complex tasks in the design of cognitive assessments:

- First, complex tasks allow integration of more requisite performance dimensions. This provides a basis for better assessing qualitative differences among individuals in their capacity to integrate what they know for task performance.
- Second, complex tasks provide multiple "snapshots" or ways of representing performance. The resulting larger set of potentially useful variables can provide the patterns of convergent and diver-

gent relationships and interactions that will evidence the construct validity of the skill assessments.

- Third, complex tasks allow for the assessment of awareness. Evidence of awareness is important in order to establish that the targeted cognitive skill is being applied.

- Finally, measures derived from performance on complex tasks are better at classifying individuals with respect to their stage of development. Qualitative assessments of complex tasks can thus allow assessments of current readiness for acquiring new knowledge—that is, future potential—thus providing an important link to the development of training interventions.

Skill Specificity

Second, most measures of complex skills are skill-specific. For example, planning skill is elicited by a task involving planning, and reading comprehension by one in which people read complex material. Thus, for tasks assessing high-level complex skills, the face- and content-validity of the task must carry a good deal of the burden for helping to establish inferences that the targeted complex skill is being elicited. Of course, tasks that are face- and content-valid can be constructed to reflect job content, such as simulations or job sample tests. Tasks reflecting job content allow stronger inferences to be made about the likelihood that assessed performance will generalize to actual performance on the job.

Fidelity

Third, measures of complex skills generally mimic real-world tasks; that is, they have a relatively high level of fidelity when compared with traditional psychometric assessments. However, they generally are not as realistic as work samples or assessment centers. A measure's fidelity, or the extent to which it mimics a real-world task, is, however, an issue when designing any assessment.

When designing an assessment intended to assess complex skills, it is important that the performance requirements of the tasks being assessed correspond to the performance requirements of the targeted real-world performance enough so that the skills required to perform the real-world task would be elicited. Thus, it is not necessary to provide elaborate simulations. Instead, there is evidence that well-designed low-fidelity simulations elicit requisite skills and permit reliable observations, as described in Chapter 9. Specific examples of a class of viable low-fidelity tasks are represented by what Mislevy (1993) calls "controlled simulation" tasks. Controlled simulations are complex tasks that represent a compromise between rigid, traditional, tester-controlled observational settings and the wholly unstructured observational setting found in the real world.

The purpose of any simulation is to approximate a realistic situation so that one can generalize from simulation performance to real-world performance. Controlled simulations satisfy this generalizability criterion. Controlled simulations include the use of scenarios, which have been most prominently used in the area of medical education in patient management problems (Assmann, Hixon, & Kacmarek, 1979). For example, a simulated patient (via written or oral dialogue) presents the examinee with initial symptoms; the examinee requests tests, considers their results, prescribes treatments, and monitors their effects, generally attempting to identify and treat the initially unknown disease. The controlled simulation model of assessment allows identification of patterns of performance that might suggest specific associations among facts in examinees' schema, or show the use of effective or ineffective problem-solving strategies (Pople, 1981).

Response Variety

Fourth, measures of complex skills provide people with a variety of response alternatives, ranging from think-aloud protocols to multiple-choice to time-on-task (*not* response latency).

Scoring

Finally, inferences regarding the application and level of the targeted cognitive skills are made based on the nature of the task and accompanying responses. In these kinds of measures, scoring is based on sound inferences regarding the application of the targeted high-level skills because the task has been judiciously structured and thus allows the observation of qualitative differences in the content of responses. It is this incorporation of qualitative assessment into the measurement design that helps capture individuals' application of processes and strategic differences that become manifest in high-level complex skills.

PSYCHOMETRIC CHARACTERISTICS OF COMPLEX SKILLS ASSESSMENTS

RELIABILITY

Because we have shown that newer assessments of complex skills are extensions, combinations, or elaborations of more traditional assessments, there is no simple way to summarize the evidence for their reliability. Instead, reliability estimates will vary according to the complexity of the skill, the type of scoring, and the number of tasks comprising the assessment. These assessment parameters vary widely because assessments of complex skills are tailored for specific skills, populations, and modes of administration. Chapter 6 summarizes broad considerations that apply equally when considering the reliability of any educational or psychological assessment, and suggests relevant sources to consult.

Newer assessments, however, can provide both a reliable overall performance score and reliable scores for performance-related constructs, strategies, procedures, or processes. For example, a computer-administered measure of information encoding was developed to assess the types of information people use when solving complex problems (Mumford, Baughman, Supinski, & Maher, 1996). Participants in the study read four novel, ill-defined problems drawn from managerial case studies and public policy studies, and typed a one-paragraph solution after reading each problem. Each case study was presented on a series of six overlapping panels on the computer display as if they were index cards in a card file. Each card provided one paragraph of information bearing on the problem, and only one card at a time could be fully displayed on the screen. People read each case study problem and had the option of reviewing any of the cards before typing their solution. The computer program recorded the time people spent viewing each card.

To obtain a total score reflecting effective information encoding, three judges familiar with the management and public policy case studies used benchmark rating scales to assess the quality and originality of the one-paragraph solutions generated by study participants (Mumford, Baughman, Supinski, Costanza, & Threlfall, 1993). The ratings of solution quality yielded a mean interrater agreement coefficient of .74, while the ratings of solution originality yielded an interrater agreement coefficient of .72. These reliability estimates are typical of those obtained for performance ratings from this number of raters using benchmark or related scales.

To obtain scores reflecting the tendency to attend to certain types of performance-relevant information during encoding, the type of information presented on the cards was manipulated. On all four problems, three of the cards presented crucial facts needed to solve the problem (drawn from the relevant case study material), and the remaining three cards presented information reflecting other types of relevant or irrelevant information. A score representing preferences for or attention to crucial facts was computed for each problem from the time spent viewing the three cards presenting crucial facts.

The internal consistency estimate of reliability for a four-item scale representing preferences for or attention to crucial facts was .80, showing that people tended to be very consistent in the types of information they referred to, whether crucial facts, other relevant information, or irrelevant information. (Relative time spent viewing cards presenting crucial facts was most strongly related to performance.) Thus, reliable measures of specific kinds of responding can be obtained when the number of tasks and their observational design provide an adequate number of observations (i.e., items) from which to construct a scale or other composite measure.

VALIDITY

As noted earlier, performance on assessments of complex skills should call forth the intended skills and be related in the expected way to real-world performance. Of course, this is the essence of validity, and assessments of complex skills tend to provide excellent validity evidence. The primary reason for this lies in the task design characteristics described in this chapter. The design considerations ensure that validity is "built into" the assessments. Tasks designed to assess complex skills must be face- and content-valid, require expression of the targeted skill, be complex enough to elicit complex responding, and be scoreable in terms of skill-relevant dimensions or constructs. Enhanced validity is an important payoff for the extra effort involved in developing these kinds of assessments. Several recent studies have used these kinds of measures, providing evidence for their criterion-related and construct validity.

Mumford and his colleagues developed computer-administered measures of four problem-solving skills using a construct-based approach: problem construction (Mumford, Baughman, Threlfall, Supinski, & Costanza, 1996), information encoding (discussed earlier; Mumford, Baughman, Supinski et al., 1996), category selection (Mumford, Supinski, Threlfall, & Baughman, in press), and category combination (Mumford, Baughman, Maher, Costanza, & Supinski, in press). In a study using 137 undergraduates, these measures not only predicted performance ($R = .43$) on a problem-solving scenario of the sort encountered in organizational settings (Mumford, Supinski, Baughman, Costanza, & Threlfall, in press), but also provided significant incremental prediction when added to basic ability measures in a hierarchical regression (change in $R^2 = .08$; $R = .55$). In two other studies, measures of these four skills were related to problem-solving strategies reflecting the effective application of the skills (Mumford, Baughman, Supinski, Costanza, & Threlfall, 1993).

Fleishman and his colleagues (Marshall-Mies et al., 1996) used a construct-based approach to develop computer-administered measures of six cognitive and metacognitive skills intended to predict the leadership potential of military officers: general problem solving, planning and implementation, solution construction, solution evaluation, social judgment, and metacognitive process. In a study carried out at the National Defense University with 84 military officers, these researchers found that the measures of general problem solving and social judgment predicted performance on a work sample ($R = .60$); the measures of solution construction and metacognitive process predicted performance on a criterion of academic excellence (i.e., Distinguished Graduate [DG]; $R = .47$).

HOW TO DEVELOP A MEASURE OF COMPLEX SKILLS: A CONSTRUCT-BASED APPROACH

The most useful kinds of measures of complex skills are those that provide information both about level of performance and the different capacities influencing performance. As noted earlier, traditional performance assessments correctly emphasize the face- and content-validity of the tasks to call forth the targeted skill. We refer to this as a "content-based" approach, without reference to relevant strategies, processes, or other constructs that may contribute to performance.

We refer to an alternative, representing an extension of traditional content-based performance assessment, as a "construct-based" approach. Here, tasks are also face- and content-valid, but scoring is based on constructs hypothesized to underlie performance.

ISSUES TO CONSIDER WHEN DEVELOPING MEASURES OF COMPLEX SKILLS

A construct-based approach for assessing complex skills and performance addresses some specific problems of the content-based approach. Typically, measures of complex skills, such as planning and decision making, are based on only a few samples of performance (as in an assessment center). This is because these realistic exercises are time- and labor-intensive relative to other kinds of assessments. However, limiting the number of assessment exercises may not provide an adequate opportunity for an individual to display the relevant skill. In contrast, a construct-based approach uses a greater number of tasks that, while less realistic, nevertheless call forth the targeted skill, and thus provide better opportunity for display of the individual's skill level.

This more limited but targeted approach addresses three other problems inherent in content-based assessments. First, structuring the tasks so that responses are linked to underlying constructs provides evidence supporting the construct validity of exercises (Messick, 1995). Second, using a larger number of exercises reduces exercise-specific effects by aggregating performance across multiple exercises (Epstein & O'Brien, 1985). Third, more limited and targeted exercises enable the development of simpler and more accurate scoring systems, thereby reducing administration and scoring costs and reducing the problems associated with rater error (Klimoski & Brickner, 1987; Reilly, Henry, & Smither, 1990; Russell, 1987; Russell & Kuhnert, 1992; Sackett & Hakel, 1979).

AN EXAMPLE OF THE CONSTRUCT-BASED APPROACH

To illustrate a construct-based approach, consider the assessment of writing skills. The content-based approach would involve asking examinees to write an essay to be rated by a number of judges. The construct-based approach, however, involves identifying and assessing constructs related to the strategies, procedures, and processes underlying writing skills. Studies by Frederiksen, Warren, and Rosenberg (1985) and Hayes and Flower (1986) are examples of this approach. These researchers began with a theoretical model stating that writing involves three key processes: planning, generation, and revision. Planning could be assessed by asking people to develop outlines for essays on several topics. Revision could be assessed by presenting people with several short essays and having them revise each essay. Performance on these exercises could be scored by comparing examinees' outlines and revisions to those suggested by experts (more objective scoring) or by having judges rate their clarity (more subjective scoring).

TASK DEVELOPMENT STEPS

Following we describe the four major steps required to develop a construct-based measure of a complex skill. To illustrate each step, we have chosen "teamwork" as the skill for which a measure is required. The basic approach can be used to develop an assessment for a range of administration formats from paper-and-pencil to computer-based multimedia.

Teamwork is a dimension of performance identified in the critical incident analysis of the inside wireman occupation described in Chapter 4. Ordinarily, teamwork is very difficult to measure, especially those aspects of team effectiveness that require effective interactions with others (i.e., so-called "teamwork skills"). Thus, developing a measure of teamwork may well be worthwhile and provide a cost-effective and valid predictor measure. To develop such a measure, four steps are required. These are:

1. Define the skill.
2. Identify the skill application requirements.
3. Develop tasks that elicit the skill.
4. Develop a scoring system.

Step One: Define the Skill

Job-relevant skills emerge from the KSAO analysis that we described in Chapter 3 and from the synthesis of critical incidents we described in Chapter 4. These skills should be defined so as to link them to existing skill taxonomies supported by the theoretical and applied literatures. For example, as we discussed in Chapter 2, Mumford, Peterson, and Childs (1997) identified 46 complex skills grouped into 6 broad domains representing the major kinds of skill-based activities required across a variety of educational and occupational settings (i.e., learning, problem solving, social, technical, systems [e.g., visioning and judgment], and resource management). These are the broad skills used to describe occupations in the Department of Labor's new on-line database of occupations (O*NET) slated to replace the *Dictionary of Occupational Titles.* Procedures for identifying occupation- or function-specific skills (Sager, Mumford, Baughman, & Childs, 1997) might be used to define more specialized skills related to the broad skills taxonomy.

The teamwork performance dimension is defined for electricians working as inside wiremen as "Communicating clearly with other workers, helping other team members, following the instructions given for completing a task, asking for help if needed." The O*NET's five broad social skills—social perceptiveness, coordination, persuasion, negotiation, instructing, and service orientation—seem most strongly linked to this definition of teamwork. Linking the complex skill (teamwork) required for the occupation of inside wireman to an existing skill taxonomy provides validation of the skill label and definition. In addition, linking teamwork to broad skills in the O*NET skill taxonomy may serve to help identify additional relevant constructs.

Step Two: Identify Skill Application Requirements

Once we define the skill, we identify the constructs, strategies, procedures, and processes required to apply the skill. These are the skill application requirements. A variety of techniques can be used to identify these elements of performance, including expert–novice comparisons (Chi, Glaser, & Farr, 1988), think-aloud protocols (Ericsson & Simon, 1993), structured interviews (e.g., Diederich, Ruhmann, & May, 1987; Gordon & Gill, 1992), or reviews of prior studies (e.g., Chi, Glaser, & Rees, 1982; Gitomer & Rock, 1993; Khandwalla, 1993). Regardless of the performance analysis technique applied, it is essential that it provide a clear definition of the constructs contributing to the application of a particular skill—in this case, teamwork.

A review of the teamwork and team training literature suggests a number of sources that might help identify the constructs, strategies, procedures, and processes related to or required for effective teamwork (Campion, Papper, & Medsker, 1996; Denson, 1981; Friedman & Yarbrough, 1985; Glickman et al., 1987; McGrath, 1984; Prince, Brannick, Prince, & Salas, 1992; Swezey & Salas, 1992). These sources should be collected and thoroughly reviewed.

Campion, Papper, and Medsker (1996), for example, refer to five themes and related characteristics that contribute to team effectiveness criteria, such as productivity, satisfaction of team personnel, and ratings of effectiveness. The five themes are: (1) job design, (2) interdependence, (3) composition, (4) context, and (5) process. Each theme has between three and five specific characteristics that influence performance. For example, the theme of interdependence includes variables representing both task and goal interdependence. Interdependence of team members, whether with respect to tasks or goals, is therefore one of the skill application requirements we will attempt to represent as we develop the assessment.

Step Three: Develop Tasks That Elicit the Skill

After we define the constructs, strategies, procedures, and processes required to apply the skill (skill application requirements), we develop tasks to elicit the skills. In developing these performance tasks, we try to develop exercises that only take a short time to complete. Critical incidents obtained from the job analysis, as described in Chapter 4, are excellent sources of material from which to develop task scenarios.

Other sources might include role-play exercises developed for training or documented case studies.

Here is an example of a procedure that might be used to develop tasks for the assessment of teamwork skills for the inside wireman occupation:

- Organize the critical incidents most related to teamwork into categories that represent the full range of situations and activities involving teamwork. We want to make sure to develop at least one task targeting the expression of teamwork skills for each important but different kind of situation and activity. For example, critical incidents describing inside wireman teamwork could be organized with respect to process-related activities primarily involving (1) workload sharing, (2) social support, and (3) communication and cooperation. In addition, we can categorize the critical incidents by performance effectiveness into three levels: "Needs Improvement," "Meets Standards," and "Superior." This suggests that we might develop tasks constructed to represent each of the three activity categories at various levels of performance effectiveness. Here is a critical incident for the inside wireman occupation representing low teamwork performance effectiveness with respect to communication and cooperation:

  > Two journeymen had to box and pipe men's and women's bathrooms together in a short time. They got into an argument when one journeyman decided to split from the other journeyman and pipe the rooms one way, refusing to listen to the other's suggestions. The bathrooms were completed the wrong way, and it took four people to redo the work of the two.

- Develop at least one scenario for each major situational or activity category so that elements in the scenario are related to or reflect the skill application requirements. It is especially important to establish clear, strong relationships between skill application requirements and specific behaviors required of the examinees. These are the linkages that make it possible to develop low-fidelity simulations that require the application of the complex skill. Make sure that each scenario is complex enough to elicit complex responding. That is, make sure that each scenario incorporates elements related to a variety of skill application requirements. Keep scenarios as generic as possible, so that the exercises will generalize, for example, across different groups and geographic areas, and remain valid over time. Following we present a scenario based on the critical incident just shown, after it has been modified to represent the skill application requirements. The scenario is now worded to contain information linked to all five themes influencing team effectiveness defined by Campion, Papper, and Medsker (1996):

> Two journeymen started to box and pipe men's and women's bathrooms. The job would be completed the next day by another pair of journeymen [Job Design: low task identity], who did not really expect the job to be started so soon [Context: low communication/cooperation between teams]. The journeymen had pretty much the same experience and skills [Composition: homogeneous], and normally worked different shifts with different crews [Interdependence: low interdependent feedback and rewards]. They got into an argument when one journeyman decided to split from the other journeyman and pipe the rooms one way, refusing to listen to the other's suggestions [Process: low communication/cooperation within the team]. The bathrooms were completed the wrong way, and it took four people to redo the work of these two journeymen so that the job could be finished in time.

Once the scenario has been generated, it must be translated into a performance task for the examinees. This consists of developing questions or other prompts, where the intent is to link the responses of examinees to the skill application requirements (e.g., type in an open-ended response).

■ Obtain expert reviewers (e.g., senior managers who have worked in the field) to evaluate and revise the scenarios. There usually are several occasions during the development of measures like these for which expert review is essential, especially with respect to their face- and content-validity. Using expert reviewers will ensure that the targeted skill is, in fact, being represented and that the scenarios are plausible.

Step Four: Develop a Scoring System

While we construct the task stimulus materials, often in the form of a computer-administered problem-solving scenario, we must develop the response requirements that define the scoring system. Response requirements (Lohman & Ippel, 1993) are specific behaviors (i.e., performance products) elicited from people by such variable task parameters as instructions, structure, sequencing, and prompts.

In addition to one overall performance score, we develop a score for constructs related to effective skill application. If the exercise has been properly structured, it is relatively easy to identify performance products (responses) that serve as indicators of specific skill application.

Developing the task instructions, structure, sequencing, and prompts defining a task's response requirements, however, requires a good deal of practice and familiarity with a variety of response formats and alternative scoring methods.

Of course, we have not waited until now to think about the response requirement of the assessments. The nature and proper sequencing of the response requirements are determined by the nature of the targeted skill, the skill application requirements, and the structure of the scenarios. For example, some scenarios may be only one paragraph long and ask people to type in an open-ended response; other scenarios may be sequential, presenting parts of the scenario, each of which requires selecting from among different printed alternatives; still other scenarios may consist of independent components, allowing people the discretion to elect the order with which to respond to components.

In the following paragraphs, we describe one way to develop response requirements for the scenario developed to represent the five themes influencing team effectiveness. The approach yields easily scoreable fixed-format tasks that nevertheless can represent complex responding. Our purpose is to show how measures of complex skills can be developed that use, combine, or extend familiar, more traditional methodologies. Of course, other approaches for developing task response requirements might be equally valid.

We identify ways that responses to the tasks would reflect the application of the targeted skill, and ways to strengthen the response-to-task relationship. For example, it is reasonable that an individual's real-world teamwork skill should depend, in part, on an implicit understanding of the five broad themes identified by Campion, Papper, and Medsker (1996). It also is reasonable that a role-playing or evaluation exercise might be an effective way to activate teamwork-relevant schema. Here is the example incident reworked to represent a task requiring the examinee to assume a particular role:

> You are working with another journeyman, and have just started to box and pipe some men's and women's bathrooms that you won't be able to finish. The job is actually going to be completed the next day by another pair of journeymen, who don't even expect the job to be started so soon. You both have pretty much the same experience and skills, but normally work different shifts with different crews. You get into an argument with each other because you have different ways you want to pipe the rooms. Neither of you listens to the other's suggestions, and you split up and work alone. The bathrooms get completed the wrong way, and it takes four people to redo your work so that the job can be finished in time.

Following are five example statements restating or interpreting information from the stimulus task worded to represent five themes relevant to teamwork effectiveness. These five statements are worded so that they could be used as response options to the stimulus task.

- We couldn't finish the whole job, so the job wasn't much fun.
- The guys coming the next day didn't really expect anything to be done at all.
- One of us was just as good as the other, so we could get away with working alone.
- We didn't try hard enough to get along because we worked different shifts.
- We didn't make the effort to listen to each other's suggestions.

People high in real-world teamwork skill should be better able than people low in real-world teamwork skill to distinguish these five statements related to team effectiveness from plausible distractor statements containing information unrelated to team effectiveness. Example distractors include:

- There was too much pressure to finish in time, so the job wasn't much fun.
- We were probably trying too hard to do our best on our part of the job.
- We were trying to impress each other, since it was the first time we had worked together.
- Shift work creates a lot of stress, and makes it more difficult to get along sometimes.

We can now define the response requirements as a set of fixed response options for the measure of teamwork skill that represent qualitatively different expressions of the targeted skill. In responding to each prompt (e.g., "What are the things you think helped to create this situation?") people select more than one response from several apparently equally attractive alternatives.

In the case of our teamwork measure, we could present ten equally plausible statements after each scenario, five of which did and five of which did not represent skill application requirements of team performance. After reading a teamwork scenario, examinees would review all ten statements and select the five "most preferred" statements in response to the prompt. We would then analyze the responses to generate a profile of scores for each examinee based on the content of his or her most frequently selected alternatives. Of course, selecting all five (equally plausible) statements representing the skill application requirements would yield the highest score. An overall score may be obtained by summing the total number of statements representing the skill application requirements across all tasks comprising the test. For validation or research purposes, scores may also be obtained for each of the five themes to examine the existence of reliable individual differences in the preferences examinees express for certain themes and their relationship to performance.

Clearly, the nature of the response options is critical to the success of this strategy. The content of the response options must reflect important qualitative differences in the way people might complete the task. Here, we have linked teamwork skill application requirements to five responses but not to five others. From the number of teamwork skill-linked responses chosen, we make inferences about the processes being applied in task performance, and these scores may be related to other indices of learning, development, and achievement.

Having people critically evaluate and select responses from a set of equally plausible responses represents complex responding. Bennett (1993) suggests that the design of tasks to capture complex responses should be the real focus of assessment. Further, Grote and James (1991) and Kilcullen, White, Mumford, & Mack (1993) have successfully used related approaches to structuring response options. This general strategy also provides a solution to important issues of practicality and cost of administration and scoring.

Linking fixed-response options to performance-relevant skill application requirements represents a viable approach to construct measurement. When combined with a strategy of allowing the selection of more than one response, the approach conforms to an important requirement for the assessment of complex skills—namely, that people should not be constrained to provide responses in which there is only one right or wrong answer (Bennett, 1993; Feltovich, Spiro, & Coulson, 1993). The responses elicited, furthermore, reflect different strategies or approaches that can be used to perform a task. Like traditional assessment exercises, we can elicit complex responses. In addition, however, we potentially can provide a more comprehensive description of the individual's performance capabilities.

SUMMARY

This chapter has provided an overview of one of the mainstreams in assessment: the application of substantive theory and research to the development of assessments in applied settings. Though possibly requiring more time and effort to develop, assessments of complex skills can predict performance as well as traditional trait-based assessments and are potentially more useful for a variety of purposes. Until recently, it has been difficult to develop measures that combine effective performance prediction with assessment of the components underlying performance. The methodologies based on the general principles discussed in this chapter combine prediction with understanding.

There is an urgent need for innovative assessment in organizations. The current move toward "skill-based" human resource management and personnel systems will probably continue for a variety of practical and political reasons. In this chapter, we described how to develop measures of complex skills as well as an example of such a measure for the construct "teamwork."

REFERENCES

Anastasi, A. (1988). *Psychological testing* (6th ed.). New York: Macmillan.

Assmann, D. C., Hixon, S. H., & Kacmarek, R. M. (1979). *Clinical simulations for respiratory care workers.* Chicago: Year Book Medical Publishers.

Baker, E. L., O'Neil, H. F., & Linn, R. L. (1993). Policy and validity prospects for performance-based assessment. *American Psychologist, 48,* 1210–1218.

Baker, L. (1989). Metacognition and the adult reader. *Educational Psychology Review, 1,* 3–38.

Bejar, I. I., Chaffin, R., & Embretson, S. (1991). *Cognitive and psychometric analysis of analogical problem solving.* New York: Springer-Verlag.

Bennett, R. E. (1993). Toward intelligent assessment: An integration of constructed-response testing, artificial intelligence, and model-based measurement. In N. Frederiksen, R. J. Mislevy, & I. I. Bejar (Eds.), *Test theory for a new generation of tests* (pp. 99–123). Hillsdale, NJ: Erlbaum.

Binet, A., & Henri, V. (1895). La psychologie individuelle. *Année Psychologique, 2,* 411–463.

Binet, A., & Simon, Th. (1905). Methodes nouvelles pour le diagnostic du niveau intellectuel des anormaux. *Année Psychologique, 11,* 191–244.

Campion, M. A., Papper, E. M., & Medsker, G. J. (1996). Relations between work team characteristics and effectiveness: A replication and extension. *Personnel Psychology, 49,* 429–452.

Carroll, J. B. (1976). Psychometric tests as cognitive tasks: A new "Structure of Intellect." In L. Resnick (Ed.), *The nature of intelligence* (pp. 27–56). Hillsdale, NJ: Erlbaum.

Chi, M. T. H., Glaser, R., & Farr, M. J. (Eds.). (1988). *The nature of expertise.* Hillsdale, NJ: Erlbaum.

Chi, M. T. H., Glaser, R., & Rees, E. (1982). Expertise in problem solving. In R. J. Sternberg (Ed.), *Advances in the psychology of human intelligence* (pp. 94–149). Hillsdale, NJ: Erlbaum.

Denson, R. W. (1981). Team training: Literature review and annotated bibliography (AFHRL-TR-80-40,A9-A099994). Wright Air Force Base, Patterson, OH: Logistics and Technical Training Division, Air Force Human Resources Laboratory.

Diederich, J., Ruhmann, I., & May, M. (1987). KRITON: A knowledge-acquisition tool for expert systems. *International Journal of Man-Machine Studies, 26,* 29–40.

Embretson, S. E. (1983). Construct validity: Construct representation versus nomothetic span. *Psychological Bulletin, 93,* 179–197.

Embretson, S. E. (1985). Introduction to the problem of test design. In S. E. Embretson (Ed.), *Test design: Developments in psychology and psychometrics* (pp. 3–17). New York: Academic Press.

Epstein, S., & O'Brien, E. J. (1985). The person-situation debate in historical and current perspective. *Psychological Bulletin, 98,* 513–553.

Ericsson, K. A., & Simon, H. A. (1993). *Protocol analysis: Verbal reports as data* (2nd ed.). Cambridge, MA: MIT Press.

Feltovich, P. J., Spiro, R. J., & Coulson, R. L. (1993). Learning, teaching, and testing for complex conceptual understanding. In N. Frederiksen, R. J. Mislevy, & I. I. Bejar (Eds.), *Test theory for a new generation of tests* (pp. 181–217). Hillsdale, NJ: Erlbaum.

Frederiksen, J. R., Warren, B. M., & Rosenberg, R. S. (1985). A componential approach to training reading skills: Part I. Perceptual units. *Cognition and Instruction, 2,* 91–130.

Frederiksen, N., Mislevy, R. J., & Bejar, I. I. (Eds.). (1993). *Test theory for a new generation of tests.* Hillsdale, NJ: Erlbaum.

Friedman, P. G., & Yarbrough, E. A. (1985). *Training strategies from start to finish.* Englewood Cliffs, NJ: Prentice-Hall.

Gagne, E. D. (1985). *The cognitive psychology of school learning.* Boston: Little, Brown.

Gerace, W. J., & Mestre, J. P. (1990). *Materials for developing concept-based problem solving skills in physics.* Unpublished manuscript, University of Massachusetts, Amherst.

Gitomer, D. H., & Rock, D. (1993). Addressing process variables in test analysis. In N. Frederiksen, R. J. Mislevy, & I. I. Bejar (Eds.), *Test theory for a new generation of tests* (pp. 243–268). Hillsdale, NJ: Erlbaum.

Glaser, R. (1984). Education and thinking: The role of knowledge. *American Psychologist, 39,* 93–104.

Glickman, A., Zimmer, S., Montero, R., Guerette, P., Campbell, W., Morgan, B., & Salas, E. (1987). *The evaluation of teamwork skills: An empirical assessment with implications for training* (Technical Report No. 87-016). Orlando, FL: U.S. Naval Training Systems Center.

Gordon, S. E., & Gill, R. T. (1992). Knowledge acquisition with question probes and conceptual graph structures. In T. Lauer, E. Peacock, & A. Graesser (Eds.), *Questions and information systems* (pp. 29–46). Hillsdale, NJ: Erlbaum.

Gordon, S. E., Schmierer, K., & Gill, R. T. (1993). Conceptual graph analysis: Knowledge acquisition for instructional system design. *Human Factors, 35,* 459–481.

Greeno, J. G., & Simon, H. A. (1987). Problem solving and reasoning. In R. C. Atkinson, R. J. Herrnstein, G. Lindzey, & R. D. Luce (Eds.), *Steven's handbook of experimental psychology* (pp. 589–672).

Grote, G. F., & James, L. R. (1991). Testing behavioral consistency and coherence with the situation-response measure of achievement motivation. *Multivariate Behavioral Research, 26,* 655–691.

Hayes, J. R., & Flower, L. S. (1986). Writing research and the writer. *American Psychologist, 41,* 1106–1113.

Hershey, D. A., Walsh, D. A., Read, S. J., & Chulef, A. S. (1990). The effects of expertise on financial problem solving: Evidence for goal-directed, problem-solving scripts. *Organizational Behavior and Human Decision Processes, 46,* 77–101.

Khandwalla, P. N. (1993). An exploratory investigation of divergent thinking through protocol analysis. *Creativity Research Journal, 6,* 241–260.

Kilcullen, R. N., White, L. A., Mumford, M. D., & Mack, H. (1993). Assessing the construct validity of rational biodata scales. *Military Psychology, 7,* 17-28.

Klimoski, R. J., & Brickner, M. (1987). Why do assessment centers work? Puzzle of assessment center validity. *Personnel Psychology, 40,* 243–260.

Lesgold, A., Lajoie, S., Logan, D., & Eggan, G. (1990). Applying cognitive task analysis and research methods to assessment. In N. Frederiksen, R. Glaser, A. Lesgold, & M.G. Shafto (Eds.), *Diagnostic monitoring of skill and knowledge acquisition* (pp. 325–350). Hillsdale, NJ: Erlbaum.

Lohman, D. F., & Ippel, M. J. (1993). Cognitive diagnosis: From statistically based assessment toward theory-based assessment. In N. Frederiksen, R. J. Mislevy, & I. I. Bejar (Eds.), *Test theory for a new generation of tests* (pp. 41–71). Hillsdale, NJ: Erlbaum.

Lohman, D. F., & Kyllonen, P. E. (1983). Individual differences in solution strategy on spatial tasks. In R. F. Dillon & R. R. Glaser (Eds.), *Individual differences in cognition: Vol. 1* (pp. 105–135). New York: Academic Press.

Marshall-Mies, J. C., Martin, J. A., Fleishman, E. A., Zaccaro, S. J., Baughman, W. A., & McGee, M. L. (1996). *Development and evaluation of cognitive and metacognitive measures for predicting leadership potential* (Report No. SBIR A92-154, U.S. Army Research Institute for the Behavioral and Social Sciences). Bethesda, MD: Management Research Institute.

Massaro, D. W., & Cowan, N. (1993). Information processing models: Microscopes of the mind. *Annual Review of Psychology, 44,* 383–425.

McGrath, J. E. (1984). *Groups: Interaction and performance.* Englewood Cliffs, NJ: Prentice-Hall.

Means, B., & Gott, S. P. (1988). Cognitive task analysis as a basis for tutor development: Articulating abstract knowledge representations. In J. Psotka, L. D. Massey, & S. A. Mutter (Eds.), *Intelligent tutoring systems: Lessons learned.* Hillsdale, NJ: Erlbaum.

Messick, S. (1995). Validity of psychological assessment: Validation of inferences from persons' responses and performances as a scientific inquiry into score meaning. *American Psychologist, 50,* 741–749.

Mislevy, R. J. (1993). Foundations of a new test theory. In N. Frederiksen, R. J. Mislevy, & I. I. Bejar (Eds.), *Test theory for a new generation of tests* (pp. 19-39). Hillsdale, NJ: Erlbaum.

Mumford, M. D., Baughman, W. A., Maher, M. A., Costanza, D. P., & Supinski, E. P. (in press). Process-based measures of creative problem-solving skills: IV. Category combination. *Creativity Research Journal.*

Mumford, M. D., Baughman, W. A., Supinski, E. P., Costanza, D. P., & Threlfall, K. V. (1993). *Cognitive and metacognitive skill development: Alternative measures for predicting leadership potential* (Report No. SBIR A92-154, U.S. Army Research Institute for Behavioral and Social Sciences). Bethesda, MD: Management Research Institute.

Mumford, M. D., Baughman, W. A., Supinski, E. P., & Maher, M. A. (1996). Process-based measures of creative problem-solving skills: II. Information encoding. *Creativity Research Journal, 9,* 77–88).

Mumford, M. D., Baughman, W. A., Threlfall, K. V., Supinski, E. P., & Costanza, D. P. (1996). Process-based measures of creative problem-solving skills: I. Problem construction. *Creativity Research Journal, 9,* 63–76.

Mumford, M. D., Peterson, N. G., & Childs, R. A. (1997). Basic and cross-functional skills. In N. G. Peterson, M. D. Mumford, W. C. Borman, P. R. Jeanneret, & E. A. Fleishman (Eds.), *O*NET: An Occupational Information Network.* Washington, DC: American Psychological Association.

Mumford, M. D., Stokes, G. S., & Owens, W. A. (1990). *Patterns of life history: The ecology of human individuality.* Hillsdale, NJ: Erlbaum.

Mumford, M. D., Supinski, E. P., Baughman, W. A., Costanza, D. P., & Threlfall, K. V. (in press). Process-based measures of creative problem-solving skills: V. Overall prediction. *Creativity Research Journal.*

Mumford, M. D., Supinski, E. P., Threlfall, K. V., & Baughman, W. A. (in press). Process-based measures of creative problem-solving skills: III. Category selection. *Creativity Research Journal.*

Nunnally, J. C. (1978). *Psychometric theory* (2nd ed.). New York: McGraw-Hill.

Perkins, D. P., Jay, E., & Tishman, S. (1994). *Assessing thinking: A framework for measuring critical thinking and problem solving skills at the college level.* Washington, DC: National Center for Education Statistics.

Pople, H. E. (1981). Heuristic methods for imposing structure on ill-structured problems: The structuring of medical diagnostics. In P. Szolovitz (Ed.), *Artificial intelligence in medicine* (pp. 119–185). Boulder, CO: Westview Press.

Prien, E. P. (1977). The function of job analysis in content validation. *Personnel Psychology, 30,* 167–174.

Prince, A., Brannick, M., Prince, C., & Salas, E. (1992). Team process measurement and implications for training. *Proceedings of the Human Factors Society 36th Annual Meeting* (pp. 1351–1355). Santa Monica, CA: Human Factors Society.

Reilly, R. R. S., Henry, S., & Smither, J. W. (1990). An examination of the effects of using behavior checklists on the construct validity of assessment center dimensions. *Personnel Psychology, 43,* 71–84.

Royer, J. M., Cisero, C. A., & Carlo, M. S. (1993). Techniques and procedures for assessing cognitive skills. *Review of Educational Research, 63,* 201–243.

Russell, C. J. (1987). Person characteristics versus role conservancy explanations for assessment center ratings. *Academy of Management Journal, 30,* 817–826.

Russell, C. J., & Kuhnert, K. M. (1992). New frontiers in management selection systems: Where measurement technologies and theory collide. *Leadership Quarterly, 3,* 109–136.

Sackett, P. R., & Hakel, M. D. (1979). Temporal stability and individual differences in using assessment information to form overall ratings. *Organizational Behavior and Human Performance, 23,* 120–137.

Sager, C. E., Mumford, M. D., Baughman, W. A., & Childs, R. A. (1997). Occupation-specific descriptors: approaches, procedures, and findings. In N. G. Peterson, M. D. Mumford, W. C. Borman, P. R. Jeanneret, & E. A. Fleishman (Eds.), *O*NET: An Occupational Information Network.* Washington, DC: American Psychological Association.

Sizer, T. (1985). *Changing schools and testing: An uneasy proposal.* Proceedings of the 1985 ETS Invitational Conference: The Redesign of Testing for the 21st Century (pp. 1–7). Educational Testing Service, Princeton, NJ.

Snow, R. E., & Lohman, D. F. (1989). Implications of cognitive psychology for educational measurement. In R. L. Linn (Ed.), *Educational measurement* (3rd edition). New York: Macmillan.

Snow, R. E., & Peterson, P. (1985). Cognitive analyses of tests: Implications for redesign. In S. E. Embretson (Ed.), *Test design: Developments in psychology and psychometrics* (pp. 149–166). Orlando, FL: Academic Press.

Sternberg, R. J. (1977). *Intelligence, information processing and analogical reasoning: The componential analysis of human abilities.* New York: Wiley.

Sternberg, R. J. (1985). *Beyond IQ: A triarchic theory of human intelligence.* New York: Cambridge University Press.

Sternberg, R. J. (1986). Synopsis of a triarchic theory of human intelligence. In S. H. Irvine & S. E. Newstead (Eds.), *Intelligence and cognition* (pp. 161–221). Dorrecht, Germany: Hijhoff.

Swezey, R. W., & Salas, E. (1992). *Teams: Their training and performance.* Norwood, NJ: Ablex.

Yerkes, R. M. (Ed.). (1921). Psychological examining in the United States army. *Memoirs of the National Academy of Sciences,* Vol. 15.

DEVELOPING MEASURES OF JOB PERFORMANCE

Ratings of Job Performance

Elaine D. Pulakos

OVERVIEW

Rewarding and promoting effective performance in organizations, as well as identifying ineffective performers for developmental programs or other personnel actions, are essential to effective human resource management in organizations. The ability to perform these functions relies on assessing employee performance in a fair and accurate manner.

There are different types of measures that can be used to evaluate employee job performance, and they can be classified into two general categories: objective performance measures and subjective performance measures. Some examples of objective performance measures include dollar volume of sales, number of words typed per minute, number of pieces produced, number of errors made, and number of days absent from work. While some useful information can be obtained from objective performance indices, there are some serious inadequacies associated with these types of measures that preclude their use in many jobs (Dunnette, 1966; Guion, 1965). One problem is that objective measures often are deficient; that is, they do not provide an assessment of all aspects of the job that contribute to performance. Consider, for example, the job of an electrician. Although number of construction projects completed within budget may be a useful indicator of performance effectiveness, the ability to complete projects within budget is only one aspect of the electrician's job. There are other important aspects of performance, such as maintaining good customer relations, for which no objective measures of performance may exist. If one were to focus only on the objective "number of projects completed within budget" criterion, other aspects of performance would be neglected, leaving an incomplete picture of the electrician's effectiveness. Thus, number of projects completed within budget would be a deficient performance measure—a common problem with many objective performance indices.

A second major problem associated with objective performance measures is that they are often affected by factors that lie beyond the employee's direct control. Again using the example of number of projects completed within budget, there are many factors beyond the electrician's ability or motivation to perform effectively that may impact the number of projects completed within budget. For example, some of these factors might include the effectiveness of suppliers or the knowledge level of customers. An electrician who happens to have good material suppliers and knowledgeable customers may be more likely to complete projects within budget than an electrician with poor suppliers and customers who do not understand the business. Such unequal circumstances create difficulties in comparing the performance of different electricians using the number of projects completed within budget criterion.

The problems associated with objective performance measures have led researchers and managers to place more emphasis on subjective measures of job performance. Subjective measures usually are some type of performance rating instrument. In fact, the most common measures used in organizations to provide developmental feedback to subordinates, make personnel decisions, or validate testing or other human resource programs are performance rating scales. One important advantage of using ratings to collect information about individuals' job performance is that all of a job's performance requirements can be described on a set of rating scales (Borman, 1987). Thus, subjective rating measures are not plagued by the criterion deficiency problems just discussed that often are inherent in objective performance measures. Also, subjective measures can be developed to focus on behaviors that lead to effective performance, which helps to alleviate the problems imposed by unequal opportunities to perform effectively. Using our example, an electrician who happens to have poor suppliers and inexperienced customers could be expending as much time and effort completing projects within budget as the electrician with good suppliers and knowledgeable customers. Using rating scales, both electricians would be given credit for behaviors on a scale that dealt with effort expended completing projects within budget, even though the number of projects completed would be fewer for the electrician with poor suppliers and inexperienced customers. Thus, job performance rating scales can be developed to safeguard against some of the problems inherent in objective performance measures.

This is not to suggest that subjective measures are without problems of their own. Because ratings rely on human judgment, they are prone to certain kinds of rating errors. These errors and strategies for dealing with them are discussed in more detail later in this chapter. The key point is that it is possible to define a job's performance requirements comprehensively and fairly using performance rating scales.

The remainder of this chapter describes the psychometric characteristics of performance ratings, how to develop rating scales using a variety of behaviorally based formats, and how to train raters to use these kinds of scales effectively.

PSYCHOMETRIC CHARACTERISTICS OF PERFORMANCE RATINGS

Evaluation of the psychometric adequacy of a set of ratings minimally involves an examination of descriptive statistics (e.g., means and standard deviations) and rating reliabilities. Researchers also frequently examine the underlying factor structure of a set of ratings to better understand the dimensions measured by the instrument.

Examination of the means and standard deviations for a set of ratings provides important information about their psychometric adequacy. One frequently observed problem, especially with operational performance ratings, is a relatively high mean rating and low variability in the ratings. This is because raters tend to evaluate most ratees using the high end of the rating scale. When pay, promotion, or other important organizational rewards are based in whole or in part on a ratings score, evaluators often have difficulty providing and justifying less than generally effective ratings. On the other hand, when ratings are used for staff development or for research purposes (e.g., as criteria for a validation study), rating distributions tend to be less skewed than in operational situations. If one is using a 7-point scale, a mean rating between 4.00 and 5.00 and a standard deviation between 1.00 and 1.50 are reasonable and indicative of an adequate rating distribution. It is reasonable to expect rating distributions to be somewhat skewed because most truly unsatisfactory performers are likely to have left the organization, or if an effective selection system is in place, unsatisfactory performers would not have been hired.

Reliability of criteria has been cited as an important consideration by numerous authors writing about job performance measurement. From a research perspective, low levels of criterion reliability lead to underestimates of the validity of predictors. There are several different ways that reliability of a set of ratings can be evaluated. One is to assess the internal consistency of ratings using coefficient alpha. Coefficient alpha indicates the extent to which ratings across different dimensions of performance are similar within ratees. However, many raters are prone to committing "halo" error, which means that they assign ratings based on an overall global impression of the ratee, rather than distinguishing among the ratee's strengths and developmental areas. The result of halo error is that ratees are evaluated at roughly the same level of effectiveness across all performance dimensions. Accordingly, a high internal consistency reliability may simply be the result of high levels of halo error. Halo error can similarly affect ratings made by the same raters at different points in time. For these reasons, a more appropriate means for assessing the reliability of a set of ratings is interrater reliability. Interrater reliability assesses the level of agreement between two or more raters regarding ratee performance levels.

There have been many studies investigating the reliability of ratings. Two meta-analytic reviews, in which large numbers of studies were quantitatively cumulated, are described here. Rothstein (1990) presented empirical evidence from 79 organizations, in which ratings on 9,975 ratees were collected. She found that as the opportunity to observe performance (as measured by the number of years supervised or observed) increased, the interrater reliability increased, but the level of reliability reached an asymptotic maximum of .60 at about the two-year point. This is consistent with King, Hunter, and Schmidt (1980), who conducted a meta-analysis of the reliability of ratings and found that the value of .60 represents the upper bound on reliability of supervisor ratings made by a single rater. Rothstein's results suggested that ratings made of employees who have been observed for less than 12 months are likely to be fairly unreliable, and thus recommended that organizations not use the ratings of one supervisor to evaluate the performance of employees with less than one year of job experience.

Visweswaran, Ones, and Schmidt (1996) compared various kinds of reliability estimates. They found that supervisory ratings appeared to have higher reliability than peer ratings and that the mean interrater reliability of supervisory ratings was .52 (using 40 reliability coefficients and a total sample of 14,650 participants) for the Overall Job Performance rating dimension. They also found that interrater reliability (the extent to which different raters agree on the performance of different individuals) was lower than intrarater reliability (the extent to which there is single rater agreement across dimensions or over time).

In summary, the primary means for assessing the psychometric properties of ratings involves examining descriptive statistics and rating reliabilities. Rating distributions are likely to be somewhat skewed, even when used for development or research purposes, because very poor performers usually do not remain in their jobs. Ratings for operational purposes are often highly skewed and thus inadequate from a psychometric perspective. Interrater reliability is the most appropriate form of reliability to compute with rating data. Reliability estimates in the .50–.60 range are typical for performance ratings. The following sections of this chapter discuss methods for creating rating cales using a variety of formats and for training raters how to use such scales.

HOW TO CREATE RATING SCALES USING VARIOUS FORMATS

Over the years, many different types of rating formats have been developed in both research studies and practice. The motivation behind much of this work and experimentation was based on the assumption that rating format characteristics would be related to rating accuracy. In fact, some research has shown that rating scales anchored with specific job behaviors yield ratings with less psychometric error (e.g., halo) than other types of rating scales (Borman & Dunnette, 1975; Campbell, Dunnette, Arvey, & Hellervick, 1973; Keaveny & McGann, 1975). Overall, however, literature reviews of format comparison studies (Bernardin, 1977; DeCotiis, 1977; Landy & Farr, 1980; Schwab, Heneman, & DeCotiis, 1975; Zedeck, Kafry, & Jacobs, 1976) have led researchers to conclude that no one rating format consistently produces psychometrically superior ratings (e.g., more reliable, valid, or accurate). In fact, Landy and Farr (1980) estimated that as little as 4% of the rating variance in psychometric rating quality can be accounted for by rating format, leading them to call for a moratorium on rating format research. Other researchers have argued that it is premature to suspend format-related research (Guion & Gibson, 1988).

Although rating format may have little impact on the psychometric quality of performance ratings, there are other aspects of the performance appraisal process for which format issues are relevant. For example, one issue is the ease with which raters are able to understand and use the format. Another is the extent to which raters and ratees accept the rating instrument and view it as appropriate. A third issue is how well the rating format supports the provision of meaningful developmental feedback to ratees. A fourth issue is the degree to which the rating format meets legal standards. Finally, although no one rating format has been shown to be superior with respect to psychometric rating quality, research (McIntyre, Smith, & Hassett, 1984; Pulakos, 1984, 1986) has shown that well-developed behaviorally based rating formats, coupled with appropriate rater training, can produce ratings with impressive levels of reliability and accuracy.

The following sections of this chapter describe several different types of rating scale formats that are useful for collecting job performance information, how they are developed, and their relative advantages and disadvantages. Although several different types of rating formats have been developed and evaluated (see Bernardin & Beatty, 1984; Borman, 1991), we focus on five of the more common ones: graphic rating scales (Paterson, 1922–1923), behaviorally anchored rating scales (Smith & Kendall, 1963), behavioral summary scales (Borman, 1979), behavioral observation scales (Latham & Wexley, 1981), and mixed standard scales (Blanz & Ghiselli, 1972). We then describe implementation issues surrounding the use of rating scales in general and strategies for ensuring that the ratings collected are as accurate and effective as possible.

GRAPHIC RATING SCALES

One of the more widely used rating formats is the graphic rating scale (Paterson, 1922–1923). Graphic rating scales are designed to elicit ratings on dimensions of performance relevant to a particular job. As described in Chapters 2 through 4, performance dimensions are typically identified via a job analysis in which job experts describe the major aspects or categories of performance for a job. The scale developer must decide how many rating scale points will be included on the scales. A generally accepted guideline is somewhere between four and nine. Use of fewer than four scale points tends to provide insufficient discrimination among ratees, while more than nine yields unimportant distinctions. The scale points are usually defined on a continuum, but the scale developer must decide how these points will be anchored—for example, with verbal anchors, numerical anchors, or a combination of both. Examples of graphic rating scales are shown in Figure 11.1.

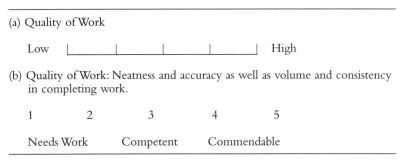

(a) Quality of Work

Low |_____|_____|_____|_____| High

(b) Quality of Work: Neatness and accuracy as well as volume and consistency in completing work.

1   2   3   4   5

Needs Work   Competent   Commendable

FIGURE 11.1   Examples of Graphic Rating Scales

The first graphic rating scale shown in Figure 11.1 (type a) contains qualitative end anchors only, while the second (type b) includes both numerical and verbal anchors. A major problem with many graphic rating scales is that the scale points are not thoroughly defined, leaving raters to develop their own interpretations of what is meant by the different rating levels. One consequence of allowing raters to apply their own standards to the rating task is that they often do not agree about the types of behavior or performance that constitute different effectiveness levels. Consider the following example. Two raters observe an electrician performing a series of job tasks. Using scale (b) in Figure 11.1, one rater may evaluate the performance he or she observes as a "3," while the other rater may evaluate that same performance as a "5." Because the anchors on the rating scales are not well defined, there are no guidelines presented for what types of behavior should be rated a "3" versus a "4" or "5." The main problem, then, with graphic rating scales is that they do not adequately define the meaning of different performance levels. Not only does this make the rater's job of distinguishing between the different effectiveness levels very difficult, but also the standards applied by different raters are variable and inconsistent across ratees.

It also is difficult to provide feedback to ratees using graphic rating scales. A rater can inform the ratee that his or her "quality of work" is a "3," but why that rating was given versus another is often difficult to explain. Graphic rating scales also provide little, if any, information about what the employee must do to achieve a more effective rating.

In the next sections of this chapter, we focus on the development of four types of behavior-based rating scales: Behaviorally anchored rating scales (BARS), behavioral summary scales (BSS), behavioral observation scales (BOS), and mixed standard scales (MSS). Behavior-based scales address the lack of specificity and definitional problems inherent in graphic rating scales.

HOW TO DEVELOP BEHAVIORALLY ANCHORED RATING SCALES

Behaviorally anchored rating scales (BARS; Smith & Kendall, 1963) are used to assess performance dimensions that represent major requirements of a job. Actual examples of behaviors that incumbents may exhibit on the job are used to anchor different levels of performance effectiveness within each dimension. These behaviors help raters make accurate assessments of performance by matching their observations of ratee performance to an appropriate effectiveness level on each dimension.

The development of BARS relies on input from job incumbents and/or their supervisors. These subject matter experts provide the information necessary to construct the rating scales (i.e., the rating dimensions and the behaviors that define different levels of effectiveness for each dimension). The behaviors are derived from critical incidents (Flanagan, 1954), as described in Chapter 4. After the critical incidents are collected from subject matter experts and edited by psychologists, subject matter experts are then asked to sort the critical incidents into dimensions and rate them on an effectiveness rating scale. Often, a 7-point scale is used. The percentage of subject matter experts sorting each incident into a particular dimension and the means and standard deviations of the effectiveness ratings for each incident are computed. Examples of results from an analysis of critical incidents are provided in Appendix B of Chapter 4.

The scale developer must then decide which reliably rated incidents will be used as anchors for each performance dimension. Two criteria typically are used to select incidents to anchor each dimension: (1) Each incident should have a small standard deviation for the effectiveness rating (indicating high agreement among raters), and (2) each incident should be placed in a particular dimension by a high percentage of the raters. If a 7-point scale is used to make the effectiveness ratings, a standard deviation of 1.5 is often used as a cutoff for retaining behavioral incidents (any incident with a standard deviation greater than 1.5 would be eliminated). A frequently used cutoff for the percentage of raters agreeing that a given incident belongs in a particular dimension is 60 to 70%. Behavioral incidents that meet these criteria are used to anchor the rating scale points. Usually between 7 and 12 representative incidents are

Planning, Preparing and Organizing Work: Plans work prior to performing tasks; reads blueprints carefully before beginning work; and anticipates tool and material needs of journeymen before being asked to order and retrieve materials.

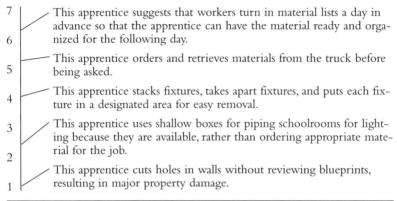

7

6   This apprentice suggests that workers turn in material lists a day in advance so that the apprentice can have the material ready and organized for the following day.

5   This apprentice orders and retrieves materials from the truck before being asked.

4   This apprentice stacks fixtures, takes apart fixtures, and puts each fixture in a designated area for easy removal.

3   This apprentice uses shallow boxes for piping schoolrooms for lighting because they are available, rather than ordering appropriate material for the job.

2

1   This apprentice cuts holes in walls without reviewing blueprints, resulting in major property damage.

FIGURE 11.2   Example of a Behaviorally Anchored Rating Scale for the Dimension "Planning, Preparing, and Organizing Work" for Apprentice Electricians

selected to anchor the different levels of effectiveness for each rating dimension. Figure 11.2 shows an example of a BARS developed for inside apprentice electricians for the dimension Planning, Preparing, and Organizing Work. Notice that in Chapter 4, the fifth incident in Appendix B, about piping school rooms for lighting using shallow boxes, was categorized into the dimension Planning, Preparing, and Organizing Work by 12 of the 20 respondents (60%). Also, the mean effectiveness rating was 2.45 with a standard deviation of .66. Since this incident is within the limits just described, it was chosen to anchor the scale shown in Figure 11.2 near the low end.

To evaluate a worker's performance using BARS, raters are first asked to record behavioral observations of a ratee's performance relevant to each performance dimension. Because these observations may occur over a six-month to one-year time period, raters are encouraged to keep notebooks in which they record performance examples as they occur. At the end of the rating period, raters compare the effectiveness of the ratee behaviors they have observed with the effectiveness levels represented in the scaled behavioral examples. A rating is then assigned based on this comparison process. Thus, in using BARS, raters are encouraged to attend to and record actual behaviors rather than relying on general impressions as a basis for making their ratings. Further, the scaled behavioral anchors serve as comparison points against which a ratee's observed performance can be evaluated.

HOW TO DEVELOP
BEHAVIORAL SUMMARY SCALES

Although the BARS rating format was an important step in the development of well-defined rating scales, a potential problem with BARS is that raters may have trouble matching a ratee's actual performance to the specific behavior examples used to anchor the rating scales (Borman, 1979). Using the BARS rating scale shown in Figure 11.2, imagine the difficulty a rater might have comparing a ratee's performance to the very specific scale anchors shown there. Even though a ratee may be performing at an effectiveness level represented by one of the anchors, it is unlikely that he or she will have exhibited the exact behavior depicted on the rating scale. This puts the rater in the position of having to decide which of the relatively few scaled behaviors best matches the ratee's actual job performance. Such judgments can be very difficult to make, leaving raters unsure about how to use the scaled effectiveness levels to guide their ratings.

In response to this problem with BARS, the behavioral summary scale (BSS) rating format was developed by Borman, Hough, and Dunnette (1976). A BSS is similar to a BARS because both scales are anchored with behavioral descriptions of effective and ineffective performance to guide raters' evaluations of employee job performance. However, rather than using a few specific behaviors to anchor the different scale points, the BSS contains anchors that are more general descriptions of effectiveness at the different performance levels. To develop these more general behavioral anchors, the highly specific behavioral incidents that were assigned to a specific category and effectiveness level using the criteria outlined earlier are examined for similar underlying content. Statements are then written to represent a wider range of behaviors that are characteristic of the specific incidents scaled at each effectiveness level. Formulating broader scale anchors that capture the content of several behavioral incidents enables the scale developer to include information on the rating scales that will be relevant to the performance of a larger number of ratees.

To develop a BSS, one would collect and analyze critical incidents using the process described in Chapter 4. Then, as mentioned, rather than anchoring the rating scales with a few specific behavioral examples,

Please rate the apprentice on the following scale by reading the description of each performance level and selecting the number that most closely corresponds to the behavior exhibited by the ratee.

LOW	MEDIUM	HIGH
Starts to perform tasks without checking blueprints/plans; uses inappropriate but available materials for jobs; hurries through work before considering additional tasks that need to be performed before job is completed; misjudges time to complete tasks.	Plans tasks before performing them; organizes tools and materials so that they are easily retrievable when needed; writes down information needed for jobs so that work is completed efficiently; makes adjustments to material before starting jobs so that work is completed efficiently.	Reviews blueprints/plans before starting tasks; makes suggestions about organizing material so that preparation time is minimized; creates lists of tasks to be completed and orders material on own initiative; keeps foreman informed of progress of jobs; anticipates needs for jobs and retrieves tools and materials before they are requested.
1 2	3 4 5	6 7

FIGURE 11.3   Example of a Behavioral Summary Scale Developed for the Dimension "Planning, Preparing, and Organizing Work" for Apprentice Electricians

the scale developer must write statements that capture as much content as possible of all of the behavioral incidents that were reliably sorted into each performance dimension or category.

Typically, several hundred behavioral incidents are categorized into dimensions and rated for effectiveness using a 1 = highly ineffective to 7 = highly effective rating scale. To develop summary statements, the incidents are categorized into levels of effectiveness as follows: incidents rated between 1.00 and 2.49 are considered *low*-level behaviors; incidents rated between 2.50 and 5.49 are considered *average*-level behaviors; and incidents rated between 5.50 and 7.00 are considered *high*-level behavioral incidents. Behavioral statements are written to capture the content of the behavioral incidents in each dimension at each effectiveness level.

Figure 11.3 shows an example of a BSS for the same dimension of electrician performance (Planning, Preparing, and Organizing Work) measured by the BARS shown in Figure 11.2. As shown in Figure 11.3, the BSS anchors cover more of the behavioral domain of the dimension than do the specific behavioral incidents used to anchor the BARS. For example, the anchor for high performance states, "Reviews blue-prints/plans before starting tasks." This statement could summarize several incidents, including the third and fourth incidents in Appendix B in Chapter 4. By providing a more comprehensive definition of the behaviors that constitute different levels of effectiveness, it is more likely that one of the anchors will describe a ratee's observed performance on each dimension. Accordingly, the rater's task of matching observed behaviors to the scaled behavioral anchors should be facilitated. While research comparing different rating formats has shown no consistent differences in the quality of ratings obtained using one versus another rating format (Landy & Farr, 1980), our experience has been that raters react more favorably to the BSS format than to the BARS because they feel it is easier to see the relevance of the BSS anchors for the employees they are evaluating.

How to Develop
Behavioral Observation Scales

Behavioral observation scales (BOS; Latham & Wexley, 1981) contain a large number of very specific effective and ineffective behaviors on which each employee is evaluated. There are no average behaviors included on the rating scales. For each behavioral incident on the scale, raters are asked to evaluate the frequency with which they have observed each employee exhibit the behavior. Latham and Wexley recommend that a 1 = Almost never performs the behavior to 5 = Nearly always performs the behavior rating scale be used for these ratings. Thus, rather than evaluating the effectiveness of a ratee's performance on each of several job-relevant dimensions, as is the case when using BARS or BSS, a BOS requires raters to evaluate the frequency with which they have observed several specific behaviors listed on the rating scales.

BOS performance dimensions and behavioral incidents are obtained during a series of workshops to generate performance dimensions and incidents, as described in Chapter 4. However, rather than only using selected incidents (as one would when developing a BARS) or summarizing the content of many incidents into more general behavioral anchors (as one would when developing a BSS), the procedure for developing a BOS retains all of the behavioral statements generated for use on the scales. One difference between the BOS and BARS or BSS

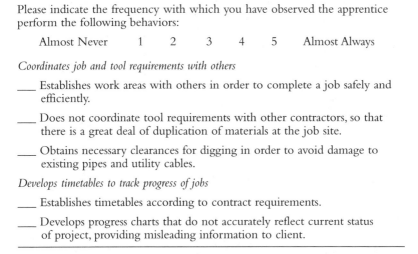

Please indicate the frequency with which you have observed the apprentice perform the following behaviors:

Almost Never   1   2   3   4   5   Almost Always

Coordinates job and tool requirements with others

____ Establishes work areas with others in order to complete a job safely and efficiently.

____ Does not coordinate tool requirements with other contractors, so that there is a great deal of duplication of materials at the job site.

____ Obtains necessary clearances for digging in order to avoid damage to existing pipes and utility cables.

Develops timetables to track progress of jobs

____ Establishes timetables according to contract requirements.

____ Develops progress charts that do not accurately reflect current status of project, providing misleading information to client.

FIGURE 11.4   Example of a Behavioral Observation Scale Developed for the Dimension "Planning, Preparing, and Organizing Work" for Apprentice Electricians

development procedures is that participants in BOS incident generation workshops are instructed to write only ineffective and effective behavioral examples. The rationale is that average behaviors do not help supervisors to make distinctions between effective and ineffective performers, nor do they effectively pinpoint employee actions that should be rewarded or those that should be remediated.

The behavioral statements are placed into a format similar to that shown in Figure 11.4. Note that behavioral examples are typically organized under the title of the performance dimension for which they are relevant. Ratees can be scored on each performance dimension by summing their ratings across all of the items contained in each dimension and then dividing this total by the number of items listed under each dimension. Note that negatively worded statements would need to be scored such that high ratings would lower the individual's overall rating. It is then possible to give feedback to employees that is structured around their performance on each major dimension of performance as well as on more specific aspects.

Latham and Wexley (1981) argued that an important feature of a BOS is that raters are required to focus on relatively specific ratee behaviors and to record the frequency with which they have observed those behaviors. They argued that this relatively straightforward rating process should result in more accurate ratings since raters are not required to make complex evaluative judgments about performance effectiveness, as when a BARS or BSS format is used. Research has shown that raters may experience some difficulty integrating complex performance information to arrive at an accurate assessment of performance (Cooper, 1981; Feldman, 1981), suggesting that appraisal formats like BOS that make fewer cognitive demands on raters might be advantageous. However, other research has shown that a BOS measures traitlike judgments rather than simply frequency of performance data (Murphy, Martin, & Garcia, 1982). Thus, the expected major advantage of the BOS format may not be realized in practice.

HOW TO DEVELOP
MIXED STANDARD RATING SCALES

Mixed standard scales (MSS), developed by Blanz and Ghiselli (1972), are similar to some of the scales described earlier in that they contain performance dimensions and examples of ineffective, average, and effective behaviors. Again, dimensions for these rating scales can be identified and behavioral incidents generated using the procedures described in Chapter 4. Similar to the BARS format, only a few incidents are selected for each MSS performance dimension. Specifically, three incidents are selected per dimension, one effective, one average, and one ineffective. The scale developer must take care to ensure that the content of the rating dimension is as well represented as possible by the incidents selected. Once all of the items are selected (i.e., three times the number of dimensions), they are then randomly arranged to form a single list of behaviors. An example of this format for the electrician's job is shown in Figure 11.5.

To use these rating scales, raters are instructed to read each behavioral statement and decide whether the ratee's performance exceeds the performance described in the statement (+), falls below the performance described in the statement (-), or is accurately described by the statement (0). MSS dimensions are scored from 1, indicating that all minuses were received, to 7, indicating that all pluses were received. The rules for deriving dimensional scores using MSS are shown in Figure 11.6. These scoring procedures not only produce a final ratee performance score but also enable an assessment of "logical" evaluation errors. One example of a logical error would be when, within a given dimension, a ratee receives a "+" on the average performance statement and a "-" on the ineffective

Read each item and decide if the typical behavior of the apprentice to be rated fits the description, is better than the description, or is worse than the description. If the item is an accurate description of the apprentice's typical performance, then place a (0) in the space next to the column. If the apprentice's typical performance is better than the item, then place a (+) in the space. If the apprentice's typical performance is worse than the item description, then place a (-) in the space.

____ Occasionally reads blueprints before starting a job.

____ Orders required material in appropriate amounts after reviewing a job's material requirements.

____ Loads, hauls, and unloads inappropriate supplies, resulting in the apprentice having to go back to obtain required materials.

____ Often assembles tools and equipment incorrectly, typically requiring some reassembly by the journeyman or foreman.

____ Loads, hauls, and unloads appropriate supplies in an efficient manner.

____ Orders required material, but occasionally orders too much, resulting in waste; or too little, resulting in lost time because more material has to be ordered.

____ Reads blueprints carefully before starting a job.

____ Assembles tools and equipment accurately and efficiently, resulting in little or no reassembly by journeyman or foreman.

____ Rarely reads blueprints before starting a job.

____ Loads, hauls, and unloads appropriate supplies, but makes stops along the way, resulting in lost time for the journeyman.

____ Orders material without reviewing the material requirements of the job, nearly always resulting in waste, or lost time because of reorders.

____ Assembles tools and equipment inaccurately, typically requiring some reassembly by the journeyman or foreman.

FIGURE 11.5   Example of a Mixed Standard Scale Developed for the Dimension "Planning, Preparing, and Organizing Work" for Apprentice Electricians

performance statement. Consistent errors of this type indicate either that a rater is incapable of using the rating scales or that there are problems with the effectiveness levels represented by the behavioral statements.

One major impetus behind the design of MSS was to minimize halo error, which is one of the most pervasive errors made when one indi-

Effective Statement	Average Statement	Ineffective Statement	Derived Rating
+	+	+	7
0	+	+	6
−	+	+	5
−	0	+	4
−	−	+	3
−	−	0	2
−	−	−	1

FIGURE 11.6   MSS Dimension Scoring Guidelines

vidual evaluates another. It occurs when a rater assigns ratings based on a global, overall impression of a ratee rather than distinguishing the ratee's strengths and weaknesses on different performance dimensions. Halo error results in ratings across different dimensions that are at about the same level when the employee's performance is, in fact, variable across these dimensions. By randomizing the behavioral statements relevant to the different dimensions and requiring that raters rate each behavior in the manner described earlier, Blanz and Ghiselli (1972) hypothesized that halo error would be minimized when using MSS compared to other rating formats in which the evaluation(s) for each dimension were clearly discernible to raters. Unfortunately, research has shown that mixed standard scales have not resulted in the reductions in halo that had been anticipated (Finley, Osburn, Dubin, & Jeanneret, 1977; Saal & Landy, 1977). MSS may, however, be somewhat easier to use than BARS or BSS. The rater must simply compare observed ratee behavior to the effectiveness reflected in single behavioral statements, rather than integrate performance information to arrive at a rating on a continuum of effectiveness.

HOW TO SELECT A RATING FORMAT

In deciding what type of rating format is most appropriate, consideration should be given to several factors, including adherence to legal standards, rater acceptance, ease of use, ease of providing feedback, and quality of ratings produced. Each of these factors is discussed in turn.

A number of factors have been considered by the courts when evaluating the adequacy of different rating formats and performance appraisal systems in general. Some of these relate to technical standards outlined in the *Uniform Guidelines on Employment Selection Procedures* (EEOC, CSC, DOL, & DOJ, 1978), while others can be considered personnel practices that help to safeguard against discrimination in employment decisions. There are four major characteristics of performance rating formats and appraisal systems that researchers have concluded are important based on legal defensibility and fairness criteria: (1) Performance standards should be based on an appropriate job analysis; (2) performance evaluation should be based on a set of specific job dimensions rather than on a global or overall measure; (3) ratings should be made on behaviorally based performance dimensions rather than on vague personality traits or personal characteristics; and (4) supporting evidence for the ratings given should be accurately and comprehensively documented (Bernardin & Beatty, 1984; Cascio & Bernardin, 1981; Nathan & Cascio, 1986). Scale developers should ensure that these criteria are met when selecting a rating format.

Certainly, another important factor to consider when selecting a rating format is rater acceptance. One advantage of all of the behavioral instruments described here is that they tend to be well liked by both employees and their supervisors. This is likely due to scale development processes that incorporate a high level of organizational member involvement. Because the scales are based on performance dimensions and behavioral examples generated by organizational members (e.g., electricians), the final instrument is customized for both the job and the specific organization for which it was developed. Not only are the scales written in the user's "language," but they also reflect the organization's specific values and orientation.

Another issue that impacts on rater acceptance is the type of rating format organizational members prefer. It is important for the scale developer to lead decision makers through the scale format selection process, outlining the advantages and disadvantages associated with different options. For example, one issue concerns the number and type of ratings raters prefer to make. With formats like BARS or BSS, raters are required to make one effectiveness rating for each performance dimension. Thus, if there are 10 performance dimensions, a total of 10 ratings per ratee will be made. With a BOS or MSS format, raters will be required to make ratings of several behavioral examples for each rating dimension. Another issue when considering a BARS or MSS format is the comfort raters feel extrapolating ratee performance levels from a relatively small number of very specific behavioral examples that may or may not describe what they have observed ratees do on the job.

The extent to which provision of feedback about performance will be facilitated by various formats also should be considered. For instance, BSS and BOS formats provide more information that can be used as the basis for a performance discussion than BARS or MSS. A BSS contains comprehensive descriptions of the behaviors that are associated with different levels of effectiveness for each rating dimension. A BOS lists numerous effective and ineffective behaviors relevant to each dimension. Using either a BSS or a BOS, supervisors have a guide not only for describing what has been observed (and thus a rationale for their ratings), but also for advising subordinates about what behaviors must be exhibited to achieve a higher rating. BARS and MSS formats are less useful when providing feedback because these formats contain only a few very specific behaviors describing each dimension. In addition, these behaviors may or may not be relevant for a given employee's performance. BARS and MSS formats thus provide employees and their supervisors with less information on which to base a performance feedback discussion or to design a developmental action plan than BSS or BOS formats.

A final important issue to consider is which rating formats can be expected to produce ratings that are more accurate and of higher psychometric quality than others. As mentioned earlier, most of the evidence from research investigating different rating formats indicates that no consistent differences in rating quality exist among different behaviorally based rating instruments. However, other research (McIntyre, Smith, & Hassett, 1984; Pulakos, 1984, 1986) has shown that when appropriate rater training is provided in conjunction with behaviorally based rating formats, rating quality can be improved. While use of one of the behaviorally based rating formats may be necessary to ensure an accurate assessment of performance, it probably is not sufficient. To ensure high quality ratings, it also is necessary to provide appropriate training on how the scales should be used to evaluate ratee performance. Accordingly, we now turn to a discussion of rater training techniques.

HOW TO CONDUCT RATER TRAINING

A major problem with performance appraisal ratings, regardless of the type of rating format used, is that they are contaminated by various rater errors. Rater errors are systematic faults in judgment that regularly occur when one individual evaluates another. Although there are several different types of rating errors, some of the most common are:

- *Halo*—The rater's ratings are based on his or her general impression of the ratee rather than reflecting the ratee's strengths and weaknesses on different performance dimensions.
- *Leniency*—The rater tends to rate all ratees at the high end of the rating scales.
- *Severity*—The rater tends to rate all ratees at the low end of the rating scales.
- *Central tendency*—The rater tends to rate all ratees around the midpoint of the rating scales.

Such rating errors cause appraisals to be of questionable reliability, accuracy, and thus usefulness. The problems associated with rating errors have led to the development of rater or observer training programs to improve the quality of performance evaluations.

CHARACTERISTICS OF EFFECTIVE RATER TRAINING PROGRAMS

Rater training programs that apply the basic principles of learning will be more effective than training that does not focus on these principles. In particular, successful training programs have been characterized by four key learning components as follows:

- *Lecture*—Rater trainees should receive instruction on such issues as the importance of providing accurate ratings, how to use the rating scales, and how to avoid common rating errors.
- *Practice*—Rater trainees should be given practice evaluating ratee performance. Often this is accomplished by showing trainees videotapes of ratees performing the job. Trainees evaluate these videotaped performances using the rating instruments on which they are trained.
- *Group discussion*—Rater trainees should be given an opportunity to discuss their ratings and provide rationales for them. Discussing personal examples of rating problems and generating solutions can also be a part of the group discussion.
- *Feedback*—Rater trainees should be given feedback on the appropriateness of their practice ratings. Feedback should be given as close as possible to the time the ratings are made, with opportuni-

ties for more practice and feedback. The content of the feedback should be specific and reflect the training objectives.

Training programs, to be maximally successful and effective, should incorporate all four key learning components. If an organization does not have sufficient resources to conduct comprehensive training, however, research has shown that some positive effects can be obtained from less extensive rater training approaches (e.g., Borman, 1975; Pulakos, 1984). For example, although lecture alone is not the recommended training strategy, some rater training is preferable to no training at all.

APPROACHES TO RATER TRAINING

The remainder of this section will describe different approaches to rater training. There are two basic types of programs that have been used to improve the quality of performance ratings: error training and accuracy training. Error training programs are concerned with teaching raters how to avoid one or more of the common rating errors described earlier. Accuracy training programs focus on teaching raters how to use particular rating formats.

Rater Error Training
Traditional rater training programs (e.g., Latham, Wexley, & Pursell, 1975) have focused on teaching raters to eliminate systematic rating errors such as halo, leniency, severity, and central tendency. The rationale for these programs was that by eliminating rater errors, performance rating accuracy and/or validity would increase. Rater training typically involves teaching raters about the types of rating errors and how to avoid them when evaluating performance. To teach raters to eliminate halo, for example, trainees would be told *not* to give a ratee the same rating across multiple performance dimensions. Instead, they would be told to spread their ratings out across the different performance dimensions. Or, to reduce leniency, raters would be told to evaluate ratees using both the low and high ends of the rating scale. Thus, error training essentially involves telling raters how to avoid making rating errors when evaluating performance.

Although error training programs have been shown to be successful in reducing common rating errors defined statistically (e.g., Bernardin & Buckley, 1981; Latham et al., 1975), they have not been particularly effective for increasing rater accuracy. Rater accuracy is the extent to which ratings of performance reflect the ratee's true performance levels. The primary reason error training approaches have not been successful for increasing accuracy is that they focus on teaching raters particular response sets (e.g., spreading ratings across dimensions; using all scale points rather than concentrating ratings at only the low, middle, or high end of the rating scale). The problem is that response sets like these may or may not reflect a ratee's true performance level. For instance, some ratees may actually perform at about the same level of effectiveness across many of the rating dimensions. In an attempt to reduce halo, however, rater error training may actually lead a rater to provide inaccurate ratings of such a ratee. The main problem with error training approaches is that they focus attention on the rater's rating style rather than on accurate observation and evaluation of the ratee's behavior. This problem has led to the development of training programs that focus more specifically on rating accuracy.

Rater Accuracy Training
Rather than focusing on elimination of common rating errors, accuracy training approaches attempt to improve raters' observational skills and teach them the appropriate use of the rating scales. Basically, accuracy or frame-of-reference training (Bernardin & Pence, 1980) attempts to convey to raters that performance is multidimensional, to familiarize raters with the content of each performance dimension, and to teach raters the requirements of the rating task. Although research has shown that no one rating scale format is superior to others with respect to yielding higher quality ratings, different rating scale formats do place different cognitive demands on raters. For example, BARS and BSS formats require raters to make evaluative judgments of ratee effectiveness, while the BOS format requires raters to report the frequency with which they have observed several specific behaviors. Alternatively, some scales require raters to evaluate ratees' job-relevant knowledges, skills, abilities, and other characteristics, while others involve rating behavioral performance dimensions. Researchers (e.g., DiNisi, Cafferty, & Meglino, 1984; Feldman, 1986) have argued that the particular demands placed on raters by different rating formats have important implications for how raters should be trained to make accurate performance evaluations. In fact, rater accuracy training should begin with an assessment of the rating task itself. Training should then be designed to teach raters to make the particular types of judgments required by the given rating format.

As an example of the type of training just discussed, Pulakos (1986) developed a training program for increasing accuracy with the BARS format. Recall that the rater's task in using BARS is to select a level of effectiveness on each rating dimension by matching observations of the ratee's job behavior to the most similar scaled behavioral anchor. In order to perform the BARS rating task accurately, raters need to have a thorough knowledge of the rating dimension content as well as the different types of behaviors that constitute the various effectiveness levels within each dimension. Accordingly, a rater training program was developed consisting of the following activities:

1. Trainees were first lectured on the multidimensional nature of job performance and the need to pay close attention to ratee performance in terms of these dimensions.
2. Several BARS used to evaluate performance were distributed to trainees.
3. The trainer reviewed each performance dimension and the types of behaviors associated with each level of effectiveness. For instance, behaviors that would be expected of a ratee performing at the "1" level were contrasted with behaviors that would be expected of a ratee performing at the "3" level, "5" level, and "7" level.
4. A videotape of a ratee performing the target job was then shown to trainees.
5. Trainees evaluated the videotape using the BARS dimensions.
6. Trainees' ratings were placed on a flip chart.
7. Differences in the ratings were discussed among the group of trainees.
8. The trainer provided feedback on the accuracy of trainees' ratings by discussing how the ratee's behaviors should have been matched to the behavioral examples anchoring the different effectiveness levels. Steps 4 through 8 were repeated using several videotaped ratee performances.

By providing an understanding of the rating dimensions themselves along with examples of the types of behaviors defining the various effectiveness levels, the training strategy promoted accuracy by facilitating the match between observed behaviors and levels of effectiveness described in the rating scales. In fact, the training strategy just described was shown to be more effective for increasing rating accuracy than no training at all or only rater error training (McIntyre et al., 1984; Pulakos, 1984). However, this general approach to training was only effective when coupled with the BARS format for which it was developed (Pulakos, 1986). This training strategy had no effect when used with other rating formats.

Pulakos (1986) also developed an accuracy training program to be used with the BOS format. As discussed earlier, the BOS differs from the BARS in that the BOS requires assessing the frequency of specific behaviors rather than dimensional effectiveness levels. Given the particular demands placed on raters by the BOS format, training that focused on matching observations of ratee behavior to appropriate effectiveness levels did not seem reasonable. Instead, it was hypothesized that accuracy would be better facilitated by fine-tuning raters' observation skills and by ensuring that target BOS behaviors were quickly recognized and accurately recorded. Accordingly, a rater training program was developed that focused on these objectives (see Pulakos, 1986, for details of this training). This training, which included the four key training components (i.e., lecture, practice, group discussion, and feedback), was shown to be the most effective strategy for increasing accuracy with a BOS format. In summary, rater training research shows that rating accuracy can be increased, provided that training matches the demands of the rating task.

SUMMARY

This chapter discussed the development and implementation of various rating formats. As general conclusions, the following are offered. There is no one rating format that will consistently provide ratings with superior psychometric qualities compared with others. When coupled with appropriate rater training, however, high-quality ratings have been produced using several of the behavioral formats described here. In addition, behavioral formats are likely to better meet legal defensibility criteria than vague and ill-defined rating scales. One can also expect high levels of user acceptance when these types of rating formats are employed. In addition, due to their comprehensive definition of different performance effectiveness levels, behavioral rating formats can facilitate providing feedback and conducting developmental planning with subordinates.

It is important to recognize, however, that even the most well developed instruments and training programs may not yield high-quality ratings. Raters must also be motivated to use the performance appraisal measures appropriately. In operational performance appraisal situations, there are numerous extraneous factors that can profoundly affect performance ratings, even when instrumentation and training have been provided (Pulakos, 1991). Some of the organizational factors that can have substantial effects on ratings include rater–ratee interpersonal relationships, the purpose of the appraisal (i.e., whether it will be used for operational personnel decisions, development, or validation), time constraints for completing ratings, the opportunities raters have to observe ratee performance, political and union pressure on raters, and the extent to which raters are accountable for their ratings. For example, if a rater is evaluated on how well his or her employees perform, there will be little incentive to rate an employee unsatisfactorily. Also, one of the most unpleasant tasks a manager must face is giving negative feedback to a subordinate or having to tell a subordinate that he or she will receive a low raise based on the subordinate's performance. While supervisors and managers should be provided with training to deal with such situations, these are still difficult matters that managers often avoid. The point is that performance appraisal does not occur in a vacuum; it occurs in the wider context of an organization. In order to gain the maximum benefits of training or of a well-developed rating format, broader organizational issues must also be addressed. This is because performance appraisal outcomes are a function of organizational contextual variables that directly affect rater motivation as well as rater ability to generate effective, accurate performance appraisals.

There are several steps that might be taken to deal with various organizational factors that affect appraisals. First, support from upper management and other relevant parties (e.g., unions) for the performance appraisal system and process is crucial for effective implementation. Also, the purposes for which performance appraisals will be used and the consequences of ratings, particularly ineffective ratings, should be made clear to raters and ratees. It always is easier to obtain accurate, high-quality ratings in a "for research only" validation setting than when the ratings are intended for operational decision making. Sufficient time for completing appraisals should be provided for raters and ratees, and ratees should participate in the process to the degree possible. One idea is to make the performance appraisal process a formal part of all employees' jobs. Raters should be made accountable and be rewarded for providing high-quality, accurate appraisals rather than "punished" for doing so by the organization or ratees. Finally, raters should be provided with training in how to provide useful feedback to subordinates and in how to deal effectively with performance problems. Ratees should be trained in how the system will operate and how they can effectively participate in their own appraisal process. The point is that although there are a number of organizational variables that may impact the validity of ratings, there are strategies organizations can use to deal with them. Whatever steps are feasible to mitigate factors that interfere with accurate ratings in organizations are strongly recommended.

REFERENCES

Bernardin, H. J. (1977). Behavioral expectation scales versus summated scales: A fairer comparison. *Journal of Applied Psychology, 62,* 422–428.

Bernardin, H. J., & Beatty, R. W. (1984). *Performance appraisal: Assessing human behavior at work.* Boston: Kent-Wadsworth.

Bernardin, H. J., & Buckley, M. R. (1981). Strategies in rater training. *Academy of Management Review, 6,* 205–212.

Bernardin, H. J., & Pence, E. C. (1980). Effects of rater training: Creating new response sets and decreasing accuracy. *Journal of Applied Psychology, 65,* 60–66.

Blanz, R., & Ghiselli, E. E. (1972). The mixed standard scale: A new rating system. *Personnel Psychology, 25,* 185–200.

Borman, W. C. (1975). Effects of instruction to avoid halo error on reliability and validity of performance evaluation ratings. *Journal of Applied Psychology, 60,* 556–560.

Borman, W. C. (1979). Format and training effects on rating accuracy and rating errors. *Journal of Applied Psychology, 64,* 410–421.

Borman, W. C. (1987). Behavior-based rating scales. In R. A. Berk (Ed.), *Performance assessment: Methods and application.* Baltimore, MD: Johns Hopkins University Press.

Borman, W. C. (1991). Job behavior, performance, and effectiveness. In M. D. Dunnette & L. M. Hough (Eds)., *Handbook of industrial and organizational psychology* (Vol. 2). Palo Alto, CA: Consulting Psychologists Press.

Borman, W. C., & Dunnette, M. D. (1975). Behavior-based versus trait-oriented performance ratings: An empirical study. *Journal of Applied Psychology, 60,* 561–565.

Borman, W. C., Hough, L. M., & Dunnette, M. D. (1976). *Development of behaviorally based rating scales for evaluating U. S. Navy Recruiters.* (Technical Report TR-76-31). San Diego, CA: Navy Personnel Research and Development Center.

Campbell, J. P., Dunnette, M. D., Arvey, R. D., & Hellervick, L. V. (1973). The development and evaluation of behaviorally based rating formats. *Journal of Applied Psychology, 57,* 15–22.

Cascio, W. F., & Bernardin, H. J. (1981). Implications of performance appraisal litigation for personnel decisions. *Personnel Psychology, 34,* 211–216.

Cooper, W. H. (1981). Ubiquitous halo. *Psychological Bulletin, 90,* 218–244.

DeCotiis, T. A. (1977). An analysis of the external validity and applied relevance of three rating formats. *Organizational Behavior and Human Decision Processes, 19,* 247–266.

DiNisi, A. S., Cafferty, T. P., & Meglino, B. M. (1984). A cognitive view of the performance appraisal process. *Organizational Behavior and Human Performance, 33,* 360–369.

Dunnette, M. D. (1966). *Personnel selection and placement.* Belmont, CA: Brooks/Cole.

Equal Employment Opportunity Commission, Civil Service Commission, Department of Labor, & Department of Justice (1978, August). Uniform guidelines on employee selection procedures. *Federal Register, 43,* (166) 38290–38315.

Feldman, J. M. (1981). Beyond attribution theory: Cognitive processes in performance appraisal. *Journal of Applied Psychology, 66,* 127–148.

Feldman, J. M. (1986). Instrumentation and training for performance appraisal: A perceptual-cognitive viewpoint. In K. M. Rowland & J. R. Ferris (Eds.), *Research in personnel and human resource management.* (Vol. 4). Greenwich, CT: JAI Press.

Finley, D. M., Osburn, H. G., Dubin, J. A., & Jeanneret, P. R. (1977). Behaviorally based rating scales: Effects of specific anchors and disguised scale continua. *Personnel Psychology, 30,* 658–669.

Flanagan, J. C. (1954). The critical incident technique. *Psychological Bulletin, 51,* 327–355.

Guion, R. M. (1965). *Personnel testing.* New York: McGraw-Hill.

Guion, R. M., & Gibson, W. M. (1988). Personnel selection and placement. *Annual Review of Psychology, 39,* 349–374.

Keaveny, T. J., & McGann, A. F. (1975). A comparison of behavioral expectation scales. *Journal of Applied Psychology, 60,* 695–703.

King, L. M., Hunter, J. E., & Schmidt, F. L. (1980). Halo in a multidimensional forced-choice performance evaluation scale. *Journal of Applied Psychology, 65,* 507–516.

Landy, F. J., & Farr, J. (1980). Performance rating. *Psychological Bulletin, 87,* 72–107.

Latham, G. P., & Wexley, K. N. (1981). *Increasing productivity through performance appraisal.* Reading, MA: Addison-Wesley.

Latham, G. P., Wexley, K. N., & Pursell, E. D. (1975). Training managers to minimize rating errors in the observation of behavior. *Journal of Applied Psychology, 60,* 550–555.

McIntyre, R. M., Smith, D., & Hassett, C. (1984). Accuracy of performance ratings as affected by rater training and perceived purpose of rating. *Journal of Applied Psychology, 69,* 147–156.

Murphy, K. R., Martin, C., & Garcia, M. (1982). Do behavioral observation scales measure observation? *Journal of Applied Psychology, 67,* 562–567.

Nathan, B. R., & Cascio, W. F. (1986). Technical and legal standards. In R. A. Berk (Ed.), *Performance assessment: Methods and application.* Baltimore, MD: Johns Hopkins University Press.

Paterson, D. G. (1922–1923). The Scott Company graphic rating scale. *Journal of Personnel Research, 1,* 351–376.

Pulakos, E. D. (1984). A comparison of rater training programs: Error training and accuracy training. *Journal of Applied Psychology, 69,* 581-588.

Pulakos, E. D. (1986). The development of training programs to increase accuracy with different rating tasks. *Organizational Behavior and Human Decision Processes, 38,* 76–91.

Pulakos, E. D. (1991). Rater training for performance appraisal. In J. W. Jones, B. D. Steffy, & D. W. Bray (Eds.), *Applying psychology in business: The manager's handbook.* New York: Lexington Books.

Rothstein, H. R. (1990). Interrater reliablity of job performance ratings: Growth to asymptote level with increasing opportunity to observe. *Journal of Applied Psychology, 75,* 322–327.

Saal, F. E., & Landy, F. J. (1977). The mixed standard rating scale: An evaluation. *Organizational Behavior and Human Performance, 18,* 19–35.

Schwab, D. P., Heneman, H. G., III, & DeCotiis, T. (1975). Behaviorally anchored rating scales: A review of the literature. *Personnel Psychology, 28,* 549–562.

Smith, P. C., & Kendall, L. M. (1963). Retranslation of expectations: An approach to the construction of unambiguous anchors for rating scales. *Journal of Applied Psychology, 47,* 149–155.

Viswesvaran, C., Ones, D. S., & Schmidt, F. L. (1996). Comparative analysis of the reliability of job performance ratings. *Journal of Applied Psychology, 81,* 557–574.

Zedeck, S., Kafry, D., & Jacobs, R. (1976). Format and scoring variations in behavioral expectation evaluations. *Organizational Behavior and Human Performance, 17,* 171–184.

Tests of Job Performance

Daniel B. Felker
Andrew M. Rose

OVERVIEW

This chapter is about assessing job performance and measuring how well people perform their jobs. In contrast to several earlier
chapters that have focused on ways to predict human performance, here (as
in Chapter 11)we are explicitly concerned about criterion performance—
specifically, job performance. As Siegel (1986) and Borman (1991) have
pointed out, measures of criterion performance are useful to and necessary
for virtually any personnel research application in organizations. Performance criteria are needed to assess the impact of personnel actions on
individual or group performance. Criteria are essential for assessing the
effectiveness of training programs, determining employees best qualified for
special tasks or advancement, deciding optimal job assignment procedures,
and many other personnel-related actions and interventions.

The most complete and, in a sense, truest picture of job performance
would involve continuously observing and evaluating job incumbents as
they complete their assigned job tasks under all possible working conditions at their job sites. This, of course, is not feasible for many practical
reasons: job disruption, cost, inconvenience, infrequency of occurrence

of some tasks, and the time needed to make the observations, to name several. A step back from this "true" ideal would be to observe and evaluate job incumbents as they work on a sample (rather than all) of their assigned tasks under selected working conditions. While this approach may be logistically feasible, it still intrudes on work routines and is inefficient. Moreover, since conditions of performance—in terms of both environmental conditions and specific job task requirements—could vary substantially from one set of observations to the next, this observational approach is unlikely to produce reliable or generalizable measures.

One step further removed from observing and evaluating actual on-the-job performance would be to measure job performance using tests. Tests can be developed that cover a representative and generalizable sample of work tasks and they can be administered to incumbents in controlled and standardized test settings. This kind of assessment can be accomplished using two kinds of tests: (1) work sample tests, in which examinees perform tasks using the same equipment, materials, and procedures required to perform tasks on the job; and (2) performance-based job knowledge tests, in which examinees answer multiple-choice items that demonstrate that they know how to complete job tasks. How to develop, administer, and score these tests is the focus of this chapter.

CHARACTERISTICS AND USES OF JOB PERFORMANCE TESTS

BACKGROUND

Job performance tests, including work sample tests and performance-based job knowledge tests, are ways to measure work performance. Work sample tests require examinees to perform tasks under conditions that are identical or highly similar to those they encounter in the workplace and to make decisions comparable to those made at work. Performance-based job knowledge tests require examinees to apply knowledges, skills, abilities, and other characteristics when answering multiple-choice questions. When both kinds of job performance tests are properly constructed and administered, performance on a relatively small number of tests can provide a basis for assessing how well incumbents perform job tasks. Both work sample tests and performance-based knowledge tests have been developed and administered to many kinds of workers and in many work contexts, including vehicle maintenance, electronic installation, clerical and administration, regulation writing, nursing, law enforcement, sales, physicians, and pilots, among many others (Campbell et al., 1990; Felker et al., 1992; Felker et al., 1988).

In organizational settings, interest in performance testing has stemmed from the need to know how well workers can apply job knowledge and demonstrate job skills. This interest historically has led to the use of performance tests as predictor measures more commonly than as criterion measures (Knapp & Campbell, 1993). For example, Asher and Sciarrino (1974) reviewed the validity of performance tests as predictors and Siegel (1986) described the use of work sample tests as predictors of trainability for selected jobs. Nevertheless, because performance tests elicit the same type of behavior required in job settings, their value as a criterion measurement method has long been recognized.

The state-of-the-art technology to develop, administer, and score performance tests was advanced by research and development work done to support U.S. military requirements. For instance, in response to the performance-based training movement, the Army in 1973 changed its approach to soldier evaluation from norm-referenced paper-and-pencil tests to criterion-referenced performance tests. This change meant that soldiers' proficiency would be based on whether they met specific standards of performance rather than on their test scores relative to test scores of other soldiers.

In the new system, soldier performance was measured by Skill Qualification Tests (SQTs) where soldiers performed and were evaluated on carefully selected tasks. The overriding requirement of SQTs was that they be job relevant. Test content was tied to critical job tasks that were identified through job and task analysis (e.g., as described in Chapter 3). Because the Army had to implement SQT testing worldwide within a short time span and their existing test developers were technically inexperienced in developing performance tests, the Army sought research support to assist in the transition to performance testing. Osborn and his colleagues at the Human Resources Research Organization (e.g., Osborn, 1974; Osborn, Campbell, & Ford, 1976) did much of the research and development work to specify the requirements and procedures for developing performance tests—both work sample and performance-based job knowledge tests—and to provide training to Army test developers. The development standards and procedures generated from this research are still widely followed today.

A distinguishing characteristic of job performance tests is that they are measures of actual or nearly equivalent job performance. As such, they require demonstrating and applying the knowledges, skills, abilities, and other characteristics needed to complete the task being tested. It is because of this feature that work sample tests especially have been touted as being the highest-fidelity performance measurement available and the most valid indicator of job performance (e.g., Green & Wing, 1988). While all personnel psychologists may not totally agree with this assertion, there nonetheless is a strong basis for arguing that these tests can have excellent face validity and can be more objective than other types of performance measures (Borman & Hallam, 1991; Knapp & Campbell, 1993; Sackett, Zedeck, & Fogli, 1988). Moreover, these tests are focused on integrated components of whole task performance, rather than on relatively molecular components of job performance. For example, if we wanted to test an electrician lineman on climbing tall wooden light poles, we would present him or her with the necessary materials and observe actual pole climbing rather than only some component of the task, such as donning climbing gear.

Applications of Job Performance Tests

Job performance tests are useful in a variety of human resources applications. For example, they can be used to evaluate the effectiveness of training programs. If the terminal objectives of a job training program are to teach specific job tasks, tests that require demonstration of those tasks, given at the completion of training, can be used as a measure of performance and can provide evidence for determining whether the terminal objectives were achieved. If the objectives were achieved, the training program can be judged effective; if they were not, the training may be deemed deficient and in need of revision.

Another use of job performance tests for evaluating training effectiveness is to administer them to job incumbents after they have been working for several months (or some other meaningful time frame) following training. If performance on the tests demonstrates that incumbents can perform the tasks at the desired level of competence, then there is evidence that transfer of training has occurred (i.e., that the knowledge and skills taught in training are being applied in the work setting).*

---

*The presentation of these two training applications is an oversimplification. When evaluating training effectiveness, proper care must be taken to obtain performance data from comparable contrasting groups, such as an untrained control group and trained groups. The main point is that job performance tests can play an important role in evaluating training effectiveness.

Tests that measure job performance also may be used when it is important to establish that someone is qualified to hold a job. For occupations that routinely affect the safety and well-being of others, incumbents frequently need to be certified to ensure that they are qualified to perform tasks expected of them. Some obvious examples include aircraft pilots, medical specialists, nuclear power plant operators, and law enforcement officers. In these situations, it is critical to establish that those who are working or want to work in these positions are able to perform their jobs. Clearly, it is not sufficient for pilots to demonstrate that they have the knowledge necessary to land a plane; they need to demonstrate actual performance before they can be certified. These are criterion-referenced testing situations, in which the test requires the examinee to demonstrate proficiency at or above specified standards.

In a similar vein, tests measuring job performance are used in performance appraisal systems to make personnel decisions about such issues as salary and promotions. This entails using tests to collect information on incumbents' current proficiency in critical job tasks. Test results can provide the basis for establishing that individuals meet expected work standards and for ranking individuals by their levels of proficiency. Used in this way, job performance tests provide valuable input to support personnel, pay, and promotion decisions.

In addition to these uses, tests of job performance also have applications in personnel selection research. Performance tests often serve as the criterion—or, more likely, as one of several criteria—for validating personnel selection instruments and procedures. This application typically involves having both job incumbents and job seekers complete selection (predictor) instruments. Scores on measures of job performance are then correlated with scores on selection instruments to determine if the selection instrument discriminates among examinees. Validation designs and procedures are described in detail in Chapter 13.

In all of these personnel applications, the value of job performance tests is that they are a means of measuring how well individuals can perform actual job tasks. More specifically, these tests are most useful, as Siegel (1986) has noted, for assessing the proficiency of job-experienced persons or those who have already been trained. These kinds of tests have the advantage of having high physical fidelity for measuring performance and having face validity; in addition, they provide objective measures of job performance.

LIMITATIONS OF JOB PERFORMANCE TESTS

There are technical and practical constraints associated with developing and using tests of job performance. Work sample tests can be especially expensive to develop and, depending on the equipment and materials involved in performing the task being tested, they can be relatively complex to administer and score.

In addition, others have noted (e.g., Borman, 1991; Sackett, Zedeck, & Fogli, 1988) that what workers actually do on the job might not reflect what they *can* do as much as what they are *willing* to do. Job performance tests are considered "can do" measures of performance because they measure what people can do in a testing situation, rather than what they will do on the job. Workers who are capable of performing a task well—as demonstrated in a testing situation—may often not do so on the job because they lack motivation, have poor supervision, or are working with defective tools. Also, job performance tests (in which examinees perform under controlled circumstances) usually contain some degree of reactivity in which the testing process itself affects what is being measured. In other words, if examinees know they are being tested, it may affect how they perform. Thus, restricting the measurement of job effectiveness to only job performance tests could result in missing information about typical worker performance. (Information about typical job performance can be gathered using rating scales, as discussed in Chapter 11.) For this reason, when assessing job performance, it is important to use more than one kind of measure, such as supervisor ratings, job knowledge tests, and work sample tests, so that all aspects of job performance are covered.

JOB PERFORMANCE TESTS: PROCESSES AND PRODUCTS

Job performance tests can measure both the processes needed to complete a task and the products that result from performing a task. Work sample tests and performance-based job knowledge tests accommodate both of these situations. Whether task processes or task products or both should be measured depends on the task and what is deemed important to assess. For tasks in which the end result is important (and can be attained via several acceptable methods), the quality of the product should be measured. Examples include:

- Identifying a legal statute: This can be accomplished in different ways, including searching a database, looking at a printed index, or from memory; the result is important, not the method.
- Installing an electrical alarm system in accordance with electrical code specifications: Within safety constraints, this can be done using a variety of tools; whether the alarm is installed and whether all code specifications are met are the important things to measure.
- Diagnosing a mechanical problem: This can be accomplished using different sequences of diagnostic tests, examining different components and system elements, and using different troubleshooting strategies; finding the problem is the important measure.
- Finding the distance and location of a road junction on a map: Several methods of determining distance and location are acceptable, including using a compass, a measuring stick, or some other informal technique; the correct answer is critical, not the method used.

On the other hand, when the process itself is inherently important, we want to measure each step required to complete a task. In these cases, the correct process may be essential to ensure safety, to preclude damage to equipment or material, or to enable proper operation at the end of the process. Examples include:

- The process followed in drawing blood: It is vital that sterilized needles are used and that the needle is not jabbed into the donor's arm.
- The process used to shut down a nuclear plant in an emergency: Steps must be precisely followed in the prescribed order.
- The process used by an outside lineman to move "hot wires" to different positions: It is critical that appropriate insulated tools be properly used to prevent serious injury.
- The process used to handcuff and arrest criminal suspects: Suspects must not be injured, must be safely secured, and their legal rights read to them prior to booking.
- The process used to land a passenger plane: It is essential that the pilot reads the right gauges correctly, operates the right switches and controls at the appropriate time, and follows all safety procedures.

There can be many occasions when it is desirable to measure both task processes and the task product. One instance is when the quality of the product is inextricably linked to the procedures used to produce the result—when variations in methods to achieve a product are not equivalent. For example, while one could imagine a situation in which a pilot could land an aircraft smoothly and safely (the product) without also reading gauges and manipulating controls and switches in specified sequences at particular times (the processes), variations in procedure indicate deficits in proficiency. Other situations when it is important to test and measure both processes and products occur when safety is critical to attaining the desired result and when certifying proficiency. For example, it is not sufficient for outside linemen to demonstrate that they can remove a heavy transformer from a pole that is carrying "hot" electrical lines (the product); journeyman proficiency also requires the use of proper tools and prescribed procedures during removal (the processes) in order to safeguard themselves and others working nearby against serious injury. The specifics of the testing situation as well as the nature of the task will dictate whether testing the process or product of a task or both is called for.

PSYCHOMETRIC CHARACTERISTICS OF JOB PERFORMANCE TESTS

The quality of job performance tests is assessed by the same general psychometric considerations as any other type of personnel measure: reliability and validity. A body of research from the military's extensive work on job performance measurement is one source of evidence that speaks to these first two considerations for job performance tests. A third consideration, measurement bias, has rarely been examined in the context of criterion measurement. Oppler, Campbell, Pulakos, and Borman (1992) discuss and present results of several approaches to investigating subgroup bias in performance measurement, primarily based on Army data (Project A). In these analyses, however, the focus was on supervisor and peer ratings rather than on hands-on performance measurement.

RELIABILITY

Psychometric properties of job sample tests are of special interest because these tests are relatively expensive to develop and are logistically complex to administer and score. The reliability of job sample tests is of particular concern because they require test scorers to observe test performance directly and interpret the quality of the performance. This observation and interpretation, even if recorded in terms of pass/fail or go/no–go standards, potentially adds variability to measurement.

Interrater agreement scores for these types of tests have been reported by all the military services and have been consistently high (Knapp & Campbell, 1993). This is noteworthy because the military services have developed and administered job sample tests to thousands of examinees across a wide range of occupational specialties and have used different types of scorers. For example, Carey (1990) and Felker et al. (1988) reported interrater agreements exceeding .90 between test scorers and "shadow" scorers for a variety of Marine Corps job sample tests. Hedge, Lipscomb, and Teachout (1988) reported pairwise agreements ranging from about .75 to .90 across three different teams of test administrators and three Air Force occupations; moreover, interrater agreement tended to improve over time. Doyle and Campbell (1990) reported comparable interrater indices for Navy radioman tests.

The generally high interrater agreement reported by the military has led to some speculation about the reasons for this outcome (e.g., Wigdor & Green, 1986). Plausible explanations lie in the serious approach taken to develop, administer, and score job sample tests. The military services treated job sample tests as benchmark criterion measures and devoted considerable effort to designing and conducting job performance tests. The care that was taken during task analysis and test construction had an obvious effect on interrater agreement. As will be described in more detail in later sections, careful segmentation of tasks into small, individually observable units of performance, and pilot testing to ensure that all steps could be consistently scored, were typical components of job sample test development.

In addition, the military services assigned and/or recruited competent job experts as test administrators. While differing in details, test administrator training was a rigorous process that involved demonstrations of the task to be scored, an emphasis on the importance of standardized test conditions, and repeated practice with scoring tests. The important lesson from this for any organization is that experienced and well-trained test administrators can reliably score well-constructed proficiency tests across time, different examinees, and varying test content.

Test–retest reliability evidence also is available from military job performance measurement research. A sample of 188 Marine Corps infantrymen was retested after 7 to 10 days with an alternate job sample test form. This yielded a test–retest reliability estimate of .77 (Mayberry, 1990). In other research, reported test–retest reliabilities were .79 for a sample of 88 Marine Corps automotive mechanics and .88 for a sample of 67 helicopter mechanics (Mayberry, 1992).

Job performance research conducted by the military has also encompassed the development of performance-based job knowledge tests. The content of these tests is based on job tasks and focuses on performance requirements by asking questions about how to do something rather than asking what something is. Pictures and drawings often are used to illustrate the problem and minimize verbal demands on examinees. These tests can be reliable: Reported internal consistency reliability estimates ranged from .89 to .92 for Army performance-based job knowledge tests (Campbell, 1988) and .91 to .97 for Marine Corps tests (Mayberry, 1990, 1992). Mayberry (1992) also reported split-half reliability estimates for automotive and helicopter mechanic tests ranging from .92 to .97.

VALIDITY

Establishing the validity of job performance tests is a bit more oblique than it is for predictor tests. Indeed, it is difficult to think about criterion validity of job performance measures themselves, since they normally are the standard against which predictor tests, training programs, and other personnel interventions are validated. It is generally acknowledged (e.g., Borman & Hallam, 1991) that job sample tests have excellent face validity. That is, most observers who look at a job sample test (or even a performance-based job knowledge test) can readily see the relevance of the test to the job. Face validity of a test is enormously important for acceptance by decision makers who are not test specialists. A test that does not "look" like it is suited for the measurement task at hand is a hard sell in almost any organization.

The general notion of content validity in job performance tests centers on the relevance and representativeness of the test to performance required on the job. As pointed out by Guion (1979a, 1979b, 1979c, 1979d) and more recently by Borman (1991), the determination of validity in this sense relates to how closely the test shares important content, such as tasks and performance conditions, with the content of the job. Tests that ask for performance that is highly similar to the performance required on the job are content-valid tests. Content validity is almost automatic if the performance test is developed on the foundation of a systematic analysis of job requirements, working conditions, and use of equipment and materials. The importance of job and task analysis for identifying the content domain of a job and for selecting test content that reflects the domain is discussed in the next section.

HOW TO SELECT TEST CONTENT

In the ideal human resources management world, all tasks would be tested under all conditions under which they are likely to occur on the job. However, there are several factors that limit which tasks can reasonably be tested:

1. There typically are too many tasks associated with a job to test. That is, the number of tasks that people could perform as part of their job—their job performance domain—is too large to test every task. For example, the performance domain for inside wireman electricians contains over 200 tasks requiring over 150 different knowledges, skills, abilities, and other characteristics (KSAOs). Even if tests could be developed for all 200 tasks, they would take too long to administer, it would be too expensive, and it would require training a very large number of people to administer and score them.
2. Some tasks are more important to the job, some are more difficult to perform, some are more frequently performed, and some are more representative of the job than others. These characteristics may be used to select tasks to be tested. Certainly, unrepresentative, unimportant, and infrequently performed tasks are unlikely candidates for testing.
3. Practical and logistical considerations limit what can be tested. Issues of safety, equipment requirements, and standardization of testing conditions limit what can be tested.

Clearly, the first and most important decision when constructing job performance tests is to determine what part of the performance domain should be tested. For the applications we have considered—for example, selecting tasks to assess job proficiency—the necessary requirement is to be able to generalize the test performance to the entire job domain. Therefore, representativeness and generalizability of test content to the entire performance domain are critical. To ensure representativeness and generalizability, there are two necessary requirements: (1) The complete job performance domain must be specified, and (2) a valid and defensible sampling strategy must be used to select tasks from that domain. The remainder of this section describes methods for meeting these requirements. We then describe two applied research projects in which different procedures were used to select test content.

SPECIFYING THE JOB PERFORMANCE DOMAIN

A job performance domain defines the totality of tasks that are performed in a job and describes how the tasks are organized under major job functions. A complete enumeration of tasks is the necessary first step to provide an empirical basis for selecting representative and generalizable tasks to test. Job and task analysis methods are used to develop job performance domains through such procedures as observing job incumbents while they work, interviewing the incumbents and their supervisors, and reviewing existing task descriptions and inventories of tasks. Typically, job and task analysis employs several procedures to compile the tasks of a job domain. Chapter 3 describes some of these job and task analysis methods.

To support the development of performance tests, the results of a job and task analysis should consist of more than a complete listing of tasks in the domain. It is critical that the contextual conditions of task performance also be identified. These contextual conditions include the circumstances (e.g., environmental conditions) in which the tasks are performed, chronological dependencies of a task (e.g., when a task is performed in a sequence of activities), and interaction requirements (e.g., where other people's performance affects task performance conditions). Test developers use this information to determine suitable testing conditions and logistical requirements.

SAMPLING STRATEGIES FOR SELECTING TASKS

The process of selecting tasks for testing has a long history. In particular, branches of the U.S. military have developed methods of selecting test content that have been adapted and widely applied to civilian occupations. These structured methods are described in detail in various research technical reports (e.g., Guion, 1979a, 1979b, 1979c, 1979d) and military documents (e.g., the U.S. Army's TRADOC PAM 351-4[T], U.S. Army, 1979). We describe two of these methods next.

The 4- and 8-Factor Models

In the first method, analysts and test developers rate (or collect data for) each task in the domain on the following eight descriptors:

1. Percent of the workforce performing (e.g., what proportion of electricians splice wire?)

2. Task delay tolerance (e.g., how much flexibility is there in terms of time before this task must be performed?)
3. Consequences of inadequate performance (e.g., how much damage will occur to equipment, workers, or the completion of the job if this task is not performed adequately?)
4. Task learning difficulty (e.g., how long will it take to learn how to do this task?)
5. Percent time spent performing (e.g., what proportion of time is spent performing this task on the job?)
6. Probability of deficient performance (e.g., what are the chances that the worker cannot perform the task?)
7. Immediacy of performance (e.g., how urgent is task performance?)
8. Frequency of performance (e.g., how often is this task performed?)

The first four of these descriptors comprise the 4-factor model; the entire set is the 8-factor model. Job analysts and subject matter experts (SMEs) rate each task in the domain on each of the 4 or 8 factors. For example, job experts might rate tasks on how difficult they are to learn and on the seriousness of the consequences if those tasks are not performed correctly; information about the percent of incumbents who perform a task might be compiled from supervisors' records or other work-related documents. After each factor has been rated or relevant data collected, SMEs decide which factors are most important. They then set cutoffs for each of these relevant factors. Example cutoff scores might be:

	Cutoff
1. Percent of the workforce performing	40% or more
2. Task delay tolerance (1 = high tolerance, 7 = no tolerance)	3
3. Consequences of inadequate performance (1 = minor, 7 = major)	5
4. Task learning difficulty (1 = low, 7 = high)	4

Tasks that meet these criteria are selected for testing.

The DIF Model

Another method for selecting test content is the DIF (Difficulty, Importance, and Frequency) model. The basic procedures are the same as those used for the 4- or 8-factor models. Analysts and SMEs rate each task on the following descriptors:

1. Difficulty: either task learning difficulty or probability of deficient performance or both
2. Importance: the consequences of inadequate performance, task delay tolerance, percent performing, and time spent performing (importance has often been rated for different scenarios, such as peak and nonpeak production periods)
3. Frequency: how often the task is performed

If simple "Yes–No" responses are provided for each of the three DIF dimensions, there are eight potential outcomes:

Difficult?	Important?	Frequent?	Decision
Yes	Yes	Yes	Select
Yes	Yes	No	Select
Yes	No	Yes	Select
Yes	No	No	Do Not Select
No	Yes	Yes	Select
No	Yes	No	Select
No	No	Yes	Do Not Select
No	No	No	Do Not Select

The last column presents a particular decision rule—select all important tasks, and also select all tasks that are both difficult and frequently performed, even if rated as not important. This rule eliminates easy and unimportant tasks and tasks that are unimportant and infrequently performed, even if they are difficult; this latter category might be included if more resources were available. More elaborate decision rules can be used, depending on the purposes of selection and resource constraints. For example, when considering tasks for initial training, the "Yes–Yes–No" tasks (difficult, important, not frequently performed) are candidates for overtraining to protect against forgetting.

Suppose one were to select tasks to be used as criteria to validate a set of predictors. Ideally, we would like to select tasks that reflect underlying abilities and skills that job seekers may possess; tasks that reflect on-the-job learning and extensive practice would be poor choices. Thus, the decision rule might be to select infrequently performed tasks. Similarly, we would select more difficult tasks, since they would be more likely to discriminate among incumbents.

Variants on this primarily judgmental DIF approach frequently appear in the literature. For example, Rose, Radtke, and Shettel (1984) were concerned with predicting tasks that were likely to be forgotten if not practiced. They developed a method to determine difficulty based on 10 task characteristics, such as number of steps in the task, its cognitive demands, and the presence and adequacy of job aids. Thus, a task that is comprised of 20 steps, involves rapid calculations and decisions, and has no job aids would be judged very difficult and prone to forgetting. Tasks identified by such procedures could be singled out for special treatment such as giving them additional training time.

Selecting Test Content: Two Examples

Perhaps the largest effort ever initiated involving the measurement of performance was the Joint Services Job Performance Measurement (JPM) Project, commissioned by the Department of Defense (Harris, 1987). The scope and content of this initiative reflect both traditional and innovative approaches to developing job performance tests. In 1980, the Department of Defense directed each branch of the military services to develop and validate procedures for measuring job performance. These measures were to be used as criterion measures to determine the validity of military selection and classification procedures. In this section, we describe two of these efforts: the U.S. Army's Project A and the U.S. Marine Corps' JPM Project.

The U.S. Army's Project A

As described by Campbell et al. (1990), Project A defined the total domain of performance for entry-level enlisted personnel in several Army jobs, or Military Occupational Specialties, such as infantryman and vehicle driver. Reliable and valid measures of the major tasks and duty areas of each job then were developed. These measures were used as criteria against which to validate both existing and project-developed selection and classification tests.

Major components of the Project A job performance measures included work sample tests and performance-based job knowledge tests. Since the procedures for selecting test content for Project A were fairly typical and are applicable to civilian performance domains, we discuss these steps in detail.

1. *Specify the entire task domain for a particular job.* As mentioned earlier, this is a necessary requirement for selecting test content, especially when we are concerned with estimating the representativeness of the test. During Project A, enumeration of tasks within each job domain was done using three sources of information: (1) Army doctrine (e.g., soldier's manuals and technical manuals), which consists of policy statements regarding what soldiers should know and should be able to do; (2) survey data from soldiers concerning what they actually do on the job; and (3) interviews with representatives from the Army agencies responsible for training in the specific jobs.

2. *Edit and describe tasks uniformly.* The typical task list generated using the methods just described often includes tasks that contain widely differing levels of description. For example, one infantryman task was "Move individually." This task involves several different activities, such as "Perform low crawl" (on elbows and knees) and "Move through barbed wire." Another task was "Take immediate action on the Light Antitank Weapon," itself consisting of several procedures to follow if the weapon failed to fire. The goal of this editing step is to describe all tasks at a comparable level of specificity, so that the tasks can provide essentially equivalent amounts of information about the domain. For Project A, after the complete task list was generated, it was reviewed and edited by project staff and then reviewed by SMEs for consistency and uniformity of scope. Occasionally, overly inclusive "supertasks" were separated into several tasks of comparable scope.

3. *Rate or judge task characteristics.* Practically all test content selection procedures involve sampling tasks (or subtasks) from the performance domain. To aid in this sampling, a typical procedure is to rate each task on a number of characteristics (e.g., the 4- and 8-factor or DIF models), and then to systematically use the ratings when selecting content. For Project A, a relatively large number of SMEs—between 15 and 30 for each job—performed three rating activities. First, they clustered all of the tasks according to similarity of behavior described in the task. That is, they sorted tasks into an unspecified number of groups, with the instructions to make the tasks within a group as similar as possible and to make the groups as dissimilar as possible. Next, the SMEs rated the importance of each task on a 7-point scale ranging between "Not at all important to unit success" to "Absolutely essential for

unit success." The SMEs rated importance in three different military scenarios: (1) peacetime training, (2) increasing international tension, and (3) combat conditions. Finally, the SMEs rated each task on task performance difficulty: they were asked to judge the level of performance that a typical group of soldiers would reach on a task. The range of levels within the typical group of soldiers was used as the measure of expected performance variability, which in turn was used as an indirect measure of task difficulty; more variable tasks tend to be more difficult.

4. *Select tasks to be tested.* Using the information just given and ratings, tasks were selected by panels of military experts and project staff. As described in Campbell et al. (1990), "No strict rules were imposed on the analysts in making their selections, although they were told that high importance, high performance variability, a range of difficulty, and frequently performed tasks were desirable and that each cluster should be sampled" (p. 282). Following initial selections, the panels developed a consensus list of most representative and critical tasks. The consensus list was reviewed by several committees and review panels as the final step in selecting the tasks to be tested.

The Marine Corps JPM Project

In this project, researchers attempted to improve on consensus procedures for selecting test content (Felker et al., 1988). The approach focused on representativeness and generalizability of the tests and the desire to include aspects of random selection in the process, rather than solely relying on SME consensus. The theory was that each task consisted of a series of "behavioral elements," which are general behaviors that are included in and performed across many different tasks or subtasks. Performance of these elements was presumed to be transferable if Marines who can perform the elements in one task can perform the elements in other tasks. Behavioral elements are the task components that are sufficiently similar in two tasks to lead one to predict that performance on the two tasks will be correlated.

Table 12.1 shows the behavioral elements derived for a Marine Corps electrician job (Felker, et al., 1992). In the Marine Corps, individuals receive training and qualify to work on specific pieces of electrical equipment (e.g., Linear Actuator, Controllable Spotlight). They perform three types of activities on these pieces of equipment: Troubleshoot and Test (T/T), Remove and Replace (R/R), and Align and Adjust (A/A). In Table 12.1, these activities are displayed across the top of the matrix.

TABLE 12.1 Electrician Task/Behavioral Elements Matrix

Behavioral Element	Linear Actuator			Controllable Spotlight			Power Lever Control Quadrant			RPM Limit Detector			Master Switch Control Panel			Trim Actuator		
	T/T	R	A/A	T/T	R	A/A	T/T	R	A/A	T/T	R	A/A	T/T	R	A/A	T/T	R	A/A
1. Read technical manual	X		X	X	X		X	X		X	X		X	X		X	X	X
2. Follow safety procedures	X		X	X	X		X	X		X	X		X	X		X	X	X
3. Remove/replace screws, nuts, bolts	X		X	X	X		X	X		X	X		X			X	X	X
4. Connect/disconnect wires/cables	X		X	X	X		X	X		X	X		X			X	X	X
5. Visually inspect for physical damage	X		X	X	X		X	X		X	X		X			X	X	X
6. Remove/replace cover/panel assembly	X		X	X	X		X	X		X	X		X			X	X	X
7. Read/interpret schematics	X		X	X	X		X	X		X	X		X			X	X	X
8. Read/observe indicators	X			X			X			X			X			X		
9. Connect probes across items	X			X			X			X			X			X		
10. Set switch to proper position	X			X	X		X			X			X			X		
11. Remove/replace components														X			X	X
12. Align mechanical/electrical parts			X			X			X						X		X	X

Behavioral Element	Linear Actuator T/T	R/R	A/A	Controllable Spotlight T/T	R/R	A/A	Power Lever Control Quadrant T/T	R/R	A/A	RPM Limit Detector T/T	R/R	A/A	Master Switch Control Panel T/T	R/R	A/A	Trim Actuator T/T	R/R	A/A
13. Clean parts																		
14. Tag wires													X					
15. Align/adjust screws using turning tool		X																
16. Remove/replace module/PCB								X			X					X		
17. Apply lubricating/sealing/cleaning compound																		X
18. Release switch								X		X			X				X	X
19. Remove/replace wire/lead								X										
20. Read/interpret oscilloscope																		
21. Engage/hold switch				X	X		X			X			X			X		
22. Remove/replace sealing compound																		
23. Remove/replace gasket/seals					X		X			X						X		
24. Remove/replace safety/lock wire							X			X								
25. Measure time using stopwatch						X												

T/T = Troubleshoot & Test; R/R = Remove & Replace; A/A = Align & Adjust

Having defined the performance domain, we then specified the behavioral elements that comprised each activity. "Connect/disconnect wires/cables" occurred in many of the task activities electricians were expected to do. Of course, electricians did not connect and disconnect the same wires and cables in all activities; furthermore, the specific procedures or performance requirements differed in various circumstances. Nonetheless, if a person could perform "Connect/disconnect wires/cables" for troubleshooting one piece of equipment (e.g., the Linear Actuator), we considered it likely that the person could also "Connect/disconnect wires/cables" when troubleshooting other pieces of equipment (e.g., the Trim Actuator). Similarly, further down the list in Table 12.1, the behavioral element "Set switch to proper position" was embedded in fewer task activities, but the thinking was the same: This element would transfer across the different tasks that included it. Operationally, behavioral elements are verb–noun statements that are larger than the typical steps done to perform a task and smaller than the typical subtask.

Behavioral element matrices were developed for all "testable units" in the performance domain for each job. Because many Marine Corps electrician tasks were very comprehensive, "testable units" served as the uniform level of description. Conceptually, a testable unit is roughly equivalent to a subtask (i.e., a meaningful segment of performance that is relatively independent, while maintaining its overall fidelity to the task, and can be performed in a reasonable time period; Mayberry, 1987). Using these matrices, test content was selected on the basis of coverage of behavioral elements. Essentially, columns of the matrix—that is, testable units—weighted by the number of elements they contained, were randomly sampled. Thus, a testable unit with 20 behavioral elements was weighted more heavily than a testable unit with 12 behavioral elements. After a column was selected, the weights were regenerated by deleting the behavioral elements from those sampled and randomly sampling the domain for another column. This process was repeated until all testing time—the chief logistic constraint—was accounted for. This procedure enabled documentation of the representativeness of the test and generation of hypotheses regarding the likelihood of performance success for any task in the domain. More specifically, the hypothesis was that performance on behavioral elements transferred across tasks; performance on tasks that had more elements in common would be more highly correlated, a hypothesis that was generally supported in analyses of the Marine Corps data.

HOW TO CONSTRUCT
JOB PERFORMANCE TESTS

All of the methods described here—4-factor, 8-factor, DIF, consensus approach, behavioral elements approach—have the same goal. They are used to help test developers select content using an empirical and defensible approach to ensure representativeness of test content to the entire job performance domain. Once this content is selected, test development can begin. In this section, we discuss methods for developing work sample tests and performance-based job knowledge tests.

WORK SAMPLE TESTS

A work sample test requires examinees to perform a task or an essential part of a task (e.g., a subtask or testable unit) under conditions similar to those in which the task is performed on the job. As with all types of tests, it is essential that work sample tests always be administered in the same way and under the same testing conditions so that all examinees have the same opportunity to demonstrate their ability to perform without any undue advantage from the test setting. As with any other form of testing, the instructions for administering work sample tests are of utmost importance for standardizing how the test is administered and scored.

Drawing on the task/behavioral element matrix detailed in Table 12.1, an example of a work sample test is shown in Figures 12.1 and 12.2. The illustrative work sample test is a Marine Corps task that required examinees to troubleshoot a Trim Actuator, an aircraft electrical component. Since the process of troubleshooting is critical to proficiency on this task, the test was developed so that each step of the process could be observed and scored by the test administrator as it was performed.

Figure 12.1 shows the "setup sheet" for the test, which helped to standardize the test conditions for each person tested. The setup sheet gives specific instructions to the test administrator for preparing the test station. It lists the materials and equipment required for the test, the procedures to set up the test station, and the procedures to be performed before testing each examinee. Work sample tests often require fairly elaborate setup procedures; test administrators need to be trained in how to both prepare the test station and administer and score the test.

Figure 12.2 is the score sheet for the test. The score sheet includes space for biographical information about the examinee and lists the steps

---

Troubleshoot: Trim Actuator

Equipment/Materials Required

1 Trim Actuator
1 Multimeter (AN/PSM-4C)
1 DC Power Supply (0-30VCD, LH-125)

Procedure to Set Up Station

1. Open retract switch (Item #12) by disconnecting wire.
2. Remove sealing compound.

Procedures to be Performed Before Testing Each Marine

1. Open retract switch (Item #12) by disconnecting wire.

Testable Units

1. Calibrate Multimeter (Steps 1-5)
2. Troubleshoot Actuator (Steps 6-12)

FIGURE 12.1   Setup Sheet for Electrican Task

of the process that must be followed that will be scored. (Work sample tests often use some type of "go/no-go" or "pass/fail" format.) It also includes the exact words that the test administrator should say during the testing and when they should be said.

Figure 12.2 demonstrates why task analysis results are crucial for the development of work sample tests. A good task analysis used to develop work sample tests will indicate not only what tasks are performed on the job but also how they are done, any materials and equipment used, what constitutes acceptable performance, and the mandatory or preferred sequence of performing task steps. All this information is used in constructing draft and final versions of work sample tests and in deciding what performance conditions to incorporate into the test setting. While the intent always is to make these tests as "real" as possible, compromises often have to be made in the degree of authenticity to accommodate practical considerations. Decisions to compromise reality in testing are affected by the following issues.

Degree of Physical Fidelity

It may not always be possible to duplicate the exact working conditions for all tasks. Thus, some conditions may need to be simulated; however, these simulated conditions must still elicit use of the same essential skills and knowledge needed to perform the actual task. For example, it is infeasible, if not impossible, to test truck drivers in all possible driving

Troubleshoot: Trim Actuator

Test Date: _____

Scorer: _____   Examinee: _____

Scorer ID: _____   Examinee ID: _____

Say: *The Trim Actuator before you is not working properly. You are to find the problem or problems. You may use the test equipment provided. Do you have any questions? Begin.*

Performance Steps	Go	No-Go
1. Removed all power to the Trim Actuator.	_____	_____
2. Set AC/DC switch to +DC on multimeter.	_____	_____
3. Set function selector switch to R x 1k on multimeter.	_____	_____
4. Touched two leads of multimeter together.	_____	_____
5. Read 0 on multimeter.	_____	_____
Note: Ask examinee for multimeter reading.		
6. Touched first lead to Pin C of connector.	_____	_____
7. Touched second lead to Pin A of connector.	_____	_____
8. Touched first lead to pin C of connector.	_____	_____
9. Touched second lead to Pin B of connector.	_____	_____
10. Engaged retract switch.	_____	_____
11. Performed steps 6–10 in sequence.	_____	_____
Note: Ask examinee what he/she found.		
12. Indicated there is an open in the retract circuit.	_____	_____

FIGURE 12.2   Score Sheet for Electrican Task

conditions in a standardized way. But requiring examinees to maneuver around portable obstacles at certain speeds and braking at different speeds (based on job analysis) may adequately simulate driving skills needed in many conditions such as wet roads and heavy traffic.

Whole/Part-Task Testing

Some job tasks may be too long to test or consist of steps that are repetitive or trivial. In such cases, testing may be restricted to the portion of the task that involves the use of critical skills or the key steps or behavioral elements of the task. For example, the task of "Replacing brakes" on a car encompasses jacking up the car, removing hubcaps, and other steps that are peripheral to the essence of replacing brakes. In the interest of saving testing time and focusing on critical skills, testing only that part of the task that actually relates to replacing brakes would be prudent and adequate.

Equipment/Material Needs

Some job tasks may require the use of equipment and materials that only can be adapted for testing with great difficulty, or at great expense, or are found only in the work setting. The use of these materials or equipment would have to be carefully planned and justified. For example, testing avionics specialists on their skill in removing electronic equipment from actual aircraft would involve the use of a very expensive airplane. Similarly, testing maintenance technicians on their skill in assembling a part by shutting down a factory production line may not be feasible. Testing requirements like these need to be planned for in advance, or the testing situation must be altered so that such testing conditions are unnecessary.

Safety

A paramount consideration for many work sample tests is the safety of the examinee. Some job tasks are dangerous and some working situations cannot safely be simulated under standardized conditions. Examples include cleaning up toxic materials, controlling fires, quelling riots, and caring for patients with highly contagious diseases.

Expense and Time

Work sample tests often are relatively costly to develop and administer. With enough money and support, very elaborate and expensive work sample tests can be developed and administered under standardized conditions (for example, flight simulators). However, for most work environments, compromises are often necessary to develop and administer reasonable tests that approximate some working conditions. Test developers almost always have to balance the cost of developing good work sample tests that measure critical knowledge and skills with the time available for testing and the proportion of the performance domain that is covered by the sample of tasks tested. It is often useful to supplement these measures with performance-based job knowledge tests and various types of rating scales to reduce cost and increase comprehensiveness of assessment.

SCORING WORK SAMPLE TESTS

Devising objective and reliable schemes for scoring work sample tests also is a creative and challenging exercise. The results of job and task analyses are critical inputs for scoring, too, since they will specify how tasks are performed and describe the level of competency and quality expected.

Score Task Processes

Developing procedures for scoring task processes requires familiarity with how the task is performed. This is because scoring is done in real time as the task is being performed step-by-step by the examinee. At times, some task steps might be very quickly performed and others might legitimately be completed in different sequences, both of which complicate observing and scoring performance. To ensure that the performance steps of a task can be accurately and reliably scored, the test must require the test administrator to make as few subjective decisions as possible. Several principles are typically followed when developing scoring procedures for process-based work sample tests. These are described as follows.

MAKE PERFORMANCE STEPS OBSERVABLE: Since performance on each step of the task process is to be scored, the steps must consist of observable behavior. For example, Step 3 in Figure 12.2, "Set function selector switch to R x 1k on multimeter," is a behavior that can be observed and is therefore scorable. Steps that call for "checking," "inspecting," "reading," and "observing" something are unobservable behaviors. The scorer does not know if the examinees are really "inspecting," or "reading" and, if they are, what they are inspecting for or what they are actually reading. Step 5 in Figure 12.2 avoids this problem by having the test administrator prompt examinees to verbalize what they read on the multimeter.

SPECIFY PERFORMANCE STEP BEGINNING AND ENDING POINTS: Each performance step should be a behavioral unit such that observers can tell when it begins and when it ends. The example just given fits this description. The step has a clear starting point ("Set function switch") and ending point ("to R x 1k on multimeter").

USE OBJECTIVE STANDARDS OF PERFORMANCE: For steps that can be performed at different levels of proficiency, the standard of performance should be objective and quantitative rather than subjective. For example, the first-aid task step "Ties bandage on arm adequately" is not particularly useful for a performance test because there is no standard for assessing "adequately." Different scorers can interpret adequacy in different ways. But saying "Ties bandage on the arm so you can insert your little finger under the edge of the bandage" provides an objective standard of performance that can be accurately and reliably scored.

SCORE SPECIAL PERFORMANCE CONDITIONS: For tasks that require certain steps to be performed in sequence or to be accomplished in a certain amount of time, the conditions should be scored as separate performance steps. Step 11 in Figure 12.2 provides for scoring the performance of steps in proper sequence. In the case where the time to perform a step (or number of steps) is important, the score sheet could include separate performance steps for scoring the task steps and for scoring the time taken to complete the task steps. That is, some steps on the score sheet would be for scoring individual task steps (e.g., "adjusted xyz correctly") and a separate one would be included for scoring the time taken to perform the task steps (e.g., "performed xyz within two minutes"). This would distinguish examinees who knew how to perform a task from those who not only knew how to do the task but also could do it within the specified time.

AVOID TESTING TRIVIAL STEPS: Some task steps that are tangential to the core requirements of tasks should not be tested or scored. For example, removing the protective cap of a needle before administering an injection tells very little about the ability to give an injection and is better left unscored.

INCORPORATE JOB AIDS IN TESTS: Job aids are typically used in work when incumbents are not expected to memorize lengthy or complicated tasks or to perform certain procedures unaided. Examples include steps to follow when making a medical diagnosis, or repairing complicated equipment, or performing mathematical transformations or calculations. Tests that require examinees to look up answers in manuals, use checklists, or follow procedures in the order shown on a schematic, just as they would on the job, can be very realistic. An example is a troubleshooting task in which the job aid graphically depicts the proper sequence to follow. At defined points in the troubleshooting process, some kind of decision or action may be required. By incorporating the job aid, a test can measure an examinee's ability to follow the proper sequence and make the appropriate decision. Examinees can be required

Electrician Task: Installation of Service Entrance Conductors

Test Date: _____

Scorer: _____   Examinee: _____

Scorer ID: _____   Examinee ID: _____

Read to examinee: *Your supervisor has told you to use the tools that have been given to you to bring electrical power from poles and lines in this neighborhood into the residence identified. Any questions? Your work will be checked after you finish. Begin.*

Performance Steps	Pass	Fail
1. Maintained at least three feet of clearance over house roof.	_____	_____
2. Installed service line where the pitch of the roof was at least 4/12.	_____	_____
3. Terminated conductors from main supply line at a through-the-roof raceway.	_____	_____
4. Installed so that at least 18 inches clearance is maintained above the overhanging portion of the roof.	_____	_____

FIGURE 12.3   Score Sheet for Product Scoring

either to say what they would do at the decision points or to perform the expected task.

TRAIN TEST ADMINISTRATORS: Administering work sample tests that measure task processes and scoring them are intricate procedures and require competent test administrators. This is particularly true when many steps are performed rapidly. It always is beneficial for test administrators to practice performing the tasks they will score as well as to observe others performing the tasks as part of their training.

Score Task Products

Figure 12.3 shows an example of a score sheet for scoring a task product. This particular test required an electrician apprentice to bring electrical power into a residence from electrical poles and lines running through a residential neighborhood. Examinees were scored by how well they "dropped service entrance" (i.e., brought electrical power into the house) and met electrical code standards. Since the method of installation was less important than meeting electrical code, only the end product was scored. The scorer did not need to be present when the apprentice examinee performed the task.

Scoring task products typically is easier than scoring a task as it is performed. Most task products—for example, a completed form, a finished letter, a manufactured ball bearing, the identification of correct information, a calculation—have definite specifications and these can be used to assess quality of performance. For example, certain parts of a form need to be completed to be correct, or ball bearings must meet precise specifications for size and smoothness, or there is a correct answer to a mathematical application. All have precise specifications. As such, these "products" can be determined and scored with some certainty. Sometimes decisions need to be made about the acceptability of products that do not meet standards of perfection and whether they should be scored as "failures" or "partially correct." Decisions on scoring exceptions also will be guided by task analysis results and input of job experts.

PERFORMANCE-BASED JOB KNOWLEDGE TESTS

Another approach to measuring job performance is through the use of a specialized form of written test called performance-based job knowledge tests. These tests resemble multiple-choice tests that are typically administered in paper-and-pencil or computer-based formats. They are different from typical job knowledge tests in that they attempt to measure knowledge about how examinees would perform a task rather than just knowledge about the task. Indeed, Osborn et al. (1976) have pointed out that the key requirement for these tests is that the test questions be methodically anchored in task procedures. Adequately constructed, these tests can provide wider coverage of the job domain at less cost as compared to work sample tests.

Job knowledge obviously is important for job performance. As DuBois (1996) has noted, job knowledge consists of the concepts, procedures, principles, and other information that support job performance. Since job knowledge conceptually includes both declarative knowledge and procedural knowledge—information about what to do and how to do it—it affects performance by guiding which tasks get performed and how these tasks are completed. Research has shown job knowledge to be a link between abilities and performance (Borman, White, Pulakos, & Oppler, 1991). Research also has shown that knowledge tests predict performance—for example, apprentice performance in a large manufacturing firm (Hattrup & Schmitt, 1990).

By focusing on procedural knowledge, performance-based job knowledge tests are likely to tell us how an examinee would perform on

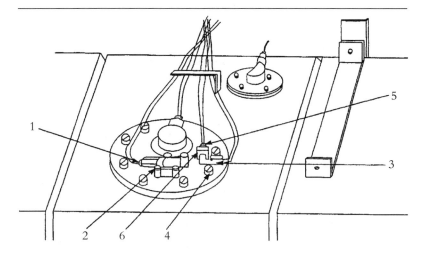

Your first step is to take the electrical connector off the fuel pump receptacle. What numbers in the figure refer to those items?

     A. 3 and 4
     B. 5 and 6
     C. 4 and 6
     D. 1 and 2

FIGURE 12.4   A Job Knowledge Test Item

a work sample test. To distinguish the typical job knowledge test item from a performance-based job knowledge test item, consider the item shown in Figure 12.4 for a vehicle maintenance troubleshooting task.

The job knowledge test item shown in Figure 12.4 tests whether the examinee recognizes a particular part of a fuel pump. The item asks for knowledge, not performance. Someone who has memorized the names of all parts of a fuel pump could correctly answer this item and not know anything at all about how to replace the pump. In contrast, a performance-based item would get at the performance aspect, the "how to." For example, the same job knowledge item shown in Figure 12.4 could be made performance-based by asking the test question in the following way, still using the same options:

"If you must replace this fuel pump, what parts should you remove first?"

While a correct answer to this item would not guarantee that examinees could actually physically replace the fuel pump, it at least demonstrates that they know the first thing they should *do* to replace the pump.

There are a number of ways to tap into the performance aspects of a task with a performance-based job knowledge test. Test items using words such as those that follow reflect different ways of measuring whether someone knows how to perform a task:

> What is the first step to install the . . .
>
> After you have . . ., you next should . . .
>
> If you have tried . . . and it didn't help, you then should . . .
>
> To replace the . . . you should first . . .
>
> If the customer objects to . . ., you should say . . .
>
> If ... is damaged, what must be replaced?
>
> Before removing the . . . you should . . .
>
> If the decision is . . . you must notify . . .
>
> The work team did . . . and . . . and . . ., so they now need to . . .
>
> The gauge reads . . . ; in what sequence should the four switches be operated?
>
> If Part 1 shown in the figure malfunctions, you should first . . . and then . . . .
>
> Given the conditions of the accompanying scenario, you should . . .

These phrases show that performance-based test items often require action of some kind as the correct answer. The examinee needs to know what to do given certain conditions, when to perform a step in a sequence of steps, and how different task steps relate to each other. To create realistic contexts for examinees, performance-based items often use pictures and other graphic material and detailed scenarios to set up the decision or performance requirement the examinee is to demonstrate.

For both work sample tests and performance-based job knowledge tests, the examinee's performance is typically scored by some variant of the number of things done "right." In the case of work sample tests, each test is built around a set of task steps (see Figure 12.2). Since each step of a task—process or product—is individually observable and scorable, we can compile the "pass/fail" (or "go/no-go") status of each step. The individual step scores can then be aggregated to produce total task pass/fail scores, or proportion of steps passed by task or across tasks. In the case of performance-based job knowledge tests, the number of test items answered correctly is usually calculated and summed over all items to derive a performance score.

SUMMARY

Job performance tests are relatively direct measures of what people can do at their work. Work sample tests, one type of job performance test, attempt to duplicate the essential working requirements of the job setting. These tests measure proficiency in using equipment and materials found on the job to complete representative job tasks under standardized but realistic working conditions. Work sample tests have often been proposed as a benchmark measure of job performance. On the other hand, performance-based job knowledge tests, another type of job performance test, typically are paper- or computer-based multiple-choice tests. Performance-based job knowledge tests go beyond the traditional job knowledge test (e.g., "Fuel pump's main function is...;" "Tourniquets are used to ...") by asking about how to carry out job tasks. Job performance tests are useful for most personnel research and can be used to support many practical personnel decisions in organizations.

REFERENCES

Asher, J. J., & Sciarrino, J. A. (1974). Realistic work sample tests: A review. *Personnel Psychology, 27,* 519–533.

Borman, W. C. (1991). Job behavior, performance, and effectiveness. In M. D. Dunnette & L. M. Hough (Eds.), *Handbook of industrial and organizational psychology.* Palo Alto, CA: Consulting Psychologists Press.

Borman, W. C., & Hallam, G. L. (1991). Observation accuracy for assessors of work-sample tests: Consistency across task and individual-differences correlates. *Journal of Applied Psychology, 76,* 11–18.

Borman, W. C., White, L. A., Pulakos, E. D., & Oppler, S. H. (1991). Models of supervisory job performance ratings. *Journal of Applied Psychology, 76,* 863–872.

Campbell, C. H., Ford, P., Rumsey, M. G., Pulakos, E. D., Borman, W. C., Felker, D. B., DeVera, M. V., & Riegelhaupt, B. J. (1990). Development of multiple job performance measures in a representative sample of jobs. *Personnel Psychology, 43,* 277–300.

Campbell, J. P. (Ed.). (1988). *Improving the selection, classification, and utilization of Army enlisted personnel: Annual report, 1985 fiscal year* (ARI TR 792). Alexandria, VA: U.S. Army Research Institute for the Behavioral and Social Sciences.

Carey, N. B. (1990). *An assessment of surrogates for hands-on tests: Selection standards and training needs* (CRM 90-47). Alexandria, VA: Center for Naval Analyses.

Doyle, E. L., & Campbell, R. C. (1990). *Navy: Hands-on and knowledge tests for the Navy radioman*. Paper presented at the 32nd Annual Conference of the Military Testing Association, Orange Beach, AL.

DuBois, D. A. (1996). *The construct validity of job knowledge: A meta-analytic review and critique*. Paper presented at the Eleventh Annual Convention of the Society for Industrial and Organizational Psychology, San Diego, CA.

Felker, D. B., Bowler, E. C., Szenas, P., Rose, A. M., Barkley, P., Helgerman, D., Keil, C., & Shade, R. (1992). *Analysis of job requirements and development of model job performance measures for Marine Corps electronic maintenance occupational areas* (AIR-89500-6/92-FR). Washington, DC: American Institutes for Research.

Felker, D. B., Crafts, J. L., Rose, A. M., Harnest, C. W., Edwards, D. S., Bowler, E.C., Rivkin, D. W., & McHenry, J. J. (1988). *Developing job performance tests for the United States Marine Corps Infantry occupational field* (AIR-47500-9/88-FR). Washington, DC: American Institutes for Research.

Green, B. F., & Wing, H. (1988). *Analysis of job performance measurement data: Report of a workshop*. Washington, DC: National Academy Press.

Guion, R. M. (1979a). *Principles of work sample testing: I. A non-empirical taxonomy of test uses* (ARI TR-79-A8). Alexandria, VA: U.S. Army Research Institute for the Behavioral and Social Sciences.

Guion, R. M. (1979b). *Principles of work sample testing: II. Evaluation of personnel testing programs* (ARI TR-79-A9). Alexandria, VA: U.S. Army Research Institute for the Behavioral and Social Sciences.

Guion, R. M. (1979c). *Principles of work sample testing: III. Construction and evaluation of work sample tests* (ARI TR-79-A10). Alexandria, VA: U.S. Army Research Institute for the Behavioral and Social Sciences.

Guion, R. M. (1979d). *Principles of work sample testing: IV. Generalizability* (ARI TR-79-A11). Alexandria, VA: U.S. Army Research Institute for the Behavioral and Social Sciences.

Harris, D. A. (1987). Job performance measurement and the joint-service project: An overview. In *Proceedings of the Department of Defense/Educational Testing Service Conference on Job Performance Measurement Technologies.* San Diego, CA.

Hattrup, K., & Schmitt, N. (1990). Prediction of trades apprentices' performance on job sample criteria. *Personnel Psychology, 43,* 453–466.

Hedge, J. W., Lipscomb, M. S., & Teachout, M. S. (1988). Work sample testing in the Air Force job performance measurement project. In M. S. Lipscomb & J. W. Hedge (Eds.), *Job performance measurement: Topics in the performance measurement of Air Force enlisted personnel* (AFHRL-TP-87-58). Brooks Air Force Base, TX: Air Force Human Resources Laboratory.

Knapp, D. J., & Campbell, J. P. (1993). *Building a joint-service classification research roadmap: Criterion-related issues* (AL/HR-TP-1993-0028). Brooks Air Force Base, TX: Armstrong Laboratory, Manpower and Personnel Research Division.

Mayberry, P. W. (1987). *Developing a competency scale for hands-on measures of job proficiency* (CRC 570). Alexandria, VA: Center for Naval Analyses.

Mayberry, P. W. (1990). *Validation of the ASVAB against infantry job performance* (CRM 90-182). Alexandria, VA: Center for Naval Analyses.

Mayberry, P. W. (1992). *Reliability of mechanical maintenance performance measures* (CRM 91-246). Alexandria, VA: Center for Naval Analyses.

Oppler, S. H., Campbell, J. P., Pulakos, E. D., & Borman, W. C. (1992). Three approaches to the investigation of subgroup bias in performance measurement: Review, results, and conclusions. *Journal of Applied Psychology Monograph, 77* (2), 201–217.

Osborn, W. C. (1974). *Process versus product measures in performance testing* (HumRRO professional paper 16-74). Alexandria, VA: Human Resources Research Organization.

Osborn, W. C., Campbell, R. C., & Ford, J. P. (1976). *Handbook for development of skill qualification tests* (HumRRO Final Report FR-CD[L]-77-1). Alexandria, VA: Human Resources Research Organization.

Rose, A. M., Radtke, P., & Shettel, H. H. (1984). *User's manual for predicting military task retention.* Washington, DC: American Institutes for Research.

Sackett, P. R., Zedeck, S., & Fogli, L. (1988). Relations between measures of typical and maximum job performance. *Journal of Applied Psychology, 73,* 482–486.

Siegel, A. I. (1986). Performance tests. In R. A. Berk (Ed.), *Performance assessment: Methods and applications* (pp. 121–142). Baltimore, MD: Johns Hopkins University Press.

U.S. Army. (1979). *Job and task analysis handbook* (TRADOC Pam 351-4[T]). Ft. Monroe, VA: U.S. Army Training Developments Institute.

Wigdor, A. K., & Green, B. F. (Eds.). (1986). *Assessing the performance of enlisted personnel: Evaluation of a Joint-Service research project.* Washington, DC: National Academy Press.

CONDUCTING STUDIES TO ASSESS THE QUALITY OF THE MEASUREMENT PROGRAM

Validation of Selection Instruments[*]

Deborah L. Whetzel
Scott H. Oppler

OVERVIEW

As mentioned in Chapter 1, one of the reasons for conducting a job analysis is to generate information that can be used to develop predictor instruments as well as measures of job performance. That same information can be used to support validation of selection measures. In this chapter, we describe validation designs and discuss issues related to collecting and analyzing validity data.

The objective of a validation study is to obtain evidence to support the interpretation and use of predictor scores. Note that in this chapter we discuss validating inferences made from "test" scores (e.g., a cognitive ability test as described in Chapter 6). But pencil-and-paper multiple-choice tests are only one kind of predictor; inferences from other predictors, such as interviews (as described in Chapter 7), background data

---

[*]Sections of this chapter are adapted by permission from *A Guide to Test Validation* compiled by the ERIC Clearinghouse on Tests, Measurement and Evaluation and the American Institutes for Research.

(as described in Chapter 8), and situational inventories (as described in 9) also should be validated. According to the *Standards for Educational and Psychological Testing*, (APA, AERA, & NCME, 1985, p. 9) validity

> refers to the appropriateness, meaningfulness, and usefulness of the specific inferences made from test scores. Test validation is the process of accumulating evidence to support such inferences. A variety of inferences may be made from scores produced by a given test, and there are many ways of accumulating evidence to support any particular inference.

This definition emphasizes the idea that validity is not a characteristic of a test or assessment procedure, but, instead, of inferences made from test or assessment information (Binning & Barrett, 1989). As Nunnally (1978) states, "one validates not a measuring instrument but rather some use to which a measuring instrument is put" (p. 87).

This definition also emphasizes that valid inference must be supported by sound evidence. The collection and analysis of such evidence will be discussed in this chapter. The definition also implies that predictor validation is a special case of hypothesis testing and theory development. In employment testing, the hypothesis is that test scores can be used to predict job performance. In achievement testing, the hypothesis is that test scores can be used to describe mastery of relevant skills.

Historically, validity evidence was defined by three "types" of validity: content, criterion-related, and construct (EEOC, CSC, DOL, & DOJ, 1978). Content validity is based on professional judgments about the relevance of the predictor content to the content of a particular behavioral domain of interest (i.e., job performance) and about the representativeness with which the predictor items cover that domain. As such, content validity provides judgmental evidence in support of domain relevance of the content of the predictor, rather than evidence in support of inferences made from predictor scores. Tenopyr (1977) argued that content validity should be thought of as "content-oriented test construction" (p. 62) since it really refers to sound methods of test or predictor development rather than to methods for providing validity evidence. Criterion-related validity is based on the degree of empirical relationship, usually expressed in terms of correlations and regressions, between predictor scores and criterion scores. This approach focuses on specific relationships with measures used for an applied purpose (i.e., predicting job performance). Construct validity is based on an integration of evidence that supports the interpretation or meaning of predictor scores. Almost any kind of information about a predictor can contribute to an understanding of construct validity, but the contribution becomes stronger if the theoretical rationale underlying the predictor scores is evaluated.

Many researchers have supported a unified conception of validity (Binning & Barrett, 1989; Dunnette & Borman, 1979; Guion, 1977, 1978, 1980; Messick, 1980; Tenopyr, 1977; Tenopyr & Oeltjen, 1982). The argument is that content evidence and criterion-related evidence offer an incomplete understanding of validity. Binning and Barrett (1989) argued that validation is theory building, and the various strategies provide different but complementary sources of evidence to support understanding and interpretation of constructs. Therefore, the different strategies cannot be logically separated. In the next section of this chapter, we describe how to develop a research plan for validating the inferences made from predictor measures.

HOW TO DEVELOP A
VALIDATION RESEARCH PLAN

Insofar as possible, research projects should be designed and carried out according to the *Principles for the Validation and Use of Personnel Selection Procedures* (Society for Industrial and Organizational Psychology, 1987) and the *Standards for Educational and Psychological Testing* (APA, AERA, NCME, 1985). Although neither document is legally binding, the importance of following the *Principles* "depends on the consequences of error which may result in physical, psychological, or economic injury to people or reduce the safety or operating efficiency of the organization" (p. 3). Whereas the *Principles* primarily address the problems of making decisions in such areas as employee selection, placement, and promotion, the *Standards* primarily address psychometric issues. This section describes psychometric and methodological issues to consider when planning to conduct validation research in accordance with both documents.

SPECIFY OBJECTIVES

All validation efforts should begin with a research plan. Such a plan should explicitly state the purpose for conducting the study and the steps to be followed. The purpose for conducting the validity study must be based on an understanding of the work performed on the job, the needs of the organization, and the rights of current and prospective employees. Of primary importance in the decision-making process is the validity of the final selection decision.

An important step for describing the objectives of the research plan is to conduct a literature review to determine what studies already have been conducted on the construct in question for predicting performance on the job(s). It is important to determine whether the objectives have already been met by previous research or how the new effort might build on previous research. Conducting the literature review is described in Chapter 5.

DESCRIBE VALIDATION STRATEGY

If an objective of the validation strategy is to assess the accuracy of inferences from predictor scores, then a criterion-related validation approach is required. There are two kinds of strategies that can be categorized according to the timing of the collection of predictor and criterion data. When predictor data (e.g., test scores) and criterion data (e.g., performance ratings or scores) are collected from job incumbents at or around the same time, the design is referred to as a *concurrent design*. On the other hand, when predictor data are collected at a particular time, usually from job applicants, and criterion data are collected at a later time from job incumbents, then the design is referred to as a predictive or *longitudinal design*. The most important difference between concurrent and longitudinal designs is the timing of the collection of predictor and criterion information.

Concurrent Designs

Designs of this type use a sample of examinees who are currently performing the job that is the focus of the study. Once the job analysis is conducted and the predictor(s) are developed, each predictor (e.g., test or interview) is administered to a sample of job incumbents. Around the same time, performance data (e.g., ratings; measures of task or course proficiency) are also collected from these incumbents. There are several advantages and disadvantages associated with this design. An important practical advantage is that this design often produces relatively timely results. The predictor administration is economical, since the total number of persons to be tested is known or can be readily determined in advance. Disadvantages of this design are that current job incumbents may be quite strong in the constructs measured by the predictors, and therefore there will likely be some restriction in the range of ability for incumbent samples. This restriction in range will cause the correlation between the predictors and the criterion to appear lower than if there were a greater amount of variance in the predictor scores (as might be observed in the applicant population). On the other hand, to the extent that performance on the predictors is affected by experience on the job, it is possible that the correlation between predictor scores and criterion scores may be overestimated in a study using a concurrent design. Another disadvantage is that it may prove difficult to obtain examinees. Employers, for example, often are reluctant to take examinees off the job for the necessary test administration. A related concern is the motivation of current employees to take the predictor and criterion tests seriously.

Longitudinal Designs

The basic distinguishing feature of the longitudinal validation design is the separation in time between collection of predictor and criterion data. In a study using a longitudinal design, the sample usually consists of applicants tested at the time they applied for a job. An advantage of this design is that the selection situation closely parallels the operational situation, because the sample is drawn from the same population of applicants on which the predictors will be used for selection purposes, and the entire range of scores is represented. Another advantage is that the predictor scores on untrained individuals are used in the prediction of performance (i.e., this design rules out any possibility of the predictor scores being influenced by job-specific training and experience, since the sample is tested before acquiring that training and experience).

Note that use of a longitudinal design does not necessarily eliminate the problems associated with range restriction, as described earlier. This is because the correlation between predictor scores and criterion scores can only be estimated using data from job applicants who were actually selected and remained on the job long enough for criterion data to be collected. These applicants will often have higher scores on the constructs being measured than applicants who were not selected, even when the tests being validated are not being used to make the selection decisions. Because of this possibility, it also is important to retain predictor data collected from all applicants, not just those with criterion data. These data can be used to estimate the variability of the test scores in the applicant population, which in turn can be used in a formula to correct the correlation between scores on the new predictor and the criterion. A formula for making such a correction is provided later in this chapter.

Other disadvantages of the longitudinal design are mainly practical. Typically, the time lag between predictor and criterion data collection ranges from six months to one year, and many companies may not wish to wait that long for study results. Further, in many cases, applicants who were tested do not remain on the job long enough for suitable criterion data to be obtained, and it is seldom possible to determine if their reason for leaving was related to job performance. Thus, it is important to assess the level of turnover so that rates of attrition can be analyzed and sample sizes can be estimated. Another disadvantage is that the accumulation of samples of sufficient size usually requires long periods of time during which new employees are hired, tested, and added to the sample.

It should be noted that empirical comparisons of validity estimates for cognitive ability tests using both longitudinal and concurrent designs indicate that the two types of designs do not yield significantly different estimates (Barrett, Phillips, & Alexander, 1981; Schmitt, Gooding, Noe, & Kirsch, 1984). On the other hand, there is some evidence that the same cannot be said of scores from personality/biodata instruments. Specifically, Oppler, Peterson and Russell (1992) found that the validities of such measures were considerably lower when estimated using a longitudinal design, rather than a concurrent design.

DEVELOP THE SAMPLING PLAN

The sampling plan describes who will be included in the study. It must address two important issues. The first issue is the sample size. How many examinees will be required in order to meet the study's objectives? The second issue is specification of the characteristics of the sample to be selected. How will examinees be selected to be representative of the population of interest? The validation design will dictate the general characteristics of those to be tested (e.g., whether they are applicants, trainees, or employees), but further specification is required to ensure a sample that is representative with respect to demographic characteristics, experience, and the nature of the job and/or work setting.

Sample Size

The first issue in deciding on the appropriate sample size is to identify the statistics that will be computed and to determine the level of reliability desired for these statistics (statistical reliability refers to the consistency or repeatability of measurement). Generally, the larger the sample of examinees included in the validation study, the more dependable the statistics will be, provided that the sample is representative of the target population. The analysis of the relationship between sample size and statistical reliability for hypothesis testing is termed *power analysis*. In a power analysis, the probability that a null hypothesis will be rejected is specified as a function of the true (population) value of the statistic of interest and the size of the sample. Generally, it is desirable that the sample size be selected so that there is a 90% chance, or greater, that differences of practical significance are also statistically significant. The power of a significance test of a correlation for various sample sizes is provided by Schmidt, Hunter, and Urry (1976). Later in this chapter, we discuss the use of confidence intervals for evaluating study results.

Decisions about sample size reflect a practical trade-off between statistical reliability and the cost of conducting the research. The sample size is related to costs in a number of ways, beginning with the resources required to obtain study participants and continuing on to the administration and scoring of both the predictor and criterion measures.

Sample Characteristics

It is important for the sample to be representative of the target population (i.e., the applicant pool). From a scientific perspective, the greater the similarity between the sample and the population, the more likely it will be that the results of the study will hold up when the predictor scores are used operationally. For instance, if a test is going to be used to predict performance in training, then it would not be advisable to include in the sample individuals with many years of job experience. On the other hand, if a test is to be used to predict longer term performance, it is important for examinees participating in a concurrent validity study to have at least a minimum amount of experience, defined as successfully completing a probationary period and functioning at a satisfactory level. A person who has just begun a job may not yet be performing at his or her optimum level. If criterion data are collected on relatively inexperienced employees, the criterion scores may be lower than they would be if the employees had more job experience. This would affect the correlation obtained (e.g., if someone who had a high predictor score performed poorly on the criterion due to minimal job experience, the coefficient would likely be artificially low). Further, if employees at one site do not perform the same tasks as employees at another site (even if they have the same job title), the job requirements may be different and the predictor may be more valid for one job/site than for another.

From a legal perspective, it is important to have numbers of minorities and women in the study sample comparable to the numbers who are likely to apply for the job. If the selection system is challenged, one question likely to be asked concerns the makeup of subjects in the validation study. Of course, if certain statistics (e.g., correlations between predictor and criterion scores) are to be computed separately for members of different groups, it may be necessary to oversample from these groups in order to obtain results that are statistically reliable.

SELECT THE CRITERION
MEASUREMENT INSTRUMENTS

The criterion-related validation of a predictor battery for use in selection requires evaluation of the ability of the test(s) to predict performance on the job or task. The criteria used in such a validation study are the particular measures of performance that are used to infer true performance. Obtaining satisfactory measures of performance is a difficult problem and one that requires attention during the planning phase of the study. Detailed discussions of how to develop rating instruments and tests of job performance are provided in Chapters 11 and 12, respectively. In this section, we describe issues regarding the choice of criterion measures.

There are several characteristics that make criteria useful for a validation study. Some of these are:

1. Validity or relevance: A criterion measure is relevant when the knowledges, skills, and abilities and other characteristics related to the measure are the same as those required to perform the job duties.
2. Reliability: When evaluating the reliability of a criterion such as ratings, one can investigate the amount of agreement between the ratings provided by two different raters or between the ratings provided by one rater at two different times. Rothstein (1990) found that the reliability of supervisor ratings increased with opportunity to observe, but appeared to asymptote at about .60.
3. Freedom from bias: Bias may occur whenever individuals or subgroups of a sample are evaluated in systematically different ways. Brogden and Taylor (1950) classified the various types of criterion bias in raw criterion data as either the omission of pertinent elements from the criterion (criterion deficiency) or the introduction of extraneous elements into the criterion (criterion contamination).
4. Practicality: There are very real limits to the effort that may be exerted or the disturbance of routine procedures that will be tolerated during data collection. Unless the validity study is being well supported by the operating personnel, any program for

gathering criterion information that calls for additional work on their part may be resisted. It is important to give supervisors a realistic evaluation of the burden imposed by the collection of criterion data.

One should guard against using operational performance appraisal systems in which the data are collected for administrative purposes as criteria for a validation study. Although they are relatively easy to collect, they are subject to a variety of contaminating factors. Wherry and Bartlett (1982) hypothesized that ratings collected solely for research purposes would be more accurate than ratings collected for administrative purposes. Several studies have demonstrated that ratings collected for administrative purposes are significantly more lenient and exhibit more halo than ratings collected for research purposes (Sharon & Bartlett, 1969; Taylor & Wherry, 1951; Veres, Field, & Boyles, 1983; Warmke & Billings, 1979).

Whenever possible, more than one set of criterion measures should be obtained in validation studies. One reason for collecting more than one set of criterion data is the multidimensionality of jobs. For example, in a study conducted by the Army, known as Project A, Campbell, McHenry, and Wise (1990) showed that supervisor ratings were more highly indicative of "will do" or motivational aspects of job performance, and work sample and job knowledge tests were more indicative of "can do" or maximal proficiency aspects of job performance. Hence, it is important to consider a wide variety of criteria when designing validation studies.

HOW TO COLLECT DATA

Several kinds of data must be collected in a validation study. These include personnel data, predictor data, and criterion data. Following is a description of each of these kinds of data. In addition, we describe methods for preparing data to ensure their quality.

COLLECT PERSONNEL DATA

It is necessary to collect background data for two key reasons: (1) Professional and scientific research practices require thorough documentation of the nature of the sample of subjects studied, and (2) selection methods are subject to public and legal scrutiny. In the event that the research practices are questioned, information regarding sample representation needs to be made available. In addition, if subgroup analyses are conducted, one must be able to differentiate among various groups.

Typical personnel data include identification or social security number, age, education, gender, ethnicity, and amount of work experience. Other data may be specified by the research plan, such as information concerning specific types of work experience, training, or equipment operated. Other subsample information may include data collection site name, and the *Dictionary of Occupational Titles* (U.S. Department of Labor, 1991) code number of the job being studied.

Personnel data collected directly from examinees should be placed on various research forms specified by the research plan. These forms should be designed for the convenience of the examinees completing them and for ready, efficient entry into electronic form for data analysis. Note that one of the most important forms for examinees to complete is a privacy or confidentiality agreement. Such agreements, signed by examinees, usually state that participation in the research is voluntary and that their data will be reported as part of group statistics only, not individually. It may be very difficult to obtain applicant or employee information if these conditions are not communicated and imposed. Under no circumstances should the researcher release individual data to organization officials after confidentiality has been promised to participants.

COLLECT PREDICTOR DATA

When collecting predictor data on instruments that can be administered to groups, there are several issues to be considered to ensure standardization across data collection sites. These include organizing the physical facilities of the room, ensuring that there are adequate supplies, maintaining security of test materials, and writing clear instructions to examinees.

Physical Facilities of Test Room

A well-lit and properly ventilated room with tables, chairs, and adequate space for testing is required. Preferably, the room should have no telephone and be situated so that there will be no distracting noises, so that the testing session can be conducted without interruption. Also, the room should have sufficient space to allow the test monitor easy access to all examinees. When testing at a site for the first time, it is a good idea to arrive at the site prior to testing to ensure that the facility is the same as was originally agreed upon.

All booklets and answer sheets should be examined prior to the testing session for misprints, pencil marks, and missing pages. Also, if there are several forms of each booklet, the examiner must check to see that answer sheets match forms being used. Sharpened pencils with erasers should be provided to each examinee. Scratch paper also should be provided to examinees, if necessary. If any of the predictor instruments are to be completed within a specific time limit, the examiner should have an extra timing device (e.g., a stopwatch) in case one malfunctions. Also, if more than about 20 examinees are being tested at once, it may be useful to have an assistant to help distribute materials and monitor examinees during the session.

Test Security

Testing materials should be kept secure at all times. In preparation for test sessions, researchers may be asked to set up ahead of time. This may be especially useful if special equipment or apparatus is required for testing (e.g., computers or pegboards). Written test materials should always remain under tight control. When the testing session is completed, the test administrator must count booklets and answer sheets to ensure that all test materials are accounted for. Numbering test booklets is helpful for ensuring that all test booklets have been retrieved at the end of a session.

Instructions to Examinees

All examinees participating in test research should understand the purpose of their participation for ethical reasons and to ensure cooperation. Typically, a presentation by a researcher immediately prior to the administration of the tests will put the examinees at ease and will enable them to understand the purpose of their participation. When job incumbents are tested, it may be desirable for management to distribute a specially prepared statement to employees who are asked to take the tests. When validity data are being collected, the written or oral statement should include the following points:

1. Name the exact purpose of the study and who is sponsoring the research. For example, "ABC Company is conducting this research in order to identify procedures for selecting persons who have a good chance of succeeding on the job."

2. Tell the examinees exactly what will be done with their predictor scores. For example, "Your scores will be compared to other data describing your job performance. Your scores will not be seen by your supervisors or anyone else outside the Research Department."
3. Inform them that their participation is voluntary and that not participating will have no effect on their chances of getting or keeping a job.
4. Encourage examinees to do their best on the test so that the research will be successful.
5. Tell the examinees about how long it will take to complete the tests and/or other instruments.
6. Ask whether examinees have any remaining questions and address any concerns that are voiced.

Following such a statement, the tests should be administered using specific instructions developed for each test. Adherence to the specific test administration procedures published and prepared for each test is crucial to ensure standardized data collection across sites and sessions. See Chapter 6 for a discussion of such instructions.

COLLECT CRITERION DATA

The procedures used for collecting criterion data depend on the type of criterion measures used. If a job knowledge test is used as a criterion, the procedures may be similar to those just described above for collecting predictor data. If objective criterion data are collected (e.g., productivity rate or error rate), procedures need to be developed to ensure their accuracy. Such indices should focus on individual rather than group performance, since scores on these measures will be correlated with individual performance on predictors. It is important that employees have approximately equal opportunity to perform the criterion behavior (i.e., employees must have been on the job long enough to be able to be accurately measured by the criterion or have had equal access to and equal time on any machines used). Procedures for collecting such data will be specific to the organization and criterion measure. For example, when collecting data using work sample measures, as described in Chapter 12, one must ensure that those who score such measures are knowledgeable enough about the task to be able to distinguish correct and incorrect performance, and they need to be trained to score such measures uniformly.

If subjective criterion data are collected (e.g., peer or supervisor ratings), it is useful to collect more than one rating for each examinee in order to assess reliability. To collect ratings, it is advisable to meet with each rater individually, or in small groups, to provide instructions for making ratings. Rater training techniques, including error training and accuracy training, are described in Chapter 11.

PREPARE DATA TO ENSURE QUALITY

Quality control of the data begins with the data collector. The data collector is in the best position to detect any significant departure from design specification and data collection standards. Irregularities in test administration or in examinee behavior may not be detectable after the data collection is complete, which makes it especially important for the data collector to conscientiously monitor all phases of data collection. Irregularities should be documented so that questionable data can be excluded from the study (e.g., data from examinees responding randomly). However, clear justification must be demonstrated before data can be excluded. Careful monitoring and documentation of the data collection effort are necessary to provide such justification.

To the extent that the data collected are inaccurate, the data analyses and the conclusions drawn from the analyses will be flawed. Inaccurate data are defined as follows:

1. Data that are not true measures of the variables, or data that are not representative of the individuals or jobs being studied
2. Data that are irregular due to administration problems (e.g., insufficient lighting in a testing room) or due to individual performance on the measure that may be exaggerated or attenuated

A form for documenting data collection should be developed and used to document the date, location, and circumstances of data collection, and to provide descriptive information about each subsample to enable researchers to decide whether data should be included in data analysis. The exact form of these records should be specified during the research design.

Preparing the database prior to conducting analyses is another important step for ensuring quality research. Preparing the database involves specifying how data are to be entered (e.g., using scannable forms or keypunching), editing the data (e.g., for out of range values), and resolving issues surrounding missing data (e.g., eliminating an examinee's incomplete data on an instrument or statistically imputing the missing values). Resolving these issues will require a number of decisions that will impact on how the data are analyzed. We now turn to methods for analyzing data.

HOW TO ANALYZE VALIDITY DATA

This section of the chapter describes a wide range of statistical techniques that might be used by analysts examining predictor validity. It covers topics ranging from the computation of means and standard deviations to regression and bias. The latter topics are discussed at a conceptual level. In the event that a more thorough understanding of these topics may be useful, references are made to appropriate texts.

COMPUTE BASIC DESCRIPTIVE STATISTICS

Descriptive statistics are used to describe the characteristics of the data and to make appropriate inferences based on statistical measures. In this section, we focus on three common types of descriptive measures: measures of central tendency, measures of variability, and correlations. For more discussion of basic statistics, one might consult *Introduction to Classical and Modern Test Theory* by Crocker and Algina (1986).

Measures of Central Tendency

There are three commonly used measures of central tendency: the median, the mode, and the mean. The *median* of a set of scores is defined to be the middle value when the set of measurements is arranged in order of magnitude. The median is most often used to measure the midpoint of a large set of measurements, such as the median age of all persons providing criterion data in the study. This is a useful statistic, since it is not influenced by extreme data points (known as outliers). The *mode* of a set of scores is defined to be the measurement that occurs most often. The mode is commonly used to determine the most frequently occurring test score. This measure of central tendency also is not influenced by outliers. The *mean,* or arithmetic average, of a set of scores on a variable (e.g., ages of workers, scores on a predictor, ratings on a dimension of job performance) is simply the sum of all the scores divided by the number of scores. The mean usually is the preferred measure of central tendency and is used in the calculation of other more complex statistics. Following we provide an example of a set of Reading Comprehension scores for currently employed electricians participating in a validation study for which a mean was computed. The formula used to calculate the mean for a set of scores is:

$$M_x = \frac{\Sigma x}{n}$$

where: M_x = the mean of a set of scores,
x = a score in the set,
Σ = sum of, and
n = the total number of individuals in the sample who provided a score.

By way of illustration, assume that predictor data (Reading Comprehension scores) and criterion scores (job knowledge test scores) have been collected from a sample of 10 electricians. The Reading Comprehension scores and the job knowledge test scores of the electricians are as follows:

Examinee	Reading Comprehension Scores (x)	Job Knowledge Criterion Scores (y)
A	16	9
B	12	6
C	14	12
D	10	5
E	11	12
F	7	4
G	9	3
H	12	9
I	7	10
J	8	3
Sum	106	73

In order to compute the mean predictor test and criterion scores for this sample, the following calculations are performed.

Let: x = the test score of each examinee
y = the criterion score of each examinee
n = the number of electricians = 10
Compute: Σx = the sum of Reading Comprehension scores = 106
Σy = the sum of job knowledge scores = 73

Substitute the appropriate values in the formula for the mean:

$$M_x = \frac{\Sigma x}{n} = \frac{106}{10} = 10.6$$

$$M_y = \frac{\Sigma y}{n} = \frac{73}{10} = 7.3$$

The mean Reading Comprehension score for this sample is 10.6; the mean criterion score for this sample is 7.3. The primary disadvantage of the mean as a measure of central tendency is that outlier values may greatly affect the value of the mean. For example, if we changed worker J's score on the criterion from 3 to 60, M_y would increase from 7.3 to 13.0, a value greater than any of the other nine actual observations.

Measures of Variability

Just as there is more than one measure of central tendency, so are there multiple measures of variability. Among these are the range, the interquartile range, and the standard deviation. The range is a rough measure of dispersion that is expressed by referring to the lowest and highest values in a distribution of scores. Computing the range of a set of scores is a simple way to check whether the scores are within the expected limits. For example, if a researcher found that the range of scores for a sample was 7 to 25 and knew that it was not possible to obtain a score above 20, he or she would be alerted to the fact that at least one score must be incorrect and could take steps to correct it. Related to the range is the interquartile range. This is expressed by ranking the observations from lowest to highest and referring to the values occurring at the 25th and 75th percentiles of the distribution. For example, if there are 20 scores ordered from lowest to highest, the fifth score would represent the 25th percentile, and the fifteenth score would represent the 75th percentile. Whereas the interquartile range is the measure of variability most closely aligned with the median, the measure of variability associated with the mean is the standard deviation.

The standard deviation is a measure of dispersion that describes the extent to which scores scatter or vary about the mean score. It is defined as the square root of the average squared deviations of a set of scores from their mean. A small standard deviation means that scores tend to cluster closely around the mean; a large standard deviation means that scores tend to range from very high to very low and there is greater dispersion around the mean. Note that the square of the standard deviation is the variance. The formula for calculating the standard deviation of a set of scores is:

$$SD_x = \sqrt{\frac{\Sigma(x - M_x)^2}{n}}$$

where Σ, x, M_x and n were previously defined.

To compute the standard deviation of the Reading Comprehension scores in our example, we would first calculate the following:

Examinee	Reading Comprehension Scores (x)	$x - M_x$	$(x - M_x)^2$
A	16	5.4	29.16
B	12	1.4	1.96
C	14	3.4	11.56
D	10	-0.6	0.36
E	11	0.4	0.16
F	7	-3.6	12.96
G	9	-1.6	2.56
H	12	1.4	1.96
I	7	-3.6	12.96
J	8	-2.6	6.76
Sum	106	0	80.40

Substituting the appropriate values into the formula as follows, the result is a standard deviation of 2.84.

$$SD_x = \sqrt{\frac{\Sigma(x - M_x)^2}{n}} = \sqrt{\frac{80.40}{10}} = 2.84$$

After similar calculations, the standard deviation of the criterion scores (y) reported earlier is found to be 3.35.

COMPUTE STANDARD SCORES FROM RAW SCORES

It often is inappropriate to compare the raw score on one measure with the raw score on another measure because of differences in the units of measurement. For example, a score of 30 on an aptitude test with a mean of 50 and a standard deviation of 10 is not equivalent to a score of 30 on a different test that has a mean of 20 and a standard deviation of 5. Transforming raw scores to a particular type of scaled score, known as standard scores, permits comparisons to be made. By comparing standard scores, it can be determined whether an examinee's performance on the first measure is better or worse than his or her performance on the second measure. Standard scores are typically expressed in "standard deviation units." That is, to transform an examinee's raw score on a given measure to a standard score, the raw score is subtracted from the average test score (as computed in the example just given) and this difference is divided by the test's standard deviation. The distribution of a set of standard scores, so defined, will always have a mean of zero and a standard deviation of 1.

For example, suppose one wanted to compare the test score of one electrician from the sample just given with his or her criterion score. To do so, one would first calculate the standard scores of each. The formula for converting raw scores on a variable to standard scores on the same variable is:

$$Z_x = \frac{x - M_x}{SD_x}$$

where: Z_x = the standard score in a set of scores
x = the raw score in the original set of scores,
M_x = the mean of the original set of scores, and
SD_x = the standard deviation of the original set of scores.

Substituting the appropriate values for electrician A into the formula:

$$Z_x = \frac{x - M_x}{SD_x} = \frac{16 - 10.6}{2.84} = 1.90$$

$$Z_y = \frac{y - M_x}{SD_y} = \frac{9 - 7.3}{3.35} = 0.51$$

Based on these calculations, electrician A's standard Reading Comprehension score is 1.90, which is higher than his or her standing on the criterion, represented by a standard score of 0.51. That is, his or her Reading Comprehension score is 1.90 standard deviations greater than the mean, whereas his or her criterion score is only 0.51 standard deviations greater than the mean.

COMPUTE CORRELATION COEFFICIENTS

Correlational methods are used in predictor validation work to analyze the relationships between variables. The size and direction of the relationship between two variables can be expressed in terms of a correlation coefficient computed from data obtained from a sample. Although there are many types of correlational indices, the most appropriate one for use in validation work is the Pearson product–moment correlation coefficient, r_{xy} (Crocker & Algina, 1986). Correlation coefficients can have values ranging from 1.00 to -1.00. A positive correlation coefficient indicates that two variables are related in such a way that high scores on one variable tend to be associated with high scores on the other variable, and that low scores on one variable tend to be associated with low scores on the other variable. In contrast, a negative correlation coefficient indicates that high scores on one variable tend to be associated with low scores on the other variable. The size of the correlation coefficient (regardless of the sign) is an index of the degree of linear relationship, with a value of 0 indicating no relationship between the two variables, and a value of 1.00 or -1.00 indicating a perfect relationship. Hence, the correlation between a set of predictor and criterion scores indicates the degree to which an individual's relative standing on the predictor corresponds to his or her relative standing on the criterion.

The formula for computing the product–moment correlation between any two variables is:

$$r_{xy} = \frac{N\Sigma xy - \Sigma x \Sigma y}{\sqrt{N\Sigma x^2 - (\Sigma x)^2} \ \sqrt{N\Sigma y^2 - (\Sigma y)^2}}$$

Compute: r_{xy} = the Pearson product–moment correlation between predictor scores and criterion scores,

N = the number of individuals in the sample,

Σxy = the sum of the cross products of predictor and criterion scores,

Σx = the sum of the predictor scores,

Σy = the sum of the criterion scores,

Σx^2 = the sum of squares of the predictor scores, and

Σy^2 = the sum of squares of the criterion scores.

Today, most statistical software packages include programs for computing the product–moment correlation coefficient between two variables. The following example, using the small sample of electricians described earlier, is provided for illustrative purposes.

Examinee	Reading Comprehension Scores (x)	Criterion Scores (y)	x^2	y^2	xy
A	16	9	256	81	144
B	12	6	144	36	72
C	14	12	196	144	168
D	10	5	100	25	50
E	11	12	121	144	132
F	7	4	49	16	28
G	9	3	81	9	27
H	12	9	144	81	108
I	7	10	49	100	70
J	8	3	64	9	24
Sum	106	73	1204	645	823

Substituting the appropriate values in the formula:

$$r_{xy} = \frac{(10)(823) - (106)(73)}{\sqrt{10(1204) - (106)^2}\ \sqrt{10(645) - (73)^2}} = .518$$

Only when a correlation coefficient is computed using accurate measurements for the total population, consisting of all members of the group of interest, can the assumption be made that it represents the true relationship. In validation work, it is not possible to measure all members of the population. Therefore, samples of the total population are used. Correlation coefficients computed using data obtained from samples are subject to chance error, known as sampling error, with the result that, in general, the values of the obtained correlation coefficients differ to some degree from the value of the population correlation coefficient. The degree of confidence that can be placed in a correlation coefficient computed from sample data depends on the number of cases in the sample. The larger the sample, the more confidence one can have that the value of the obtained correlation coefficient approaches the value of the population correlation coefficient. It is a general rule in statistical analysis that the stability of any statistic is greater for large samples than for small samples. For this reason, validation studies should be based on samples that are as large as possible. Because of the inaccuracy of sample-based correlation coefficients, it may be helpful to consider the correlation coefficient not as a single value, but as a range of values. For this purpose, it is useful to calculate a confidence interval, which is a range of values that has a given probability of containing the population value. The formula for calculating a 95% confidence interval is:

$$r_{xy} - 1.96 S_e \leq p \leq r_{xy} + 1.96 S_e$$

where S_e is the standard error of the correlation.

To calculate the confidence interval for a given correlation, one must first compute the standard error for that correlation. The formula for the standard error of a correlation is:

$$S_e = \frac{1 - r_{xy}^2}{\sqrt{n - 1}}$$

In our example, the standard error of the correlation would be calculated as:

$$S_e = \frac{1 - .518^2}{\sqrt{10\text{-}1}} = .244$$

Using this value in the formula for the confidence interval just presented, the confidence interval is calculated as follows:

$$.518 - (1.96 \times .244) \leq p \leq .518 + (1.96 \times .244)$$
$$.0398 \leq p \leq .996$$

Note that the confidence interval does not contain zero, indicating we can be confident, with 95% accuracy, that the population correlation will be greater than zero. However, the size of the interval encompasses nearly the entire range of positive correlations, from zero to one. This indicates that little confidence can be placed in the precision of the .518 correlation as a point estimate of the correlation in the population. The reason for this was alluded to earlier; that is, the accuracy with which a correlation can be estimated is highly dependent on the number of cases included in the analysis, and in our example, the sample size is only 10.

Tests of statistical significance are also used to determine whether the obtained correlation coefficient is significantly different from zero or from some other specified level. Tables for testing the significance of correlation coefficients can be found in most statistical textbooks (Hays, 1981, Appendix D). Although tests of statistical significance are quite frequently used to evaluate predictor validity (i.e., the correlation between a predictor and criterion measure), data indicate that statistical significance tests are susceptible to large Type II error, defined as accepting the null hypothesis (e.g., that the predictor is not valid) when it should be rejected (e.g., the predictor really is valid; Schmidt & Hunter, 1977). In fact, Hunter (1996) and Schmidt (1996) have called for a ban on significance testing, arguing that significance tests have led researchers to discard useful findings due to the stringency of these tests. Following we describe reasons why observed correlations may be artificially low.

CORRECT FOR FACTORS AFFECTING THE CORRELATION COEFFICIENT

Range Restriction

When a validation study is conducted, the correlation between a predictor and the criterion is affected by several factors. One such factor, sampling error, was described earlier. Now we will describe two other factors: range restriction and criterion unreliability. The intent of validation research is to determine the true validity of a predictor for members of the applicant population. However, concurrent validation studies use employee samples (e.g., current workers, screened by some form of operational selection procedure). If the operational selection procedure happens to be correlated with the predictor being validated, then the distribution of predictor scores in the employee population will differ from the distribution of predictor scores in the applicant population. Specifically, employees' predictor scores will be less variable than applicants' scores. This phenomenon is known as *range restriction*. The effect of range restriction is to artificially reduce the size of the correlation coefficient. As a consequence, the correlation between predictor scores and criterion scores for the examinee population will underestimate the correlation for the population at large. To estimate the correlation for the population, one needs to know: (1) the correlation between the predictor and criterion in the job incumbent sample (r_w), (2) the standard deviation of predictor test scores in the job incumbent sample (SD_W), and (3) the standard deviation of predictor test scores in the applicant population (SD_A).

One formula for estimating the correlation between the test and the criterion in the population r_A, is:

$$ r_A = \frac{r_W \dfrac{SD_A}{SD_W}}{\sqrt{1 - r_W^2 + r_W^2 \left(\dfrac{SD_A^2}{SD_W^2}\right)}} $$

where r_A, r_W, SD_A, and SD_W are defined as earlier.

As calculated in the preceding section, the correlation between the Reading Comprehension scores and the criterion scores for the sample of 10 electricians is 0.518. Suppose that the standard deviation of Reading Comprehension scores is 5.0 for the applicant population, although the standard deviation of test scores for this sample of job incumbents is only 2.84. To estimate the validity of the test in the population, the formula is used in the following way:

$$r_A = \frac{.518\left(\frac{5}{2.84}\right)}{\sqrt{1 - .518^2 + .518^2\left(\frac{5^2}{2.84^2}\right)}} = .729$$

Using the correction formula, the correlation between the Reading Comprehension test and the criterion would be estimated at 0.729 in the population being studied. This procedure may be referred to as correcting the correlation coefficient for the effects of range restriction.

The primary problem associated with the use of the range restriction correction formula concerns the estimation of the standard deviation of test scores for the population. Only in situations where test scores are available for applicants who were rejected, as well as for those who were accepted, can the standard deviation of the applicant population be determined. In concurrent validation research, this value must be estimated from other sources of information. When conducting longitudinal test validation research, it is important to collect test data on all applicants, not just those selected for the job.

Criterion Unreliability

When a test validation study is conducted, the correlation to be determined is that between a given predictor measure and a particular performance measure. However, since pure measures of performance do not exist, criterion measures that contain some amount of random error must be used. This random error is referred to as criterion unreliability. The more random error a criterion measure contains, the more unreliable it is. The correlation obtained between a test and a criterion will tend to decrease as the reliability of the criterion decreases, and will tend to increase as the reliability of the criterion increases. As a result, the effect of criterion unreliability is to cause the correlation computed in a test validation study to underestimate the true size of the relationship between test scores and job performance.

However, if the actual reliability of the criterion is known, the correlation obtained between any test and the criterion can be corrected for criterion unreliability by the following formula:

$$r'_{tc} = \frac{r_{tc}}{\sqrt{r_{cc}}}$$

where: r'_{tc} = the estimated correlation between a test that is not perfectly reliable and a criterion that is perfectly reliable

r_{tc} = the observed correlation between a test and a criterion, neither of which is perfectly reliable, and

r_{cc} = the reliability of the criterion.

For example, suppose, for our sample of 10 electricians, that the criterion has a reliability of 0.60. The correlation between the test scores and the criterion scores, as calculated earlier in this chapter and corrected for the effects of range restriction, is 0.729. The formula just given can be used as follows to estimate the predictor-criterion correlation (r'_{tc}) that would have been obtained if the criterion were perfectly reliable.

$$r'_{tc} = \frac{r_{tc}}{\sqrt{r_{cc}}} = \frac{0.729}{\sqrt{.60}} = .941$$

Thus, it is estimated that if the criterion were perfectly reliable, the obtained predictor-criterion correlation would have been 0.941, instead of 0.729.

It is important to remember that a coefficient corrected for criterion unreliability represents the correlation that would be obtained between a perfectly reliable criterion and predictor scores that are not perfectly reliable. The obtained predictor-criterion correlation is usually not corrected for the lack of perfect reliability of the predictor, since under normal circumstances, the same imperfect predictor will be used in both the validation and operational situations.

For a more detailed discussion of both range restriction and criterion unreliability corrections, a good source is *Applied Psychometrics* by Thorndike (1982).

CONDUCT REGRESSION ANALYSIS

In the previous section, the use of correlations to assess the strength of the relationship between a set of predictor scores and a set of criterion scores was discussed. Correlation is used to describe the relationship between the two specific sets of scores. Regression is used to predict an individual's score on one measure (e.g., the criterion), using that individual's score on one or more other measures (e.g., the predictors). The term *simple linear regression* refers to the special case where there only is one predictor measure. The adjective *linear* refers to the description of the relationship as a straight line; that is, as the values of one variable (e.g., scores on a test of cognitive ability) increase, so do the values of the other variable (e.g., ratings of job performance), and they do so in the same proportion at any level of the first variable (Nunnally, 1978).

The basic equation for simple linear regression is

$$y' = a + bx$$

where: y' = an individual's predicted score on the criterion measure, such as job knowledge test scores,

x = the score on the predictor measure,

a = the y-intercept (the value of the criterion when the value of the predictor measure is zero), and

b = the slope of the straight line (the unit change in the criterion for a unit change in the predictor score).

Using the regression equation

$$y' = 10 + .9x$$

a person with a predictor score (x) of 50 would be expected to have a y score of $10 + .9(50) = 55$. In actual practice, a group of individuals each with an x score of 50 would likely have y scores scattered above and below 55, but 55 would be the best guess for any one of them, if all we knew was their performance on x.

Multiple regression techniques differ from simple linear regression in that more than one predictor is used to predict performance on a criterion variable. For example, performance on a test of job knowledge may be related to (1) cognitive ability, (2) grade-point average in college, and (3) years of experience on the job. Multiple regression techniques can be used to determine both the unique and combined contribution of these variables to the prediction of performance on that criterion. Various results may be found using multiple regression. For example, regression techniques may reveal that all three variables contribute to the prediction of performance, or regression techniques may reveal that once the contribution of one variable is taken into account (e.g., cognitive ability), most of the variance in performance on the criterion is explained, and the contributions of the other variables are minimal. Similarly, one can assess the extent to which a measure predicts performance on several criterion variables, such as a job knowledge test, a work sample measure, and supervisor/peer ratings. Since different predictors are likely to predict performance on different criteria, one would conduct these analyses separately. If there are different measures of the same criterion construct, one may create a combined score and conduct the analyses on that measure as well. A good description of the concept of regression is provided in Crocker and Algina (1986).

ASSESS BIAS

The term *test bias* has been used to refer to a wide range of test issues, including differences between groups in average scores, language demand, validity, content relevance, content offensiveness, and selection rates (Flaugher, 1978). In employment testing, these issues are embedded in a history of complex and emotionally charged debates regarding the purposes of testing, the constitutional legality of certain testing procedures and employment selection policies (Bolick, 1988), and the appropriateness of a variety of analytic procedures used for designing tests, evaluating outcomes, and distinguishing the fine line between adverse impact and reverse discrimination (Baldus & Cole, 1980). Adverse impact is defined as a substantially different rate of selection in hiring, promotion, or other employment decision that works to the disadvantage of members of a race, gender, or ethnic group (Cascio, 1987). This is different from test bias, which focuses on differences in subgroup regression lines.

A commonly accepted definition of test bias, used in the *Uniform Guidelines on Employee Selection Procedures* (EEOC, CSC, DOL, DOJ, 1978) has focused not on mean subgroup differences in test scores, but rather on subgroup differences in the relationship between test scores and performance on the criterion that the test is being used to predict (Cleary, 1968, p. 115):

> A test is biased for members of a subgroup of the population if, in the prediction of a criterion for which the test was designed, consistent nonzero errors of prediction are made for members of the subgroup. In other words, the test is biased if the criterion score predicted from the common regression line is consistently too high or too low for members of the subgroup.

According to this regression model, a test is considered to be biased if use of an overall regression equation results in the systematic underprediction or overprediction for one or more subgroups. A generally accepted method used to assess whether a particular measuring instrument meets this definition of bias has been the comparison of the regression line of some criterion on the test scores for members of one subgroup with the regression line of the same criterion on the test scores for another group. If differences between the two regression values exist, then criterion prediction based on the total group will result in systematic errors of prediction.

A source of some confusion concerns the distinction between test bias and fairness of test use. Although often used interchangeably, the notions of test bias and fairness of test use are conceptually different. Whereas test bias is exclusively concerned with the equality of the prediction error across subgroups for each test score level, fairness of test use is concerned with equality across subgroups regarding a wider variety of outcomes resulting from the use of test scores in selection. Since people have differed in their opinions regarding which specific outcomes of selection should be equated, different definitions of fairness of test use have been proposed. The fairness model that has received widespread acceptance is the Cleary (1968) regression model. As Jensen (1980) pointed out, fairness of test use is a subjective concept that is affected by moral, legal, and philosophical ideas, rather than scientific or statistical analyses. In addressing the distinction between bias and fairness, Cole (1981, p. 1069) wrote:

> Testing scholars and the courts must clearly recognize that test validity and the appropriateness of social or educational policies are separate issues. Thus, even as the scholarly community affirms its concern with (and belief in the value of) validity-type evidence about test bias, it must not be blinded to the limitations of this evidence in answering the essentially different question of the relative desirability of alternate social policies.

For a more extensive discussion of the use of regression in assessing bias, see Bartlett, Bobko, Mosier, and Hannon (1978), Cleary (1968), and Linn (1982).

DOCUMENT THE RESEARCH DESIGN AND STUDY RESULTS

As described earlier, conducting a validity study requires making many research design decisions (e.g., sampling, data collection, and data analysis). The rationale underlying these decisions needs to be documented so that their effects on the results can be considered. Further, study results should be documented so that, if challenged, the use of a measure for predicting performance of an individual on a particular job is defensible, both legally and scientifically.

SUMMARY

In this chapter, we have discussed various methodological and statistical techniques used to conduct a validation study. These techniques included how to develop a validation research plan, procedures for collecting data, and methods of data analysis. We recognize that portions of this chapter are written at different levels of technical sophistication. While sufficient information is probably provided for relatively simple statistical processes (i.e., descriptive statistics), more information may be required about advanced kinds of analyses. Toward that end, we have made reference to more technical texts.

REFERENCES

American Psychological Association, American Educational Research Association, & National Council on Measurement in Education (Joint Committee). (1985). *Standards for educational and psychological testing.* Washington, DC: American Psychological Association.

Baldus, D. C., & Cole, J. W. L. (1980). *Statistical profile of discrimination.* New York: McGraw-Hill.

Barrett, G. V., Phillips, J. S., & Alexander, R. A. (1981). Concurrent and predictive validity designs: A critical analysis. *Journal of Applied Psychology, 25,* 499–513.

Bartlett, C. J., Bobko, P., Mosier, S. B., & Hannon, R. (1978). Testing for fairness with a moderated multiple regression strategy: An alternative to differential analysis. *Personnel Psychology, 40,* 37–47.

Binning, J. F., & Barrett, G. V. (1989). Validity of personnel decisions: A conceptual analysis of the inferential and evidential bases. *Journal of Applied Psychology, 74,* 478–494.

Bolick, C. (1988). Legal and policy aspects of testing. *Journal of Vocational Behavior, 33,* 320–330.

Brogden, H. E., & Taylor, E. K. (1950). The theory and classification of criterion bias. *Educational and Psychological Measurement, 3,* 159–186.

Campbell, J. P., McHenry, J. J., & Wise, L. L. (1990). Modeling job performance in a population of jobs. *Personnel Psychology, 43,* 313–334.

Cascio, W. F. (1987). *Applied psychology in personnel management.* Englewood Cliffs, NJ: Prentice-Hall.

Cleary, T. A. (1968). Test bias: Prediction of grades of negro and white students in integrated colleges. *Journal of Educational Measurement, 5,* 115–124.

Cole, N. (1981). Bias in testing. *American Psychologist, 36,* 1067–1077.

Crocker, L., & Algina, J. (1986). *Introduction to classical and modern test theory.* Fort Worth, TX: Harcourt Brace Jovanovich.

Dunnette, M. D., & Borman, W. C. (1979). Personnel selection and classification. *Annual Review of Psychology, 30,* 477–525.

Equal Employment Opportunity Commission, Civil Service Commission, Department of Labor, & Department of Justice. (1978, August). Uniform guidelines on employee selection procedures. *Federal Register, 43* (166), 38290–38315.

Flaugher, R. L. (1978). The many definitions of test bias. *American Psychologist, 33,* 671–679.

Ghiselli, E. F., Campbell, J. P., & Zedeck, S. (1981). *Measurement theory for the behavioral sciences.* New York: Freeman.

Guion, R. M. (1977). Content validity, the source of my discontent. *Applied Psychological Measurement, 1,* 1–10.

Guion, R. M. (1978). "Content validity" in moderation. *Personnel Psychology, 31,* 205–213.

Guion, R. M. (1980). On trinitarian doctrines of validity. *Professional Psychology, 11,* 385–398.

Hays, W. L. (1981). *Statistics* (3rd ed.). New York: CBS College Publishing.

Hunter J. E. (1996, April). *Why all arguments for using statistical significance tests are wrong!* Paper presented at the Eleventh Annual Conference of the Society for Industrial and Organizational Psychology, San Diego, CA.

Jensen, A. R. (1980). *Bias in mental testing.* New York: Free Press.

Lemke, E., & Wiersma, W. (1976). *Principles of psychological measurement.* Boston: Houghton Mifflin.

Linn, R. (1982). Ability testing: Individual differences, prediction and differential prediction. In A. K. Wigdor & W. R. Garner (Eds.), *Ability testing: Uses, consequences, and controversies. Part II: Documentation section.* Washington, DC: National Academy Press.

Messick, S. (1980). Test validity and the ethics of assessment. *American Psychologist, 35,* 1012-1027.

Nunnally, J. C. (1978). *Psychometric theory.* New York: McGraw-Hill.

Oppler, S. H., Peterson, N. G., & Russell, T. (1992). Basic validation results for the LVI sample. In J. P. Campbell & L. M. Zook (Eds.), *Building and retaining the career force: New procedures for accessing and assigning Army enlisted personnel. Annual report, 1991 fiscal year* (ARI Technical Note). Alexandria, VA: U.S. Army Research Institute for the Behavioral and Social Sciences.

Rothstein, H. R. (1990). Interrater reliability of job performance ratings: Growth to asymptote level with increasing opportunity to observe. *Journal of Applied Psychology, 75,* 322–327.

Schmidt, F. L. (1996, April). *Data analysis methods and cumulative knowledge in psychology: Why significance testing should be abandoned.* Paper presented at the Eleventh Annual Conference of the Society for Industrial and Organizational Psychology, San Diego, CA.

Schmidt, F. L., & Hunter, J. E. (1977). Development of a general solution to the problem of validity generalization. *Journal of Applied Psychology, 62,* 529–540.

Schmidt, F. L., Hunter, J. E., & Urry, V. W. (1976). Statistical power in criterion-related validity studies. *Journal of Applied Psychology, 61,* 473–485.

Schmitt, N., Gooding, R. Z., Noe, R. A., & Kirsch, M. (1984). Meta-analysis of validity studies published before 1964 and 1982 and the investigation of study characteristics. *Personnel Psychology, 37,* 407–422.

Sharon, A. T., & Bartlett, C. J. (1969). Effect of instructional conditions in producing leniency on two types of rating scales. *Personnel Psychology, 23,* 251–263.

Society for Industrial and Organizational Psychology (1987). *Principles for the validation and use of personal selection procedures.* (3rd ed.). College Park, MD: Author.

Taylor, E. L., & Wherry, R. J. (1951). A study of leniency in two ratings systems. *Personnel Psychology, 4,* 39–47.

Tenopyr, M. L. (1977). Content-construct confusion. *Personnel Psychology, 30,* 47–54.

Tenopyr, M. L., & Oeltjen, P. D. (1982). Personnel selection and classification. *Annual Review of Psychology, 33,* 581–618.

Thorndike, R. L. (1982). *Applied psychometrics.* Boston: Houghton Mifflin.

U.S. Department of Labor (1991). *Dictionary of Occupational Titles* (4th ed.). Washington, DC: Government Printing Office.

Veres, J. G., III, Field, H. S., & Boyles, W. R. (1983). Administrative versus research performance ratings: An empirical test of rating data quality. *Public Personnel Management, 12,* 290–298.

Warmke, D. L., & Billings, R. S. (1979). Comparison of training methods for improving the psychometric quality of experimental and administrative performance ratings. *Journal of Applied Psychology, 64,* 124–131.

Wherry, R. J., Sr., & Bartlett, C. J. (1982). The control of bias in ratings. *Personnel Psychology, 35,* 521–551.

Contributors

Lance E. Anderson is research scientist for the American Institutes for Research. He received his M.A. (1987) and Ph.D. (1989) degrees from Bowling Green State University in industrial/organizational psychology. His research interests include personnel selection, job classification, and research on employment of persons with disabilities.

Wayne A. Baughman is research scientist for the American Institutes for Research. He received his B.M.Ed. degree (1973) from the Eastman School of Music, an M.A. degree (1993) from the Catholic University of America in music performance, and both M.A. (1993) and Ph.D. (1997) degrees from George Mason University in industrial and organizational psychology. His research interests include developing performance assessments and interventions to enhance performance in applied settings.

Ruth A. Childs is research scientist for the American Institutes for Research. She received her B.S. degree (1988) from Duke University in psychology and both her M.A. (1991) and Ph.D. (1992) degrees from the University of North Carolina at Chapel Hill in quantitative psychology. Her research interests include individual assessment and the application of quantitative methodologies in both employment and educational settings.

Jennifer L. Crafts is a former senior research scientist for the American Institutes for Research. She received her B.S. degree (1980) from the University of Illinois in psychology and her M.S. (1983) and Ph.D. (1985) degrees from the University of Houston in industrial/organizational psychology. While at AIR, her main areas of concentration included job analysis, test development, and job performance measurement.

Daniel B. Felker is senior research fellow for the American Institutes for Research. He received his B.A. degree (1960) from Creighton University in psychology, his M.A. degree (1962) from the University of Nebraska, Omaha, in psychology, and his Ph.D. degree (1973) from the University of Pittsburgh in educational communication and technology. His research experience includes instructional systems analysis, design, and evaluation; job performance measurement; and program evaluation in military, government, criminal justice, and business settings.

Mary Ann Hanson is research scientist at Personnel Decisions Research Institutes, Inc., in Tampa, Florida. She received her Ph.D. degree (1994) from the University of Minnesota in industrial/organizational psychology. Most recently, she has been involved in the application of industrial psychology to less traditional problems, including the integration of technology in the workplace, training, and career guidance.

P. Richard Jeanneret, Ph.D., is founder and managing principal of Jeanneret & Associates, Inc. (J & A), a cofounder and president of PAQ Services, Inc., and adjunct professor in the Department of Psychology at the University of Houston. He is coauthor of the *Position Analysis Questionnaire* (PAQ), a widely used job analysis instrument, and is one of the principal investigators of the U.S. Department of Labor's project to develop the O*NET (the replacement for the *Dictionary of Occupational Titles*). Jeanneret was the 1990 recipient of the Distinguished Professional Contributions Award of the Society for Industrial and Organizational Psychology.

Charles T. Keil, Jr. is senior research associate for the American Institutes for Research. He received his B.A. degree (1990) from Wabash College in psychology and his M.A. degree (1997) from George Mason University in industrial/organizational psychology. He is currently completing his Ph.D. studies at George Mason University in industrial/organizational psychology. His research interests include individual differences, performance measurement, and the application of quantitative methodologies in employment settings.

Michael A. McDaniel is associate professor of psychology at the University of Akron. He received his Ph.D. degree (1986) from the

George Washington University in industrial/organizational psychology. His research interests include employment interviews, applicant deception, and the aging worker.

Stephan J. Motowidlo is professor of management and director of the Human Resource Research Center at the University of Florida. He received his B.A. degree (1969) from Yale University in psychology and his Ph.D. degree (1976) from the University of Minnesota in industrial and organizational psychology. His research interests include job simulations, selection interviews, performance appraisal, models of job performance, work attitudes, and occupational stress.

Michael D. Mumford is principal research scientist for the American Institutes for Research and associate director of AIR's Personnel Assessment Group. He received his B.A. degree (1979) from Bucknell University in psychology and his M.S. (1981) and Ph.D. (1983) degrees from the University of Georgia in psychometrics. His research interests include background data, creativity, and leadership.

Scott H. Oppler is principal research scientist for the American Institutes for Research and associate director of AIR's Personnel Assessment Group. He received his B.S. degree (1985) from Duke University in psychology and his Ph.D. degree (1990) from the University of Minnesota in industrial and organizational psychology. Oppler's research interests include individual differences, test development and validation, and performance measurement.

Norman G. Peterson is senior research fellow for the American Institutes for Research and director of AIR's Personnel Assessment Group. He received his B.A. (1969) and Ph.D. (1980) degrees from the University of Minnesota in psychology. He has conducted research in job analysis, test development and validation, classification systems, and other applied topics for a variety of government and private sector sponsors.

Elaine D. Pulakos, director of Personnel Decisions Research Institutes' Washington, D.C., office, has spent her career conducting applied research and consulting in organizations. She received her Ph.D. degree (1984) from Michigan State University in industrial and organizational psychology. A fellow of APA and SIOP, she has published widely on selection and performance appraisal issues. She has served as consulting editor of *Journal of Applied Psychology, Personnel Psychology,* and *Frontiers in I/O Psychology.* She is president-elect of the Society for Industrial and Organizational Psychology.

Andrew M. Rose is principal research scientist at the American Institutes for Research and chief scientist of AIR's Washington Research Center. He received both his M.S. (1972) and Ph.D. (1974) degrees from the University of Michigan in experimental psychology. His research interests include communication effectiveness, information design, and technological solutions to applied problems.

Teresa L. Russell is senior research scientist for the American Institutes for Research. She received her B.S. (1980), M.S. (1983), and Ph.D. (1988) degrees from Oklahoma State University in psychology. Her primary research interest is in human performance measurement in industrial and organizational settings.

Christopher E. Sager is senior research scientist for the American Institutes for Research. He received his B.A. degree (1985) from San Diego State University and his Ph.D. degree (1990) from the University of Minnesota, both in psychology. His research interests include job analysis, selection, and performance assessment.

George R. Wheaton is a vice president of the American Institutes for Research and Director of AIR's Washington Research Center. He received his A.B. degree (1961) from Bowdoin College in psychology and his M.Sc. (1963) from McGill University in clinical psychology. His research interests include taxonomies of performance and the application of job and task analysis methods to transfer of training phenomena and criterion measurement.

Deborah L. Whetzel is a psychologist in Corporate Training and Development at the U.S. Postal Service. Prior to her employment with the Postal Service, she was a senior research scientist at the American Institutes for Research. She received her B.S. (1981) and M.A. (1983) degrees from George Mason University in psychology and her Ph.D. degree (1991) from George Washington University in industrial and organizational psychology. Her research interests include developing and validating personnel selection instruments, and evaluating training programs.

Kristen M. Williams is a principal with C² Multimedia, a firm specializing in the development of custom training programs. She received her A.B. degree (1971) from Stanford University in psychology, her M.S. degree (1972) from the University of Pennsylvania in education, and her Ph.D. degree (1981) from Johns Hopkins University in sociology. Williams has conducted job analysis for the purposes of selection and the identification of training needs.

Sandra R. Wilson is senior research fellow and director of the Institute for Health Care Research for the American Institutes for Research. She is also clinical associate professor of medicine at Stanford University School of Medicine. Wilson received her B.A. degree (1963) from the University of Minnesota in psychology and zoology and her Ph.D. degree (1968) from Stanford University in psychology. Her research interests include understanding disease self-management and health risk behaviors and the application of behavioral analysis and psychological measurement methods to the definition and assessment of patient self-management competencies and disease outcomes.

Index